The Huk Rebellion

The Huk Rebellion

A Study of Peasant Revolt in the Philippines

BY BENEDICT J. KERKVLIET

UNIVERSITY OF CALIFORNIA PRESS

Berkeley   Los Angeles   London

The author gratefully acknowledges permission to quote
from books published by International Publishers.

University of California Press
Berkeley and Los Angeles, California

University of California Press, Ltd.
London, England

First Paperback Printing 1982
ISBN 0-520-04635-8
Library of Congress Catalog Card Number: 75-22656
Printed in the United States of America

1 2 3 4 5 6 7 8 9 0

To
John B. and Dorothy M. Kerkvliet
and
Amerigo (Spagg) and Rhoda Grasseschi

CONTENTS

TABLES AND MAPS

Tables

Maps

PREFACE

THIS IS a study about a peasant revolt in the Philippines commonly known as the Huk rebellion. Although by no means the only case of agrarian unrest in modern Philippine society, it was perhaps the most important and certainly the largest. Its roots go back to smaller uprisings and scattered incidents of peasant anger early in the twentieth century. By the 1930s, discontent had grown to a rage that united a few hundred thousand peasants in the important rice- and sugar-producing plain of Central Luzon. This widespread unrest developed into a rebellion between 1946 and the early 1950s. Although the Huk rebellion eventually petered out, the peasant discontent that had been its backbone persists in many guises until today, reminding us that conditions are still harsh for most Filipino villagers.

My purpose in this book is to understand the Huk movement from the point of view of its participants and sympathizers. This is a perspective other social scientists have ignored when writing about the Huks and one frequently absent in studies of peasant movements in general. Scholars have tended instead to see these movements from the point of view of government policy makers and counterinsurgency strategists or regard them as incidents worthy of mention, but not of central focus, when analyzing national and international events. I hope to illustrate a simple but important point: seeing a peasant revolt through the eyes—or as nearly so as possible—of those who rebelled reveals much and makes more reasonable the actions of people who otherwise might appear irrational.

Keeping in mind the perspective of people who rebelled or were sympathetic to the Huks, I researched several questions that seemed central to the nineteenth- and twentieth-century agrarian uprisings in "Third World" countries. First, were qualitative changes in relations between local elites and villagers significant in explaining why people revolted? Were there other major causes for the rebellion? Second, what did peasants want? Did they want, as many scholars contend, to escape from the tenancy system and become landowners? Did they organize in order to challenge the local landowners and displace them as local political powers? Third, why did participants feel that rebellion was justified? Fourth, who were the leaders of the movement, what were their backgrounds? Were they, as several theories argue, from nonpeasant classes and from outside the villages, such as urban intellectuals? Fifth, how important was communism as an ideology, and the

Philippine Communist Party in particular? Did the Communist Party control the movement, as most previous scholarship has said? Sixth, at what point did peasants in Central Luzon rebel? Did rebellion develop quickly, or did it come after a long struggle? What were the circumstances immediately prior to it? Seventh, why did the revolt end? Was it, for example, because the government made reforms and gave land to the peasants, or was it because local elites and the villagers came to terms, or was government military force superior?

These questions and the perspective I have emphasized necessarily limit my study. This book does not consider, for instance, the psychology of rebels, the continuities and discontinuities between the Huks and other rebellions in Philippine history, or the cultural significance of the peasant movement in Central Luzon. Furthermore, this book does not try to see the unrest from the viewpoint of government soldiers or the landed elites. Nor does it contrast Central Luzon with other parts of the Philippines where there was no rebellion or compare conditions in Central Luzon with those in other countries.

In short, this is not an exhaustive study. Rather, this book is concerned with a few important political and economic questions about the rebellion and the region in which it was strong. And the analysis tries to approximate the viewpoint of the villagers who participated.

The approach I have taken explains my sources and the organization of the material. I have relied heavily on documents from the Huk rebellion and the Philippine Communist Party (Partido Komunista ng Pilipinas, or PKP) and on discussions with former Huks and other persons in Central Luzon, particularly in the municipality of Talavera, Nueva Ecija.

A Filipina research assistant and I examined roughly 1,200 documents during the course of five months. As they were not adequately stored or catalogued, I undoubtedly missed some. The documents were captured from the Huks and PKP by the Philippine military and most are still kept on military bases. The Philippine army only recently allowed researchers to examine large numbers of these documents, so scholars have not used them extensively before. More accessible, however, are a smaller number of captured papers submitted to courts in the 1950s as exhibits during trials for several accused rebels. Those exhibits I found most useful were from the trials of the PKP politburo and of Amado V. Hernandez.

I discussed the Huk rebellion with three types of people: fourteen former Huks (twelve who were still in prison and two who had already served prison sentences as a result of their rebellious actions), people who participated in the rebellion or supported it in some fashion, and others who lived in Central Luzon during this period. Persons in the second two categories included both key informants whom I sought out in different parts of Central Luzon and individuals whom I met randomly and in the specially selected village of San Ricardo.

Conversations with these people covered a wide range of subjects related to the origins and growth of the Huk rebellion and to each person's biography. I discovered early that structured interviews stifled discussion and seemed to insult people. For each interview, therefore, I had in mind several questions in which I was particularly interested but which I asked during the course of rather casual conversations. Sometimes these discussions lasted two or three hours each. Most lasted about an hour. In several instances I spoke more than once with the same person. During these conversations I took notes, which I used as soon as possible afterward to record in detail what was said.

Making arrangements to interview former Huks in the military prison at Camp Crame required assistance from generous people. Mrs. Ruth Lava asked her brother-in-law Jesus Lava and several of his fellow inmates if they would be willing to talk to me. After they indicated they would, I approached Camp Crame authorities. Mr. Dominador Arañas, a civilian employee who was the Camp's chief accountant and an uncle to my research assistant, introduced me to the officers in charge of the prison. After I explained my purpose, the officials said I cold talk to these men as frequently as I wished so long as the men themselves consented. My request, I later found out, was not unusual; several people, including other Americans, had interviewed these prisoners.

Generally, former Huks were willing to discuss the movement and their activities. Only one declined; his case was being reviewed by a government agency, and he did not want to speak about his experiences to anyone except his lawyer. Several Huk veterans were actually eager to talk, partly because my visits to the prison relieved their boredom and partly because they were proud of what they had done. Three of the twelve men in prison felt that by telling me their experiences, their version of the Huk's story would be recorded. They themselves did not feel able to write about it. Proper introductions, initially from Mrs. Lava and thereafter from one former Huk to the next, helped to create a friendly and candid atmosphere for these interviews. Also helpful was the fact that two decades had passed since the rebellion. Finally, the former Huks with whom I spoke, whether inside or out of prison, knew that I had read many documents and done other research prior to talking to them. I think this was important evidence for them that I was genuinely interested in learning about them. From this they also knew I had other sources with which to cross-check information.

The interviews themselves were conducted in a large airy room where visitors routinely met with prisoners. I talked with each person individually. Frequently only the two of us were in the room, for I confined my visits to days when relatives and friends of the men were usually unable to come. No guards lingered to eavesdrop, nor did anyone restrict our conversations or check my notes. Most of the time the guards were not even in earshot or in sight. In short, rules for prisoners and visitors at the stockades in 1970, prior to martial law, were lax compared to today.

After I had spent several months studying documents, reading newspapers, and doing library research in metropolitan Manila, I wanted to talk about the rebellion with villagers who had experienced it. I therefore looked for people in Central Luzon who were former Huks, former leaders of extinct peasant associations, long-time residents who could recall events covering several decades, and so on. After several sojourns to Central Luzon and numerous conversations, I decided to concentrate on one village. So, from March through June 1970, the people in San Ricardo, a barrio in Talavera, Nueva Ecija, educated me about their lives and their village.

I selected San Ricardo because many of its residents were involved early in the unrest, because I had acquaintances who kindly introduced me there, and because people in the area spoke Tagalog, the only Filipino language I know. As I was primarily interested in talking to people who remembered conditions and events before and during the Huk rebellion, I concentrated on those who were forty years old and over. Although I wanted to interview both men and women, most of my conversations were with men. From these interviews I gathered fairly detailed biographical information for fifty-six household heads, representing about 30 percent of the total number of houses (190) in the village. Forty-three of the people were in the forty-and-over age group, which represented about one-half of all men in the village in that group. Thirteen of the biographies were for people between twenty and thirty-nine years old. These fifty-six people lived in all parts of the barrio and, I am confident, were representative of the village. In addition, I had numerous casual discussions that did not result in biographical sketches. These supplementary interviews were valuable for piecing together the history of San Ricardo.

In San Ricardo and other villages, I talked to people wherever I found them—inside their homes, working in the fields, standing on the roadsides, resting under shade trees, chatting at village hang-outs. Each morning I came to San Ricardo by bus from the Talavera municipal center, where I roomed with a family, and stayed until late afternoon. The barrio captain and his wife introduced me to several people in the first few days I was in San Ricardo; thereafter everyone was aware of my presence, although not clear about my purpose. I spent several days making a crude map of the barrio, as much to explain my presence to residents as to number each house in order to prepare an interviewing procedure. People naturally were curious about why I wanted to talk to them, especially about events that had happened so long ago. I said I was a student doing research for a degree and that I wanted to learn about how people lived and what had happened during the last several decades. After I had been coming regularly to the village for three or four weeks, I became a familiar figure. I had made several friends who lived in different parts of the village, and they introduced me to other neighbors and relatives. In this way I was able to meet and talk with at least one person in most of the barrio's households. Most people willingly discussed their lives and what they had seen during the Huk rebellion, the Japanese occupation, and the agrarian unrest of the 1930s. Some spoke freely about their own participation in the rebellion; others talked only a little about involvement with the Huks or other organizations; some would not talk at all about their political activities even though they did discuss other facets of village life; and some said they had not been involved in any of the unrest.

Because I had several different types of sources, I could check the veracity of what people told me not only by comparing it to what others said but also by comparing it to information found, for instance, in captured documents, government reports, and newspaper articles. Similarly, I compared the documents not only to other documents, but to other sources. This method enhances the credibility of the data on which I base my analysis.

Each major section in this book begins by examining what was happening in San Ricardo, thereby starting the analysis with villagers themselves and setting the tone for the entire section. This method also helps to demonstrate one important finding: the movement began small, in villages scattered across Central Luzon, before building upward into large organizations. After looking at San Ricardo, each section analyzes the agrarian situation and the peasant movement for Central Luzon in general. As often as possible—but not nearly as often as desirable—I have used people's own words to relate their impressions and experiences. The names for villagers, however, are pseudonyms.

The book is divided into six chapters and a conclusion. Each chapter analyzes an important period in the genesis of the rebellion. The first two chapters argue that traditional patron-client relationships between landed elites and peasants deteriorated, from the peasantry's viewpoint, into exploitive relationships. In response, villagers tried to force landlords to live up to their obligations as patrons; later they petitioned the government to make landowners do this. Gradually, peasants organized, and agrarian unrest spread.

Chapter 3 discusses the importance of the Japanese occupation for the growth of the peasant movement in Central Luzon. The Japanese military and its Filipino collaborators abused villagers to such an extent that people resisted. The peasants' anti-Japanese resistance movement in Central Luzon, called the "Hukbalahap," built on the peasant organizations that had emerged during the 1930s. The Hukbalahap not only became an effective guerrilla army but also a popular-based organization. Its success and strength also increased rural people's political power. Consequently, peasants who had been in or supported it were incensed after the war when Filipino and American governments denounced the Hukbalahap, imprisoned many of its leaders, and hunted down former particpants.

The fourth chapter focuses on the crucial period between 1945 and late 1946. Peasants continued to push for agrarian reforms. They also wanted the government and landed elites to stop harassing Hukbalahap veterans and peasant leaders. Now peasant organizations were larger and stronger than they had been in the 1930s. And in 1946 they nominated and elected six out of the eight congressmen from Central Luzon. The elites in Central Luzon and in Manila, however, would not tolerate this threat to their control. They ousted the congressmen-elect and intensified their repression against the peasant movement. This combination forced large numbers of villagers to revolt.

The fifth and sixth chapters analyze the Hukbong Mapagpalaya ng

Bayan (HMB) or the Huk rebellion itself. They argue that peasants resorted to organized violence in order to pursue the limited objectives they had sought for years and to defend themselves against repression. The movement had considerable support in the villages of Central Luzon, and it grew stronger until the early 1950s. It died down, however, after 1951 when the government reduced significantly the military's abuses of villagers and began some agrarian reforms that spoke to the objectives of most rebels. Because people were also weary of fighting, many decided to resume nonviolent efforts to get agrarian reforms. These two chapters also argue that the Communist Party joined the rebellion after first disapproving it. The objectives of the Communist Party's top leadership differed, however, from those of most Huks. In general, the Communist Party advocated changes that were more radical than what peasants supported. These differences remained unresolved during the rebellion and contributed to its weakness.

The last chapter discusses eight major conclusions. Although this book examines only one rebellion, these conclusions help to appreciate peasant rebellions in general.

Before turning to the Huks, I should describe briefly the national political setting. Between 1930 and the mid-1950s, Filipino national leaders and the American colonial rulers were absorbed in such issues as deciding trade relations between the United States and the Philippines, finalizing the terms of independence from the United States, and, after 1946, establishing a viable government for the new republic. Government leaders seemed to have no time to deal thoughtfully with numerous problems inside the country, such as the continuous Muslim resistance to Christian Filipino nationalism in Mindanao and unrest in Central Luzon. The government, whether in the provinces or at the national center in Manila, was also exclusively in the hands of American officials and Filipino landowners and businessmen. The distance in life style and political power between the elites and the masses of Filipinos was as wide then as the chasm that exists today in the country. Only those few Filipinos who were educated and could compete successfully in a capitalistic economy enjoyed the democratic and libertarian principles that were so eloquently praised in the halls of the Philippine Congress and during the luncheons of the civic clubs of the wealthy.

Nevertheless, there were ties, sometimes strong ones, between elites and average Filipinos. Extended families, for example, were still important and often cut across social classes. So did the traditional system of patronage, which obligated those who were fortunate and well-to-do to help those who were not. The significance of these ties for binding Philippine society together in spite of the striking inequalities was demonstrated in Central Luzon itself when this social fabric began to unravel, resulting in rebellion.

NOTATIONS FOR FOOTNOTES

Biographical Information
Miscellaneous biographical information from records among documents captured from the Hukbalahap, HMB, and PKP.

CapDoc, Ag.
Captured Hukbalahap, HMB, and PKP documents held by the Armed Forces of the Philippines and located at Camp Aguinaldo, Quezon City.

CapDoc, Cr.
Captured Hukbalahap, HMB, and PKP documents held by the Philippine Constabulary and located at Camp Crame, Quezon City.

Federal Records, Suitland, Md.
Documents deposited in the Federal Records Center of the United States National Archives, Suitland, Maryland.

HDP
Historical Data Papers, usually followed by the name of the municipality described in a particular volume.

Hernandez Exh. _____ ; CFI, Manila
Documents entered as exhibits in the trial of Amado Hernandez in the Court of First Instance, Manila.

Military Records, National Archives, Washington, D.C.
Documents deposited in the Military Records section of the United States National Archives in Washington, D.C.

Politburo Exh. _____ ; CFI, Manila
Documents entered as exhibits in the trials of several persons accused of being members of the PKP and its politburo in the Court of First Instance, Manila.

PF
Personal folder of the person cited in a particular reference. (When the name of the person whose folder is being cited is not obvious, that person's name comes after the PF.) These folders are among the captured documents. Hence, *PF, CapDoc, Ag.* means Personal Folder (of the person cited in the note), Captured Documents, deposited at Camp Aguinaldo, Quezon City.

RG
Record Group in the United States National Archives. The titles for Record Groups used are the following:
RG 94 The Adjutant General's Office
RG 126 Office of the Territories
RG 165 War Department General and Special Staffs
RG 319 Army Staff
RG 350 Bureau of Insular Affairs

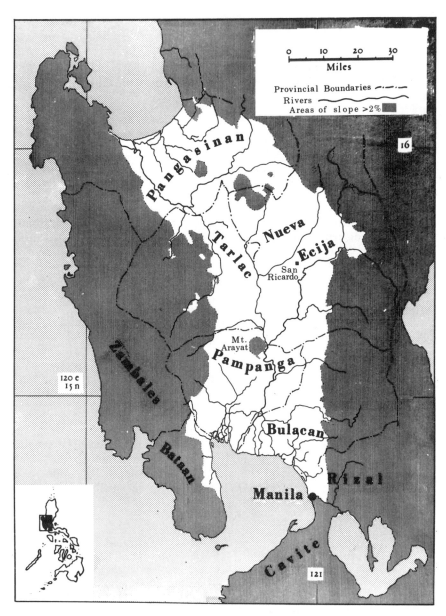

Map. 1. The Central Plain of Luzon.

Chapter 1

ORIGINS OF REBELLION

THE PEOPLE of the Huk rebellion lived in Central Luzon. This is the extensive lowland area on Luzon, the most populated and largest island in the Philippines. The Central Plain stretches north 125 miles from the Manila Bay to Pangasinan's picturesque fishponds and beaches on the shores of the Lingayen Gulf. The imposing Sierra Madre Mountains to the east and the Zambales mountain ranges to the west rise on each side of the plain. Several river systems, which drain the monsoon rains, wind their way through rice and cane fields and around villages and towns dotting the landscape. In the 1930s and 1940s, the time period for this study, nearly one and one-half million of the country's sixteen million people lived in the four Central Luzon provinces of Bulacan, Pampanga, Tarlac, and Nueva Ecija, and most of them were peasants.

Today, as it was thirty years ago, it is easy to reach Central Luzon from Manila. You can hop on a bus on the city's outskirts and within a half hour you can be well into Bulacan, with its serene rice fields, busy market towns, and the quiet, yet active, villages (barrios) that line the roads. From Bulacan there are two national roadways through Central Luzon. One heads in a north-northwestern direction through the heart of Pampanga's rice and sugar cane lands, skirting the foothills of the Zambales mountains, past the perimeter of the American's huge Clark Air Force Base outside of Angeles City, and into eastern Tarlac, where cane fields and a smattering of rice land dominate the landscape. The alternative route is nearly straight north, across rice fields that stretch as far as the eye can see. Within two hours' time the bus passes through the bustling market of Baliwag, Bulacan, several villages, and the municipal center of San Ildefonso, and is headed for San Miguel, the last municipality of the province before reaching Nueva Ecija. One hour more and the bus makes its way along the streets of Cabanatuan, the capital of Nueva Ecija.

There, as in every other town in which the bus momentarily stops to take on or leave off passengers and cargo, dozens of vendors swarm, exchanging icedrops, *pinipig, tsitsaron,* and other snacks for the coins that passengers thrust through the paneless windows of the bus.[1] Everyone seems to be

---

[1] Ice-drops are the Filipino forerunners of American popsicles; *pinipig* is a type of candy made of pounded rice that is lightly toasted and mixed with molasses; and *tsitsaron* is fried pork skin that is eaten like a potato chip.

1

talking at once, a baby cries, a jeepney driver outside honks for the bus to move, and women on their way to market seem not to notice the commotion as they walk behind and in front of both vehicles. Still, there is a relaxed, pleasant atmosphere about it all; everything is colorful, people are friendly, and no one seems in too much of a hurry.

One particularly striking physical feature about Central Luzon is Mount Arayat. It is the only mountain for miles around, standing like a giant who reigns over the land that sprawls in all directions beneath it. Its base nearly touches the boundaries of Tarlac, Nueva Ecija, and Pampanga; and it is readily visible from almost any place in those three provinces and Bulacan. The mountain belongs to the people of Central Luzon. It has long been a source of wood for peasants living in its shadow. It has also been the home for numerous folk heroes and spirits, and it is said to possess mystical powers that wise and good persons can tap to benefit others. Through the centuries, Mount Arayat has also hidden many outlaws and bandits. Huk rebels, too, used the cover of its forest slopes for their headquarters during the height of the movement and later for their retreats as the rebellion crumbled. Mount Arayat cannot describe those Huk days, but middle-aged and elderly people in Central Luzon can, and they remember well.

San Ricardo, Talavera

The barrio of San Ricardo in the municipality of Talavera, Nueva Ecija, is a good place to begin to study the causes of the Huk rebellion.[2] Like many barrios in Central Luzon, San Ricardo was in the thick of the Huk movement, and numerous residents participated actively in it. As one source recorded, "the Huk movement in Talavera had its roots in this barrio."[3] Because the roots of the Huk rebellion in San Ricardo go deep, one must look back to understand why people eventually rebelled. And because the barrio's experience was not an isolated event, its recent history reflects Central Luzon's history, too.

Setting
Today San Ricardo is one of forty barrios in Talavera; during the time of the Huk movement, it was one of seventeen. It is about nine miles north of Cabanatuan, the capital of Nueva Ecija, and four miles east of Talavera's *bayan* (municipal center, or *poblacion*). Most of the houses line the two unpaved roads in the barrio. Their architectural style and building materials have changed little in the last four decades: small homes with one, sometimes two bedrooms, no furniture to speak of, constructed of nipa, bamboo, and wood. Many of the houses rest on husky timbers to keep out floods during the monsoons. Underneath these stilted homes,

---

[2] Provinces in the Philippines are divided into municipalities. Each municipality has a municipal center, called in the local vernacular *poblacion* or *bayan*, which has such institutions as the municipal government offices, churches, marketplace, and granaries. In addition to the bayan, municipalities are broken down into several villages or barrios (*nayon* in Tagalog), where most people in the municipality live. Sometimes barrios, in turn, have smaller settlements called *sitio*.

[3] *HDP, Talavera.*

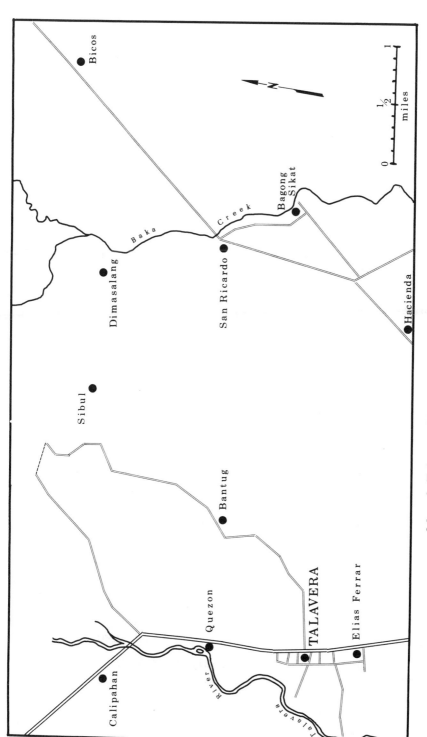

Map. 2. Talavera, Nueva Ecija (partial), circa 1950.

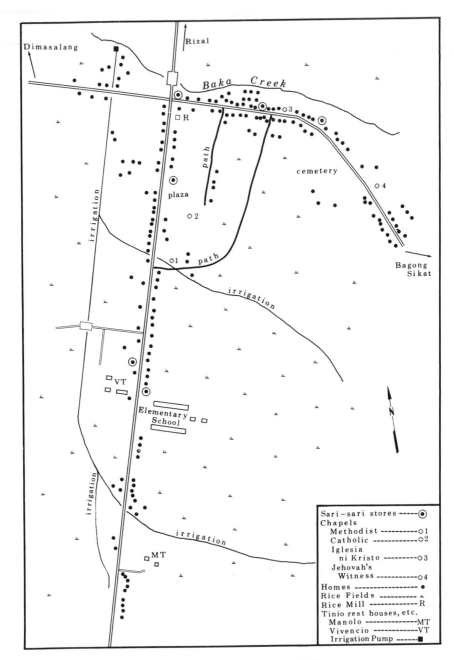

Map 3. San Ricardo, Talavera (1970).

families frequently keep stacks of wood, farming tools, and a stall for the carabao. Pigs and chickens also scrounge for scraps of food that fall through the cracks in the floor above. The village has many bushes and large trees, including acacia, *santol,* and mango, although the general appearance of this barrio, like most in Central Luzon, is drab and dusty in the dry season and wet and muddy during the wet one.

Rice fields surround San Ricardo. Lush and emerald green while the rice is growing, but parched and cracked stubble fields for months after harvest, the fields seem to stretch for miles in all directions. All that breaks the view are shallow dips and rises and clumps of bamboo and acacia trees with a few houses peeping through, indicating barrios. Criss-crossing the fields are the low dikes that hold water when the rice seedlings are planted from late June through August. Harvest comes in late October through January, depending on weather conditions and type of seed. Until today, few peasants in the barrio plant a second crop of *palay* (the Tagalog name for unhusked rice), largely because they have no year-round irrigation. A few people do plant tomatoes, onions, or other vegetables during the dry season, but rarely was this possible before the 1950s.

When standing on the fringes of the barrio, you can see the Sierra Madre mountains far away to the east. To the north, toward San Jose municipality, the rice fields continue endlessly. To the west a long line of trees crosses the fields, marking the national road that passes through Talavera from Cabanatuan. A couple of church steeples poke above the trees to identify the bayan of Talavera. And to the south, rising above the plain, is Mount Arayat. From San Ricardo, it appears to be an oversized straw hat of the sort men in the barrios wear. As you scan the area, a slight breeze rustles the bamboo and carries the familiar smell of an outdoor fire. Someone is cooking *bigas* (husked or polished rice). There are noises in the background, too: a fighting cock crows, several children giggle as they play in the road, someone is chopping wood, a carabao shuffles along a path and its rider, a middle-aged man, clicks his tongue to urge the animal on. These and other familiar sights and sounds would have been in the barrio years ago, too, even at the height of the Huk rebellion.

Prelude to Unrest in San Ricardo

Eighteen hundred souls lived in San Ricardo by 1918, over twenty-six hundred by 1939.[4] The principal occupation was farming rice on small parcels of land. If they were lucky, villagers harvested enough each year to live at a subsistence level. The vast majority of people were share tenants *(kasamá);* they worked the land that someone else owned and divided the harvest with the landowner on a percentage basis. Because people lived so close to the land, land tenure arrangements were central to the area's history. An elderly tenant farmer in San Ricardo put it well: "You know,

---

[4] Philippines, Census Office, *Census of the Philippines, 1918,* 2: 211; and Philippines, Commission of Census, *Census of the Philippines, 1939,* vol. 1, pt. 3, Nueva Ecija section.

before the time of the Japanese, the most important thing that affected this area, not just San Ricardo but all over, was that relations between tenants and big landowners went from decent to indecent."

Years ago, one of the largest landowners in Talavera was Manuel Tinio.[5] This former general in the Filipino Revolutionary Army of 1898 had 400 hectares that sprawled across San Ricardo and neighboring barrios. At the turn of the century, much of his land was still virgin forests and meadows. But between 1900 and the 1920s, Tinio took on more and more peasants, who staked out small parcels and laboriously turned the land into neatly diked rice fields.

Some of these peasants who worked Tinio's land in San Ricardo had been tenants for the wealthy Tinio clan elsewhere in the province. Most, however, had migrated to San Ricardo from more populated areas of Nueva Ecija, from Bulacan province, and from the Ilocos region.

One of these migrants was Carlos Rivera. In 1970, this kindly looking man was ninety years old. As he prepared and chewed a wad of juicy betel, he talked about his early years:

> I came to San Ricardo as a young man. For fourteen years, from 1910 to 1924, I worked two and one-half hectares of land that belonged to General Manuel Tinio. Like most of us farming in this area at that time, I had to clear the land first before turning it into decent rice fields. That took two years. My landlord and I shared agricultural expenses. And after the harvest, I gave him 55 percent; the remainder was for me.

Rivera and other tenants also did odd jobs for Tinio; they built irrigation canals on the hacienda, and generally were at his beck and call.

But Rivera did not simply give to Manuel Tinio; he also received things that, in his view, compensated his subordination. First, of course, he had the right to farm a plot of land and to keep a share of the harvest. The specifics of the tenancy agreement were not written down, nor were they grounded in formal law. They were simply based on custom. Rivera was free to plant and keep vegetables and fruits on his home lot, cut wood from Tinio's uncleared land for fuel and lumber, and catch fish in the irrigation canals and streams that ran through Tinio's land. Perhaps most important of all, Rivera could ask Tinio to help him when someone in the family was sick, borrow a carabao, or borrow rice. To illustrate, Rivera said, "General Tinio was my *kompadre* because he was the godfather [*ninong*] of my eldest child. Actually, he was a sponsor at weddings and baptisms of many tenants I knew. He even came to my house occasionally just to see how things were."

Loans of rice and, less frequently, cash were important to tenants. "My wife and I had a big family—twelve children," Rivera explained. "And as

---

[5] The following account of the Tinio hacienda in San Ricardo is based on interviews and conversations with residents in this and other Talavera barrios, including three persons who had been tenants for both Manuel Tinio and his successors. Also included are two interviews with Manolo Tinio and one interview with Vivencio Tinio, sons of Manuel.

the family got bigger, we needed more food. It got to the point that I only had enough *palay* left after harvest to last for a few months. I had to get extra from my landlord." Each year between June or July and harvest time in December, Rivera borrowed rice from Tinio, sometimes as much as a cavan of palay each week.[6] "During the 1920s, I was borrowing about 20 cavans of palay per year just for eating purposes. This was called *rasyon* [rations]. I also borrowed sometimes for other expenses. Of course, there was no interest for any of this, and General Tinio was always willing to lend." Manuel Tinio was even known to overlook unpaid loans when he knew the tenant was hard up.

Both the tenants and Manuel Tinio assumed that they were entitled to ration loans. Because villagers took a ration loan when they had no other rice to eat, the rasyon was a kind of guarantee that their families would at least always have food for minimal subsistence. To a poor peasant whose crops were vulnerable to typhoons, floods, and other unpredictable disasters, this guarantee was vital.

Manuel Tinio, too, benefited from this paternalistic relationship with his tenants. At practically no expense to him, peasants cleared and cultivated his land, of which he owned a great deal. Besides what he owned in San Ricardo, Manuel Tinio paid fifty to a hundred pesos per hectare for several hundred hectares of public land elsewhere in Nueva Ecija during the early years of the American occupation. Some elderly residents in Talavera even suspected that Tinio abused his position as Director of Lands (1913-1916) in the American regime to add more real estate. Whatever the case, once tenants had converted his land into rice fields, it was worth much more than the purchase price. Although he kept most of this land, he did sell some later and made a handsome profit. Tinio also benefited by using his developed agricultural land as collateral for bank loans in order to buy more land and make investments in Manila. In addition, whenever he wanted anything done on his haciendas, he asked his tenants to do it without pay.

Beyond these economic gains, Manuel Tinio profited because his tenants constituted a personal following that swelled his status and political power. He was not just a landowner. He was a *hacendero* in the traditional sense of the word: a large landowner with many tenants who were more than tillers of his land. They were people on whom he could rely to promote his interests out of gratitude to him. They were *his* tenants. He could ask them, for example, to defend his property against bandits or rival claimants and to vote for his favorite candidates. He himself was elected provincial governor in 1908. Moreover, his tenants were loyal. They did not suddenly leave to farm for other landowners; rather, they generally stayed for years, even a lifetime. This was important to Tinio because the number of people who would tenant farm was relatively small for the amount of land to be cultivated. Furthermore, losing a good tenant was a noticeable loss to hacenderos like Tinio. Loyalty required time in order to grow and hence

[6] A cavan is a measure for grain. One cavan of palay is about forty-four kilograms.

could not be duplicated simply by replacing the old tenant with a new one.

Tremendously significant in this type of landlord-tenant relationship was that Rivera and other tenants for landowners like Manuel Tinio believed the tenancy system was judicious and that their landlords' requests were legitimate. Even though they worked hard and lived in poverty, they did not feel exploited. The commonly heard judgment among older tenants in San Ricardo and surrounding barrios was that "the old hacenderos were generous and good men." Rivera and another former tenant of Manuel Tinio remembered him as their "benefactor" and "protector." They had reciprocal relationships with landlords that carried both benefits and obligations. A tenant generally did not object to doing what a landlord asked because he was confident that the landlord would do, in turn, what the tenant expected of him. As one man in the barrio said, "A man of his [Manuel Tinio's] means was supposed to lend his tenants rice and help them when times were hard. That's part of being a landlord." Peasants expressed the same idea in cultural terms: Tinio and the other old hacenderos had *"utang na loob"*—they complied with their moral obligations to reciprocate to the peasants. And they were not *"walang hiya"*—unscrupulous or disrespectful—toward their tenants.

Manuel Tinio's hacienda was one of many in Talavera and in the province. While Carlos Rivera and other tenants were developing Tinio's property, thousands of others in Nueva Ecija were doing the same for other landlords. Between 1900 and 1940, according to census figures, the population in Talavera quadrupled and it doubled in Nueva Ecija as a whole. During these forty years peasants cleared nearly 200,000 hectares in the province, compared to only 5,000 hectares during the thirty years prior to 1900.[7] By 1939, 77 percent of all farm land was cultivated compared to only 30 percent at the turn of the century (see Table 1). Families like the Tinios jumped quickly to take advantage of the colonial government's decision to sell several hundred thousand hectares of "public land." The kasamá or share tenancy system expanded right along with the development of new farm land. In 1939, 76 percent of all farmers in Talavera and 67 percent in Nueva Ecija were tenants[8] (see Table 2). Unfortunately for rural folks, however, the quality of the landlord-tenant relationship declined over the years.

According to people on the Tinio hacienda, conditions definitely became worse after 1924. In that year Manuel Tinio died. Replacing him was Manolo Tinio, an elder son of the deceased hacendero. Carlos Rivera recalled those years:

[7] In 1870 only about 22,000 hectares of land were cultivated in Nueva Ecija. Tomas I. Pagaduan, "Kasaysayan ng Talavera, Nueva Ecija," [History of Talavera, Nueva Ecija], (unpublished manuscript, 1967), p. 220.

[8] Because land tenure data from the two earlier censuses in this century are not comparable to the 1939 census data, one cannot readily say what tenancy percentages were earlier. See Benedict J. Kerkvliet, "Peasant Rebellion in the Philippines: The Origins and Growth of the HMB" (Ph.D. dissertation, University of Wisconsin, 1972), pp. 70-71.

General Tinio died in the early twenties. His son, Manolo, took over the hacienda. I continued to farm for Manolo Tinio; most of us did. But things weren't the same. At first there were just the little changes; Manolo became stricter about what we could and couldn't do, and he was so difficult to see and talk to. I was intimidated by him, yet I didn't think I should be. Then came the final blow. Manolo quit giving loans, including the rasyon. That was terrible! All us tenants had to borrow. Everyone knows that. It's been that way all along. Now what was I to do? I was forced to borrow outside from a money lender. So after a couple of years of that, I left San Ricardo to find another landlord like General Tinio.

Others agreed with Rivera's description of Manolo Tinio's hacienda. "As far as I know," a middle-aged tenant said, "Manolo never gave presents to tenant families who had had a baptism or wedding." "Well, I recall that he did at first, at least on one occasion," said another tenant who had farmed for

Table 1
BASIC CENSUS DATA, TALAVERA AND NUEVA ECIJA*

	1903	1918	1939	Percentage increase
Population				
Talavera	3,300	8,700	20,400	490
Nueva Ecija	134,000	227,000	417,000	210
Number farms				
Talavera	*n.a.*	1,000	4,500	310
Nueva Ecija	13,000	34,000	78,000	500
Farm area (ha.)				
Talavera	*n.a.*	7,100	17,200	140
Nueva Ecija	90,000	205,000	289,000	220
Cultivated area (ha.)				
Talavera	*n.a.*	4,900	13,700	180
Nueva Ecija	27,000	97,000	222,000	720

Sources: Philippines, Bureau of Census, *Census of the Philippine Islands, 1903.*
Philippines, Census Office, *Census of the Philippines, 1918.*
Philippines, Commission of Census, *Census of the Philippines, 1939.*

* Rounded figures.

n.a. Not available in census data.

ha. Hectare(s).

Table 2

NUMBER OF FARMS BY TENURE: 1939*

	Number of farms	Number of owners	Per-centage	Number of tenants	Per-centage
Talavera	4,500	1,100	24	3,400	76
Nueva Ecija	78,000	26,000	33	52,000	67

Source: Census of the Philippines, 1939, vol. 3.

* Rounded figures.

both Tinios, "just like his father had done. But pretty soon he didn't." Manolo Tinio also became increasingly "*mas mahigpit*," as it was frequently put—more strict, businesslike, and impersonal. He even went so far as to require all tenants to sign a contract with rules and regulations. One illustration of Tinio's strict policies involved grain for livestock. Earlier, landlords did not mind if tenants took a few handfuls of palay from the field to give to their chickens and ducks. But Manolo Tinio would not allow it. One peasant named Roberto Aspia remembered when his father, a tenant for Tinio, "was accused of being a thief because he took a few grains from the field at harvest time to feed our chickens. That was in the mid-thirties. It wasn't actually Tinio himself who accused and threatened my father. It was Tinio's *katiwala* [overseer], who said that my father had gone against Tinio's orders and that he was going to report this to Tinio himself." Several recalled how strict Manolo was about *pulot,* a long-standing practice of peasants gleaning recently harvested fields. Whatever fallen grain the peasants picked up, they could take home. "But Manolo was so hawk-eyed about it," complained one man. "Only certain fields could be gleaned and his katiwala enforced some rules about pulot that I never understood nor did anyone else so far as I know."

The katiwala or overseers were an important part of Manolo Tinio's hacienda. In the 1930s he always had one and sometimes two or three. There had been overseers before; General Manuel Tinio, for example, had one katiwala in San Ricardo. What changed, peasants noticed, was what the katiwala did and represented. Previously, the katiwala had been an intermediary between the tenants and the landlord. Tenants had gone to him when the hacendero was away to make a complaint and to ask about loans. But later, according to villagers, a katiwala was mainly there to enforce Manolo Tinio's orders and to manage the hacienda in the land-lord's absence, which was frequent. Because the katiwala was the enforcer of the landlord's policies, other peasants tended to look on him with disfavor. This unpleasant and sometimes hostile relationship between tenants and katiwala caused some tenants to turn Tinio down when he offered them the job. Benjamin Bueno was one: "A katiwala was the landlord's tail. He wagged whenever the landlord told him to. Tinio asked me to take the job, but I didn't want to be his tail and still have to face my neighbors."

Eventually, according to many in San Ricardo, Manolo Tinio hired armed guards who helped the katiwala to enforce hacienda policies. People said that Tinio had four, six, sometimes twenty guards all of whom he paid a monthly salary.

Another criticism against Manolo Tinio was his insistence that tenants work for him without pay. "I did work around General Tinio's house, but that was different. It was part of the custom," Rivera said, "I'd be damned though if I was going to cut wood for his son when he wouldn't even give us rasyon." Another elderly tenant, Benjamin Bueno, said, "Several tenants were pushed off Tinio's land in the thirties because he said they were 'lazy.' But you know what that meant? It meant that the tenants had refused to do odd jobs around the hacienda without pay. I didn't blame them, although I did the work because I wanted to keep my parcel of land."

The most dramatic change for tenants on the Tinio hacienda was the end to ration loans in the early 1930s. Rarely could tenants go from one harvest to the next without running short of rice to eat. Household budgets of San Ricardo residents during the 1930s showed this (the data are synthesized in Table 3). That portion of the deficit (45 cavans and 25 cavans in the table's two examples) which a tenant could not earn by working for a harvest crew or by his wife and children transplanting seedlings, he had to borrow. Usually that amount was large. Tenant families in San Ricardo during the 1930s borrowed between 5 and 50 cavans of palay per year. A common range was 20 to 40.

From the tenants' point of view, Manolo Tinio's decision to stop rations and other loans was a grave breach in his responsibilities as a landlord. Manolo Tinio, they said, was *walang hiya* and had no sense of *utang na loob*. One sixty-year-old tenant summed up the feeling of others: "Tinio and others like him in those days no longer upheld their end of the relationship between the tenant and his landlord. They were being unfair to the peasants; it was unjust. Besides that, we had no protection anymore, and not enough to eat. But Tinio, de Leon, Jacinto, and the other big landowners had their protection. They had their guards and the constabulary."

Manolo Tinio, however, believed his actions and policies were justified. While sitting in his "rest house" one humid May day in 1970, he talked about the changes he had made years before. (Tinio stays in this house when visiting San Ricardo. It sits on the edge of the barrio, and is a wooden building of simple design that is several times larger than any of the villagers' houses nearby.) "In the old days, when I was still small," he said in American English, "the tenant-landlord system was a real paternalistic one. The landlord thought of himself as a kind of grandfather to all his tenants, and so he was concerned with all aspects of their lives. That's

Table 3

BUDGET OF A TYPICAL SAN RICARDO FAMILY OF SIX
SHARING NET HARVEST 50-50 WITH THE LANDLORD (1930s)

Example *A*: 3 hectares, averaging 45 cavans of palay per hectare

Gross harvest: 3 ha. X 45 cav./ha. =		135 cavans
Net harvest:		
Expenses for planting and harvesting		
binhi[a]	2.40 cavans	
gapas[b]	9 cavans	
telyadora[c]	6.75 cavans	
Subtotal	18.15 cavans[d]	
Net harvest		116.85 cavans
Tenant's share of net harvest:		58 cavans
Tenant's expenses:		
kanin[e]	36 cavans	
cash expenses[f] (200 pesos)	67 cavans[g]	
Subtotal	103 cavans	
Balance (tenant's net share minus his expenses):		(-45) cavans

- -

Example *B*:[h] 4 hectares, averaging 45 cavans of palay per hectare

Gross harvest: 4 ha. X 45 cav./ha. =		180 cavans
Net harvest:		
Expenses for planting and harvesting		
binhi[a]	4 cavans	
gapas[b]	12 cavans	
telyadora[c]	9 cavans	
Subtotal	25 cavans[d]	
Net harvest		155 cavans
Tenant's share of net harvest:		78 cavans
Tenant's expenses:		
kanin[e]	36 cavans	
cash expenses[f] (200 pesos)[i]	67 cavans[g]	
Subtotal	103 cavans	
Balance (tenant's net share minus his expenses):		(-25) cavans

Table 3 (continued)
BUDGET OF A TYPICAL SAN RICARDO FAMILY OF SIX
SHARING NET HARVEST 50-50 WITH THE LANDLORD (1930s)

[a]*Binhi* is the palay seed; usually 1 cavan of binhi is needed to plant 1.25 hectares. The normal practice was (and still is) for the landlord to advance the binhi but then be reimbursed from the gross harvest.

[b]*Gapas* here refers to payment made to harvesters — roughly three cavans per hectare in the 1930s. Typically, it was an expense both landlord and tenant shared (as it was on the Manolo Tinio hacienda). But sometimes it was borne entirely by the tenant himself, in which case it was not removed from the gross harvest but the tenant had to pay the harvesters from his share of the net harvest.

[c]*Telyadora,* or threshing machine, the rental fee for which was commonly 5 percent of the gross harvest. Not all peasants used a telyadora but most did (Manolo Tinio had one; so did a barrio resident who owned a small rice mill or *kiskisan*). Peasants figured it was more efficient than the traditional way of threshing palay. Usually the expense was shared between tenant and landlord.

[d]Not included here in the expenses for planting and harvesting are wages for transplanters (*upa tanim*), which ran about 10-15 pesos per hectare in those days. The landlord was responsible for this expense, paid from his share of the net harvest. Rice transplanters were from San Ricardo or nearby barrios. Usually rice transplanters were women (probably young); by custom the only males who transplanted were then (as now) boys and *binata* (unmarried men).

[e]*Kanin* is palay used for home consumption. With but one or two exceptions all informants' figures average 6 cavans per capita per year. (At 2 cavans of palay for 1 cavan of bigas, this means 3 cavans of bigas per capita, or 168 kilograms.)

[f]Cash expenses were the most difficult for informants to remember. Under this category fall expenses for additional food purchased, clothing, cigarettes, miscellaneous household items, any school supplies for children, and, undoubtedly for many, gambling. It also includes expenses for *pagaararo* — literally, ploughing, but more generally includes repairs of farming implements, and other expenses related to ploughing and tending the crop. It would not, however, include the purchase of a carabao. The figure of 200 pesos for the 1930s is the best average I could arrive at, although the range of estimates of peasants went from less than 150 pesos to 300 pesos per year. Unlike kanin, cash expenses did not seem to vary proportionately to size of family.

[g]In the 1930s, one cavan of palay was roughly equivalent to 3 pesos. This is more accurate for harvest season or in months when palay was abundant, which is usually the time peasants repaid cash loans in equivalent palay value or, in a few cases, sold extra palay for cash.

[h]The more typical size of a parcel was about 3 hectares. The upper limit was just about 4 hectares, although a few had more. Frequently, parcels over 4 hectares, however, were supporting two family units, such as a father and son's family or two brothers sharing the parcel. That 3, or even less, was more typical is confirmed in interviews, but also in the 1939 census. For Talavera, there were 10,272 hectares of cultivated land and 11,183 hectares of farm land operated by 3,334 share tenants (*kasamá*), for an average of 3.08 hectares of cultivated land or 3.26 hectares of farm land. For Nueva Ecija as a whole, the respective averages are 2.90 and 3.18 (147,158 hectares of cultivated land; 161,700 hectares of farm land; 50,831 kasamá). *Census of the Philippines, 1939,* vol. 3, pp. 1308-1311.

[i]This assumes expenses did not go up for the extra hectare of land farmed.

how my father, Manuel Tinio, was, for instance. My father's tenants thought very highly of him, too. But that system had to change over time as haciendas had to be put on a more sound economic footing. You see, the landlord-tenant relationship is a business partnership, not a family. The landlord has invested capital in the land, and the tenants give their labor."

Manolo Tinio had set out immediately to put the hacienda on a "sound economic footing." He saw many wasteful practices, which his father's way had fostered. "Take the rasyon and the other loans, for example. I put a stop to that. If the tenants needed to borrow rice or money, they could go somewhere else to get it. I decided to lend to only a few tenants, if they paid interest on it. But to give rasyon loans and charge no interest, and then sometimes not be repaid, is certainly an unbusinesslike way to handle money. Also, I stopped the rasyon because I got tired of seeing or hearing about sad faces. By the time the tenants had paid back their loans after harvest, they didn't have much left. Then they felt hurt. Pretty soon they'd be coming to me or my katiwala for another loan. No loans also saved book work."

Contracts, which Manolo Tinio insisted on beginning in 1933 or 1934, also resulted from his efforts to turn the hacienda into an efficient business operation. He felt it important to put the terms of partnership in writing, particularly things that were expected of the tenant. That way there would be no room for argument were a tenant later to question what he was supposed to do. "I got tired," he said, "of tenants agreeing to do something like removing stumps from the land without pay, and then later complaining that they weren't reimbursed." Contracts also helped to prevent tenants, he said, "from cheating me. My father never had this problem because the tenants were better people then. But tenants became lazy, and they would try to take rice and other things that didn't belong to them. So each year I had them all sign contracts. Anyone who didn't want to could go someplace else. And those who didn't abide by the contract were told to leave."

Actually Manolo Tinio would have preferred in the 1930s to turn his hacienda into a mechanized farm. When he took over his father's lands in San Ricardo and other parts of Nueva Ecija, he had just returned to the Philippines from the United States, where he had graduated in engineering from Cornell University. "I was enthused about putting machinery to work like the modern farms I'd seen in the U.S. But the estate of my father was unsettled; none of his relatives knew for sure what lands they would end up owning. So, I had to postpone the use of tractors. The only machine here before the Japanese occupation was a rice thresher, something most big landowners had. Meanwhile I tried to get the tenants to do as I said, impose some discipline on them so that the land would produce better." As the years went along, however, Manolo Tinio became more frustrated with the tenancy system and increasingly anxious to replace his one hundred tenants with machinery. He observed, "If you tell a machine to do something, it'll do it. It's not that way with tenants."

Conditions Elsewhere in Central Luzon

Carlos Rivera of San Ricardo left Manolo Tinio's hacienda in the early 1930s thinking he could find another landlord like General Tinio. He found, however, things were no easier elsewhere. He and his family went first to a barrio in Santo Domingo, a municipality neighboring Talavera. "I farmed 3 hectares for a landowner. We divided the crop 50-50, and I could get rasyon. But the whole area was cleared of all timber. There wasn't any wood left, nor any fruit trees. This meant added expenses for firewood and food. It was too hard. So we left." The next place was a barrio in Muñoz, north of Talavera. "I was told about a landlord who needed a tenant. Even though my wife was sick, we went. But we lasted only one year. The harvest was very poor, and the landlord refused to give loans. He had promised that he would, but he backed out. He would only lend at 50 percent interest." The third try was further north, in the municipality of San Jose. "At least there the harvests were OK, and there were trees for fuel. But the landlord was bad, although not as bad as Manolo Tinio. He rarely came, only at harvest time to get his rent. He had two katiwala who were lemons. You know, sour-faced and grumpy to the tenants. But we could get loans. The interest was one bag of palay for every two borrowed. From what I heard, it seemed like all landlords were charging interest. I think I was fortunate just to be able to get loans."

The same year that Rivera had left San Ricardo, another man moved into the barrio from San Isidro, Nueva Ecija. Carrying their belongings on their backs and on a bamboo sled pulled by a carabao, he and his family came to Talavera to look for "better arrangements with a landowner." They picked San Ricardo because his wife had relatives there. The hacienda where he had tenant farmed in San Isidro had become intolerable. "The landowner had been charging interest on loans for several years. The bad thing, though, is that the amount kept going up; first one bag, then two, and then three for every three bags of palay borrowed. He was the only person there was to borrow from. He was really an unscrupulous man." In San Ricardo, he said, "I was lucky. A small landowner who lived in the bayan of Talavera had just lost a tenant. The tenant had died and had no son to farm the land. So, I got his 3 hectares. The landowner and I split the crop 50-50, and I could borrow rice at 50 percent interest. Also the landowner was a nice, personable man."

A third peasant's experience also illustrated the times. In 1922, at the age of thirty-eight, he came to Talavera with his wife, eight children, a carabao, and a few possessions. He had been a kasamá for a large landowner in Bulacan, Bulacan. But he left because his share of the harvest was only 45 percent, the landlord refused to pay for seed and transplanting even though he had before, and loans, which had previously been interest-free, now had a 30 percent annual interest. "I had also heard that there was land available in Nueva Ecija and that it was very fertile." For two years he was a tenant for Manuel Tinio. After the latter's death, he continued to farm for

Manolo Tinio. "When the conditions with Manolo Tinio became so bad," he said, "I went to another landowner. After a couple of years, I went to another, and then another. Between 1922 and the mid-1930s I worked for five different landlords, all in this vicinity. I kept looking for better conditions: a larger share of the crop, fewer agricultural expenses for me to pay, low interest loans, and a fair landlord. At first I was looking for a landowner who gave interest-free loans like General Tinio had done. But that was impossible. The question became how much interest would be charged, from 25 percent all the way up to 150 percent. The landlords had us trapped. Most of them didn't care whether we farmed or not, lived or died."

Conditions described by residents in Guimba, a municipality north of Talavera, also fit the pattern of deteriorating relations between peasants and landlords.[9] In fact, the situation in Guimba was worse. One of the large haciendas there was De Santos Hacienda #5, which had 1,000 hectares. (As the "# 5" indicates, the De Santos family owned numerous haciendas.) Several hundred tenants, each with 3 or 4 hectares, split their harvests 45-55 or 50-50 with the landlord. According to one villager, "Practically no tenant got enough to live on." Consequently, most tenants were in debt to the hacienda and often paid interest rates of 100 percent. In addition, the tenants had to pay yearly fees for irrigation, fish caught in streams running through the hacienda, the use of the hacienda's chapel, and doctor's services. Years before, when relations between landlords and tenants were paternalistic, things like these would have been included automatically, without payments, in the tenancy system. Now, according to elderly tenant farmers in Guimba, "even when we paid we didn't get these things. Usually there was no irrigation, the chapel was locked, and the doctor was never around." The landlord, too, was rarely present. For years tenants did not see him. "We saw only De Santos's fancy white house and new cars," one man said with a smile. "Twelve katiwala ran the hacienda," added a woman. "Sometimes the landowner didn't even pay the katiwala. Then they'd get mad at us. They'd take rice and the vegetables I had grown during the dry season."

South of Talavera in Cabiao, the Nueva Ecija municipality bordering Pampanga, peasants emphasized that landlords had become removed from barrio life.[10] While several peasants squatted on a dusty road, one sixty-six-year old tenant farmer described a typical harvest scene in the late 1920s: "The hacendero I farmed for only came around to collect his palay. His katiwala saw to it that we harvesters had stacked the bags of thrashed palay in piles along the road. At night they'd guard the stacks. Then in the morning the landowner, driving a black car, would come, count the bags, do some calculations on a piece of paper, and then order the katiwala to load so

[9] HDP, Guimba and several interviews with residents of that municipality, including Juan T. Alano (4 February and 24 June 1970) and a Mr. Catabona (24 June 1970). The latter two men, one an attorney and the other a former tenant on the De Santos hacienda, were actively involved with peasant organizations there in the 1930s.

[10] Interviews with residents of two barrios in Cabiao, 11 and 12 March 1970.

many bags on a wagon. Then he was gone again until next year. I couldn't get help from him. To get a loan I had to walk to the bayan and talk to his sister, who lived in a big house there. Sometimes I got it, sometimes not. One thing, though, the interest on his loans was less than the Chinese rice dealers charged." Several people illustrated the landlord's absence with examples about barrio fiestas. Traditionally, the fiestas were the one time in the year when everyone shared food and celebrated the barrio's patron saint. Local landlords would come, too, even if they lived in the bayan. Usually they helped pay the expenses, and they contributed a roasted pig. By the 1930s, however, this had changed. "I never saw a big landowner in this barrio during the fiesta," one fifty-seven-year-old tenant said. "Small landowners with only three or four tenants came. But the big ones, no." Alluding to the hacenderos' rich life style, he added with a smile, "Maybe they only liked beef, not pork, and potatoes, not rice."

Perhaps Benito Santos, a ninety-nine-year-old man in San Ricardo who tenant farmed all his adult life, best summarized the changed situation. Before coming to Nueva Ecija in the late 1930s, Santos was a tenant in San Miguel, Bulacan. As a young man during the Revolution, he had fought the Spanish army, he said, "side by side with my hacendero who was our commanding officer." Afterward he farmed 3 hectares of rice land that this hacendero owned, and lived what he considered a good life. "Landowners and peasants used to be like this," he said, and he folded his two hands together. "But times changed until tenants and landlords became separated." To illustrate, he unclasped his fingers and moved his two hands apart. "And they kept getting further and further apart. Then there was trouble; peasants against landlords. That's why I left San Miguel and came here, to Talavera. I didn't want to get caught up in the chaos there. But you know, I found the same situation here. I just decided to stay and join other peasants to demand what was ours. It wasn't right for the wealthy to leave us poor people like that."

"Progress" in Central Luzon

Carlos Rivera and other peasants in San Ricardo thought at first that the drastic changes on the Tinio hacienda were merely consequences of the new landlord. Gradually they discovered, however, that landlords like Manolo Tinio had become predominant, whereas paternalistic hacenderos had become exceptional. The reasons went beyond the behavior of individual landowners. The cause was "progress." In particular, rapid population growth, capitalism, and the expansion of the central government dramatically changed Central Luzon.[11]

Between 1903 and 1939, the population in the Philippines more than doubled, from seven million to sixteen million people. In the four principal

[11] For more about the causes of changes in Central Luzon, see John A. Larkin, *The Pampangans* (Berkeley and Los Angeles: University of California Press, 1972), chapters 4, 7, and 8; and Kerkvliet, "Peasant Rebellion," pp. 38-56.

provinces of Central Luzon, the population increased from 717,000 to over
1.3 million people (see Table 4). Most people needed to farm in order to live,
so they turned virgin land into cultivated fields. But whereas the amount
of usable land was finite, the number of people continued to grow. In parts
of Nueva Ecija, population growth was slower than the conversion of virgin
lands into cultivated fields, but in Tarlac the amount of cultivated land
barely kept pace with the rising numbers of people. And in Bulacan and
Pampanga, the ratio between population and cultivated land increased
rapidly; they became two of the most densely populated rural areas in the
country. Even in Nueva Ecija there were several municipalities like Talavera
where population increased much more rapidly than did hectares of
cultivated land (see Table 1). According to people there, grasslands and
woodlands became palay fields so rapidly that practically no unused land
remained by the beginning of the Japanese occupation in 1942. They also
emphasized that land scarcity necessitated the farming of less fertile land,
which people previously would have rejected.

By the 1930s, the peasantry was desperate for land. Moreover, as few
people owned land, almost everyone depended on landowners for a parcel to
farm. If for some reason a landowner forced a tenant to leave, the tenant had
less hope than before of finding another landowner. The other side of the
coin was that landowners could demand more from tenants and threaten to
replace anyone who refused their terms. And as they became more concerned about making profits, their terms became stiffer and more strictly
enforced.

Landowners like Manolo Tinio realized they could make money from
cash crops. And they reasoned that by using their land, their capital, and
their tenants' labor more efficiently, they would have more harvest to sell.
Capitalism, which had been creeping into Philippine society long before the
Americans came, picked up speed in the twentieth century. Landowners in
Central Luzon helped the spread of capitalism and a cash economy by
responding to the market for agricultural produce. Far more than before,
land ownership became a means to wealth. Land speculation—buying low
and selling high—was one route; selling the land's produce was another.

Among the crops in greatest demand from 1910 onward were rice and
sugar cane. The market for rice was automatic in a country whose
nonfarming population grew so rapidly and whose staple food was rice. The
sugar cane market was worldwide, and the Philippines' principal customer
was the United States.

Rice and sugar cane particularly thrived in Central Luzon. Indeed, these
crops accounted for practically all the produce grown in Nueva Ecija,
Bulacan, Pampanga, and Tarlac. As Nueva Ecija and Bulacan had no cane
to speak of, palay consumed 80 to 90 percent of their cultivated land.
Throughout the Philippines, the amount of land planted in palay surged
upward, from 11 million cavans on 590,000 hectares in 1902 to over 55
million cavans on 2.3 million hectares in 1942. The Central Luzon provinces
of Bulacan, Nueva Ecija, Pampanga, and Tarlac accounted for a sizable
proportion of that increase (see Table 5). From 1930 to 1934, when rice

Table 4

BASIC CENSUS DATA FOR CENTRAL LUZON PROVINCES AND THE PHILIPPINES*

	1903	1918	1939	Percentage increase
Population				
Bulacan	224,000	249,000	333,000	49
Nueva Ecija	134,000	227,000	417,000	210
Pampanga	224,000	258,000	375,000	67
Tarlac	135,000	172,000	264,000	96
Philippines	7,000,000	10,300,000	16,000,000	129
Number farms				
Bulacan	21,000	44,000	36,000	71
Nueva Ecija	13,000	34,000	78,000	500
Pampanga	10,000	28,000	24,000	140
Tarlac	11,000	35,000	29,000	164
Philippines	800,000	1,900,000	1,600,000	100
Farm area (ha.)				
Bulacan	90,000	92,000	91,000	11
Nueva Ecija	90,000	205,000	289,000	220
Pampanga	106,000	149,000	121,000	14
Tarlac	78,000	108,000	111,000	42
Philippines	2,800,000	4,600,000	6,700,000	140
Cultivated area (ha.)				
Bulacan	61,000	71,000	73,000	20
Nueva Ecija	27,000	97,000	222,000	720
Pampanga	64,000	100,000	89,000	39
Tarlac	37,000	64,000	87,000	135
Philippines	1,300,000	2,400,000	3,900,000	200

Sources: Census of the Philippines, 1903, 1918, and 1939.

* Rounded figures.

Note: A major reason for apparent decreases in farms and area in some cases between 1918 and 1939 is that the two censuses defined "farm" in two different ways.

production prior to the Japanese occupation was at its peak, these four provinces plus Pangasinan to the north were among the top six rice producers in the country. Nueva Ecija was first among all provinces with a yearly average of nearly 9 million cavans of palay.[12]

More importantly, Central Luzon consistently produced more rice than people living there ate. Landowners, therefore, sold much of their harvests in Manila's rice markets. Between 1930 and 1934, Nueva Ecija was the country's leading rice-surplus province with 3.5 million cavans of rice (bigas). The next three leading provinces were Pangasinan, Tarlac, and Bulacan. In 1936, an estimated 220,000 cavans of bigas per month flowed from the Central Plain into Manila. About half of this came from Nueva Ecija alone. Other major exporters were Pangasinan, Tarlac, Pampanga, and Bulacan.[13] As a consequence of increased population, the country nearly became self-sufficient in rice. Rice imports declined from over 3 million cavans in 1910 to a little more than 200,000 cavans in 1941, even though at the same time the population had doubled.[14]

Sugar cane was another principal cash crop. It had long been prominent, but in the twentieth century it mushroomed from 72,000 hectares in 1910 to 306,000 hectares in 1934. Pampanga and Tarlac had nearly one-fourth (74,000 hectares in 1934) of the country's sugar land and ranked second and third—behind Negros Occidental in the Bisayas region—for cane growing in the 1930s.[15] Indicative of the expanding sugar industry in these two provinces were the numerous modern centrals, which Pampangan and Tarlac capitalists had built during the 1920s and 1930s to mill high-grade centrifugal sugar.

The large landowners were the ones who prospered from the rice and sugar boom. Peasants barely had enough for subsistence from one year to the next, even though it was they who grew, harvested, and milled the rice and cane. Rarely did villagers in San Ricardo, for example, have even a single cavan of rice to sell. Instead they often borrowed in order to eat. So meager was their income that most villagers could not send their children to public schools, which the government built in the provinces. At most they could afford to enroll their children only until the third or fourth grade. Meanwhile, the landed elite eased into a life style of fashionable clothes, homes, and cars. Their children went to public grade schools and high schools conveniently located in the bayan; afterward they attended universities in Manila or abroad. The contrast between the rich and the poor became greater than before. It angered peasants that landed families refused to share their good fortune with them. To share would have been in keeping

[12] Philippines, Rice Commission, *Report of the Rice Commission to the President of the Philippines* (Manila: Bureau of Printing, 1936), pp. 63, 67.

[13] Ibid., pp. 28-29, 63, 67.

[14] Kerkvliet, "Peasant Rebellion," p. 47.

[15] Philippines, Bureau of Commerce and Industry, *Statistical Bulletin of the Philippine Islands* (Manila: 1921), table 26; Philippines, Department of Agriculture and Commerce, *The Philippine Statistical Review* (Manila: 1935), p. 71; and Kerkvliet, "Peasant Rebellion," pp. 80, 84-85.

Table 5

PALAY CROPS IN CENTRAL LUZON AND
THE PHILIPPINES FOR SELECTED YEARS

Year[a]	Central Luzon[b]		Philippines	
	Area *(1,000 ha.)*	*Production* *(1,000 cavans)*	*Area* *(1,000 ha.)*	*Production* *(1,000 cavans)*
1902	150	2,834	593	11,166
1912	240	1,868	1,079	11,319
1922	395	13,621	1,661	43,437
1928	411	15,574	1,787	49,921
1934	417	16,857	2,004	53,001
1938	398	12,522	1,830	41,492
1942	456	12,587	2,318	55,494

[a]Each year ending June 30.

[b]Bulacan, Nueva Ecija, Pampanga, and Tarlac.

Sources: For palay data for Central Luzon provinces in most years between 1902 and 1942, see Benedict J. Kerkvliet, "Peasant Rebellion in the Philippines: The Origins and Growth of the HMB" (Ph.D. dissertation, University of Wisconsin, Madison, 1972), pp. 41, 81-83. The original sources for crop data by province are the following: 1902 and 1912 – Philippines, Bureau of Commerce and Industry, *Statistical Bulletin of the Philippine Islands* (Manila: 1921), table 24; 1922 – *Statistical Bulletin* (Manila: 1923), table 25; 1928 – *Statistical Bulletin* (Manila: 1930), table 41; 1934 – Philippines, Department of Agriculture and Commerce, *The Philippine Statistical Review* (Manila: 1935), p. 69; 1938 – *Census of the Philippines, 1939,* vol. 2, pp. 1033-1042, 1185-1189; and 1942 – Philippines, Department of Agriculture and Natural Resources, *Philippine Agricultural Statistics,* vol. 2 (Manila: 1956), tables 43, 45.

with traditional values, but it was not part of a developing capitalistic society. On the contrary, by imposing strict rules and contracts, denying rations and other loans, hiking rents, and doing other manipulations, landlords extracted more from the peasantry, gave less in return, and passed down to their tenants and laborers losses they encountered.[16]

The third important change during the American occupation was the

[16] Because prices for rice and sugar dropped sharply in the 1930s compared to the 1920s, possibly as a result of the worldwide depression, large landowners may have made less profit and some may have lost money. Probably hardest hit were those who had borrowed large sums of money to invest in other business ventures or live beyond their means. Whether low market prices meant grave losses to many landlords depends on the magnitude of fixed costs and other variables for which I have insufficient information. Were this true, however, it would add to our understanding of why landlord policies became increasingly harsh.

impact of an expanding central government on rural society.[17] This generally affected peasants adversely because they were weak competitors compared to local elites when seeking favors from the government or taking advantage of the regime's laws and policies.

A significant illustration here was the government's policy to survey and properly title, according to Western law, all land in the Philippines. Once this "cadastral survey" was completed, the government would know exactly who owned what land. Although perhaps unintended, a principal consequence of the survey was to strengthen further the landlord's hand and to weaken the tenant's. It placed landownership, based on a government-recognized title, above the peasant's traditional right to landholding, based on his ties to the landlord and on his continued use of the land. In the event of any dispute between a landlord and a peasant about rights to the land, the landlord's legal title carried far more weight than the peasant's appeals to traditional rights and verbal agreements with the landowner. Moreover, the landlord could invoke the whole legal system, including the police, to support his claim. The cadastral survey, coupled with the accelerating value of land for cash-crop purposes, also prompted local elites to overpower weaker claimants to lands by "fixing" the titles in assessors' offices and winning court cases against peasant landowners who did not understand the law and who lacked "connections" in government agencies.

The major effect of American colonial rule on the local officials' rural society was to transform the local elite's relationship to the community. Up until the nineteenth century, one could argue, most local elites had little reliable support from the outside. Rather, their support and an important basis for their prestige and power came from a local following of "little people," mainly peasants. They cultivated a following by extending patronage and protection. It was in their interest, therefore, to minimize any claims on the local communities from the outside, particularly the central government. Gradually, however, colonialism broke the local elites' dependence on the peasantry in the barrios. Simultaneously, it inflated the landlords' power, reduced their need for a loyal following, and as a consequence whittled away their incentives to serve the community by protecting it against the government. Although this transformation had begun under Spanish rule, it accelerated during the American occupation. Working through the elites in the municipalities and provinces, the American colonial regime reached much further into the countryside than had the

[17] In addition to my own analysis of Central Luzon, I have drawn on the following sources for the argument presented in the next four paragraphs: Larkin, *The Pampangans*, chapters 6-8; Teodoro A. Agoncillo and Oscar M. Alfonso, *History of the Filipino People* (2d ed. rev.; Quezon City: Malaya Books, 1967), chapters 19-21; Pedro E. Abelarde, *American Tariff Policy towards the Philippines* (New York: Kings Crown Press, 1947); Amado Alejandro Castro, "The Philippines: A Study in Economic Dependence," (Ph.D. dissertation, Harvard University, 1953); Theodore Friend, *Between Two Empires* (New Haven: Yale University Press, 1965); Garel A. Grunder and William E. Livezey, *The Philippines and the United States* (Norman: University of Oklahoma Press, 1951); Shirley Jenkins, *American Economic Policy Toward the Philippines* (Stanford, California: Stanford University Press, 1954).

Spanish and it governed through more numerous Filipinos. In addition, the American regime fostered a national political arena—particularly the national assembly and the central bureaucracy—which the traditional elites dominated and used to protect their economic and political interests in their home provinces.

Finally, American colonialism encouraged the expansion of the capitalistic economy, which favored American investors and wealthy Filipinos. The U.S. tariff policies stimulated cash crops (especially sugar cane) for export (principally to the United States) but inhibited the development of a diversified Philippine economy. And the regime's credit and banking allowances helped Filipino capitalists to invest in export-oriented business ventures. At the same time, the regime made the Philippines an open market for American manufactured goods and undermined Filipino industries. This not only stifled production of local consumer goods, but denied rural people alternative sources of jobs and income.

Capitalism and colonialism did not spread evenly across the country. Central Luzon was probably more affected than most regions because agricultural conditions for cash crops were excellent, the commercial and political capital of Manila was close, and roads and other infrastructures there were relatively good at the turn of the century. Consequently, society in Central Luzon may have suffered the ravages of progress more than other regions did, resulting in more serious hardships for the peasantry there than elsewhere. This has implications for understanding the Huk rebellion.

Unrest and rebellion correlated strongly with the high percentage of tenant farmers in Central Luzon provinces, where tenancy exceeded all other provinces except one (see Table 6). Yet as testimonies from villagers suggest, tenancy alone was not sufficient for discontent. Additionally important was the quality of relationships between tenants and landlords. Peasants resisted and detested landlords who exploited them but not those who were paternalistic to them. One might reasonably infer the same for peasants living elsewhere in the Philippines. If true, one can understand why rebellion would not necessarily sweep across all areas with high tenancy, for according to available information relations between landlords and tenants in several high tenancy provinces remained relatively paternalistic or did not deteriorate nearly so rapidly or extensively as they did in Central Luzon.[18]

[18] James N. Anderson, "Kinship and Property in a Pangasinan Barrio," (Ph.D. dissertation, University of California, Los Angeles, 1964); James N. Anderson, "Land and Society in a Pangasinan Community," in Socorro C. Espiritu and Chester L. Hunt (eds.), *Social Foundations of Community Development* (Manila: R. M. Garcia Publishing House, 1964), p. 171-192; Richard W. Coller, *Barrio Gacao: A Study of Village Ecology and the Schestosomiasis Problem* (Quezon City: University of the Philippines Community Development Research Council, 1960); George H. Fairchild, *Facts and Statistics about the Philippine Sugar Industry* (Manila: Philippine Sugar Association, 1928); Frank Lynch, *Social Class in a Bikol Town* (Chicago: Philippine Studies Program Research Series, University of Chicago, 1959); Philippines, Department of Labor, *Fact-Finding Survey: Report of Rural Problems to the President of the Philippines, 1936;* Generoso F. Rivera and Robert T. McMillan, *The Rural Philippines* (Manila: Mutual Security Agency, 1952); I. T. Runes, *General Standards of Living and Wages of Workers in the Philippine Sugar Industry* (Manila: Institute of Pacific Relations, 1939).

Table 6

PROVINCES RANKED BY TENANT FARMERS AS A PERCENTAGE
OF ALL FARMERS (1939)

Province	Percentage tenant farmers[a]	Province	Percentage tenant farmers[a]
Pampanga	70.4[b]	Masbate	30.3
Negros Occidental	67.9	Isabela	29.0
Nueva Ecija	66.4[b]	Lanao	28.9
Bulacan	64.2[b]	Nueva Vizcaya	27.9
Cavite	54.5[c]	Mindoro	27.8
Tarlac	53.0[c]	Sulu	26.4
Bataan	52.4[c]	Davao	26.2
Iloilo	47.4	Zamboanga	25.7
Batangas	44.9[c]	Ilocos Sur	24.2
Negros Oriental	43.8	Albay	23.5
Camarines Norte	43.6	Cotabato	23.2
Leyte	43.4	Misamis Oriental	21.4
Misamis Occidental	42.3	Cagayan	20.1
Capiz	42.0	Ilocos Norte	19.5
Cebu	41.4	Agusan	18.5
Laguna	41.3[c]	La Union	17.7
Rizal	36.6[c]	Samar	16.7
Quezon	36.3[c]	Bohol	16.5
Romblon	36.1	Antique	15.4
Bukidnon	33.3	Surigao	14.0
Pangasinan	33.1	Marinduque	13.6
Camarines Sur	32.3	Abra	11.5
Zambales	31.8	Palawan	3.5
Sorsogon	31.3	Mountain Province	1.9
		Batanes	1.8

Source: Census of the Philippines, 1939, vol. 2, p. 970.

[a]The percentages are the total number of tenant-operated farms as a percentage of all farms. Tenants here would include the share tenants (kasamá), share-cash tenants, and cash tenants appearing in the 1939 census. Except for Sulu and Bukidnon provinces, share tenants were always the overwhelming majority.

[b]Core provinces of peasant unrest and Huk rebellion.

[c]Marginal provinces of peasant unrest and Huk rebellion.

Population pressures on available land, capitalism, and colonialism had made life for a large proportion of villagers in Central Luzon far more insecure than they had known it before. Yet these same changes had made the landed elites less paternalistic and less interested in tenants as clients. Whereas before people had been the principle resource for the landed elite, now cash and land were the most important. The General Tinios of Central Luzon in an earlier, more traditional society had wanted a loyal clientele; the Manolo Tinios of the new, modernizing country wanted maximum earnings and profits. To the modern landlords, their relationship to their tenants was a business proposition—the peasants were laborers who would be employed so long as they helped turn land into profits. This attitude was also possible because these landlords were further removed from the entire traditional social and cultural system than the older generation of large landowners had been. They spent less time in the rural areas. Many had been educated in Manila and even abroad. There was little in their personal experience to make them feel attached or obligated to villagers as other than mere workers. This "psychological absenteeism" went beyond the physical absenteeism that had been common earlier. After all, General Manuel Tinio was often absent from San Ricardo. But in the eyes of the tenants, the elder Tinio's physical presence was less crucial than his paternalistic attitudes and ties to them. He and other traditional landlords were simply more personally involved with the peasantry than their successors were.

The peasantry, meanwhile, wanted traditional patronage more than ever, lest they succumb not only to such usual hazards as poor harvests and sickness, but also to new ones resulting from radical changes that had been compressed into a few years. "Progress" had not brought even modest economic gains to the peasantry, while at the same time severing numerous ties with their landlords that peasants wanted to retain and to which they felt entitled. The traditional landlord-tenant relationship included far more than a simple exchange of labor for money, so peasants wanted to keep it. They wanted the landed elites to acknowledge those ties and the obligations entailed. The stage was thus set for a conflict that was to last for years.

Chapter 2
UNREST

PEOPLE in Central Luzon tried numerous strategies to protect themselves against the worsening conditions and growing uncertainties of the 1920s and 1930s. They adapted old ways while simultaneously venturing into new ones. Gradually at first, but then with a tempo that quickened as other efforts proved unsatisfying, villagers turned to collective action. Still clinging to the tenancy system, they protested and organized in hopes of forcing the landed elites to be judicious landlords.

Trying to Adjust in San Ricardo

Many in San Ricardo reacted as Carlos Rivera had done—they simply moved away.[1] "Peasants around here were forever moving around before the Japanese occupation," Manolo Tinio recalled. "I don't know why, but they did. The turnover of tenants on my land was high." Peasants went from one landowner to another, searching for better tenancy arrangements. A few hoped to buy land, because the government had opened public lands to homesteaders. Others moved to Cabanatuan, some even to Manila.

Tenant farmers also looked for odd jobs to supplement family income: cutting wood in distant mountains and selling it in Talavera, raising pigs or poultry to sell in the Cabanatuan market, hiring out as palay transplanters and harvesters. Some men found seasonal work as laborers in Cabanatuan. A few planted vegetables in their fields after the palay had been harvested. More peasants would have done this, but because the rivers and creeks were nearly dry during the hot season, they could not irrigate their fields.

Options were few. As one man in San Ricardo put it, "What else could we do but make do. We had to suffer through as best as possible." People reduced diets that were already meager, wore worn out clothes even longer, walked to market instead of spending coins for transportation, and endured illnesses

[1] The following account is based on interviews and conversations with residents of San Ricardo and other barrios in Talavera. Included are interviews with Manolo and Vivencio Tinio.

26

without treatment. They also borrowed rice and cash from landlords and moneylenders, and typically paid interest rates of 100 to 150 percent for rice and 20 percent for money.

Peasants said that having extended families helped; as one elderly man stated, "It's easier for many relatives to bear the load than it is for just one man or a small family." Several people, including Carlos Rivera, returned to San Ricardo, after concluding that good tenancy arrangements were unavailable anywhere, in order to be with relatives again.

Villagers also practiced a kind of "share-the-poverty" ethic. For example, neighbors had customarily helped one another harvest without payment. By the 1930s, however, peasants were paying teams of harvesters 6 percent of their grain. As this amount was subtracted from the gross harvest, before the tenant and landlord divided the crop, it came from the landlord's pocket as much as from the individual tenant's. In this way, the peasants kept more of the rice in the barrio. It also made work for those who were either landless or unable to grow enough. According to the share-the-poverty ethic, those families most in need of work should be the ones hired. The same ethic prevailed with regard to gleaning the fields *(pulot)*. Because times were hard, more people than before would pulot. Several peasants remembered when fallen rice would lie for weeks without anyone bothering to pulot. In the 1930s, however, and after the Japanese occupation, this was no longer so. Custom dictated that peasants most in need had first claim to pulot. As one middle-aged tenant put it, "Without pulot, these people would have nothing left to eat. I didn't have much either, but more than they did. I would be *walang hiya* were I to pulot."

Another reaction was to demand that the landlords treat them fairly. The standard of fairness was the traditional tenancy system. Initially, peasants made these demands individually or in groups of two or three. Later several joined together and formed organizations. Because collective action like this was new to most people, it evolved gradually and sometimes painfully.

One individual who exemplified this evolution in San Ricardo was Patricio del Rosario. He was born the son of a tenant farmer in San Miguel, Bulacan, in 1881.[2] While still an adolescent and after four years of formal education, del Rosario became a tenant. He farmed in San Miguel until he was forty years old. His last three years there, however, had been extraordinarily difficult because his landlord had unilaterally altered the tenancy arrangements by charging high interest on loans. Some people protested. The next year they formed an association called Union ng Magsasaka (Peasant Union), whose main goal was to improve relations between themselves and the landlords. Del Rosario may have participated in this group, but he was not committed to it. For him there were still other possibilities.

[2] I am grateful to Ely del Rosario for the details about his father and to many other people in Talavera for their recollections of this man.

In 1922 he, his wife, and their eight children left San Miguel and went to Talavera, where he had heard good farm land was still available. He became a tenant for General Manuel Tinio. After General Tinio died, del Rosario tenant-farmed for Manolo Tinio. But he soon left because of Tinio's harsh policies. By this time his eldest son had become a tenant for another landlord in the vicinity. Perhaps for this and other family considerations, del Rosario decided to stay in San Ricardo rather than move again. He became a tenant for another Tinio in Talavera, and for still another landlord three years later. Between the mid-1920s and mid-1930s, he had at least six different landlords. Although rents were nearly the same everywhere—either 45 or 50 percent of the harvest—del Rosario was searching for a landlord who charged little or no interest on loans. Like most tenants, del Rosario was usually in debt, so loan opportunities and interest rates were critical considerations.

Eventually he abandoned hopes of finding decent tenancy arrangements. He concluded that in order to get what he and other villagers believed they deserved, they needed to organize. In 1931 and 1932, he was a member of a peasant organization in Talavera called Tanggulan (Defense).[3] An elderly man who had been a member with del Rosario said the group's purpose was "to defend peasants against the bad practices of landlords and to make relations between tenants and landowners better." Tanggulan supporters in Talavera were allied with others elsewhere in Nueva Ecija, although they acted independently. In 1934, del Rosario's landlord evicted him because he had urged tenants to unionize. The next year another landowner forced him to leave for the same reason.

By this time, del Rosario was well-known in the municipality as a leader. "He was a soft-spoken man," said Hilario Felipe, who had known del Rosario, "but very determined, very strong. He wanted all peasants to join one big organization. Only in this way, he felt, would landlords give us a fair share of the harvest, and treat us like men rather than dogs." On one occasion in 1938, after a strike against a Talavera landlord had been only partially successful, del Rosario spoke with several peasants in front of his house. His son, who was thirteen years old at the time, remembered del Rosario's message:

> Some of the people there had not joined the strike. They said they were afraid of being evicted if they joined. But my father told them that the most important thing he had learned was that peasants had to overcome their fears and to stand up to the hacenderós and moneylenders as one, like a clenched fist. He wasn't angry with those who had not joined the strike because he understood. But he couldn't support their weakness either. He wanted all peasants to be strong, together.

---

[3] *Tanggulan* is often spelled *Tangulan* in newspapers and secondary sources. As the root word in Tagalog is *tanggol,* meaning "defense," it seems more accurate to use consistently the first spelling.

Throughout the municipality, the unrest grew. The *Tribune,* a Manila daily newspaper, had fifteen reports between 1930 and 1941 of landlords evicting tenants, tenants striking, peasants petitioning the provincial governor to force landlords to divide harvests fairly, and other instances of protest. Other cases, of course, went unreported. In 1933, for example, a half-dozen tenants in San Ricardo beat up a katiwala who worked for a landlord named de Leon because he had tried to stop them from taking grain to feed their chickens. The next year about twenty people in a neighboring barrio almost killed a landlord after he had refused to give them rasyon loans. In Talavera there was at least one strike in 1935, one in 1936, two in 1938, three in 1939, and five in 1940. "Settlements" of disputes seemed to last only until the next month or the next year, when another confrontation came. Among the haciendas with numerous instances of unrest were those owned by such families as Jacinto, de Leon, Cojuangco, and Tinio.

In 1936, tenants for Manolo Tinio asked him to pay more of the agricultural expenses. He refused by saying this was not part of their contract. The next year, Patricio del Rosario, speaking on behalf of Manolo Tinio's tenants, asked a lawyer from the Department of Justice who was in Talavera to intercede because the tenants were paying over half the farming costs, which was more than they had paid previously. The next year, 1938, several disputes erupted at harvest time over payments for expenses and because Tinio had evicted several tenants. He claimed they had been lazy; they claimed he had ousted them for opposing his policies. In 1939, several tenants went on strike. They refused to harvest until Tinio promised to pay the expenses stipulated in a new law. Other tenants, believing that Tinio would ignore that law and instead abide by contracts they had signed which did not include some of the guarantees included in the law, began to harvest the palay at night when hacienda guards were not looking. Tinio then complained to the government authorities. The provincial commander of the Philippine Constabulary (PC) sent troopers, which arrested three tenants—two for cutting rice "illegally" and one for leading a strike. A few days later, the PC released the three men. Other tenants, meanwhile, decided to harvest under the watchful eyes of Tinio's katiwala and guards. Afterward, the villagers and Tinio again disagreed over expenses. Tenants cited the new law, but the landlord pointed to the contracts they had signed several months earlier. Eventually they divided the crop, although hard feelings lingered all around and carried over to following years.

Tenants on a nearby hacienda in barrio Sibul, Talavera, also struggled with their landlord, Nicanor Jacinto.[4] In January 1937, the administrator asked the Talavera police to "help maintain order" on the huge Jacinto

[4] This account of unrest on the Jacinto hacienda is based on interviews in Talavera, including barrio Sibul, and on these articles in the *Tribune:* 13 January 1937, p. 2, 14 January 1937, p. 16, 6 May 1939, p. 20, 12 January 1940, p. 4, and 1 August 1940, p. 16.

hacienda. The administrator of the hacienda claimed that tenants owed money for loans and irrigation fees. The tenants, however, refused to pay on the grounds that the contract's terms were unjust. When the administrator and a katiwala tried to collect these alleged debts while the tenants were stacking bags of threshed palay in the fields, they and the tenants nearly had a brawl. The police arrived in time to prevent it. The next day, representatives from the Nueva Ecija governor's offices mediated an agreement between Jacinto and the peasants' spokesman that included the landlord's commitment to give interest-free loans and to abolish irrigation fees.

The agreement did not last. After the next harvest, the Jacinto hacienda administrator again tried to collect interest on loans given during the year. When the tenants refused, he ordered the tenants to leave. The dispute continued from May until the December 1939 harvest. Meanwhile, both the tenants and Jacinto went to the newly established Court of Industrial Relations (CIR). A lawyer from a Nueva Ecija peasant union argued that Jacinto had failed to abide by the 1937 agreement, whereas Jacinto's lawyers argued that the tenants had violated the contract when they demanded to be reimbursed for the food they had fed to harvesters. In August 1940, the CIR ruled in favor of the tenants. By then it was too late, however, because Jacinto's armed guards had already driven away several tenant families.

In another confrontation in San Ricardo, a national government agency also ruled in favor of the peasants, but this time before it was too late. The case involved several small landowners, some of whom lived in a subbarrio (sitio) of San Ricardo.[5] In 1936 a woman named Maria Pilares, a relative of the deceased General Manuel Tinio, claimed that her hacienda included the lands that these small landowners were farming. She went to court and said that because she had been paying taxes on the land she was the owner. She also asked that the peasant families using the land be evicted. But the peasants refused to leave. Each family claimed to be the owner of the three or four hectares it farmed. With the help of Patricio del Rosario and another local peasant leader named Amando Santa Ana, the small landowners pooled their money to hire a lawyer. During the hearing, the representatives from the Bureau of Lands dismissed evidence that the peasants' attorney had offered as proof of ownership. The documents, they ruled, were forgeries. The peasants became furious. Three hundred people stormed the hacienda house of Maria Pilares and almost killed one agent from the Bureau of Lands. Several months later, the bureau ruled that the homestead applications which the peasants had held since 1925 were valid because they had in fact been paying taxes. During the celebration that followed, people gave the sitio a new name: Bagong Sikat,

[5] I pieced together this account from three sources: *Tribune,* 10 December, 1936, p. 2; Pagaduan, "Kasaysayan ng Talavera," pp. 78-79; and interviews with two men in San Ricardo who are sons of two claimants in this case and who still own and farm the small parcels that their fathers fought to keep.

meaning "Brilliant Hope," which the people there believed this triumph meant for their lives.

The Bagong Sikat case reflected the growing unity among villagers trying to survive. Another illustration was the credit cooperative several people in San Ricardo tried to form in order to avoid paying high interest rates. They began by purchasing a mechanical rice thresher *(telyadora)* on an installment basis. Members could rent the machine for 4 percent of their harvest as opposed to the usual 6 percent. With these earnings from the rentals, cooperative members hoped to pay for the thresher and have a surplus from which members could borrow. After only two years, however, the venture died. The members had to sell the thresher because they could not make their payments.

Although local conditions caused their discontent, people in San Ricardo were inspired and influenced by actions in other barrios. Through word of mouth, they learned more about resistance and protest. Hilario Felipe, for example, said,

> Several organizations in the 1930s affected our actions here in Talavera. I think the most memorable were the organizations among tenants on Hacienda Santos in Guimba and Samahang Magbubukid, a peasant union in Bulacan someplace. Also there were the peasants of Bahay Pare in Pampanga who were well organized in the 1930s and the labor union strikes in Manila. These were examples for us and the leaders here. They showed the importance of joining together because we had the same problems.

The actions of San Ricardo peasants, in turn, became examples for others such as the tenants on the Jacinto hacienda in Sibul, Talavera, or villagers in Jaen, a municipality south of Talavera, who organized a strike in 1939 partly because of San Ricardo's influence. Like ripples from a pebble tossed into still water, unrest in one barrio affected others farther away.

An important sign that people in San Ricardo were a part of a growing movement in Central Luzon was the local chapter of the KPMP— Kalipunang Pambansa ng mga Magsasaka sa Pilipinas (National Society of Peasants in the Philippines). Peasants in San Ricardo and Talavera had participated in other organizations before, but the KPMP was the largest, and in a way it was a culmination of the previous ones. By the second half of the 1930s, many who had supported earlier associations now were in the KPMP. Joining them were others who had not been involved before.

As attitude and action, not formal rules, determined membership in the KPMP, it is impossible to say precisely how many people joined. Anyone who believed peasants needed to unite in order to deal with landed elites could be considered KPMP members. Never mind, people said, whether or not an individual had paid the 70 centavo dues supposedly required of all, and never mind if he had formally joined a KPMP chapter. Hilario Felipe, who was a KPMP activist in Talavera during the 1930s, examined this question of size by saying,

Maybe 10 percent of the peasants in Talavera joined the KPMP. Perhaps it was higher in San Ricardo because this barrio was one of the most active. We used to have a simple initiation ceremony for members. A new member would prick his finger, then sign his name in blood to symbolize brotherhood and unity. But there were others who were KPMP in their hearts. KPMP had an insignia shaped like this: ⌒. Like the yoke of the carabao to pull the plow. Anyone could wear this insignia. Some tatooed it on their arm, others drew it on this shirt sleeve. I'd say 40 or maybe 50 percent of the peasants in Talavera wore this insignia, and they agreed with the purposes of the KPMP and joined KPMP actions. Yes, they were KPMP, too.

Leadership, too, was rather informal in KPMP chapters. Usually men, but in rare cases women, became the recognized leaders and spokesmen not through formal elections but by earning the respect and confidence of fellow peasants. Villagers accepted someone as a leader because of what he had done in the peasant movement.

Most barrios in Talavera had at least one leader. San Ricardo had two: Patricio del Rosario and Amando Santa Ana. Indeed, by the late 1930s these two men were recognized throughout Talavera and even in other parts of Nueva Ecija as spokesmen for the peasant movement in general and for the KPMP in particular.

Born near the turn of the century, Amando Santa Ana was originally from the municipality of Quezon in Nueva Ecija and was born in a peasant family.[6] In his youth, he moved to Cabanatuan and put himself through high school by working at part-time jobs. He had hoped to go to college but never had enough money. In 1921 he married and moved to Talavera, where his wife's relatives owned 6 hectares of land. He and several of his wife's relatives tried to live off this land, but it was too small and its soil too poor. His wife's family eventually sold the land in order to pay their debts. Santa Ana then had no permanent work. He and his wife, with their several children, built a hut in San Ricardo and earned a living by transplanting rice, harvesting, and doing odd jobs. When the children were old enough, they worked too. The family also would pulot because, his daughter recalled, "otherwise we didn't have enough to eat."

Hilario Felipe remembered that Santa Ana "was sometimes a bitter man. It irked him so much that the wealthy people were so rude and uncaring to poor people. He was also smart—a thinker as well as a doer. And he was certainly dedicated to the peasant movement. No doubt about that." Along with others from Talavera, Santa Ana joined the Tanggulan. A newspaper in May 1932 listed his name among ten Tanggulan supporters who were convicted of "attempted rebellion" after they had "sacked" the municipal government building in Talavera.[7] The stint in jail, however, did not stifle

---

[6] For the background of Amando Santa Ana, I am grateful to his surviving daughter and to several other people in the municipality who remember him.

[7] *Philippine Herald,* 18 May 1932, p. 10, and 10 June 1932, p. 1.

his activism. In 1935 he was in the Sakdal, a peasant-based organization that was strong in parts of Central and Southern Luzon in the mid-1930s. He continued to travel among Talavera's barrios to advocate reform, paying little attention to police agents who spied on him because he was a "radical." By this time, according to his daughter, "peasants in San Ricardo and other barrios gave my father contributions of palay and fish so that our family could eat. It was their expression of support for what he was doing as their spokesman." In the second half of the 1930s, Santa Ana helped several strikes. "I remember him particularly well at a strike in 1938 in barrio Pinagpanaan," said Hilario Felipe.

> He was standing among several people along the road leading to the hacendero's barrio house. They were holding flags with "KPMP" written on them. Santa Ana spoke very well as he read in a loud voice, so the landlord's administrator could hear, a list of demands that the strikers had prepared. "Fifty-five percent of the harvest because 50 percent is not enough," he said; "the landlord must pay for his half of the agricultural expenses; and all tenants who have been evicted because they joined the KPMP must be given back their parcels of land." Later that day during a discussion Santa Ana told everyone that peasants needed to pressure the government in Manila to make laws that would guarantee that tenants got what they deserved from the landlords.

People most likely to be in the KPMP, to go on strike, or otherwise to join the movement in the 1930s were tenants of large landowners. As one middle-aged tenant in San Ricardo explained, "These were the people who were the most desperate. They were the ones most cut off from their landowners. Conditions were more harsh for them than for anybody." Those who owned 3 or 4 hectares that they farmed themselves also joined the movement. These small landowners, who composed only a small fraction of the peasantry, shared tenant farmers' growing animosity toward the big landowners, and they wanted to guard against big landlords' attempts to take their lands by force or through court maneuverings. Moreover, they were also peasants, and many were related to tenant farmers.

Family ties did sometimes influence people to join the KPMP, although many emphasized, as Hilario Felipe did, that "family was much less important than a tenant's relationship to his landlord." One man, for example, said that he joined the KPMP in 1938, "because my brother in San Miguel [a barrio in Talavera] became very active there. Up until then, I had hesitated to get involved, not because I didn't have gripes, because I did, just like everybody else. But I was afraid of getting kicked off the land. My brother convinced me that if more of us would stick together, the landlords couldn't throw us out."

Certain customs in the barrios also contributed to more unity among peasants. A revealing illustration involved the custom of neighbors helping one another to build houses, plow fields, and do other tasks. Bonds of friendship became stronger when neighbors who exchanged labor also supported one another during strikes or attended demonstrations together.

One San Ricardo activist during the 1930s noted that, "Sometimes this got turned around. Peasants cooperated and exchanged work *because* they were KPMP together." As the movement in the barrio became stronger, according to Hilario Felipe, organized peasants even "excluded nonjoiners from work exchanges, using this as a way to prod hesitant people to join the movement."

A new development during the 1930s was that tenants who had the same landlord began to see their common concerns and grievances. This had not been true before when landlords were paternalistic, for tenancy arrangements were not uniform and landlords dealt with individual tenants rather than with tenants as a class. By the 1930s, however, tenants who had the same landlord shared the same predicament. Frequently, each had signed the same written contract which their landlord had prepared. Rarely did landlords like Manolo Tinio make exceptions for individual peasants. It was not long, therefore, before these homogeneous tenancy conditions drew tenants together to organize for better contracts.

Numerous peasants, of course, were not active in unrest. Some were tenants like Carlos Rivera, who explained, "There were peasant groups when I returned to San Ricardo in 1939. But I didn't want to get involved. I was already too old; and I was tired. I just wanted a piece of land to plant enough to feed my wife and me." Rivera tenant-farmed again for Manolo Tinio, despite what he thought were "bad conditions," and never participated in any of the peasant movement activities there. Other peasants were afraid. To complain, they feared, would mean eviction from the land. "Land to farm was more and more scarce," said one tenant about the late 1930s. "I was feeling lucky just to have a parcel to farm. I didn't join the KPMP or anything like that because I didn't want to be thrown off the land." A few tenants pursued another kind of strategy for survival and security: they obeyed their landlords' laws to the letter and did everything to stay on the good side of both their landlords and their katiwala. Said one man, "I was a tenant for Manolo Tinio from 1935 until the Japanese occupation. Many didn't like his conditions. But I just worked hard and didn't cause trouble. There was no choice. When he was around, Tinio treated me OK." Other people in San Ricardo said that this man was one of those whom Tinio paid to be armed guards on the hacienda. He was, they said, a *bata* (pawn) of the landlord. Among those least likely to join the movement were tenants for small landowners who had 12 or 15 hectares that three or four tenants farmed. Hilario Felipe elaborated: "This is because the small landowners often were farmers too. They worked a parcel of land right alongside their tenants. Or if not that, then at least they lived on the land and were close to their tenants. If they had any problems or complaints, the tenants could easily go talk with the landowner."

Even among those who eventually joined KPMP or participated in collective actions, many had doubts that this was the best thing to do, although they saw no alternative. Many people felt as Benito Santos did when he explained his reluctant activism: "I had left Bulacan because I didn't like the trouble between the peasants and landlords. But I ended up in the KPMP in San Ricardo. I had to. There was no other way to try to bring the landlords together again with us tenants. Yet it seemed like we just got further apart. Sometimes I wondered if we were making things worse."

Whatever their fears and reluctance, peasants in San Ricardo and other barrios of Talavera did come together as they had never done before. They were learning that this was necessary if the deteriorating tenancy system was to improve. And they were learning how to express their shared political objectives. Because of these experiences, the 1930s was a memorable decade for them.

Growing Unrest in Central Luzon

Like residents in San Ricardo, barrio residents elsewhere in Central Luzon also tried to adjust to the rapid changes. Had alternative employment been available the situation would have been eased considerably. As tenancy conditions became worse, peasants could have left the land to work elsewhere. But Central Luzon, like San Ricardo, offered little work other than in agriculture.[8] Most people were either tenants or agricultural laborers who cut and hauled sugar cane, harvested rice, and worked in sugar centrals and rice granaries. A handful tended fishponds in southern municipalities of Bulacan and Pampanga, but this was no escape from life as a tenant because wealthy families owned the ponds. There were some local industries, such as weaving, metalworking, and pottery, but the products were primarily for local consumption. Few families could subsist on earnings from handicrafts; they still had to tenant farm or work as laborers.

Peasants in Central Luzon could try to migrate to look for land elsewhere. People had done this earlier in the century, especially villagers from Bulacan and Pampanga who went to the less crowded provinces of Nueva Ecija and Tarlac. Only a small percentage were willing to move very far, however, and few among these actually found unclaimed land. Most ended up as tenant farmers anyway.

Although the colonial government opened up several thousand hectares of public land to homesteading in the 1910s, obstacles to getting a title overwhelmed all but a handful of peasants. Applying for a homestead was

---

[8] This conclusion is based on interviews and the following: Philippines, Department of Labor, *Fact-Finding Survey Report, 1936; Tribune,* 1 May 1936, p. 2; Headquarters, Philippine Department, Office of Assistant Chief of Staff for Military Intelligence, Manila, "Agrarian Unrest in Pampanga and Adjacent Provinces," 20 August 1938, p. 8 (RG 350, 1937-157; National Archives, Washington, D.C.); Larkin, *The Pampangans,* pp. 300-302; and *HDP* volumes for Central Luzon municipalities and provinces.

one thing, but actually getting it approved was another—and securing a title was still one more hurdle. Because the bureaucracy was incapable of handling the mushrooming number of applicants and because filing procedures and requirements were complex, less than a quarter of the applications in Central Luzon (29,000) and the country as a whole (150,000) had actually been approved by 1928. And only one-tenth of the applicants actually received titles to the land.[9] Moreover, the landed elite manipulated both the laws and the bureaucratic maze, whereas small landowners were rather ignorant of such matters. Using such tactics as circumventing a 16-hectare per person limit by putting land in the names of several family members and tampering with land records through bribery and influence, the landed elite walked away with most of whatever untitled land remained in Central Luzon before the Japanese occupation. The lure of these public lands plus inducements to document property ownership because of the cadasteral surveys produced a history replete with cases of land-grabbing. For example, hundreds of people in Nampicuan, Nueva Ecija, who had thought they owned land that they had laboriously cleared and planted for several years, found out differently in 1922. Owners of haciendas in the vicinity, backed by armed government police, confronted the peasants with legal titles they held to the peasants' lands. A few people resisted, feebly, and a few moved away. Most, however, could do nothing other than accept the hacienda owners' terms and become tenant farmers.[10]

Facing harsh conditions but having no way out, peasants began to protest. Signs of discontent had appeared off and on for years. There had been attacks against landlords and government officials, social bandits, millenarian groups, and local uprisings. What was different by the 1930s is that there was no longer any doubt that peasants were becoming organized. Unrest dominated Central Luzon.

By the latter half of the 1930s, scarcely a week would pass without a major incident of agrarian discontent. October through March were particularly turbulent months because then peasants and landlords disputed how to share the new harvest, who paid what expenses, and how much money or rice tenants owed. May through August were also difficult months, for landlords seemed to prefer to evict troublesome tenants then and tenants who had no more food demanded rasyon and other loans and assistance. Apparently disagreements frequently went unresolved, because

    [9] See figures by province from 1904 to 1928 in Philippines, Bureau of Commerce and Industry, *Statistical Bulletin of the Philippine Islands* (Manila: 1929), pp. 23-25.
    [10] Conflict over land and land-grabbing during the 1900-1940 period are major themes in the *HDP*s for Central Luzon. The case of Nampicuan is from *HDP, Nampicuan*. Also see Erich H. Jacoby, *Agrarian Unrest in Southeast Asia* (Bombay: P. S. Jayasinghe, Asia Publishing House, 1961), p. 201; Marshall S. McLennan, "Land and Tenancy in the Central Luzon Plain," *Philippine Studies 17* (October 1969): 673-674; and Karl Pelzer, *Pioneer Settlement in the Asiatic Tropics* (New York: American Geographical Society, 1945), pp. 90, 108-113.

names of many landlords and places with unrest reappeared year after year in newspaper reports.

Among other actions, peasants burned crops to protest against landlords who hired strikebreakers, refused to harvest until landlords had agreed to their terms regarding expenses and loans, raided the granaries of landlords to take what they believed belonged to them, held large and colorful parades in provincial capitals to demonstrate for new tenancy laws and government assistance, and defended themselves in court against the landlords' accusations of stealing or the government's charges of subversion and being communists.

Adding further cause for discontent were several bad harvests due to droughts and floods between 1935 and 1940. The result was more hunger and despair than usual. Hundreds of peasants in several municipalities in all four Central Luzon provinces begged for food and raided government rice warehouses.[11]

Peasants formed numerous organizations. Among them were Samahang Magsasaka, Kabisang Tales, Kapatirang Magsasaka, Kalipunan Mipanampon, Anak Pawis, Aklasan, Handa Na, Dumating Na, Atin Na, and Oras Na. Most were so small that people today have difficulty recalling which was where. A few, however, became large enough to encompass dozens of municipal chapters: the Sakdal movement in parts of Nueva Ecija, Bulacan, and Laguna; Aguman ding Malding Talapagobra (AMT; General Workers' Union), strong in Pampanga and Tarlac and in parts of Bulacan and Nueva Ecija from 1935 onward; and the KPMP in most municipalities of Nueva Ecija and Bulacan and in parts of Tarlac, Pampanga, Laguna, and Pangasinan during most of the 1930s. Among these organization's leaders who earned fame among the peasantry while arousing anger among government officials were Pedro Abad Santos of Pampanga, Juan Rustia of Bulacan, and Juan Feleo of Nueva Ecija, to name only three. Also scattered through the tumultuous decade of the 1930s were a handful of peasant uprisings—Tayug (1931), Tanggulan (1931), and Sakdal (1935)—all of which government troops quickly and easily put down. Giving the government even further cause for alarm were several Robin Hood-type outlaw bands of peasants who slipped in and out of various peasant organizations in the area. Two notable ones were the Lope de la Rosa band, which criss-crossed Bulacan and Nueva Ecija, and the

---

[11] Poor harvests and instances of hungry peasants begging for food and, on several occasions, trying to steal rice from warehouses are noted in *HDP*s for municipalities in Central Luzon and in several news articles, including *Tribune,* 12 October 1935, p. 20, 15 October 1935, p. 10, 28 August 1936, p. 1, 13 September 1936, p. 7, 21 October 1936, p. 14, 28 September 1939, p. 14, 3 October 1939, p. 6, 5 October 1939, p. 14, 4 January 1940, p. 8, 16 November 1940, p. 11, and 31 January 1941, p. 24. For additional evidence about relatively poor yields and bad weather conditions in Central Luzon during the latter half of the 1930s, see Philippines, Department of Agriculture and Commerce, Bureau of Plants, *Annual Reports,* 1935-1940; and the tables in Kerkvliet, "Peasant Rebellion," pp. 41, 81-85.

Asedillo-Encallado band, which was in eastern Laguna and sometimes southern Bulacan.[12]

Table 7 illustrates the growing agrarian unrest from 1930 through 1941. It shows the number of incidents of unrest in the provinces as reported in Manila daily newspapers, principally the *Tribune*.[13] The numbers are simple counts of events indicating that people were discontented or they protested against someone or something or wanted to change conditions. Included, for example, are tenants attacking a landlord's granary, peasant demonstrations, villagers petitioning government officials, strikes, arson in cane fields, landlords stationing guards around their fields to keep their tenants from harvesting, court cases between tenants and landlords, and police evicting tenants. Practically all of these incidents reflected problems of the peasantry, including tenants, peasants who owned a little land, cane-cutters, sugar central workers, and other agricultural laborers. In Rizal province and in the Bisayas, Mindanao, and Northern Luzon regions, however, a sizable number of the incidents reflected discontent among wage laborers in the towns and cities. Excluded from my tabulations were reports about conflicts and fighting between Muslim and Christian Filipinos in parts of Mindanao and Sulu.

The table suggests that peasant unrest during the 1930s was concentrated primarily in Nueva Ecija, Pampanga, and Bulacan. Several nearby prov-

---

[12] Several scholars have researched the Tayug, the Tanggulan, and the Sakdal. See, for example, Milagros C. Guerrero, "The Colorum Uprisings: 1924-31," *Asian Studies* 5 (April 1967):65-78; Roy M. Stubbs, "Philippine Radicalism: The Central Luzon Uprisings, 1925-1935," (Ph.D. dissertation, University of California, Berkeley, 1951); and David R. Sturtevant, "Philippine Social Structure and its Relation to Agrarian Unrest," (Ph.D. dissertation, Stanford University, 1958), "Sakdalism and Philippine Radicalism," *Journal of Asian Studies* 21 (February 1962):199-213, and "No Uprising Fails—Each One Is a Step in the Right Direction," *Solidarity* 1 (October-December 1966):11-21. A handful of reports about the Lope de la Rosa band and about the Esteban Asedillo and Nicolas Encallado band are in the *Tribune* during 1935 and 1936; also see Luis Taruc, *Born of the People* (New York: International Publishers, 1953), pp. 27-28. For additional details about unrest during the 1930s, also see Benedict J. Kerkvliet, "Peasant Society and Unrest Prior to the Huk Revolution," *Asian Studies* 9 (August 1971):172-204, and "Peasant Rebellion," chap. 2.

[13] I chose the *Tribune* for several reasons. Three daily newspapers from the 1930s were available in the library of the University of the Philippines: the *Manila Times, the Tribune,* and the *Philippine Herald* (Manila). After comparing each paper's reporting of provincial news, particularly news about peasants and agriculture, the *Manila Times* seemed the most appropriate. But it ceased publication in March 1930. The *Tribune*, however, was a strong second choice, and compared to the *Herald* it was definitely a better paper for my purposes. So for the first three months of 1930, I read the *Times;* for the rest of the time period (through December 1941, when the Japanese took over the press), I used the *Tribune*. The only exception to this was for the period March 14 to June 30, 1932, for which there were no copies of the *Tribune* available. For this brief time, I used the *Herald*. I picked 1930 as a starting date largely because I wanted to read newspapers from at least a full decade prior to the Japanese occupation, but had no time to do much more than that. It took a part-time assistant and myself most of three months to do twelve years. Certainly a thorough study of peasant unrest prior to World War II would have to go back at least to the 1920s.

inces had considerable agrarian unrest, too, particularly Tarlac, Pangasinan, and Laguna, A close look at the newspaper reports also shows that
most of the people involved were tenants on large landholdings in those
parts of the provinces where tenancy predominated.

The table also supports what the peasants in San Ricardo believed was
happening, namely that unrest grew rapidly during the 1930s. The increase
was especially striking in Nueva Ecija, Bulacan, and Pampanga. Not only
did it grow in terms of number of incidents but also area affected. One
measure of this is that the number of municipalities with reported unrest
increased markedly between 1930 and 1940 (see Table 8). Only in 1941,
according to newspaper reports, did the fever of agrarian discontent appear
to decline. This, however, may reflect only that newspaper publishers had
to give more attention to an expanding world war and less to domestic
problems. Even when the *Tribune* carried several stories of "widespread
radicalism" in Bulacan, Nueva Ecija, Pampanga, and Tarlac that forced the
national government to increase the ranks of the Philippine Constabulary
there and take other "peace-keeping measures."[14] And Luis Taruc, a
peasant leader in Pampanga at the time, later wrote that although "labor
struggles in Central Luzon had abated somewhat by 1941" because peasantry had achieved some gains, many tenants and sugar central workers
continued to strike and protest.[15]

Themes

Several significant themes weave among the incidents and loosely tie them
together. These themes are also important for understanding the Huk
rebellion that followed a few years later. The four major ones are the
peasants' moderate objectives or demands, the generally nonviolent course
of the peasantry's actions, the growth of peasant organizations, and the
role of leadership.

The peasants' demands were modest and remained fairly constant. They
revolved primarily around wanting to improve the tenancy system. A
statement about the 1930s by an elderly peasant leader in Talavera
epitomized the peasantry's purpose: "Our worst problems were debts, high
interest rates, and not enough rice. So we wanted three things: loans from
the landlords and from the government, low interest rates or none at all,
and a larger share of the crop—55 percent of the harvest instead of only 50
or 45." To cite another example, Juan Feleo told Department of Labor
officials in Manila in June 1939 that 10,000 restive peasants in Nueva Ecija
and Pampanga wanted landlords to give them loans to which they felt
entitled and they wanted the government to assist them.[16]

A composite list of demands reported in three newspaper stories about
major strikes in 1933, 1939, and 1940 that involved thousands of peasants

[14] *Tribune*, 4 March 1941, p. 1, 1 June 1941, p. 3, and 18 June 1941, p. 12.
[15] Taruc, *Born of the People*, p. 49.
[16] *Tribune*, 28 June 1939, p. 14.

Table 7

REPORTED INCIDENTS OF UNREST BY PROVINCE OR REGION (1930-1941)

Region or Province	1930	1931	1932	1933	1934	1935	1936	1937	1938	1939	1940	1941	Total
Central Luzon													
Bulacan	4		6	16	5	9	15	10	22	14	20	4	125
Nueva Ecija	7	3	12	4		7	8	24	8	67	38	7	185
Pampanga	1	3	6	6	4	15	1	19	37	44	64	52	252
Tarlac	1	2	2		2	1	3	1	11	3	9	4	39
Pangasinan		2	1			4	11	7	3	1	2	1	32
Bataan		1	1	1	1			1		7	15	1	28
Zambales										1			1
Subtotal	13	11	28	27	12	36	38	62	81	137	148	69	662
Southern Luzon													
Rizal	5	1	1		5	7	6	8	5	2	3		43
Laguna		1	1		2	5	5	2	1	7	6	6	36
Quezon	1		1			1	1	1	1	2			8
Batangas		2			1	4	3	5	1	2	3	2	23
Cavite	1		1	4				1	1	2	1		11
Subtotal	7	4	4	4	8	17	15	17	9	15	13	8	121

Table 7 *(continued)*

REPORTED INCIDENTS OF UNREST BY PROVINCE OR REGION (1930-1941)

Region or Province	1930	1931	1932	1933	1934	1935	1936	1937	1938	1939	1940	1941	Total
Northern Luzon	2					2		2	2	3	4	1	16
Ilocos	1					1		2	2				6
Bisayas													
Capiz									2	1			3
Iloilo	3	4		1	1	3	2		2	2	4	5	27
Negros Occidental	1	9	16	1		3		2	5	10	6		53
Other		2		2	4	3			2	5	3		21
Subtotal	4	15	16	4	5	9	2	2	11	18	13	5	104
Mindanao	1		1	4		5	2	2	3	3	1	5	22
Total	28	30	49	39	25	70	57	87	108	176	179	83	931

Source: Compiled almost exclusively from articles in the *Tribune*, 1930-1941. Note that some reports about the following were not included in this compilation: Tayug, Tanggulan, and Sakdal uprisings and social banditry groups led by de la Rosa, Asedillo, and Encallado.

Table 8

NUMBER OF MUNICIPALITIES WITH INCIDENTS OF UNREST IN
THREE CENTRAL LUZON PROVINCES: 1930, 1935, AND 1940*

Province	1930	1935	1940	Number of municipalities in the province
Bulacan	3	6	13	23
Nueva Ecija	3	5	16	27
Pampanga	1	9	17	21

*Based on incidents summarized in Table 7.

on palay and sugar cane lands throughout Central Luzon follows.[17] It indicates the range of the peasants' demands while also illustrating that the overall objective was, in the words of one elderly man in San Ricardo, "to get what was just if landlords were honorable and good men."

Loans:
- If a tenant is so heavily in debt that after paying what he owes he has little or nothing left from the harvest, "the landlord shall give him not less than 25 cavans of palay free of interest" (1933).
- Landlords and moneylenders must eliminate usurious interest "like *talindua* [50 percent] and *taquipan* [100 percent]" (1939).
- "Give the tenants a ration of 5 cavans of palay per cavan of seedlings planted, with no interest, from the time the fields are prepared up to the time of planting; and free rations to each tenant during harvest and threshing. Allow tenants to borrow money with which to buy prime necessities, with no interest . . ." (1940).

Sharing the harvest:
- Divide the net harvest 50-50 (1933).
- Seventy-five percent of the harvest belongs to the tenant (1939).

Method of dividing the harvest:
- Settlement of accounts between tenants and landlords shall be in the fields immediately after threshing, cleaning, and measuring the palay, not at the landlord's bodega (1933).
- "Landlords who refuse to recognize tenants' rights to ask for immediate liquidation [division of harvest] should be punished" (1940).

Expenses:
- Tenants have no obligations whatsoever to pay for irrigation (1933).
- "Expenses for planting, pulling, and cutting must be born share-and-share-

[17] *Tribune*, 15 June 1933, p. 1 (involved tenants in both Pampanga and Bulacan), 13 January 1939, p. 20 (involved fifteen thousand peasants in Pampanga), and 16 January 1940, p. 1 (involved "thousands" of peasants and "over fifty landlords" in Nueva Ecija).

alike by tenants and landlords." "Landlords must bear all expenses for irrigation of his farmland" (1940).

Landlord practices regarding evictions, strikes, and peasant unions:
- No tenant should be forced to quit his tenancy without sufficient reason, and he is entitled to three-months' notice (1933).
- Landlords shall not discriminate against tenants and laborers who belong to unions. Landlords shall not hire strikebreakers (1939).
- Landlords must "reinstate all tenants disposed during 1938-39 because there is no just cause for dispossession." "Landlords must recognize the KPMP's right to collective bargaining for its members" (1940).

Others:
- Tenants "who meet with accidents, fall sick, are bitten by snakes, are struck by lightning, or suffer injury in the performance of their duty shall be given relief by their landlords" (1933).
- Public rivers usurped by rich landlords for private fishponds must be opened (1939).

There were some additional minor concerns. One was higher wages for the growing number of agricultural day-laborers. Rarely was this an issue in the early 1930s, according to newspaper articles, but by the end of the decade it was. Agricultural workers demanded, for instance, 1 peso a day minimum wage for laborers without carabaos, 1.50 pesos per day for laborers plowing with their own carabaos, and 2.50 pesos to each laborer for each cavan of seedlings he pulled prior to transplanting. Another issue was that some tenants wanted to become owners of the land that they tilled. Among them were tenants, mainly in Nueva Ecija and Tarlac, who claimed that big landlords had illegally taken their lands, and tenants on church-owned estates who argued that their lands belonged to them, not to the church, or that the national government should purchase the land and resell it in parcels to the tillers. Contested lands included the Buenavista estate in Bulacan, the Dinalupihan estate in Bataan, and the San Pedro Tunasan estate in Laguna. This demand for landownership, however, was atypical; few peasants questioned their landlords' right to ownership. A third minor issue was that government officials were frequently negligent, unfair, and abusive to villagers. Peasants condemned, for example, the constabulary for helping landlords but not tenants and judges for being prejudiced in favor of landlords.

The second theme was that unrest was a mixture of violent and non-violent actions. Nonviolence, however, was more common. In any given area, such as Talavera, Bahay Pare in Pampanga, or the Buenavista estate in Bulacan, peasant activity could vary from petitioning, striking, or taking court action to burning cane fields, physically attacking strike-breakers, or killing a local landlord or one of his katiwala. Generally, only a small number of people at any one time did something violent, and their targets were usually what they believed to be immediate causes of their troubles or symbolic of those causes. As the scope of the peasantry's actions grew larger, in terms of both area and numbers of people, violent incidents rarely occurred. One reason was the orientation of the peasant movement itself—reform and protest rather than rebellion or revolution. The larger the number of villagers protesting together, the fewer who were willing to magnify their risks and take steps that might mean being arrested, beaten, or even killed.

A second reason was that leaders such as the provincewide spokesmen of the KPMP or AMT in the late 1930s, although frequently critical of the government, wanted to work through legitimate channels. In part, their backgrounds as teachers, lawyers, and politicians led them to this position; they also believed remedies could be achieved through peaceful protest. For example, spokesman Pedro Abad Santos of Pampanga, whom the government often thought too radical, said in 1940 that he was perfectly willing to work within the framework of law and was "committed to democratic constitutional methods of reform."[18] Consequently, such leaders cautioned peasants against violence and tried to steer them into legal channels of protest. They became embarrassed and angry with peasants who did something violent, like stab a katiwala, while they were in the provincial capital or in Manila negotiating with government officials and landlords to resolve the very problems that had prompted the violence.

The third theme was that peasant organizations grew larger and politically stronger. The activities of San Ricardo's and Talavera's KPMP supporters illustrated this. People from there joined other KPMP groups many times to parade and demonstrate. In May 1939, for instance, fifteen thousand villagers from throughout Nueva Ecija, including Talavera, demonstrated in Cabanatuan.[19] In 1940, KPMP supporters from San Ricardo joined twenty thousand others in the province to threaten a general strike in order to force landlords to divide harvest fairly. On the Cojuangco hacienda, close to San Ricardo, four hundred tenants had already stopped harvesting.[20] Peasant leaders like Hilario Felipe strengthened the bonds between Talavera's villagers and others in the movement by representing Talavera at a demonstration in Cabiao, Nueva Ecija, in May 1939, when eight thousand tenants from three provinces gathered to demand that landlords there reinstate several hundred tenants whom they had ejected.[21] And Patricio del Rosario and Amando Santa Ana regularly represented Talavera at provincial KPMP meetings over which Juan Feleo, the provincial leader, presided.

Many other cases showed that people increasingly organized to make landlords and government officials listen. For instance, the protests of a few tenants on the Sabani estate in Nueva Ecija in 1937 developed into a major strike by nearly all of the two thousand tenants there in 1938.[22] In

[18] Samuel W. Stagg, "Pedro Abad Santos, Demagogue or Savior?" *Philippines Free Press,* 13 April 1940, p. 11.

[19] *Tribune,* 2 May 1939, pp. 2, 16.

[20] *Tribune,* 10 January 1940, p. 12.

[21] *Tribune,* 21 April 1939, p. 1, and 18 May 1939, p. 1.

[22] *Tribune,* 23 February 1937, p. 14, 27 February 1937, p. 3, 31 May 1938, p. 1.

May 1935, three thousand peasants paraded in San Fernando, the provincial capital of Pampanga. Every year after that more and more rural folks marched, until thirty thousand tenant farmers and sugar central workers paraded on May Day 1939.[23] On the Buenavista estate, which included the large municipalities of San Rafael and San Ildefonso, Bulacan, the number of tenants who demonstrated, refused to pay rent, or protested in other ways increased from a few hundred to several thousand. In 1939 they virtually paralyzed the area.[24] In San Miguel, Bulacan, a thousand tenants farming for several landlords went on strike in June 1933. In January 1940, over four thousand KPMP supporters from San Miguel and four adjacent municipalities struck to force landlords to comply with the newly passed share tenancy law and to give loans.[25] The most dramatic expression of unity among the peasantry occurred in early 1939. The two largest peasant organizations in Philippine history up to that time, the AMT (which claimed seventy thousand members) and the KPMP (which claimed sixty thousand members), merged. Most of their supporters were in Nueva Ecija, Bulacan, Pampanga, and Tarlac. To celebrate, delegates from chapters across the region had a huge parade in Cabanatuan, Nueva Ecija.[26]

Increasingly peasants realized their shared predicament and common grievances. And they learned that individually or in small groups, they had little power. The only way to make an impression on landlords or government officials, they concluded, was to protest together. Consequently, their actions went beyond what might be considered more traditional forms of protest, such as a few villagers raiding a landlord's granary or individual peasants asking landlords for different tenancy arrangements. They did this, but much more as well. The strikes, the petitions to provincial governors or to the Philippine president himself, the court cases, and the demonstrations became the peasants' new political instruments as they sought to reestablish the paternalistic tenancy system and reaffirm their rights to at least subsistence and help from landlords.

Peasants also viewed their movement in terms of mutual protection against landlords and government officials. When they protested alone or in small numbers, peasants were liable to be evicted, be arrested, or suffer other reprisals; when they acted in large numbers, they were less vulnerable. Illustrating this mutual protection were several sympathy strikes in the late 1930s. For example, peasants in Calumpit, Bulacan, and in Balanga, Bataan, went on strike in January 1939 partly to support thou-

[23] *Tribune,* 5 May 1935, p. 4, 2 May 1939, p. 1.

[24] Kerkvliet, "Peasant Rebellion," pp. 148-154.

[25] *Tribune,* 2 June 1933, p. 9, 11 June 1933, p. 14, 13 June 1933, p. 11, 18 June 1933, pp. 5 and 40, 23 June 1933, p. 9, 28 June 1933, p. 1, 12 January 1940, p. 1, 16 January 1940, p. 6.

[26] Guillermo Capadocia, "History of the Peasant and Labor Movement in the Philippines," undated (CapDoc, Ag.), and *Tribune,* 12 February 1939, p. 4. Another version of Capadocia's "History" is located in Hernandez Exh. W 167-218; CFI, Manila, and is entitled "The Philippine Labor Movement."

sands of striking peasants in Pampanga; tenants in several barrios of
Bulacan, Nueva Ecija, and Tarlac supported strikers in Pampanga in
January 1940 by also going on strike; and several thousand tenants in
Nueva Ecija, Pampanga, and Bulacan threatened to strike in May 1939 if
landlords continued to evict those tenants who insisted that the landowners
abide by new tenancy laws.[27] Two thousand tenants from Nueva Ecija and
Pampanga supported a tenant in Jaen, Nueva Ecija, and helped him plant his
field in July 1939 after he had defied the landlord, who had tried to evict him.
The following December, a thousand tenants from nearby municipalities
again came to that hacienda in Jaen. This time they supported the same
man and many other tenants there who opposed the hacienda management's plan to pay outsiders to harvest the palay. Many *tambuli*, a bugle
made of a carabao horn, were heard through the night, calling people from
Cabiao, San Isidro, San Antonio, and Santa Rosa municipalities to help in
Jaen.[28] The tambuli became a symbol in Central Luzon for peasants
assisting one another. Hilario Felipe of Talavera said, for example, "We
used the tambuli to call for help and assemble meetings quickly. Three
short blasts, for example, signaled peasants from far around to come
because of an emergency, like landlord guards trying to take too many
bags of rice." Among the newspaper reports that cited tambuli calls, one
summarized several mayors in Pampanga who complained in 1938 that
"every night, at the sound of the tambuli, . . . hundreds of laborers gather
in remote barrios, take possession of lands where some members of the
groups have been expelled, plow and till the field in spite of protests from
the landowners."[29]

Perhaps the most significant evidence of the peasantry's growing unity
and political awareness was the 1940 election in Pampanga. Peasant
organizations there—including the AMT, KPMP, and the Pasudeco
Workers Union—and the small Socialist Party (some of whose members
were peasants) ran a slate of candidates on a Popular Front ticket. Their
candidates won nine mayorships and a majority of council seats in eight of
those municipalities. In three of Pampanga's largest municipalities, Popular Front candidates won all council seats. At least six of the mayors
elected had been prominent in Pampanga's peasant movement, and seven
were themselves peasants. Two of the municipalities had had peasant-
backed mayors and councils since 1937, when the Popular Front first
supported candidates. The Popular Front candidate for governor of Pampanga in 1937 and 1940 was Pedro Abad Santos, a major spokesman for
the peasantry. Both times he lost to Sotero Baluyut, one of the Pampanga
peasantry's arch enemies. The second time, however, Abad Santos lost by
only five thousand votes.[30] According to Casto Alejandrino, who was the

[27] See following *Tribune* reports for each of these examples, respectively: 27 January 1939, p. 1
and 31 January 1939, p. 14, 19 January 1940, p. 1, and 18 May 1939, p. 1.

[28] *Tribune,* 28 July 1939, p. 2, 7 December 1939, p. 20.

[29] *Tribune,* 2 June 1938, p. 1.

[30] Kerkvliet, "Peasant Rebellion," pp. 139-144.

Popular Front mayor elected in Arayat and who had been a principal spokesman for peasant organizations there, the most important objective after taking office was "to show by word and deed that the power of the local government was on the side of the common person and not on the side of the propertied."[31]

The fourth theme in the unrest was the role of leadership. Peasant activism started in the barrios. And although villagers did not act randomly, neither was their movement carefully planned and manipulated by a handful of leaders. Not even in the late 1930s, after the KPMP and AMT had merged, could a central leadership orchestrate the peasantry. Leaders helped to structure the growing unrest in the barrios; they did not foment or instigate it.

The largest of the peasant organizations, KPMP and AMT, had lives of their own, independent of particular leaders. They were not personal followings of particular individuals. For example, several top KPMP leaders were imprisoned on sedition and other charges between 1931 and 1933. Among them were Juan Feleo and Jacinto Manahan, both long-time and widely acknowledged KPMP activists. Yet while Feleo and others were in prison or in exile, until 1938, the KPMP swelled as agrarian unrest grew more intense. After his release, Feleo was welcomed back into the KPMP top leadership. Manahan, meanwhile, had been pardoned in 1933, and shortly thereafter KPMP leaders denounced him after discovering that he had agreed to work secretly for the government. He tried to start a separate organization, the KPMMP, that was more moderate than KPMP and had the government's endorsement. But the KPMMP apparently collapsed due to lack of support.[32]

Leaders in the movement sometimes disagreed with one another. Several prominent leaders in Pampanga, for example, publicly criticized Juan Rustia, a lawyer for several peasant groups including Atin Na (Ours Now) in Candaba, Pampanga. They said he was responsible for unnecessarily

[31] Interview with Casto Alejandrino, Camp Crame, Quezon City, 5 November 1970.

[32] KPMMP is the abbreviation for Kalipunang Pambansa ng Manggagawa at Magbubukid sa Pilipinas (Philippine National Society of Peasants and Workers). The conclusion that it failed is based on the following: The *Tribune* (16 May 1935, p. 1) said that Manahan was working to counteract "radical movements in the Philippines" and that he was the president of the new Philippine Farmers Federation (which probably was an abbreviated translation of KPMMP). But after this report, Manahan and his organization disappear from the pages of the *Tribune*. Second, a government-compiled list of "all Filipino secret societies, radical groups, and labor organizations," including "Quezonist" (government-endorsed) ones and the name of each group's top leader, does not mention either Manahan or KPMMP ["Filipino Secret Societies, Radical Groups, and Labor Organizations," memo from Colonel J. T. H. O'Rear, Assistant Chief of Staff, Military Intelligence, Headquarters Philippine Department, Manila, to Assistant Chief of Staff, G-2, War Department, Washington, 22 April 1940 (RG 165, MID 2657-2-40; Military Records, National Archives, Washington, D.C.)]. A third source is Capadocia, "Philippine Labor Movement."

militant actions among Atin Na tenants on the Bahay Pare estate. Privately several AMT and KPMP leaders distrusted Rustia and thought he was only using the peasants as a stepping-stone to public office. Rustia, in turn, said that men like Pedro Abad Santos and Juan Feleo were jealous of his popularity among villagers and the strength of Atin Na and other peasant groups with which he was identified.[33] Leaders also disagreed about tactics and strategy. For instance, those KPMP spokesmen in Nueva Ecija who opposed violent tactics accused AMT leaders in Pampanga of endorsing acts such as arson. And AMT and KPMP leaders feuded with top leaders of the Sakdal who believed in the mid-1930s that a general uprising was necessary. Occasionally, the differences seemed to be more personal. A man in Guimba, Nueva Ecija, recalled, for example, "a KPMP leader in Santo Domingo bitterly hated another guy who worked in the KPMP provincial headquarters in Cabanatuan because he suspected that this other leader had designs on his wife." Conflicts even involved members of the same family, as in the case of the Alejandrinos in Arayat, Pampanga. During a strike by sugar central workers in Arayat in 1939, both Jose Alejandrino, Jr., and his cousin Casto Alejandrino claimed to be the strikers' spokesman. And when Jose had negotiated a settlement, the AMT, in which Casto was a leader, opposed it. Jose was angry, he claimed that he, not Casto, was the elected spokesman of the Arayat workers and the AMT members opposed his agreement not because it was unsatisfactory but because they did not want him to get the credit.[34]

Disputes among top leaders in the movement seemed to cause little concern, however, among the rank and file. People in, say, Atin Na also joined AMT and KPMP despite feuds between Rustia and the provincial leaders of other groups, and many Sakdalistas were also in the KPMP in Bulacan and Nueva Ecija and in Dumating Na and Handa Na in the Buenavista estate. And there seemed to be no confrontations between, say, KPMP and Dumating Na, or Atin Na and AMT in the barrios and municipalities.

Broadly, there were two types of leaders during the unrest. Leaders in the barrios and municipalities were people like del Rosario and Santa Ana in Talavera—people who were peasants themselves and who were closely identified with villagers in a small geographical area. This type could be called local leaders. Then there were nonlocal leaders, provincial and interprovincial leaders that might be called, for shorthand purposes, top leaders. They spoke on behalf of people in many barrios and municipalities and often were elected provincial and national officers in organizations like KPMP and AMT. This second leadership group included both peasants and persons from middle-class occupations and, in a few cases, upper-class

---

[33] *Tribune,* 4 March 1939, p. 1; interview with Jose Rustia (surviving brother of Juan), Quezon City, 21 November 1970; and Alejandrino interview, 5 November 1970.

[34] *Tribune,* 22 January 1939, p. 3; 27 January 1939, p. 1.

families. Some of those from nonpeasant backgrounds identified closely with villagers and lived among them; others remained aloof.

Gaps between these two types of leaders and between top leaders and barrio activists help to explain why the movement was not controlled from the top. One illustration was the relationship between Juan Rustia and several thousand tenants in the Buenavista estate who were in two organizations—Dumating Na (It Has Come) in San Rafael, Bulacan, and Handa Na (All set) in San Ildefonso, Bulacan—of which Rustia was a recognized leader.[35] Rustia was dedicated to using his skills as an attorney to win land for the tenants of Buenavista. All the way to the United States Supreme Court he argued, unsuccessfully, that the Catholic Church did not own the land but, rather, it had illegally taken the land from the Philippine government. He worked without pay because he sympathized with the peasants and he had a passion for law. As a man who defended them before the press and in the courts, villagers greatly respected him. At the same time, they knew that Rustia was not one of them. He lived in a large house in Manila, sent his only child to exclusive schools, played poker and golf with leading personalities in Philippine politics, and enjoyed his membership in the prestigious Wac Wac country club. The fees he charged, "big, money-making legal cases," according to his daughter, supported this life style. When he went to Bulacan to defend peasant clients in court or to confer with peasant leaders on the Buenavista estate, he drove one of his two cars and dressed in American-styled suits. Consequently, although Rustia was the peasants' spokesman during negotiations with government officials and in court, he was not their leader inside the barrios. Villagers had their own leaders there. And he was not with them to help when they did such things as refuse to pay the rent and when they plowed the land even after the estate administration had tried to evict them. Sometimes, in fact, their actions went contrary to his advice, but he was unable to stop them.

Leadership on the part of the Partido Komunista ng Philipinas (PKP, Philippine Communist Party) has been a disputed subject. Some government officials and scholars have argued that the PKP controlled the peasant movement in Central Luzon; a few have even claimed that the PKP started the unrest; and occasionally the PKP itself has said

[35] This discussion of Rustia is based on several articles in the *Tribune* and on the following: Jose Rustia interview, 21 November 1970; interview with Glecy Rustia Tantoco (daughter of Juan Rustia), Manila, 25 November 1970; Jose G. Sanvictores, "A Study of the Conflicts at the Buenavista Estate in Bulacan," 21 January 1939 (Roxas Papers, Bundle 10; National Library, Manila); Patricio A. Dionisio, Confidential Agent NIB [National Investigation Bureau], "Memo for the President [Quezon], Subject: More Incitements in the Buenavista Estate," 24 March 1939 (Roxas Papers, Bundle 10; National Library, Manila); "Memorandum for the Chief, Information Division, P.C., Subject: Non-Signing of Government Lease Contract by Tenants of Buenavista Estate, San Ildefonso and San Rafael, Bulacan," 24 April 1939 (Roxas Papers, Bundle 10; National Library, Manila).

that it directed the movement. But the evidence shows otherwise.[36] Organizationally, the PKP was weak during the 1930s. Less than three years after it was formed in 1930, many of its members had dropped out or had been imprisoned or exiled because the government declared it a subversive group. Even after the government allowed the party to come back, the PKP did not grow large. More importantly, the PKP lacked strong ties with the peasantry. Few of its members were peasants, and the party did little political work in the countryside. Most of the active members lived in towns and cities where they focused on labor unions, especially those in Manila. According to the PKP's top leadership, the urban proletariat, not the peasantry, would be the backbone of any radical movement in the Philippines and hence required the party's attention. Some PKP members, however, disagreed and criticized the party for ignoring peasants and for being too removed from typical Filipinos. Guillermo Capadocia, for instance, who was a major figure in the PKP at the time and active in both labor and peasant unions, criticized the party's national officers for being unable to organize even party cells or to make themselves understood at meetings because they spoke about things that were unintelligible or irrelevant to most people. Finally, the PKP lacked a clear political position and was generally undistinguishable from several other political organizations in the country.

There were, however, a few individuals in the PKP who tried to help the peasant movement. Two of them, who were not peasants themselves and who lacked a peasant base, were Capadocia and Mateo del Castillo. They frequently came from Manila to speak at peasant demonstrations, and they lobbied in Congress for tenancy laws, negotiated many times with government officials (including President Manuel Quezon) on behalf of peasant organizations, and sat on government-initiated councils to help resolve the differences between landlords and tenants. Peasant activists in Central Luzon who were aware of Capadocia and del Castillo's activities appreciated what they did, and felt that these men were at their best when they used their skills with the English language and their understanding of national politics to communicate the movement's demands to government officials. But the distance between rural people and even those PKP leaders who were involved in the movement was illustrated when a tenant farmer recalled Capadocia speaking in Cabiao, Nueva Ecija, in the late 1930s:

> It was a large demonstration. I remember some of us carried red flags with KPMP emblems. Juan Feleo was there, too. Capadocia also came to help Feleo and others during negotiations with a bunch of landlords who were meeting in

[36] This assessment of the PKP during the 1930s is based on interviews in Talavera and on the following: Capadocia, "Philippine Labor Movement"; Jose Lava, "Milestones in the History of the Philippine Communist Party," (mimeo, circa 1950), pp. 20-21; Renze L. Hoeksema, "Communism in the Philippines" (Ph.D. dissertation, Harvard University, 1956); A. S. Araneta, "The Communist Party of the Philippines and the Comintern, 1919-30" (Ph.D. dissertation, Lincoln College, Oxford, England, 1966); and S. Carpio, "The Situation in the Philippines and the Tasks of the CPPI," *International Press Correspondence,* vol. 12, no. 51, 17 November 1932, and no. 52, 24 November 1932 (RG 350, 28342-10-with; National Archives, Washington, D.C.).

the municipal hall in the bayan. He was a nice fellow. We had heard about him and knew he was a labor leader in Manila. That night he spoke at a KPMP rally in this barrio. You know, I didn't understand why he went on that night about how good things were in Russia. It wasn't relevant to our problems. It was also dangerous. The police could have thought we were a bunch of communists and arrested us.[37]

A handful of PKP leaders did devote much of their lives to the peasant movement. Unlike Capadocia and del Castillo, they lived close to the peasantry. Two of them—Juan Feleo and Pedro Abad Santos—still have a special place in the hearts of many people in Central Luzon, not because they were officers in the PKP but because of their commitment to the movement.

Juan Feleo, born in 1896, in Santa Rosa, Nueva Ecija, was the son of a small landowner who had to mortgage his land.[38] As a young man, Feleo briefly taught school in Santa Rosa. By the early 1920s, he spent most of his time defending tenants in Santa Rosa against landlords who threatened to evict them. One of Feleo's contemporaries, novelist Lazaro Francisco, recalled: "Feleo didn't really have a job as far as I know. He was too busy working on one cause or another for one peasant organization or another to have a job. He lived on contributions and probably a small stipend from the KPMP." According to Francisco, Feleo was disgusted with some of the early peasant organizations because they had been taken over "by men who were basically trying to get publicity for themselves and hoping to work their way onto a ticket of a major political party and get elected to office, and then forget about the peasants completely." One reason Feleo worked hard with the KPMP, of which he was one of the founders in the mid-1920s, was his conviction that it should be a union for peasants, not a conduit for aspiring politicians. By the early 1930s, he was widely known in Nueva Ecija and Bulacan as a spokesman for the peasantry. He frequently spoke at meetings and demonstrations, helped to organize KPMP chapters, negotiated with landlords, and carried peasants' petitions to government offices in the provinces and in Manila. A tenant farmer in San Ricardo remembered Feleo this way: "He was a very kind man. He came to Talavera several times to speak at our meetings. He was a very good speaker; he knew how to handle the landlords, too." Another man said, "Feleo was one of us; he knew peasants, and he was honest, sincere. Some people who claimed to be concerned about the situation here were only interested in themselves. But not Feleo; he was not stuck on himself."

[37] Interview, barrio Sinipit, Cabiao, Nueva Ecija, 12 March 1970.

[38] In addition to interviews in Nueva Ecija and reports in the *Tribune,* information about Feleo's background comes from these sources: "Kasaysayan ng Kilusang Magbubukid sa Pilipinas" [History of the Peasant Movement in the Philippines], circa 1949 (Hernandez Exh. W 411-29; CFI, Manila); interview with Lazaro Francisco, Cabanatuan, Nueva Ecija, 4 June 1970; and Taruc, *Born of the People,* pp. 92-93.

Feleo was a charter member of the PKP in 1930 and was elected to its first politburo. From 1933 to 1938 he was imprisoned after being convicted of subversion for speaking about Russia and waving PKP flags. After being released, he continued in the PKP and threw himself into the peasant movement. He became president of the KPMP and served as executive secretary of the government's National Commission of Peasants. It was for what he did as their spokesman that peasants remembered him. One elderly tenant remarked, "The government said Feleo was a communist. Maybe he was. But if he was, so were I and lots of others here in San Ricardo, because he was telling the landlords and the government the things we wanted."

Pedro Abad Santos was born in 1875 and raised in a well-to-do family in San Fernando, Pampanga.[39] He attended good schools in Manila, then returned to Pampanga to practice law. He had barely begun when the revolution started. He joined General Hizon's army and fought first the Spanish and then the Americans. The American military eventually arrested him and sentenced him to execution. Only after numerous court appeals and with help from Americans and Pampanga landlords did Abad Santos's family persuade the government to reduce his sentence and finally to release him. He then resumed his profession and earned a reputation as a skilled attorney. In 1916 his province elected him to Congress, where he served until 1922. While in Congress, he became increasingly concerned about the troubles of Pampanga's rural folk. Later he recalled to a Manila journalist an incident that caused him to become more aware of social injustices: "It was in Manila. The weather was bad. I saw the rich ride by in carriages, splashing mud on the streetcleaners working in the rain. And I asked myself why these things were so."[40] He began to give free legal counsel to peasants and their organizations. For this other politicians labeled him a "radical" and dumped him from their party ticket. This rebuff, coupled with his deepening criticism of society and the government, led him to become active in the Socialist Party in the early 1930s. By then he had become a prominent spokesman for several peasant groups. He had also turned further away from his elite background, dressed as peasants dressed, decided never to marry, and generally lived an ascetic life in a small house in San Fernando. That house became an office for the AMT and the Socialist Party and a meeting place for peasant activists and leaders. He also recruited young men who were serious about working in the peasant movement. Among them was Luis Taruc, who later led the Huk rebellion.

[39] In addition to reports in the *Tribune,* specifics about Abad Santos are from these sources: Ramon Aquino, *Jose Abad Santos: A Chance to Die* (Quezon City: Almer-Phoenix Publishing House, 1967), pp. 8-14, 47, 145; interview with Luis Taruc, Quezon City, 27 January 1970; notes of an interview by Professor John Larkin with Casto Alejandrino, Camp Crame, Quezon City, 12 April 1970; and Taruc, *Born of the People,* pp. 33-48.

[40] Leon Ma. Guerrero, "Peace! Peace! . . . But There is No Peace," *Philippines Free Press,* 20 January 1940, p. 5.

In 1938, the Socialist Party and the PKP merged; Abad Santos became the new organization's vice-chairman. Although he read Marxist philosophy and advocated socialism, he was never a zealot. He said, for example, "We have no intention of importing the Russian brand of communism into this situation. Russian conditions are utterly different.... In fact, I feel free to severely criticize the Soviets. Indeed, we would welcome . . . twentieth-century capitalism in the Philippines. If our workers could approximate the living conditions, status, and rights that . . . American workers have obtained under modern capitalism, we would be satisfied."[41] Like Juan Feleo, Abad Santos was known among peasants as an advocate for their goals, which, in his words, meant first "to secure a more just division of the fruits of labor for the tenants."[42] Because he was dedicated to their movement and was close to them, peasants respected Abad Santos even though many disagreed about the value of communist ideology.

The contributions of leaders can now be summarized. The farther from their immediate vicinity peasants went to protest and find solutions, the more they relied on persons with special skills to present their petitions to the proper government officials, lobby on their behalf in Manila, defend them in court, interpret the law for them, and so on. Consequently, attorneys like Rustia, Abad Santos, Jose Alejandrino, and Ramon Diokno, teachers like Feleo, and even a few landlords like Casto Alejandrino had important responsibilities in the peasant movement. These persons were educated and knew the world beyond the barrios; many were also committed to the peasants' cause. Joining these provincial or top leaders who were not of peasant stock were a few others, like Luis Taruc in Pampanga, who came from peasant backgrounds but had also learned to deal effectively with government officials and landlords. Top leaders influenced the movement by channeling the protesting peasantry to demand new tenancy laws, pushing legal cases beyond local courts, and urging peasant-backed candidates to run for local office. Finally, top leaders helped to knit together local peasant groups and associations into larger and stronger peasant organizations.

Meanwhile, local leaders were also important, although in a different way. They were crucial because they were in the barrios and towns when peasants with shared grievances were coming together for the first time. Frequently, they had been among the first in their area to protest publicly against agrarian conditions. They undoubtedly inspired others to do the same. Second, local leaders shouldered the responsibilities that went with organizing collective actions, whether it was arranging for transportation so that people could attend demonstrations in distant places, calling meetings, or bolstering morale. Third, these leaders were the principal links between an organization in one locality and organized villagers in surrounding areas.

[41] Stagg, *Philippines Free Press,* 13 April 1940, p. 10.
[42] Ibid., p. 9.

Actions of Landlords and the Government

During the 1930s, some landlords did negotiate in good faith with tenants and abide by agreements they reached. And government officials did occasionally side with villagers against the landlords and give peasants cause to hope for satisfactory resolutions to their problems. Upper courts, for example, seemed more inclined than lower courts to rule in favor of tenants, and they did overturn several lower court decisions which tenants had lost. Newspapers also reported a few instances of Philippine Constabulary detachments protecting barrio residents against large landowners.

These actions, however, were exceptions to the rule. On the whole, landed elites were more repressive than conciliatory, and the government usually sided against the peasantry.

The Philippine Constabulary (PC), for example, was practically an army for the landed elites. When landlords needed help, whether to guard their fields against tenants who wanted to harvest early or to barge in on peasants' meetings, they only had to ask the local PC commander to send detachments. People in San Ricardo, for example, frequently described the PC as "bata" (pawns) of the landlords, and no tenant would have thought to ask the PC to help them if the landlord abused them. In 1935, a tenant farmer in a barrio of San Fernando, Pampanga, spoke for many when he said of the PC, "they only serve the rich. They do whatever the landlords tell them to do."[43] Pedro Abad Santos, who criticized the PC many times, once said that all a landlord had to do when he wanted PC troops was to telephone the provincial PC headquarters.[44] Also indicative of the PC's partisanship is that there were no newspaper reports of PC or local municipal police forces arresting or threatening to arrest a landlord. Yet the PC and local police forces arrested hundreds of tenants during the 1930s. In early February 1939 alone, an estimated four hundred peasant activists sat in jails across Pampanga.[45]

The courts, too, were no refuge for those without wealth or influence. Because local justices of the peace were appointed, they frequently were either of the landed elite or beholden to local landlords who had helped to get them appointed in the first place. A remark by a judge in the national government's Court of Industrial Relations illustrated the general thrust of the court system when it handled disputes between the rich and the poor: "While the court of industrial relations is committed to the amelioration of the laborers' lot, it does not see justice in the triumph of labor to the prejudice of capital." With that said, he ruled that several hundred tenants had no right to shares of the "benefit payments" that landlords in Pampanga and Tarlac had received from the government for sugar crops the weather had destroyed during the preceding years.[46] Pedro Abad Santos

---

43 *Tribune*, 26 May 1935, p. 1.
44 *Tribune*, 31 January 1939, p. 14.
45 *Tribune*, 11 February 1939, p. 16.
46 *Tribune*, 21 January 1938, p. 1.

spoke on behalf of many peasants when he wrote to his brother, who was then Secretary of Justice,

> I might as well tell you at the outset that the workers [including tenants and agricultural laborers] have lost faith in the courts . . . ; our ruling class has taken the place of the former [colonial] rulers and uses the courts to further their interest and privileges.[47]

The landed elites and the national government overlapped. Manuel Quezon himself, president of the Philippine Commonwealth from 1935 to 1944, owned several estates, including a two-hundred-hectare hacienda in Arayat, Pampanga. Many other officials in the national bureaucracy and in Congress also owned land in Central Luzon. Furthermore, government officials had close ties with large landowners who were not in the government. A famous example in Central Luzon in the 1930s was the close friendship between President Quezon and Sotero Baluyut. Baluyut, a prominent spokesman for landlords and an outspoken foe of AMT and similar peasant organizations, was Pampanga's governor for several years and was appointed to President Quezon's cabinet in 1941. On many occasions, leading government officials, including secretaries of justice and of labor, defended the landlords for taking firm action against "radical" and "subversive" peasants. Secretary of Labor Leon G. Guinto, for example, toured Central Luzon in 1941 to speak against "the communists" in the peasant movement and to endorse efforts by landlords to use strike-breakers. The landed elites also protected their interests by pressuring government agencies, the courts, and the legislature. New tenancy laws in the late 1930s, for example, remained weak because many lawmakers were themselves landlords and because landlord organizations from Central Luzon lobbied against proposals that threatened their power over the tenants.

Large property-owners in Central Luzon had formed associations before, but they did so more vigorously in the 1930s. In 1937, landlords in Cabiao, Nueva Ecija, for example, formed the Samahan ng mga Propietario (Association of Landowners) "to protect their interests and to get united action in case of litigation arising out of the Land Tenancy Act [1936]."[48] By 1938 large landowners from all over Nueva Ecija had formed the Nueva Ecija Rice-Growers Association; by 1939 it had more than four hundred members.[49] Landlords in Pampanga had the League of Property-Owners of Pampanga. Landowners in Bulacan, Tarlac, and other provinces had similar organizations. In addition, sugar central owners in Central Luzon had "company unions" for cane workers, and landlords helped one another to organize landless peasants from Central Luzon and import villagers

---

[47] *Tribune,* 8 March 1939, p. 1.

[48] *Tribune,* 28 April 1937, p. 14.

[49] *Tribune,* 23 November 1939, p. 1.

from other regions to use as wage laborers and tenants when local peasants went on strike or after they had evicted their previous tenants.

The largest of these landlord-led peasant groups was the Cawal ning Capayapaan (Knights of Peace) in Pampanga. Its organizer was Governor Sotero Baluyut, who said in 1940 that the Cawal had fourteen thousand members who were "pledged not to use violence, and never to strike without the approval or sanction of the government, and above all never to resort to sabotage."[50] The turnover in groups like the Cawal seemed to be high, but there were always a sufficient number of desperate tenants and agricultural workers who would be strikebreakers and do anything else property owners asked of them. Several times between 1939 and 1941 newspapers reported bloody clashes between AMT and KPMP peasants, on the one hand, and the landlords' strikebreakers and armed guards, on the other. The newspaper also cited instances, however, of Cawal peasants later joining AMT and similar organizations, and strikebreakers turning around to go on strike themselves because landlords had reneged on promises.

A perceptible, although not prominent, reaction among large landowners to agrarian unrest was to eliminate or reduce their need for tenant farmers. Some, for example, looked into mechanized farming as Manolo Tinio wanted to do in San Ricardo. Many more recruited people from other parts of the country to be seasonal wage laborers rather than replace evicted tenants with other tenants. Apparently they thought it would be more efficient to have workers only when needed rather than year-round and to limit the pay to strictly cash wages. Peasant organizations in Central Luzon objected and added this to their lists of grievances.

The government's actions were a mixture of force, intimidation, moderate legislation to govern landlord-tenant relations, and pledges of sympathy. With regard to the use of force, the national government increased the strength of the PC garrisons in Central Luzon several times during the 1930s. In Pampanga, for example, the number of PC was one hundred in June 1938, two hundred in January 1939, and nearly four hundred by March 1939. The number of PC in Bulacan and Nueva Ecija increased similarly as part of what one report called President Quezon's "mailed fist" policy in 1939 toward the "agrarian disorder."[51] On at least two occasions in 1938, President Quezon ordered the army and PC to take control of Bulacan and Pampanga. Then in June 1941, the President ordered the PC to take over all municipal police forces in Pampanga, Nueva Ecija, Bulacan, Tarlac, Pangasinan, Bataan, and Cavite so that the government could strike swiftly against what the Secretary of Interior called "subversive, rebellious, and radical elements in Central Luzon."[52] A common belief among local and national government officials was that the

[50] Guerrero, *Philippines Free Press*, 20 January 1940, p. 10.

[51] *Tribune*, 12 June 1938, p. 3, 14 January 1939, p. 1, and 5 March 1939, p. 1.

[52] *Tribune*, 9 February 1938, p. 14, 30 April 1938, p. 1, 1 June 1941, p. 3, and 18 June 1941, p. 12.

peasant movement was subversive, communistic, and manipulated by a few clever leaders. Illustrative here was a report that the PC commander in Nueva Ecija was pleased after his troops had arrested a prominent "labor agitator" because "there will be less agitation in Nueva Ecija, as he is one of the most active radical leaders in Central Luzon."[53] In addition to arresting peasant activists and spokesmen and protecting landlords, the PC also used violent methods. For example, PC commanders in 1931 in Pampanga and Nueva Ecija ordered their troops to "shoot on sight suspicious characters" during strikes and other trouble; tenants in Bahay Pare accused the PC and local police of "shooting down people like dogs" during a demonstration in 1939; and in 1940 ten PC soldiers and the provincial sheriff, with the approval of the district attorney, demolished the houses of five tenants who had refused to abide by the landlord's order to leave on the grounds that their case was still in court.[54]

Government efforts to deter peasants from organizing included harassing activists and spying on peasant organizations. Officials, especially at the local level, also obstructed meetings and denied parade permits to peasant groups. National government officials did this, too, including President Quezon. On one occasion in 1938, Quezon became angry with the mayor of Mexico, Pampanga, who had been elected on the peasant-backed Popular Front ticket the year before, because the mayor had made no attempts to stop nightly meetings of peasant organizations. The mayor argued that the Constitution guaranteed this right. But, according to a newspaper report, "the President countered that apart from the Constitutional guarantees, there is the police power that limits the use of [those] rights. . . . Quezon went on to say that the principal duty of the mayor is to first comply with his duty before talking of the Constitution." He then asked all the assembled Pampangan mayors to cooperate with his campaign to stop the "misguided laborers" in the province.[55] The national government also supported Governor Sotero Baluyut in 1941 when he and other opponents of the peasant movement tried to undermine the power of the nine Popular Front mayors and municipal councils in Pampanga and finally to remove some of them from office.[56] Another government tactic was to dissuade peasants from waging strikes by ruling through the Department of Labor and the Court of Industrial Relations that strikes were illegal. Furthermore, President Quezon and his chief cabinet officers joined with leading landlords in Central Luzon to form peasant organizations like the Cawal that would pledge not to strike.[57]

The government did adopt a handful of laws during the late 1930s that were supposed to resolve the differences between the peasants and large

[53] *Tribune,* 15 October 1939, p. 32.

[54] *Tribune,* 30 October 1931, p. 1, 7 March 1939, p. 1, and 26 June 1940, p. 9.

[55] *Tribune,* 2 June 1938, p. 1 and 7 June 1938, p. 3.

[56] Kerkvliet, "Peasant Rebellion," pp. 144-145.

[57] See, for example, *Tribune,* 21 July 1939, p. 1, 10 June 1941, p. 10, 15 July 1941, p. 20, and 26 July 1941, p. 12.

landowners. They were too weak, however, to protect the peasantry. These laws and President Quezon's "Social Justice" program of which they were a part never intended sweeping reforms. Nor did the government make significant concessions to the peasantry at the expense of the landed elites. On the contrary, the laws included protection and escape-clauses for the landlords. Even the strongest of the laws from the peasantry's point of view only protected tenants against those evictions that lacked "just cause." As the laws defined "just cause" broadly, landlords could legally deny a contract renewal to practically any tenant and oust him. The Labor Department admitted being helpless to prevent the hundreds of evictions that occurred each year. And implementing the tenancy laws remained impossible right up to the Japanese occupation. As people in San Ricardo said many times, landlords could use the laws or ignore them, depending on their needs; there was little that villagers could do because the government was on the landlords' side.[58].

When new laws, small concessions, and force failed to stem the unrest, government officials tried to persuade the peasantry to desist. National government figures traveled to Central Luzon to cajole people with speeches and to convene meetings between peasants and landowners. The most effective of them all was President Quezon. He had a degree of rapport with people in Central Luzon. To many, he seemed at least to be concerned, and according to leaders in the peasant movement, he tolerated dissent and criticism more than most officials.[59] His favorite method to reach the peasantry was travel to Central Luzon and give a speech that pleaded with people to be patient and admonished them not to be violent. Here is a taste of his message to thirty thousand peasants assembled in San Fernando, Pampanga, in February 1939 when agrarian unrest was at a high peak:

... I have always requested the capitalists to improve the living conditions of the field workers, because I would like to see the moneyed class and the poor folks associate cordially with each other, as it is by this means alone that we could insure peace and maintain order in our country. I do not like to see again what I am witnessing here this afternoon. I know that you who are gathered in this place harbor ill-feelings and have an ax to grind against the property owners in Pampanga. I do not like to behold such an ugly sight. [Shouts of "Long live President Quezon!"] ... I have a duty to defend the rights of the property owners and likewise those of the poor. I favor the laboring class not because I desire to grab the property of the rich; I side with them owing to the fact that in order that the rich may enjoy peace and his legitimate share, he must give what rightfully belongs to his

58 For more information on the limitations of the tenancy laws during the 1930s, see these sources: Philippines, *Public Laws of the Commonwealth* (Manila: Jacobo and Sons), Acts 53, 178, 271, 461, and 608; Labor Department, *Fact-Finding Survey, 1936*, pp. 2-3; Loretta M. Sicat, "Quezon's Social Justice Program and the Agrarian Problem" (Master's thesis, University of the Philippines, 1959): Francisco Nemenzo, Jr., "The Land for the Landless Program in the Philippine Government" (Master's thesis, University of the Philippines, 1959); Friend, *Between Two Empires*, pp. 156-160; and Pelzer, *Pioneer Settlement*, pp. 98-101.

59 Alejandrino interview, 5 November 1970; Taruc interview, 27 January 1970.

laborers. I beseech you to have more patience; I ask you to desist from resorting to the worst—by burning the sugar-cane fields and harvesting the palay at your will and then seizing all, including that which does not belong to you. You must not do that! . . . [I]t takes time to help you improve your condition. Just be tolerant; have some more patience. . . . If you have any complaints, present them to the Department of Labor or to the Court of Industrial Relations. . . . My friends: you can always hope for my help as long as you comply with the law. Your complaints and the alleged injustices done to you can be taken to the courts and to the proper authorities; once there you can unravel everything that is in your heart. It is, therefore, not necessary that you use guns or any other weapon. No law officer or government official can abuse you, because justice is dispensed to all alike.[60]

Results

After at least a decade of public discontent, the results for the peasantry in Central Luzon were inconclusive. Peasants had made some gains, but overall they were no better off than before. In terms of gains, more tenants by 1940 than in 1930 got 50 and 55 percent of the palay harvests. They also had laws on the books that theoretically required landlords to give loans and at reasonable interest rates. They also knew more about using the courts and government agencies. And peasants had become more organized and stronger as a class than they had ever been before. Using their local and regional associations, they compelled landlords to accede to their demands at least once in a while, and in a few cases they elected their own kind to local offices. Given the government's sympathetic rhetoric and their marginal victories, they hoped for more substantive gains and were encouraged to continue their organizations and protests.

Yet peasants remained impoverished while the elites prospered. Insufficient food, land, and security continued to oppress them. Laws that many tenants had hoped would protect their traditional rights turned out to benefit the landlords as much if not more than them. It was impossible to get a law that included all that they had been entitled to by custom. And written contracts, which many peasants had hoped in the early 1930s would protect them, became so disliked that thousands of peasants refused to sign them because they concluded that good relations with their landlords could not to be put on paper.[61] Peasants also began to learn about the national government what they had known for a long time about local governments, namely, that officials and property owners were entwined. Finally, the landed elites still had considerable ability to counteract the peasant move-

[60] Speech by President Manuel Quezon in San Fernando, Pampanga, 14 February 1939, pp. 9, 11, 12 (RG 350, 1937-176; National Archives, Washington, D.C.). Also see the account in the *Tribune*, 15 February 1939, p. 1.

[61] See, for example, *Tribune*, 6 May 1933, pp. 13 and 14, 3 April 1940, p. 10, and 22 June 1940, p. 16.

ment and to resist the peasantry's efforts, in the word of several landowners in 1940, "to cling to the antiquated tenancy arrangements."[62]

What would come of this situation in Central Luzon was unclear at the beginning of the Japanese occupation. Future developments would depend on the larger environment as well as the struggle between the elite and the peasantry. Certainly rural folks never anticipated, let alone planned, the rebellion that was to come.

[62] *Tribune,* 22 June 1940, p. 16.

Chapter 3

THE HUKBALAHAP:

Resistance to the Japanese Occupation in Central Luzon

AGRARIAN UNREST in Central Luzon showed no sign of let-up in 1941. Indeed, indications were that new alternatives had blossomed as peasants continued trying to adjust to the changes that so severely unsettled their lives. In Lubao, Pampanga, for example, two hundred tenants negotiated with their landlord to farm a 1,200-hectare sugar estate on a cooperative basis. Not far away, on the Bahay Pare estate in Candaba, Pampanga, tenants hoped to buy the land. The government had promised to purchase the estate and resell it to the tenants. Whether efforts such as these could have led to breakthroughs in the agrarian situation is unknown, because Japanese armed forces interrupted everything in December 1941. They invaded and captured the Philippines. Now people in Central Luzon faced a new problem—how to deal with this foreign intruder.

San Ricardo and Talavera, Nueva Ecija

On 9 December 1941, the newspapers in Manila screamed, "Japs Invade the Islands!" American officials in Manila, including military chief Douglas MacArthur, met hastily with President Quezon and other Filipino leaders. Soldiers scurried to prepare to defend the Manila Bay while people in the city hurriedly stocked up on food supplies or grabbed a few belongings and fled to the provinces.

Eighty miles away, in the market place of Talavera, Nueva Ecija, Carlos Rivera scrutinized a used plow. Rivera had just completed his harvest, and he thought it was a good time to replace his old plow while he still had a little bit of cash left. The harvest had only been fair; next year, he hoped, it would be better. As usual, the market place was alive with gossip. The most discussed topic was the Japanese invasion of the nation's southern islands. People wondered if the foreigners would come to Talavera, and what would happen if they did.

That evening Rivera was back home in San Ricardo. He told his neighbors what he had heard in the market about the Japanese. Another

man who had been working in Cabanatuan for the last two weeks said he
had heard that the Japanese would soon be in Luzon. Benito Santos, who
had fought in the revolution against Spain, predicted, "It'll be like when
the Americans came during the revolution. Lots of blood will wet the
ground." "Well," said another man, "I'm not going to sit here if they come.
The family and I are going to the mountains." Several other men agreed
that it would be too dangerous to stay.

Subsequent days brought more news of the Japanese army's advance.
San Ricardo residents heard that fighting between the Japanese soldiers
and Filipino and American troops was heavy; that much of the country
was falling to the invaders; that soon they would be in Manila and perhaps
even before then they would take Central Luzon. They learned that
Manolo Tinio had left Cabanatuan to join his army reserve unit in Bataan.
Many people were leaving for safer places—some to the city, others to the
mountains. "No one knew what to expect," recalled an elderly woman in
San Ricardo, "but we soon found out."

New Rulers and Filipino Responses

Japanese troops took Talavera shortly after Christmas 1941.[1] "They
came from the north," said Hilario Felipe of Talavera. "We could hear
their guns and bombs for two days before they reached us." Then they blew
up the bridge that crossed the Talavera river at barrio Calipahan only a
mile up the road from the bayan. On 6 January 1942, Japanese soldiers
stormed the bayan itself. They broke up anybody who got in the way," said a
market vendor; "they raped women, too." The soldiers seized Mayor
Ambrosio Fausto and other officials and imprisoned them in Cabanatuan.
Other troops, meanwhile, spread into the barrios.

"By the time they reached San Ricardo," said a former barrio captain,
"almost everybody had left. It was a good thing too. The soldiers charged
in, firing their guns and throwing grenades. They shot carabao and
anything else that moved." Within minutes several houses were burning.
The soldiers rushed on. Cautiously, people who had fled to nearby fields
returned to the village. They found two men and a young woman dead.

From January until about April 1942, only a few people remained in San
Ricardo. Many other barrios in the municipality were similarly deserted.
There was general confusion while people tried to figure out what they
should do. Many ran to the Sierra Madre mountains; others went to
remote barrios. Some looked for relatives in other places. Ironically, as
many left San Ricardo, others from distant places came to the village to
find their relatives. "Those first few weeks of the occupation were the worst
of the whole war," recalled Alfredo Buwan of San Ricardo. "Everything

---

[1] This account of the Japanese occupation in San Ricardo, Talavera, and the surrounding
vicinity relies heavily on conversations with persons living in the area at that time. In addition, I
have found the following sources valuable: Pagaduan, "Kasaysayan ng Talavera"; *HDP,
Talavera;* and *HDP*s for other municipalities and provinces in Central Luzon.

was so disrupted. There were the Japanese troops. There were burning barrios. People were lost, cut off from their families. Some looted what others had left behind. People were scared, and no one knew how long this would last. I took my family and hid in the nearest forest. Sometime in February we moved further into the mountains, where my youngest daughter got sick and nearly died."

However feebly, a few people in Talavera began to fight the invaders. Among the many odds against their resistance was that they had only a few guns. To help solve this problem, a few villagers who were hiding along the river planned one February night how to get weapons. "Within two days afterward," said Romeo Lapitan, who was one of these men, "we had two guns among the eight of us. We used these to steal two more the next week from a landlord in Talavera." These men soon joined others to discuss how to fight the Japanese soldiers. "We were twenty men with six guns among us," said Lapitan. "Amando Santa Ana and Patricio del Rosario were there. Most of us were KPMP members. One guy who wasn't was the young son of a tenant who had been. The Japanese had killed his father when they swept through Talavera. We agreed that we could easily get more men, and we talked about how to get them. What we wanted to do was protect ourselves and families from the Japanese and to stop the banditry." By this time the men had learned through the grapevine about similar groups elsewhere. "One that we learned about," Lapitan recalled, "was a group of men in Cabiao, Nueva Ecija, who, I was told, were also KPMP." But the biggest boost in their morale was news in March that a woman named Felipa Culala, who was a KPMP activist, and thirty others in Candaba, Pampanga, had ambushed a patrol of Japanese soldiers and Filipino policemen, killed several of them, and captured many weapons.[2] Hilario Felipe recalled, "I remember very well hearing about that Culala raid. It was the first big news of organized resistance, and everyone I was with cheered."

The Japanese, meanwhile, had begun to implant their new regime more firmly. The military command took over Talavera's municipal government and set up several outposts in strategic barrios, including San Ricardo. It released Mayor Fausto and other Filipino officials from prison on the condition that they continue in office but work hand-in-hand with the Japanese authorities. The mayor and most of the municipal councillors agreed. The Philippine Constabulary (PC) headquarters in Manila, which by this time was cooperating with the Japanese high command, assigned a PC detachment to Talavera commanded by Captain Burgosino Fausto. Its

---

[2] A newspaper article (*Tribune,* 9 February 1939, p. 1) reported that Felipa Culala was one among three hundred persons arrested in Pampanga during a wave of strikes and related incidents in 1939. The ambush she led against the Japanese is reported in two sources: Luis Taruc, *Born of the People,* pp. 63-64; and "Kasaysayan ng Kilusang Magbubukid sa Pilipinas" [History of the Peasant Movement in the Philippines], circa 1949 (Hernandez Exh. W 411-429; CFI, Manila). This latter document says that Culala and associates killed thirty-seven soldiers; Taruc reports that they killed eighty-eight and captured thirty guns.

orders were to augment the Japanese troops and to help enforce the laws of the new regime. Next, the government turned to public relations. In April 1942, it urged people to return to their barrios and plant their crops. It distributed thousands of leaflets promising that soldiers would no longer mistreat civilians and that the regime wanted to help everyone become prosperous.

Gradually people did return to San Ricardo. "We had to plant our crops," explained Buwan. "Life was too difficult in the hills. And things seemed to be settling down again in Talavera. Japanese troops no longer ran all over the place. There wasn't so much violence. There was a Filipino government again, and it promised that we wouldn't be abused any more." "But," another person said, "coming back didn't mean we gave in or liked the Japanese. The Japanese soldiers killed my wife's cousin. We could never forgive them for that. But my family and I also had to live—to plant our crops and take care of our kids." By May, almost everybody who had fled to the mountains and forests had returned to San Ricardo. In addition, there were a few new families, mainly from nearby barrios, who thought they would be safer living near more people but still be close enough to farm their lands.

Not all returned, however. Some had already left for other parts of the province. Those who had gone to Talavera's bayan seemed to prefer it there, although they traveled frequently to the barrio to farm. A few stayed in the mountains. One family, for example, lived with about ten other families in the Sierra Madre. Not all the families were from San Ricardo, but all were from that part of the province. And all were related on one side of the family or the other. For three years, they lived in the same area. They built small homes similar to the ones they had in the barrios. For food, they planted *kaingin* (swidden) rice and foraged for root plants. Occasionally, small bands of Hukbalahap—anti-Japanese guerrillas—passed through. They would rest and eat, then be on their way. The Hukbalahap paid pesos for the food, or sometimes had some of their own to share. They never attempted to recruit the men of this small group. A few times, Japanese soldiers stumbled into their village, perhaps searching for guerrillas in the mountains. "Then," said this San Ricardo man, "we were in a difficult situation. We didn't like the Japanese, of course, but we couldn't stand up and fight either. So we were just pleasant, but never said anything about the Hukbalahap. Then they'd leave."

As the occupation continued, the military government in Talavera tried to do those things a government would normally do. "In the beginning," said a woman who lived in Talavera's bayan, "the Japanese closed all the schools. But after a few months, most of them were open again but with some new courses, including Japanese language." Several Filipinos learned to speak Japanese well enough to become interpreters. "The school here in San Ricardo," said a middle-aged man, "didn't open again for several months after the one in the bayan did. But it did open, although classes met less often than before the war." The new government also imposed taxes, which it promised to use on civic projects. But as one tenant farmer in San Ricardo said, "Probably they just used the taxes to pay salaries and feed the troops." The ten or fifteen—including Japanese and Filipinos—who were stationed at the outpost in San Ricardo collected the taxes from people there and the surrounding barrios. Residents did not remember how much those taxes were, however, and no one cited it as a particularly oppressive aspect of the new government. "In addition to these taxes, though," explained one person, "we had to feed the soldiers in the outpost. Everyone in San Ricardo contributed rice and other food for that." The government also did such things as encourage peasants to try different agricultural methods, which the Japanese said would increase crop yields without additional expense. The government also wanted villagers to plant such year-round crops as *kamote* and to follow the advice of Japanese agricultural experts who occasionally visited barrios in Talavera. Some barrios, although not San Ricardo, had chapters of Kalibapi (Kapisanan sa Paglilingkod sa Bagong Pilipinas or Association for Service to the New Philippines) through which the government funneled much of its advice to farmers. Although people doubted that these agricultural programs had any significant effect on crop yields, they did remember them as the government's gestures to improve its relations with villagers.

The Japanese government did have supporters among Filipinos. First, a few fervent nationalists believed that the Japanese would give the Philippines its independence. Consequently, they embraced the Japanese as liberators. Known as "Ganaps," they were particularly helpful to the invading army during the early months. Ganaps in several Central Luzon municipalities emanated from prewar political groups, including the Sakdal movement. According to many Talavera people, Ganaps were not from the peasantry; they were frustrated politicians from middle-class backgrounds. Although never numerous in Talavera, they did hold positions in the Japanese government there.

Two larger groups of supporters were big landowners and local officials. "Most of the rich people, at least those who didn't move to Manila," said Hilario Felipe, "were pro-Japanese." Nearly all villagers in San Ricardo agreed with his observation. Many of the hacenderos left Talavera during the war; they went to Cabanatuan and, more frequently, Manila. Manolo Tinio, for example, did not return to Nueva Ecija after fighting in Bataan but instead went to Manila with his family. Vivencio Tinio, Manolo's younger brother, did also. Vivencio explained, "It was safer [in Manila] than staying in the province where the Hukbalahap [guerrillas] and Japs were fighting each other."[3] The wealthy who did remain generally assisted the Japanese, because, as novelist Lazaro Francisco explained, "many of these [elite] families were related to the very government officials who were cooperating with the Japanese. Also, they couldn't afford to be at odds with the Japanese military. They benefited, as they had in the past, from being a friend of the government authorities no matter what the govern-

[3] Interview with Vivencio Tinio, Quezon City, 15 November 1970.

ment was."[4] Furthermore, the Japanese government gave elites no cause for alarm or opposition. Its policies were similar to the previous regime's, and it made no threats against their properties. Government officials, too, not only cooperated with the new regime, but endorsed it. In short, the very Filipinos whom the peasantry had increasingly come to resent in the 1930s—the local officials and landed elites and the PC and police—supported and joined the Japanese regime. This not only contributed to the new government's lack of popular support, but further undermined whatever legitimacy local elites still had in the eyes of peasants.

Most Filipinos in Talavera disliked the new regime. A peasant who owned two hectares expressed well what most in San Ricardo said: "I couldn't forgive the Japanese for what they did. All the abuses, the destruction, the harshness, the forced labor. I saw people they had tortured. It's true, I liked some individual Japanese soldiers. There was one from the outpost here in San Ricardo that my family and I got to know well and he was nice—just a young soldier. But most of them were mean, and the Japanese government here was bad." Several villagers particularly hated such things as, "Every time you went to market in the bayan and a Japanese passed by, you had to bow to him! Even the soldiers in San Ricardo usually expected us to bow to them." Others disliked having to carry identification cards in order to travel. "If an official stopped you on the road and you didn't have a pass," one man complained, "you could be held for interrogation." Another person said, "The Japanese government also had spies who were Filipinos, and they tried forcing us to form a neighborhood association as a way of keeping an eye on us. Everyone was supposed to spy on each other."

What caused the most fear and anger, however, was repression. "The Japanese government had what they called 'zona.' Like a flash," explained Carlos Rivera of San Ricardo, "thirty or forty Japanese and PC would swoop down on a barrio or a section of town and surround the place. Anyone who moved or objected in any way could be shot, no questions asked. They were looking for people who might be in the resistance movement. Anyone whom they suspected was hauled off and detained indefinitely, frequently beaten up and tortured. One guy I knew in barrio Bantug was taken away and never heard from again." Sometimes the Japanese had Filipinos with hoods over their heads come into a room of people who had been rounded up during a zona and simply point at those who were "guilty." "These [hooded] people," explained a man in San Ricardo, "were what we called makapili. They worked for the Japanese and would do anything they were told. Sometimes we knew who they were, but sometimes not, because they were outsiders from other areas." Occa-

---

[4] Interview with Lazaro Francisco, Cabanatuan, Nueva Ecija, 4 June 1970. The early chapters of a recent novel elaborate on the lives of large landowners and others in the elite of Central Luzon during the occupation, including their cooperation with the Japanese regime: Amado V. Hernandez, *Mga Ibong Mandaragit* [Birds of Prey] (Quezon City: International Graphic Service, 1969).

sionally, the local police chief and a municipal councillor took advantage of these arbitrary procedures to settle old quarrels from prewar days by accusing enemies of being antigovernment without showing any proof. A lady who was a small merchant in Talavera during the war confirmed, "You didn't have to be part of the resistance movement to suffer Japanese government abuses. For a little while there in 1942, the government under the Japanese calmed down and seemed to be more respectful of the average person's rights. But it didn't last. For most of the occupation, the Japanese military and many of the Filipinos working with them just acted like they owned the place and everything in it. If you crossed them, you were in trouble."

The Hukbalahap Resistance

Among this majority who disliked the Japanese occupation, the "Hukbalahap" resistance movement thrived. The name was an abbreviation for Hukbo ng Bayan laban sa Hapon (People's Anti-Japanese Army). Significantly, the Hukbalahap emerged in part from the previous peasant movement. Initially, people from the KPMP, in particular, formed the core of the Hukbalahap. Moreover, the adversity of the Japanese occupation reinforced a major lesson villagers had learned during the 1930s—the necessity for collective action. "Now more than ever," explained one San Ricardo tenant who had also been active in the prewar unrest, "we needed to protect ourselves: from the Japanese, from the PC and police, and from bandits." According to Alfredo Buwan, who had been in both the KPMP and Hukbalahap, "Around 30 percent of the peasants in San Ricardo were KPMP members. But during the Japanese time, 90 percent or more of the people supported the Hukbalahap." Another villager who had been a Hukbalahap guerrilla said, "Almost everybody in San Ricardo was part of the Hukbalahap. If not actually carrying a gun, then they gave information and food to the Huk soldiers." The Hukbalahap, in short, was a popular peasant-based resistance. As one tenant described it, "We in San Ricardo swam in two rivers: one that the Japanese government forced us into and the other, our own Hukbalahap."

One reason for the Hukbalahap's support was that even those persons not directly involved had friends and relatives who were. As one San Ricardo informant explained," Almost everyone had a son or husband or close relatives and friends who were soldiers in the Hukbalahap somewhere. This was an additional reason to join the underground." People not only supported those particular Hukbalahap groups in which they had acquaintances; they also empathized with other Hukbalahaps. The wife of a tenant farmer, for example, expressed this with her own case: "My husband was a guerrilla. But we helped any Hukbalahap guerrillas who might be in the area, just as I know people elsewhere would help my husband's unit wherever it might be."

A handful of people joined the Hukbalahap for nationalistic reasons. As one such individual said, "I had no choice but to fight against the Japanese. I believed that the Philippines should be independent. The

Japanese had no more right to my land than the Americans did. When the Americans came back in 1945, I welcomed them only because they helped free us from the Japanese and because they promised us independence in one year."

Independence for the sake of independence, however, was not the key issue for most people in San Ricardo's resistance. They wanted the Japanese out because of what the new regime had done to their lives—the fear, death, destruction, and repression were worse than anything people had known before. The Japanese and Filipino authorities were their own worst enemy, for they did little to win popular support but did much to turn people against them.

On revenge grounds alone, there were plenty of people in Talavera to cause trouble. "I became a Huk guerrilla," one tenant in San Ricardo explained, "because of what happened to my father. In 1942, the PC came here looking for Huks. The officer started questioning people, including my father. The next thing I knew, they carried him off and only said he would have to answer questions in the bayan. We never saw him again. Friends learned later that he had been tortured and died. I can't describe how hard it was on my mother . . . on all of us. I couldn't take any more. Within a month a squad of Huk guerrillas accepted me, and I was with this group for the rest of the occupation." Another example was one of Patricio del Rosario's sons. He joined the Hukbalahap army in 1943 at the age of sixteen after Japanese and Filipino soldiers abused the family and killed one of his brothers.

Cases like this were common among Huk guerillas, said Alfredo Buwan of San Ricardo: "People had lots of reasons for taking up a gun. No one of them would be enough. But revenge was a powerful one for many, especially younger men. But in my case, well, it was partly vengeance because of what had happened to my best friend. But it also was because I felt I had to do my share. Many others in our KPMP group were fighting in the Huk army, and I felt I had to be there with them." Another man added, "It wasn't just what the Japanese themselves did. What I fought against was the damn PC. I know others did too. The PC had been pawns of the landlords before. Now they were even worse—pawns of the Japanese military. They were even more ruthless than the Japanese."

Not everyone who opposed the new government could or even wanted to join the Hukbalahap guerrillas. Some said simply that they were too old. Others felt as one villager did: "I couldn't leave my family; I was the only one who could take care of them." Villagers believed that every family should have at least one adult male to look after it; consequently many husbands and brothers did not feel free to join the Hukbalahap army. Other villagers frankly admitted that they chose not to join because they feared being killed or wounded. Still others simply wanted to avoid being involved with any resistance work despite their displeasure with the Japanese regime.

Hilario Felipe was a good example of a Hukbalahap participant in

Talavera. He was born in 1910, was the son of a tenant farmer in Pampanga who had moved to Talavera when Felipe was an adolescent, and had a few years of formal education. Before the Japanese occupation, Felipe farmed 3 hectares of palay for a hacendero and lived with his mother, brothers, and sisters in a barrio near San Ricardo. Previously his father had farmed the same land, but in the early 1930s his father died. "I got 50 percent of the crop, which wasn't enough to feed all of us," Felipe recalled. "It was a good thing I wasn't married yet and had kids." He said he had joined the KPMP "because I believed that we peasants had to work together to get bigger shares. Landlords were too stingy to allow us more otherwise." When the Japanese came, he continued, "I was really scared. All I could think of was how all of us could run away. We moved to the bayan. My mother insisted it would be safer there. But there was no place to hide, really. Everywhere the soldiers were stealing, killing, and raping." People formed the Hukbalahap, he said, "because they couldn't sit idly by and let this happen. People joined the Hukbalahap to fight the Japanese. It was the only way—combine what we had in order to protect ourselves. We had to defeat these invaders." The Hukbalahap also "turned against the hacenderos and big landowners. Of all things, many of them contributed to the Japanese government! They gave rice and money to the Japanese while everyone else suffered. They also left for Manila and other places." Felipe's Hukbalahap squadron had one hundred men most of the time, "but nearly two hundred before liberation. Del Rosario was one of the squadron's leaders." Felipe's major responsibilities in the resistance, he explained, were to "help arrange food and supplies. I kept in touch with the Huk governments in the barrios. Sometimes we went hungry. There were many hard times. But I'm glad I never ran away. I still have good feelings about what we did."

Most guerrillas from the San Ricardo area were, like Felipe, relatively young—in their twenties and thirties. Some, however, were only in their late teens, whereas others were middle-aged. Amando Santa Ana, for example, was in his forties. A few were even older, like Patricio del Rosario, who was in his sixties. Villagers said all the guerrillas were men.

By mid-1942, according to residents in San Ricardo, the Hukbalahap guerrilla force in Talavera had one squadron of about a hundred men. The commanders were Patricio del Rosario and Amando Santa Ana. By 1944, Talavera had three squadrons, each with about two hundred people. One called "squadron 8" operated in Talavera itself; its head officer was del Rosario. The other squadrons operated in parts of Talavera and adjacent municipalities. Santa Ana led one of these. Hilario Felipe said, "The number of people who wanted to join the Huks increased faster than we could absorb everyone. That first year we had more men than we had guns. As the number grew, we split the original squadron into smaller groups you could call squads. Eventually, Hukbalahap groups from Aliaga and Quezon [municipalities just southwest of Talavera] and some of the squads from barrio San Miguel na Munti and that area [in south Talavera] linked up and formed another squadron. By 1943, I think, there were Hukbalahap squadrons in several municipalities in this vicinity, like Cabanatuan, Quezon, Licab, Santa Rosa, and Bongabon."

Hukbalahap guerrillas moved back and forth between normal barrio life and guerrilla activities. Only a few stayed away from San Ricardo for weeks at a time. A small number, including del Rosario and Santa Ana, nearly always remained "in the field" in order to minimize the risk of being caught. Most guerrillas continued to farm and live in their villages. As one man described the situation, "we were peasants by day and guerrillas by night."

Squadron 8 in Talavera, according to an official roster prepared at the end of the war, had twelve squads, each with about a dozen men who usually were from the same barrio or nearby barrios.[5] Each acted on its own except for large battles or other activities, at which time squadron leaders would call several together. Squadron 8 also had five couriers and two groups of six persons each that specialized in gathering intelligence information.

The Hukbalahap guerrillas' major responsibilities were to police the countryside and harass the Japanese. Guerrillas in the San Ricardo area acted like a police force because, according to residents, neither Filipino nor Japanese authorities would. "So it was our job," said Hilario Felipe, "to stop the looting and stealing." They caught several carabao rustlers, thieves, and people accused of assault. "Just the fact that the Hukbalahap did police the area was a great help," explained one elderly man, "because there wasn't anyone else doing it during the occupation." The police in Talavera stuck close to the bayan and, this man continued, "the PC were chasing guerrillas, not carabao thieves."

The guerrillas' most dangerous job was to resist the Japanese government and fight its troops. The Hukbalahap was, as villagers frequently put it, *sige-sige*—aggressive and always making life difficult for the Japanese government. In late 1942, for example, a Hukbalahap squad ambushed three Japanese trucks on the small bridge near San Ricardo. The guerrillas confiscated weapons and killed one soldier. A clash in northern Talavera in 1943 with a PC detachment led by Japanese officers left several dead on both sides. "We had little military training," said one former Hukbalahap guerrilla, "so we made mistakes and learned as we went along. One thing we learned was to pick on only a small number of the PC or Japanese with

[5] "Rosters of Hukbalahap Units," Regional Command 4, Third Battalion. This document is enclosure 13 of a study entitled *History and Organization of the Hukbalahap and United Front Movement*, prepared by the staff of the Military Police Command (MPC) Headquarters, Philippines, United States Armed Forces in the Western Pacific (AFWESPAC), Intelligence Division (G-2) 20 December 1945. The study itself is 15 pages, and it has 14 enclosed documents originating from or concerning the Hukbalahap. The National Archives has a complete copy of this study (ID No. 285993, Federal Records Center, Suitland, Md.); another copy is among the captured Huk-PKP documents held at Camp Aguinaldo, Quezon City, Philippines. Hereafter, references to this source will be abbreviated as follows: MPC, *History and Organization of the Hukbalahap.*

lots of our own numbers." The Hukbalahap also sabotaged government buildings and assassinated officials. For example, they kidnapped, tried, and executed Estanislao Peralta of Talavera. According to residents, he was a cruel man, more sinister than Japanese soldiers, and a paid informant of the government. A small group of Hukbalahap also killed a Filipino interpreter who worked closely with the Japanese military. The Hukbalahap's most daring act of political violence was the assassination of Mayor Fausto early in 1943. The mayor's cooperation with the Japanese had disturbed the Hukbalahap from the beginning. Then in January 1943, he helped Japanese forces locate a small group of Hukbalahap guerrillas camped in Talavera. While twenty Japanese planes bombed, the army shelled the area, which included four barrios. Afterward Hukbalahap supporters plotted their revenge. One Sunday while the mayor watched a cockfight, they murdered him. Thereafter, the Japanese authorities had trouble convincing another Filipino to be mayor of Talavera.[6]

In addition to military proficiency, practice also taught the guerrillas to be more disciplined. To some degree, better discipline resulted from the advice given by other Hukbalahap leaders in Nueva Ecija, particularly Juan Feleo and Jose de Leon, who kept in touch with Hukbalahap leaders in Talavera and who occasionally came to the municipality. But experience was the most consistent teacher. Roberto Aspia, a tenant in San Ricardo who joined the Hukbalahap army at the age of seventeen, explained, "It was important to treat people fairly. Otherwise the Hukbalahap would be in trouble because people wouldn't support us; we'd be worse than the Japanese. The Hukbalahap wasn't a group that lived away from people in the mountains somewhere. We were from the barrios that we were trying to protect. There were some Huks, though, even in my own squadron, who were mean sometimes. One guy I remember beat up a peasant in barrio Pula. But it was our job to straighten out fellows like this or else we'd all be in trouble." Hilario Felipe pointed out, "We did have bad Huks sometimes, but we did things to change them or avoid them. At first almost anyone could join the Hukbalahap. But then there were several men who abused barrio people, misused their guns, and so on. We even had some spies in our midst. So, we started to screen potential recruits. Then, new recruits were put on probation—they weren't given guns right away. In this way, our discipline improved even while our numbers increased. So the Hukbalahap guerrillas had a good reputation with the people."

It was over disciplinary problems that one man named Carlos Nocum from barrio Pinagpanaan, Talavera, left the Hukbalahap. Originally Nocum had been with del Rosario's squadron 8. According to the Hukbalahap side of the story, del Rosario tried to discipline Nocum for mistreating civilians and stealing their chickens. Nocum also had three mistresses, which was immoral by Hukbalahap standards. But Nocum refused to be disciplined and left, taking with him friends and relatives from his home barrio. They then affiliated with other guerrillas under the

---

[6] This account concerning Mayor Fausto is documented in *HDP, Talavera*.

command of two American military officers named McKenzie and Lapham
and became "USAFFE squadron 311."[7] (USAFFE stood for "United States
Armed Forces in the Far East.")

The Hukbalahap and Nocum's squadron 311 continued to feud for the
duration of the occupation. To the Hukbalahap forces, Nocum was a
deserter. They also contended that squadron 311 had close ties with
influential Filipinos in the Japanese regime in Talavera and elsewhere in
the province. Finally, they thought squadron 311 was a bunch of thieves.

Generally, peasants in San Ricardo and others parts of Talavera had a
low opinion of all USAFFE guerrillas, including Nocum's group. "They
weren't really anti-Japanese," said one person. "They never attacked the
Japanese or PC," said another. "Instead they just hid. They were cowards."
"The Huks were aggressive," said one elderly resident of San Ricardo, "but
not the USAFFE. They helped the Japanese more than they hindered." Some
believed that the men in squadron 311 and other USAFFE squadrons were
simply waiting out the war in order to collect back pay, which American
officers had assured them would be coming from the American government. Many also said the USAFFE, which was much smaller than the
Hukbalahap, mainly included men who either were close to the government or were hoodlums whom the Hukbalahap had rejected. They stole
food and money from villagers and seemed not to care whether they had
popular support. Consequently, villagers frequently called these guerrillas
"tulisaffe"—a pun on the word tulisan, which means thief.

In addition to being a guerrilla army, the Hukbalahap was a network
through which people tried to undercut the Japanese and to govern
themselves. According to numerous villagers, "Practically everybody in
San Ricardo was in the Hukbalahap underground. People wanted to be in
it." Villagers worked hand-in-hand with the guerrillas, for the army and
this countergovernment were parts to the same movement. This distin-
guished the Hukbalahap from the USAFFE guerrillas; the latter had no
political organization.

The political organization of the Hukbalahap in San Ricardo had several
names. Some villagers called it the KPMP. Others said it was the PKM
(Pambansang Kaisahan ng mga Magbubukid or National Peasants Union),
which was the large peasant movement in Central Luzon after the Japanese
occupation. Still others simply called it the "Hukbalahap government."
This confusion over names was further proof that people in San Ricardo
saw the KPMP, Hukbalahap, and PKM as parts of a continuous peasant
movement. These groups were blurred in people's minds because their
purposes and structures overlapped, and because many individuals in one
also were in the others.

[7] Residents of Talavera said that squadron 311 was with USAFFE, as did *HDP, Talavera.* An
American officer who had been a USAFFE guerrilla in Luzon also identified squadron 311,
commanded by a certain "New-Comb" and with its headquarters in Talavera, as a USAFFE unit
(443rd CIC Detachment, USAFFE, Interrogation Report No. 348: Subject—Wilbur J. Lage,
Captain, Infantry, to Officer in Charge, 9 January 1945; miscellaneous records on guerrillas in the
Philippines, ID No. 14 and 42; Federal Records Center, Suitland, Md.).

The Hukbalahap government in San Ricardo had a president, vice-president, secretary, treasurer, and five policemen. Residents elected these officials in 1942. The same individuals held office throughout the Japanese occupation. The barrio government also had three deparments, each with a person in charge who in turn called on others in the barrio to help. One department handled communications with Hukbalahap governments in other barrios; it relied on couriers and special signals. A second department collected intelligence information about the military, the PC, and other units of the Japanese government. It also helped to police the barrio. The third arranged for supplies—especially food—for Hukbalahap guerrillas who were on the move.

Ramon Tapang was the person in charge of supplies for the Hukbalahap in San Ricardo. He was in his early thirties at the time. He and his older brother owned a small piece of land, which they farmed. Although he had not been involved with the peasant movement prior to the war, his brother had been and he himself was sympathetic to it. When the Japanese invaded, he fled with his family to the mountains, but returned to San Ricardo after a few months. Concerning the resistance movement, Tapang said,

We had to organize in order to protect ourselves from the Japanese and PC. Patricio del Rosario, who was my barrio mate, was already leading a group of Huk guerrillas, many of whom I also knew. They fought the Japanese, and we supported that. They needed food and other things, especially later in the occupation when they'd be away for days at a time, when battles with the soldiers were bigger and more often. People asked me to be in charge of San Ricardo's contributions to the Huks. Many helped me, like my brother here. For example, we'd get a message that a Hukbalahap group was camped nearby and needed food for the night and to take with them the next day. I spread the word. Women cooked *puto* [rice cakes] and other food. Then people secretly carried the food to the guerrillas. Even little children helped. Of course we had to be careful not to make Japanese and PC soldiers in the outpost here suspicious. Often, though, they were away on patrols. I'd say that we did things like this a couple times a month. Once we had to feed five hundred Huks who were in the area. Of course, San Ricardo wasn't alone. Other barrios around here helped, too.

People in San Ricardo supplied between fifty and one hundred cavans of palay a year to Hukbalahap guerrillas. They also arranged for clothing and other necessities. If people had incurred expenses for supplies other than food, the guerrillas reimbursed them. But as one man explained, "Landlords in the area were large contributors of clothing, especially shoes, to the Hukbalahap. They gave these things free, because otherwise the Huks might harm them." "It's true," said Ramon Tapang, "that hacendero families contributed to the Hukbalahap. I arranged for some of this. But most of them didn't really support the Hukbalahap. They gave because they were afraid that we might hurt them if they didn't."

The Hukbalahap government in San Ricardo was part of a larger movement that encompassed most barrios in Talavera. Pulling them all together was a Talavera leadership of a dozen or so men and women. These persons, in turn, kept in touch with Hukbalahap governments in other parts of Nueva Ecija. For security, however, most members of the Hukbalahap movement in San Ricardo did not know who all the leaders were elsewhere in the municipality. "After all," explained Hilario Felipe, "the screening of people wasn't perfect, so we had to be careful about members betraying leaders."

A few people from Talavera attended a Hukbalahap training session that convened in a remote area of Nueva Ecija early in 1943. One of those attending was Religio Felipe, brother of Hilario Felipe. He explained what happened:

> Most of the people there were young. I was nineteen. We studied why the Hukbalahap needed to be a disciplined movement, especially why we should be fair with villagers. We studied guerrilla war tactics and politics. The topics most discussed in political classes were the anti-Japanese struggle and anti-facism. We also talked about how the American army would eventually return to throw out the Japanese and then give the Philippines its independence. We also studied how to help the American army to fight the Japanese when it returned. I remember one of our teachers was Jose de Leon, also known as Dimasalang. He said that after the war, organizations like KPMP would be even stronger than before the Japanese came, and they should run candidates for office in order to change the agrarian situation. We also had a few sessions on Marxism, but I don't think anybody understood it nor saw the relevance. Anyway, hardly any time was spent on it. The whole study session lasted about a month. Afterward I returned to Talavera. I helped in the Hukbalahap government in this municipality. My major job was to coordinate intelligence-gathering and give information to the Huk guerrillas.

Although Felipe, Ramon Tapang, and others in the resistance took precautions, the Japanese military and the PC sometimes did discover them. For instance, the PC arrested the president of the Hukbalahap in a nearby barrio. After a few days the PC released him, but, according to villagers, he died on the way home from jail from wounds authorities had inflicted while interrogating him. In 1943, Ramon Tapang, too, was arrested. "Japanese and PC soldiers took me from my house to Cabanatuan," he said. "They accused me of being a Huk. I denied it. But they wouldn't believe me so they beat me several times, trying to make me talk. This lasted many days. I was in jail for two months. I was lucky they didn't kill me." After being released, he returned to San Ricardo and continued in the Hukbalahap. "Of course," Tapang added with a smile, "what the Japanese said about me was true, but they never found out."

I was surprised to learn that the Japanese government knew so little about the underground network in Talavera. But residents said that the explanation was simple: People did not inform on their neighbors. "Oh, of course, a few did from time to time," said some villagers, "but they were very few and they were outsiders—they weren't from Talavera." Because villagers held the government in such low regard, even those who never fully embraced the Hukbalahap resistance would not run to the authorities to tell what they probably knew about what went on in their barrios. Another part of the explanation was mentioned by several Hukbalahap activists. "The Japanese formed 'neighborhood associations,' " explained Alfredo Buwan of San Ricardo. "Every barrio was supposed to have one. The Japanese figured these would be watchdogs for them. But the Huks infiltrated them. In every barrio we ran them and led them, although the Japanese never knew." "Every barrio" may have been an exaggeration, but apparently the government unwittingly did provide a cover for the Hukbalahap resistance in some places.

According to Central Luzon leaders, the Hukbalahap resistance in Talavera was one of the most effective in Nueva Ecija.[8] By 1943 the Hukbalahap government reached into the municipal mayor's office itself. One of the movement's information sources about what the Japanese were up to, according to Religio Felipe, "was a Huk sympathizer in the municipal government. He was a Filipino who was close to the Japanese. But he looked forward to the day when the Americans would drive the Japanese away." Local historians recorded that, "From November 1942 to January 1944, [Talavera] was under the domination of the Hukbalahap."[9] Although "domination" was an overstatement, according to Hukbalahap activists themselves, the statement indicated the movement's strength.

Improved Economic Conditions

Even though the occupation brought added hardship, the rhythm of barrio life continued to be the cycle of palay agriculture. Villagers still had to farm in order to eat. One surprising economic change was a relative abundance of rice. When I asked, for example, what was the price of rice during the occupation, people typically responded with a surprised look and said, "Oh well, it was cheap here because practically everybody had enough, so there was no market. And if somebody needed palay, he could easily just go to a neighbor or relative to borrow."

One explanation for this was bigger harvests. Many peasants in San Ricardo remembered that some of their best palay crops came during the Japanese occupation. One tenant recalled, for example, "I cut about 200 cavans each year during the Japanese time." That was on 3 hectares of land. From 1945 to 1949, on the same land, "I'd say the harvests ranged between 120 and 160 cavans." Certainly not everyone did this well, but many did contrast higher yields during the occupation with lower yields prior to it and afterward.

Why the higher yields occurred was not entirely clear to the villagers. One explanation they offered was the weather, which happened to be particularly favorable during the occupation. Another reason, they said,

---

[8] Interview with Luis Taruc, Quezon City, 27 January 1970; and interview with Casto Alejandrino, Camp Crame, Quezon City, 5 November 1970.

[9] *HDP, Talavera.*

was that crops were poorer after the occupation because fighting during liberation killed many carabaos and destroyed much property including plows and rice fields. Finally, many believed that people farmed their land more carefully than they were able to do before or after the occupation.

The second explanation for more rice in San Ricardo concerned new agrarian conditions that benefited the average peasant. As most of Talavera's large landowners had gone and did not return before 1945, many tenants no longer paid high rents. For instance, after Manolo Tinio had settled in Manila in 1942, he sent instructions to his katiwala that he would no longer be able to pay his share of the farming expenses. So, Tinio recalled, "I said I'd only ask for 30 percent of the harvest. My katiwala would arrange for it to be delivered to me in Manila."

Tenants also reduced their expenses, partly by necessity and partly by choice. For example, the Japanese had confiscated or destroyed all machinery such as rice mills and threshers *(telyadora)*. Instead of paying for a telyadora to thresh the palay, tenants now did it by hand just as they had done before there were machines. As one man pointed out, "This was cheaper, although more work." The same for husking the palay; people did it by hand for less cost. Villagers also reverted to labor exchange practices for work that they had hired agricultural laborers to do in the 1930s, because then landlords had shared the expense and that had been one way to spread around what little wealth the barrio had. During the Japanese occupation, however, villagers said that land was more available, for some families had left and never returned to farm until after 1945. Consequently, people who previously had had to rely on agricultural wage labor now could farm instead.

With rents and expenses reduced, therefore, tenants had more palay to take home after harvesting. They saved additional rice by not paying the full 30 percent that the large landowners had asked for. Tinio said, "I figure I only got 10 or 15 percent of the harvests. The tenants cheated me." But tenants defended themselves as one man did: "Lord, no, I didn't pay Tinio 30 percent! But I wasn't stealing. I was just taking what was due to me. There had been many harvests before when he had cheated me out of my full share, so I was just making up for some of that." Other tenants in San Ricardo claimed they had given 30 percent to Tinio's katiwala but, as one explained, "I first subtracted things like contributions to the Hukbalahap and taxes and donations I had to give to the Japanese soldiers and PC. Tinio didn't know about what we had to put up with here. He was in Manila the whole time." But, Manolo Tinio countered, "Whatever people gave the Hukbalahap or Japanese should have come out of their share, not out of mine or out of the gross harvest." Still other tenants said they gave Tinio's share to his katiwala, "but the katiwala probably snitched extra for himself. He wasn't paid very much, anyway." In addition to these complications, Tinio probably lost sacks of rice while they were being transported. Bandits, USAFFE guerrillas, the Japanese military, or the Hukbalahap often hijacked trucks and wagons loaded with rice that traveled the road to Manila.

One further change that put villagers in a more enviable position was the declining importance and value of cash. First, there was less that money could buy during the occupation. Cigarettes, clothing, and household goods, for example, became scarce. People in San Ricardo and elsewhere had to improvise. Villagers, whose standard of living had never been high, were better able to make do than were many urban and town folks. Of course, there were hardships, and no one in San Ricardo thought life was easy during the occupation. But they did have the one commodity that an increasing number of others needed—palay. Manila and other urban areas depended on the farmers for rice, as they always had, but less rice was coming into the cities. Meanwhile, cash became practically worthless. People called it "Mickey Mouse" money and had to carry sacks of it to buy anything. Consequently, the barter system revived, and palay was the most sought after commodity as well as a principal medium of exchange. People in barrios like San Ricardo, therefore, were in a better position than they had been before. Illustrative here was an elderly tenant who proudly said to me, "See that chest over there?" pointing across the room of his small house to an artistically engraved four-drawer mahogany bureau with fancy knobs. "I got that for a half a cavan of palay in 1943 from a merchant in Cabanatuan."

The economic situation for peasants in San Ricardo improved because more rice stayed in the barrio and because peasants had more control over where rice would go if it did leave. This, however, was only an incidental benefit of the Japanese occupation, which otherwise brought only grief. Peasants made one point clear: They saw no reason to thank the Japanese government for the additional palay. From their point of view, they had more rice only because of God-blessed weather conditions and because most large landowners had left, not because of any Japanese policies. Furthermore, they saw no indication that the Japanese authorities would side with them were landlords suddenly to return.

The Hukbalahap in Central Luzon

The situation in Central Luzon was generally the same as in Talavera. Harvests, for whatever reason, were better, tenants were able to keep a larger share of the rice, and landlord-tenant problems were overshadowed by the question of how to cope with a military government that was foreign and drew to its side undesirable people. As in Talavera, reactions among people in Central Luzon varied: the Ganaps who welcomed the Japanese; the politicians who cooperated; and many villagers who simply tolerated. Most important for this account, however, was the Hukbalahap resistance. Two important developments, which San Ricardo and Talavera illustrated, were, first, that the Hukbalahap resistance grew out of the peasant movement of the 1930s, and second that the Hukbalahap resistance expanded the peasant movement beyond what it had become by 1941. Both of these were true for

Central Luzon as a whole and were the heart of the Japanese occupation's meaning for peasant politics there.

Hukbalahap's Continuity with Earlier Peasant Movements

When Amando Santa Ana, Patricio del Rosario, and others in Talavera began to resist soon after Japanese soldiers came, they heard of others doing the same thing. One group was to the south in Cabiao, Nueva Ecija. A former Hukbalahap in Cabiao confirmed this: "After the Japanese had rolled over this municipality, a few of us decided we had to fight. I had a gun that I'd found on a dead soldier. Some other men had guns, too. We got together with others from this area. That was in January. There were about fifteen or twenty of us who all knew each other. Some were AMT, others were KPMP like me. We had been on many parades and demonstrations together before the war."[10] Further south, in Malolos, Bulacan, another resistance group had begun. Shortly after the Japanese had taken over Manila, a young man named Agaton Bulaong left the city and returned to Malolos to be with his widowed mother and his brothers, who tenant farmed there. "I was angry and scared," Bulaong recalled, "but I wanted to fight back. I thought of going to Bicol because friends in Manila said Assemblyman Vinzons was going to form an army. But when I returned to Malolos, some friends and relatives already had guns and they talked about fighting the Japanese. I decided to join them because I knew the people in that area." When he described this group, which later became part of the Hukbalahap, he said, "Most were tenants, of course, since that's what most people were there. Many had been in the peasant movement, or their fathers had been. I know, for example, my brother and others were KPMP."[11] A man named Silvestre Liwanag found a similar situation in Lubao, a municipality in southwestern Pampanga: "I had been away for about a year, but soon after the Japanese came, sometime in January, I ran back to Pampanga. Already AMT people had formed a little armed group in the mountains nearby. They had homemade guns, and they had stolen a few rifles from homes of hacenderos. I joined them."[12] Elsewhere in Pampanga another resistance group had begun. Its leader later described this scene:

> In the month of January 1942, when the Japanese were reported entering Manila and the Central Plain of Luzon, thirteen men from Mexico [Pampanga] and nearby towns, all of them labor leaders, went around and mobilized guerrilla units with their 13 arms . . . . This was the first squadron, which stayed mostly in the barrios.[13]

[10] Interview, barrio Sinipit, Cabiao, 11 March 1970.

[11] Interview with Agaton Bulaong, Camp Crame, Quezon City, 20 July 1970.

[12] Interview with Silvestre Liwanag, Camp Crame, Quezon City, 21 July 1970.

[13] "History of Squadron #6 and Records of Encounters," with enclosure 13 in MPC, *History and Organization of the Hukbalahap*.

Its numbers increased, and shortly it became squadron 6 of the Hukbalahap. Meanwhile, in the neighboring municipality of Arayat, Pampanga, Mayor Casto Alejandrino distributed rice from government granaries when he heard about the Japanese approaching. He also broke open a small ammunition depot that retreating American troops had left and gave weapons and ammunition to residents. He and other local AMT activists then formed a "citizen's army."[14]

Between December 1941 and late March 1942, these and other resistance groups sprang up in Central Luzon. Although members of peasant organizations like KPMP and AMT had discussed possible armed resistance in the event of an actual invasion by Japan, they had made no plans. Now that it had happened, people acted on their own. Soon many realized they needed to be better organized in order to be more effective. Experienced peasant leaders and activists took the initiative. In late March 1942, in a barrio of Concepcion, Tarlac, at the foot of Mount Arayat near the Pampanga border, several of these armed bands met. Among them were Felipa Culala with people from Candaba, Pampanga; Bernardo Poblete, sometimes called "Banal," who was an AMT leader and who brought twenty to forty men from San Luis and Minalin, Pampanga; Lope de la Rosa, a social bandit and peasant activist from Bulacan; Eusebio Aquino, a peasant leader who came in with thirty or forty men from Magalang, Pampanga; Mariano Franco, a KPMP spokesman from Cabiao, Nueva Ecija; Casto Alejandrino from Arayat; and Luis Taruc, the AMT leader from San Luis, Pampanga.[15] All together they numbered about two hundred people, several of whom carried weapons. Poblete later wrote of the meeting, "It was on March 29, 1942, when different groups of anti-Fascist elements armed with *paltik* [homemade guns], *balisong* [homemade knives], bolos, and a few rifles organized into anti-Japanese forces, were baptized and given the name 'HUKBALAHAP.' "[16]

Those at the meeting accomplished three important things. First, they agreed on the major purposes of the Hukbalahap: to organize people into an anti-Japanese resistance movement, collect arms "by force if necessary" from civilians unwilling to join the movement, gather up guns that retreating United States armed forces (USAFFE) had left, and stop banditry "which is bound to exist due to the downfall of government authorities."[17] Second, they agreed on a general organizational plan for the guerrilla groups, which they now called squadrons. And third, they elected four persons to form a "military committee," which later became the "general headquarters," whose job was to help the squadrons keep together and to

[14] Alejandrino interview, 5 November 1970; and Taruc, *Born of the People*, pp. 84-85.

[15] Alejandrino interview, 5 November 1970; Bulaong interview, 20 July 1970; Liwanag interview, 21 July 1970; Taruc, *Born of the People*, p. 65.

[16] "History of Squadron 5," with enclosure 13 in MPC, *History and Organization of the Hukbalahap*.

[17] Ibid.

guide the movement. Elected were Alejandrino, Culala, Poblete, and Taruc. These four, in turn, asked Taruc to be the overall commander and Alejandrino to be the vice-commander.[18] One of Taruc's first acts as commander of the Hukbalahap was to send a message to General Douglas MacArthur, the commander-in-chief of USAFFE, which summarized the sentiments and achievements of the meeting. It said in part:

> Here in the Japanese-occupied territories, the people are furious to drive out the Japanese fascist aggressors who grabbed the properties and killed the people of the Philippines. The battle in Candaba is a sign of general counterattacks in the year of the enemy.

> The anti-Japanese people of the Philippines today form their Military Committee under which they organized the People's Anti-Japanese Army [Hukbalahap]. Both the committee and the Army inaugurate on this date and set their officers in San Fernando, Pampanga. The object of this army is to drive out the Japanese aggressors for the defense of lives, properties, and the democratic rights of the people, and for the territorial integrity and national independence of the Philippines as promised by the United States Government.

> We, the people of the Philippines, loyal to the governments of the United States and the Philippines, are determined to offer our lives for the defense of democracy and territorial rights of both the Philippines and the United States. We wish that you will kindly grant your guidance and support to this newly born but militant force of the Filipino people.[19]

Luis Taruc epitomized the continuity between the peasant movement of the 1930s and the Hukbalahap. He was the son of a tenant farmer and grew up in San Luis, Pampanga and San Miguel, Bulacan. He farmed and later learned from an older brother to be a tailor, a trade he practiced in the mid-1930s in San Miguel, Bulacan. Unlike most sons of peasants, Taruc graduated from high school (in Tarlac, Tarlac) and completed one year of college in Manila. Financial support from his eldest brother, the tailor, and his own part-time work in Manila as a ditch-digger permitted him to attend school. Despite his education, however, Taruc felt more at home in Central Luzon's towns and villages. When he returned to San Miguel in 1934 and set up a small tailor shop, the peasant movement was, as he later wrote, "beginning to roll across Central Luzon."[20] Soon he became involved. He attended meetings of peasant organizations in San Miguel and nearby municipalities; he participated in demonstrations and marches; and most important of all, he listened to tenant farmers, sugar-cane cutters, and other villagers. In 1936, he decided to devote full time to the movement, leaving his wife to mind their tailor shop and to raise their

[18] Taruc, *Born of the People*, p. 66.

[19] Luis Taruc, Chairman, People's Anti-Japanese Military Committee, to General Douglas MacArthur, Commander-in-Chief, United States Army Forces in the Far East, 29 March 1942, enclosure 13 in MPC, *History and Organization of the Hukbalahap*.

[20] Taruc, *Born of the People*, p. 26.

son. He went to San Fernando, Pampanga, and told Pedro Abad Santos, the well-known leader of the AMT, that he wanted to work in that peasant organization. Abad Santos, who was, Taruc later wrote, "a tiny, frail old man, who looked as if he could be carried away under one arm by a sturdy peasant," agreed.[21] Taruc also joined the Socialist Party and in 1938, when the socialists merged with the Communist Party, Taruc held an office in the PKP. From 1937 until the Japanese occupation, he was a major figure in the movement in Pampanga and was widely respected among the peasantry across Central Luzon. Undoubtedly, his demonstrated commitment and leadership was why those at the founding meeting of the Hukbalahap selected him to lead the resistance army.

Other links between earlier peasant organizations and the Hukbalahap were men who were younger than experienced peasant leaders like Taruc, but who nevertheless traced their involvement back to the prewar movement in which they either had participated or had watched closely. An example was Silvestre Liwanag of Lubao, Pampanga. In 1970, this soft-spoken, pleasant man discussed his past while sitting in the visitors room of the Camp Crane military prison, where he had been incarcerated for ten years as a convicted rebel: "I was born in 1919. My father was a tenant, just like my grandfather had been. There were thirteen kids in the family, and it never seemed like we had enough food or money to meet expenses, even though my father worked hard. All of us worked. If the crop was palay, half of it went to the landlord."[22] Because Liwanag's father wanted his landlord to decrease the rent, "he joined the AMT along with other peasants in our barrio. In 1938, though, my father died; he never got that rent decrease." By the time Liwanag was seventeen years old (1936), he was in "the youth arm of the AMT. It was a group that sort of helped parents and other elders with their AMT chapters or anything else that they needed help with. The overall purpose of the AMT was to get better sharing arrangements with landlords and improve general conditions for peasants." What he remembered most vividly about the peasant movement in the 1930s was the armed guards that landlords used. "Sometimes they even raided houses; a few people even died," he said. Moreover, the government supported the landlords' guards because "landlords and the government were like one." Especially upsetting to Liwanag was that "the armed men of the landlords were often peasants themselves. . . . It showed the lack of solidarity among the peasants." The AMT tried to change this; "it tried to build that solidarity." Liwanag continued to farm and participate in the AMT in Lubao until late 1939, when he heard that the Philippine army planned to draft him. Hoping that the authorities would be unable to find him, he explained, "I went to Manila and worked there. I thought of going back to school—I had seven grades in Lubao—but never did." After the Japanese invaded, he quickly returned to Lubao where he found many AMT friends and relatives preparing to fight back. "I guess it is a bit

---

[21] Ibid., p. 34.
[22] Liwanag interview, 21 July 1970. This interview is the main source for his biography.

funny," Liwanag grinned, "that I ended up fighting after I had left to avoid being pulled into the government's army." But one lesson of the 1930s "was that we had to work together to defend ourselves." This was one reason why he joined this group. "I was part of them because I was in the AMT, too," he said. But also, "I wanted to fight the Japanese; they were destroying everything." His group, led by Abelardo Dabu, who was Liwanag's brother-in-law, became a squadron of the Hukbalahap. In 1943, after Dabu had died in battle, Liwanag became its commander.

In addition to persons like Taruc and Liwanag, who were originally from the peasantry, a few individuals who came from nonpeasant backgrounds, yet who had been involved in the peasant movement, also participated in the Hukbalahap resistance movement. Juan Feleo, the KPMP spokesman from Nueva Ecija, for example, stayed with the peasantry as a resistance leader. So did Casto Alejandrino from Pampanga.

Alejandrino was certainly a unique individual in the peasant movement and Hukbalahap. He was from a well-to-do landed family in Arayat, Pampanga, and he was a landlord. He had inherited 68 hectares in Arayat, which fourteen tenants farmed in the 1930s. And he could have continued in elite Pampangan circles and probably could have held prominent government positions just as others in the Alejandrino family had done. Instead, he chose to speak on behalf of villagers in Central Luzon, including his own tenants. "I agreed with what they wanted," he said. "Peasants deserved more of the harvest and they deserved to be treated like people, not slaves."[23] Also, he said, "I could contribute because, as a landowner, I helped the AMT and Socialist Party look more respectable in the eyes of the government and the elite." He was also disgusted with traditional politics in the country and believed "the elite-controlled Nacionalista Party was incapable of accepting reforms needed in the country." During the late 1930s, Alejandrino spoke on behalf of the AMT many times and in many places, including picket lines, municipal court houses, and the palace of the Philippine president. After the Socialist Party and the Communist Party merged in 1938, he also held a position in the PKP's central committee. In 1940, he ran on the Socialist Party—and AMT-endorsed—Popular Front ticket for mayor of Arayat and won. "I was still mayor when the Japanese invaded. Guess you already know about the guns we took from that depot after Filipino and American soldiers retreated to Bataan. I had no doubts about using those guns, either." He wanted the Japanese out as quickly as possible because "they were a brutal army, and they were invaders. I was a nationalist—still am. The Philippines had to be independent, not held by the throat by another foreign power." Given these feelings, Alejandrino was one of the minority in the Hukbalahap for whom independence from foreign control was a significant

[23] Information about Casto Alejandrino comes from two interviews I had with him (5 November and 12 November 1970) and from notes that Professor John Larkin shared with me after he interviewed Mr. Alejandrino on 5 April and 12 April 1970. All the interviews were at Camp Crame, Quezon City.

reason for resisting. In the Hukbalanap, his responsibilities included vice-commander for the guerrilla army's general headquarters and top commander for several squadrons in Pampanga and Bulacan.

Table 9 provides additional evidence for the continuity between the prewar peasant movement in Central Luzon and the Hukbalahap. Obviously it is not an exhaustive list of all squadron and other leaders in the Hukbalahap; it only identifies those persons whose prewar activities I know. (Nor does the table include all those persons in Talavera who were active; it lists only the two most prominent leaders from there.) Were the information about Hukbalahap leaders more complete, the correlation with previous involvement in the peasant movement would probably be lower than the table suggests. Nevertheless, the history of San Ricardo and Talavera, statements of Hukbalahap participants, and the list itself show that the continuity between the peasant movement of the 1930s and the Hukbalahap resistance was significant. Several years after the occupation, Luis Taruc wrote in unmistakable terms about this relationship:

> The resistance movement that sprang up in Central Luzon was unique among all the groups that fought back . . . against the Japanese. The decisive element of difference lay in the strong peasant unions and organization of the people that existed there before the war. It gave the movement a mass base, and made the armed forces indistinguishable from the people, a feeling shared both by the people and by the fighters.[24]

Table 10 also illustrates this continuity. Although the figures are inexact because the sources themselves were only estimates, they make the point that the Hukbalahap guerrilla army was confined almost entirely to those provinces where agrarian unrest had been most pronounced during the 1930s. Furthermore, the Hukbalahap, according to this table and all other available evidence, was strongest in those provinces where the peasant movement had previously been the most active—Bulacan, Nueva Ecija, and Pampanga.

Expansion of the Hukbalahap Movement
While benefiting from earlier peasant organizations, the Hukbalahap also pushed the peasant movement in Central Luzon beyond what it had been prior to the Japanese occupation. The numbers of persons in the Hukbalahap increased, and by the end of the war more were involved than had been active in peasant organizations during the 1930s. Moreover, the Hukbalahap affected the quality and composition of the peasant movement.

The increased number of armed Hukbalahap guerrillas shown in Table 10 is one illustration of the movement's growth. Another is a more detailed breakdown over time of the number of Hukbalahap guerrillas (Table 11).

---

[24] Taruc, *Born of the People*, p. 56.

Table 9

HUKBALAHAP GUERRILLAS WHOSE PREWAR ACTIVITIES ARE KNOWN

Home province	Prewar activism	Hukbalahap activism
Pampanga		
Casto Alejandrino	Peasant organizations (AMT); Socialist mayor; PKP[a]	GHQ,[b] vice-commander; Reco 3 leader;[c] governor of Pampanga[d] (1945)
Eusebio Aquino	Peasant organizations (AMT); Socialist Party; PKP	Reco 3 commander
Sergio Cayanan	Peasant organizations (KPMP)	Squadron commander
Felipa Culala	Peasant organizations (KPMP)	Squadron commander; military district leader; Military Committee member
Abelardo Dabu	Peasant and labor organizations	Squadron commander; military district leader
Remedios Gomez	Peasant organizations (AMT)	Squadron leader
Silvestre Liwanag	Peasant organizations (AMT)	Squadron commander, military district leader
Bernardo Poblete	Peasant organizations (AMT)	Reco 7 commander; Military Committee member
Luis Taruc	Peasant organizations (AMT); Socialist Party; PKP	GHQ commander
Peregrino Taruc	Leftist groups (Manila); PKP	Squadron commander; GHQ, education division

Table 9 (continued)

HUKBALAHAP GUERRILLAS WHOSE PREWAR ACTIVITIES ARE KNOWN

Home province	Prewar activism	Hukbalahap activism
Nueva Ecija		
Mamerto Baniaga	Peasant organizations (KPMP); PKP	GHQ, education division
Juan Feleo	Peasant organizations (KPMP); PKP	GHQ, cultural division; Reco 9 leader; governor of Nueva Ecija (1945)
Mariano Franco	Peasant organizations	Reco 9 leader
Jose de Leon	Peasant organizations (KPMP); PKP	Reco 9 commander
Patricio del Rosario	Peasant organizations (KPMP)	Squadron commander
Amando Santa Ana	Peasant organizations (KPMP)	Squadron commander
Bulacan		
Agaton Bulaong	Labor organizations (Manila)	Squadron commander; military district leader
Iluminada Calonge	Peasant organizations	Squadron leader
Lope de la Rosa	Peasant organizations (KPMP); rebel	Squadron commander
Tarlac		
Benjamin Cunanan	Peasant organizations (AMT-Youth)	Squadron leader
Laguna		
Pedro Villegas	Peasant and labor organizations (KAP)[e]	Reco commander

Table 9 (continued)

HUKBALAHAP GUERRILLAS WHOSE PREWAR ACTIVITIES ARE KNOWN

Home province	Prewar activism	Hukbalahap activism
Manila		
Mariano Balgos	Labor organizations; PKP	GHQ, political advisor
Guillermo Capadocia	Labor and peasant organizations; PKP	Attached to GHQ
Mateo del Castillo	Labor and peasant organizations; PKP	GHQ, political advisor
Jorge Frianesa	Labor unions; PKP	PKP
Jesus Lava	Leftist groups; PKP	Manila liaison; education adviser; governor of Laguna (1945)
Jose Lava	Leftist groups; PKP	PKP, organization adviser
Vicente Lava	Leftist groups; PKP	PKP, general secretary
Celia Mariano	Leftist groups; PKP	PKP, education adviser

aPKP Partido Komunista ng Pilipinas (Communist Party of the Philippines).

bGHQ General Headquarters of the Hukbalahap guerrillas.

cReco Regional command, an organizational unit of the Hukbalahap that included several squadrons.

dHukbalahap movement's temporary governor of the province during "liberation" at the end of the Japanese occupation.

eKAP Katipunan ng mga Anak Pawis (Association of Toilers), a labor organization in the 1930s.

Table 10

ARMED HUKBALAHAP AND NUMBER OF SQUADRONS
BY PROVINCE AND YEAR

| Province | Armed Hukbalahap | | Number of squadrons |
	1942	1944	1944
Bulacan	350	1,000	10
Nueva Ecija	750	3,000	22
Pampanga	1,200	4,000	35
Tarlac	300	600	6
Laguna	100	300	2
Other*		100	1
Total	2,700	9,000	76

Sources: Interviews with Hukbalahap leaders, 1970; rosters for "recognized" Hukbalahap units, Noncurrent Records Office, Camp Aguinaldo, Quezon City; documents from the Hukbalahap and PKP; Military Police Command (MPC) Headquarters, Philippines, United States Armed Forces in the Western Pacific (*AFWESPAC*), Intelligence Division (G-2), *History and Organization of the Hukbalahap and the United Front Movement* (including enclosures), 20 December 1945; and Luis Taruc, *Born of the People* (New York: International Publishers, 1953).

*Special squadron (number 48) that had no particular province.

Table 11

GROWTH OF THE HUKBALAHAP GUERRILLAS

Date	Number of persons	Number of squadrons
April 1942	less than 300	5
September 1942	3,000	30-35
December 1942	5,000	42
February 1943	7,000 to 10,000	
June 1943	7,000	
December 1943	10,500	
September 1944	10,000 to 12,000	76

Sources: Interviews with Hukbalahap leaders, 1970; Military Police Command (MPC) Headquarters, Philippines, United States Armed Forces in the Western Pacific (AFWESPAC), Intelligence Division (G-2), *History and Organization of the Hukbalahap and the United Front Movement* (including enclosures), 20 December 1945; and Luis Taruc, *Born of the People* (New York: International Publishers, 1953).

The dates in this table are significant only because they are the ones for which I have information. Although one should not take the figures too literally, as they are only reasonable approximations based on sources that are sometimes contradictory, they nevertheless do reflect the guerrilla army's growth. Beginning with less than three hundred persons and five squadrons in April 1942, the Hukbalahap army exceeded ten thousand persons and had seventy-six squadrons near the end of the war. Although this increase was not a linear progression, for the movement did suffer setbacks partly as a consequence of the Japanese government's increased military retaliation beginning in early 1943, available evidence suggests that the majority of Hukbalahap guerrillas became active during 1942 and the first half of 1943.[25]

Squadrons, which were sometimes called companies, had between one hundred and two hundred persons each. As one squadron became too large, it divided to form two or more separate ones. For example, a Hukbalahap account recorded, "Squadron 46 was an off-spring of both Squadrons No. 3 and No. 6. It was organized from the two big squadrons to accommodate more patriotic volunteers from Mexico, Magalang [both in Pampanga] and Concepcion [in Tarlac]."[26] Another account said, "After the battle of Baliti [a barrio in Arayat, Pampanga], where 6 other squadrons participated, the Staff members of the said squadrons decided to create another squadron out of the arms they captured from the enemy. Thus was formed Squadron 50."[27]

The number of squadrons also increased as the Hukbalahap resistance spread to other areas. South of Central Luzon in eastern Laguna, for example, eight peasants formed a guerrilla group in 1942. They had guns and had been in peasant organizations in Longos and Paete municipalities. Gradually, their numbers increased under the leadership of persons such as Pedro Villegas. Of peasant background and a tenant himself, Villegas had been involved in several peasant and labor organizations in Longos, Laguna. When the Japanese invaded, he was serving a prison term in Manila for alleged seditious actions. Villegas and others in this band of guerrillas knew several Hukbalahap leaders, including Luis Taruc and Casto Alejandrino, and they requested an affiliation with the Central Luzon movement. Thereafter they became the "Southern Luzon Command" of the Hukbalahap, which had by 1944 about three hundred armed persons from five municipalities in Laguna and two in Quezon province.[28]

[25] Interviews in Nueva Ecija in 1970; rosters of several Hukbalahap units found with enclosure 13 in MPC, *History and Organization of the Hukbalahap;* and rosters for the three "recognized" Hukbalahap groups, whose records are filed at the Noncurrent Records Office, Camp Aquinaldo, Quezon City.

[26] "Brief History: Squadron No. 46," with enclosure 13 in MPC, *History and Organization of the Hukbalahap.*

[27] "Brief History: Squadron No. 50," with enclosure 13 in MPC, *History and Organization of the Hukbalahap.*

[28] Information concerning Pedro Villegas comes from Taruc, *Born of the People,* pp. 164-165, and from a folder for Pedro Villegas filed with the records of recognized guerrillas (Southern

A list of those squadrons whose locations I have been able to identify shows that armed groups did operate in much of the Central Plain (Table 12). A complete list would probably show even more municipalities with Hukbalahap forces, as this one has only forty-two of the seventy-six that existed at the movement's peak. Bulacan is especially underrepresented, for only two of the known ten squadrons in that province appear on the list. The Hukbalahap's expansion was not always the result of squadrons dividing or local spontaneous resistance. To some extent, Hukbalahap leaders ventured into barrios and municipalities that were not yet involved in the movement. They mixed, as Luis Taruc once illustrated, persuasion, intimidation, and violence to get new supporters:

> A different type of problem confronted us when we encountered a barrio in which puppets and spies were present or where there was pro-Japanese feeling; or when we were very mobile and had to enter a barrio where conditions were unknown. Here, too, we sent in contact men who obtained full information on who the puppets and spies were, where they lived, and about the movement. Then we surrounded the barrios with a heavy guard, permitting no one to leave and making those who entered stay. Our next step was to arrest all puppets and spies and to place them before a public meeting in the church or in the school. The people were told that we had come to arrest traitors. Our charges against those arrested were made on the basis of the information we had gathered, and then the people were asked if the charges were correct, and if they had anything further to add. If the people refuted the charges, the prisoners were released. If the charges were affirmed, we next found out if the persons in question had acted under force by the enemy or willingly. Those who were avowedly traitors were punished, killed if the people thought it appropriate. Those who acted under duress were lectured on the principles of the resistance movement, and urged to remain in their positions and use them as a disguise for anti-Japanese work.[29]

In addition to increasing the size of the peasant movement in Central Luzon, the Hukbalahap affected its quality. An obvious change was that thousands of villagers acquired military skills. Now there were peasants in nearly every municipality of Bulacan, Nueva Ecija, Pampanga, and eastern Tarlac who had learned to be guerrilla soldiers. During the resistance, they took weapons from dead soldiers, picked up hundreds of guns that Americans and Japanese had discarded in Bataan, and stole rifles and ammunition from landowners and government munitions depots. "But most people in the Hukbalahap, " said Peregrino Taruc, "had never held a

Luzon Command, Officers) at the Noncurrent Records Office, Camp Aguinaldo, Quezon City. For the origins and growth of the Hukbalahap in Southern Luzon, I have used the following captured documents: "Malakanang Oportunismo sa SLB" [Rightist Opportunism in the Southern Luzon Bureau], circa 1944 (CapDoc, Ag.); "Pangkalahatang Ulat ng PKP sa Timog Luzon (SLRC) Simula sa Kaniyang Pagkakatatag Hanggang Ngayon" [General Report of the PKP in Southern Luzon (Southern Luzon Regional Committee) from Its Beginning until the Present], 15 September 1945 (CapDoc, Ag.); and Taruc, *Born of the People,* pp. 162-169.

[29] Taruc, *Born of the People,* p. 118.

Table 12

HUKBALAHAP SQUADRONS AND THEIR GENERAL LOCATIONS
(INCOMPLETE)

Location		Squadron number
Province(s)	*Municipality(s) or other local description*	
Nueva Ecija	San Isidro	1
	Near Mount Arayat (probably San Antonio-Cabiao area)	2
	Foot of Mount Arayat (especially the municipality of Cabiao)	4
	Talavera	8
	San Antonio	22
	Guimba	23
	Jaen	25
	Gapan	28
	Licab	32
	Cabiao-Jaen	55
	Cabiao	88
	Santa Rosa-Aliaga	98
	Quezon	101
	Laur-Bongabon	JD-1
	Aliaga-Zaragoza	JF-2
Tarlac	Concepcion	43
	Concepcion	45
	Capas-Concepcion	50
	Southern part	56
	Lapaz-Victoria	60
Pampanga-Tarlac	Foot of Mount Arayat (to west and north)	3
	Mount Arayat area	44
	Mexico and Magalang-Concepcion	46

Table 12 (continued

HUKBALAHAP SQUADRONS AND THEIR GENERAL LOCATIONS
(INCOMPLETE)

Location		Squadron number
Province(s)	*Municipality(s) or other local description*	
Pampanga	San Luis-Candaba	5
	San Fernando-Mexico	6
	Macabebe-Minalin	12-B
	Mexico	12-C
	Macabebe	12-D
	Lubao-Floridablanca	18
	San Luis-Santa Ana	21
	Arayat	31
	Angeles	49
	Bacolor	66
	San Fernando	86
	San Luis-San Simon	87
	Apalit-San Simon	104
	Floridablanca-Lubao	Co. *B*
	Guagua-Lubao	Co. *C*
Pampanga-Bulacan	San Luis-Calumpit	77
	San Luis and San Simon-Baliwag and Santa Maria	97
Bulacan	San Ildefonso	24
	San Miguel	105

Sources: Interviews with Hukbalahap leaders, 1970; documents from the Hukbalahap and PKP; Military Police Command (MPC) Headquarters, Philippines, United States Armed Forces in the Western Pacific (AFWESPAC), Intelligence Division (G-2), *History and Organization of the Hukbalahap and the United Front* (including enclosures), 20 December 1945; Luis Taruc, *Born of the People* (New York: International Publishers, 1953).

Map 4. Central Luzon: Municipal Boundaries and Vicinity of Hukbalahap.

gun before."[30] Taruc, brother of Luis Taruc, was put in charge of training them, because he was one of the few with military experience. "I had been," he explained, "in the Philippine army reserve and had fought in Bataan against the Japanese." Despite the efforts of Taruc and others, however, only a few guerrillas received formal training. A handful of Hukbalahap

[30] Interview with Peregrino Taruc, Camp Crame, Quezon City, 8 July 1970.

soldiers did read Edgar Snow's *Red Star Over China* and other books that explained guerrilla warfare. Some more profited from a special squadron, number 48, composed of Chinese Filipinos. As some men in the squadron had learned guerrilla tactics when fighting the Japanese army in Canton before immigrating to the Philippines, they moved around Central Luzon to teach others. Most guerrillas, however, whether officers or nonofficers, acquired their military knowledge by experience.

They learned from their mistakes as well as their successes. For example, several squadrons and the general headquarters established permanent camps near Mount Arayat from which they raided Japanese-controlled municipal buildings and attacked Japanese and PC patrols. Not until several squadrons had suffered serious losses in late 1942 and early 1943, when the Japanese army bombed and shelled Hukbalahap camps, did the resistance army fully realize that it would have to be more mobile and flexible. "We learned to be more discreet, too, and collect better intelligence first," said Benjamin Cunanan who had been a young vice-commander of a squadron in Tarlac. "We also avoided long battles. One or two hours at most; usually shorter. This was partly to save ammunition and to avoid being pinned down."[31] Peregrino Taruc admitted that he himself had to learn new methods because his ROTC training had not equipped him for guerrilla fighting, and "we learned the hard way, by errors, to avoid battles near barrios. Otherwise the Japanese would come back later and destroy houses and kill people out of revenge."

The Hukbalahap army became rather effective. According to its chief commander Luis Taruc, "the Hukbalahap . . . killed more than 20,000 Japs, spies, and Puppet Philippine Constabulary men [and] weakened Japanese domination of the masses in Central Luzon and to a certain extent in southern Luzon. . . ."[32] An official history of the United States Sixth Army, which landed in Luzon during liberation, stated that "the Hukbalahap fought the Japanese furiously and unceasingly at every opportunity."[33] An American military official whose job had been to be knowledgeable about guerrilla groups in the Philippines reported that the Hukbalahap consistently fought the Japanese and was the most effective resistance organization in Luzon.[34] A justice of the peace in Tarlac told United States military authorities after the war that the Hukbalahap had kept alive the spirit of resistance and had kept down the number of crimes. And a former governor of Tarlac told American soldiers that the Hukbalahap guerrillas "constituted the only militant opposition force from mid-1942 until September 1944. During this period, he [the governor] said, the USAFFE

---

[31] Interview with Benjamin Cunanan, Camp Crame, Quezon City, 11 August 1970.

[32] Luis Taruc, Commander-in-Chief, Hukbalahap, to General Douglas MacArthur and President Osmeña, circa February 1945, enclosure 10 in MPC, *History and Organization of the Hukbalahap.*

[33] *Sixth Army on Luzon,* circa 1946, p. 58 (RG 94, WW II Operations Reports, 1940-1948, 6th Army 106-0.3; Federal Records Center, Suitland, Md.).

[34] Headquarters, Sixth Service Command, ASF, "Hukbalahap," Intelligence Report, 29 December 1945 (XL 34731, OSS Files; Military Records, National Archives, Washington, D.C.).

guerrillas maintained a passive intelligence organization."[35] The Hukbalahap's aggressiveness, in fact, aggravated bad relations between it and USAFFE
groups. USAFFE guerrillas claimed they had orders to adopt a "lie-low" policy
after 1942, to cease active resistance, and to concentrate on collecting
intelligence, which they forwarded to the United States Pacific command
outside the Philippines.[36] Partly because of this, they resented the Hukbalahap so much that they "went so far as to ambush Huk units to prevent them
from engaging the Japs."[37]

It would be a mistake, however, to picture Hukbalahap guerrillas always
engaged in battle. Luis Taruc, as commander-in-chief, encouraged each
squadron to carry out at least three actions each month, be they ambushes,
raids, or acts of sabotage. Although some squadrons may have been this
active, many probably were not. For example, squadron 3 near Mount
Arayat listed seven "encounters" in 1942 and five in 1943. In December
1942, it fought Japanese patrols twice, but between February and June
1943 it had no battles. Squadron 46 listed fourteen encounters during the
entire occupation, beginning in June 1942 and ending with a battle in
Tarlac, Tarlac, on 14 January 1945. Unlike squadron 3, this squadron had
several battles in the first half of 1943, but between the end of May 1943
and June 1944 it reported no encounters. The point is that most Hukbalahap guerrillas did more than fight; they continued to farm and otherwise
participate in the life of their home barrios. "We couldn't fight all the
time," said Liwanag, "for one thing because we didn't have enough
ammunition to do that." Besides, "there was more to guerrilla warfare than
fighting—collecting intelligence about the PC and the Japanese, for example." Members, he said, "did this best in their home towns and barrios,
and they sent their information to squadron commanders whose job was to
plan raids carefully."[38]

Liwanag went on to say, as residents in San Ricardo had emphasized,
that the Hukbalahap resistance was more than its army: "The Hukbalahap
was both a military and a political organization. The guerrillas could not
survive alone. The armed part and the barrio underground were inter-
woven." In western Pampanga, the home area of those squadrons in which
Liwanag participated, people in the Hukbalahap resistance, he said,
"secretly converted neighborhood associations [fostered by the Japanese]
into BUDC"—Barrio United Defense Corps or Sandatahang Tanod ng

[35] 441st CIC [Counter Intelligence Corps] Detachment, "Monthly Information Report of
Activities in SWPA," February 1945, pp. A17-A25 (RG 94, CIDT-441-0.2, CIC; Federal Records
Center, Suitland, Md.).

[36] Sixth Army on Luzon, p. 49; MPC, History and Organization of the Hukbalahap; and the
Combat History Division, G-1 Section, Headquarters AFWESPAC, Triumph in the Philippines:
1941-1946, vol. 3, 30 July 1946, p. 42 (RG 94, WW II Operations Reports, 1940-1948, Pacific
Theater, 98-USF6-0; Federal Records Center, Suitland, Md.).

[37] MPC, History and Organization of the Hukbalahap. Several former Hukbalahap leaders
with whom I spoke confirmed attacks of this kind by USAFFE groups.

[38] "History of Squadron 3 and Records of Encounter" and "Brief History: Squadron No. 46,"
both with enclosure 13 in MPC, History and Organization of the Hukbalahap; and Liwanag
interview, 21 July 1970.

Bayan. In this manner, Liwanag explained, villagers could appear to be doing as the Japanese government wished while in fact collecting "supplies, money, and information for the guerrillas." BUDC was the name used in documents from the general headquarters and by leaders like Liwanag, Alejandrino, and Taruc for what people in San Ricardo and other barrios called the Hukbalahap government or the KPMP and AMT of the Japanese period.

The activities of these Hukbalahap governments and leaders and the coordination among barrio organizations and guerrilla squadrons went beyond the achievements of previous peasant groups in Central Luzon. According to Liwanag and numerous other Hukbalahap sources, barrio governments governed in much the same manner as the one in San Ricardo did. Hukbalahap government leaders and guerrilla officers even officiated at weddings, baptisms, and funerals, and issued marriage licenses and baptismal certificates.[39] In a Nueva Ecija barrio, a Hukbalahap government tried a man accused of murdering a woman, whom the accused claimed was a witch. A jury of villagers found him guilty and sentenced him to imprisonment.[40] Not only did this illustrate the peasant movement's development, but it showed innovation because neither a barrio government nor a trial by jury was provided for in Philippine law. The Hukbalahap guerrilla army also had judicial procedures to investigate infractions of rules, which were outlined in a widely circulated document entitled "Fundamental Spirit." This and similar papers found among Hukbalahap records, many of them originating from its general headquarters and its education committee, set the standards for being a good soldier, an honest person in a resistance movement, and a well-mannered guerrilla among civilians. The regional command for northern Pampanga and Tarlac (Reco 3), for example, found one guerrilla guilty of malversation of funds; Reco 8 (in Nueva Ecija) found one of its commanders guilty of banditry and giving information to the Japanese; and Reco 7 (Pampanga) concluded after a long investigation, which had begun at the squadron level, that the Hukbalahap heroine Felipa Culala was guilty of stealing food from barrio residents and using her rank to accumulate wealth.[41]

The Hukbalahap movement also had a communication network consisting of couriers, codes, secret niches where messages could be left, and contact persons in barrio organizations and guerrilla squads who were responsible for circulating incoming news and sending out information that could be valuable to the resistance in other localities. Its cultural and

[39] Military Division, Region [Reco] 3, "Report No. 1, Hukbalahap, Office of the Military Division," 4 August 1944 (CapDoc, Ag.); and Luis Taruc interview, 27 January 1970.

[40] Narding [Mamerto Baniaga], P'Com [Provincial Committee], to . . . [illegible], circa 1945 (CapDoc, Ag.). Baniaga, this document's author and a prominent leader in Nueva Ecija's peasant movement, was sometimes better known as Magno Bueno.

[41] Military Division, Region 3, "Report No. 1," 4 August 1944; "Pangkalahatang Ulat ng Lupon Panglalawigan ng Nueva Ecija" [General Report of the Nueva Ecija Provincial Committee], 8 June 1945 (CapDoc, Ag.); MPC, History and Organization of the Hukbalahap; and Taruc, Born of the People, pp. 129-130, 157-158.

information committee, headed by Juan Feleo, organized shows consisting of songs, skits, and short dramas that went from barrio to barrio to counter Japanese propaganda and bolster morale. The Hukbalahap also issued publications, the most regular and largest of which was *Katubusan ng Bayan* (Redemption of the Nation). During much of the occupation, its small staff included peasants, trade unionists, and university people who, in a mountain hideout, mimeographed about three thousand copies each week. One or two pages in length, *Katubusan* praised the Hukbalahap's victories; lambasted fascism, the Japanese regime, and its Filipino "puppets"; and hailed the approaching American armed forces.

Hukbalahap publications, however, never reached all parts of Central Luzon nor even all Hukbalahap barrio governments and squadrons. Similarly, the Hukbalahap governments were weak in some barrios while strong in others, and judicial procedures worked better in some places than in others. So it would be an exaggeration to say that the Hukbalahap movement had tightly woven together all barrios of Central Luzon or that it enjoyed the undaunted support of all villagers. The important point is that the resistance had drawn the Central Luzon peasantry closer together than it had been before, thousands of villagers participated actively in the Hukbalahap, and many more sympathized with it.

At the same time, the Japanese occupation pushed peasants and local elites further apart. Whereas most villagers supported the Hukbalahap, most landlords abandoned their tenants and fled to the cities, favored and served the new regime, and endorsed USAFFE groups that quarreled with Hukbalahap squadrons.[42] And the PC, police, and other local officials were worse in the eyes of the peasantry. They not only worked with the Japanese regime, they were its instruments of oppression, a conclusion that even American officials later reached.[43] Being on opposite sides, Hukbalahap supporters and the PC and local government officials became bitter enemies. This animosity continued long after the Japanese had left.

National Level: The United Front against Japan

Prior to the Japanese invasion, several small groups, mainly in Manila, had publicly opposed fascism and Japan's foreign policies. Three of the most active were the League for the Defense of Democracy, the Friends of

[42] The point that landlords often supported USAFFE groups against the Hukbalahap comes from the following: interviews in Nueva Ecija and with former Hukbalahap leaders, 1970; and Taruc, *Born of the People*, p. 155.

[43] Office of Strategic Services, Research and Analysis Branch, *Law Enforcement in the Philippine Islands*, 25 September 1944, p. 66 (OSS R&A No. 2330; Diplomatic Records, National Archives, Washington, D.C.); J. E. Hall, Lt. Gen., Asst. Chief of Staff, OPD, "Reorganization of the Commonwealth Government of the Philippines, Summary Sheet," 1 November 1945 (RG 165, OPD 093.5 PI, case 45; Military Records, National Archives, Washington, D.C.); and 443rd CIC Detachment, USAFFE, Interrogation Report No. 348, 9 January 1945.

China, and the Communist Party (PKP). One member of the League, Peregrino Taruc, described what these groups were doing in 1941: "We were anti-Japanese. We picketed stores selling Japanese-made goods; we asked the government to boycott Japanese products so as to slow Japan down and keep it from trying to take over more countries. We also demonstrated on behalf of China, who at that time was already fighting Japanese invaders. We also had fund-raising campaigns to send money, food, and clothing to the Chinese."[44] The League and the Friends of China had both American and Filipino sympathizers, many of whom were either in college or had recently graduated, like Peregrino Taruc, or had good jobs in professions or the government. The League's founder, for example, was Vicente Lava, a world-renowned Filipino scientist who had a doctorate from Columbia University and worked in the government's Bureau of Science. He was also an officer in the PKP. "We were what I'd call 'progressives,' " said Peregrino Taruc. "We were concerned about social and economic problems, and we wanted the Philippines to be independent—something the Americans had already set a date for—and to keep the Philippines out of Japanese control." The League and similar groups, however, Taruc said, "were not involved with agrarian issues. We were aware, of course, of the peasants' problems and some members had contact with peasant leaders in the KPMP, for example. But we were mainly concerned with national issues."[45]

After the Japanese invasion had begun in December 1941, representatives from the League, Friends of China, the PKP, other anti-fascist groups, and several peasant organizations met in Manila. They agreed, first, to set aside their differences in order to form a "united front" against Japan and fascism. Second, they authorized Pedro Abad Santos and Crisanto Evangelista, the two top officers in the PKP, to announce their "national unity for an Anti-Japanese United Front" and to recommend that President Manuel Quezon and American High Commissioner Francis B. Sayre begin immediately to train and organize civilians to fight. People at the meeting decided that the PKP officers should issue this announcement because, they reasoned, the government would expect the PKP to be the least likely political group to support the war effort and thus "if the Communists were giving their support, it was to be understood that all labor and peasant groups would be also."[46] In order to make itself clear, the PKP pledged loyalty to democracy and to the governments of the Philippines and the United States.[47]

A few days later, the Japanese military took Manila peacefully. No one, inside the government or out, had had time to form a militia. Indeed, within weeks, Japanese soldiers had captured and imprisoned several who

[44] Peregrino Taruc interview, 8 July 1970.

[45] Other sources support Peregrino Taruc's view of the League and similar groups. For example, "History of the Hukbalahap Manila-Rizal Force," with enclosure 13 in MPC, *History and Organization of the Hukbalahap.*

[46] MPC, *History and Organization of the Hukbalahap.*

[47] The text of the PKP's statement is in Taruc, *Born of the People,* pp. 52-53.

had denounced Japan, including Pedro Abad Santos, Crisanto Evangelista, and Guillermo Capadocia, the three top officers in the PKP.

In early February 1942, however, representatives from those organizations that had met in December in Manila convened again, this time in a barrio of Cabiao, Nueva Ecija, near Mount Arayat. Vicente Lava, who had become the acting chairman of the PKP following the arrest of other party leaders, called the meeting and proposed an organizational structure for a unified resistance. His plan included a citizens' army led by the United Front. Among the groups represented at the meeting were the PKP, Civil Liberties Union, League for Defense of Democracy, Friends of China, Popular Front Party, Philippine Youth League, KPMP, AMT, other peasant and labor organizations including Katipunan ng mga Anak Pawis (Association of Toilers, KAP) and "other anti-Fascist elements." Among those peasant leaders and spokesmen for peasant organizations who participated were Luis Taruc, Mariano Franco, Eusebio Aquino, Jose de Leon, Juan Feleo, and Casto Alejandrino. The meeting accepted, in principal, Lava's proposal and created a national committee to direct the resistance. The committee had fifteen members representing the broad spectrum of groups attending. The participants also chose Luis Taruc, Casto Alejandrino, and another person to form a military committee and organize an army for the United Front.[48]

Meanwhile, as this chapter has shown, villagers in several parts of Central Luzon had already begun to arm themselves and resist the Japanese. And in March, a month after the United Front meeting in Cabiao, Taruc and Alejandrino presided over the founding of the Hukbalahap.

The United Front was a convergence of two phenomena in Philippine politics that had had little contact during the 1930s. One was the peasant movement. The other was the Filipino political left, which was concentrated in metropolitan Manila. It consisted of groups and individuals who were discontented with the regime, disgusted with the major political factions in the country, and in favor of making the government more representative of Philippine society. As it included, for example, opponents of the ruling elites, nationalists, civil libertarians, some trade unionists, socialists, and communists, the left was diverse. Some familiar individuals in the peasant movement—for instance, Luis Taruc, Juan Feleo, and Casto Alejandrino—were also involved in leftist groups. Another example was Mateo del Castillo, whose major involvement had been with the PKP and labor unions in Manila but who had also been a spokesman for the peasantry before the Japanese occupation. On the whole, however, these two currents in Philippine political life had stayed apart until the United Front was attempted.

Those who formed the United Front in early 1942 did share several interests. First, they were anti-Japanese—that is, they opposed the invasion, the new government, and the repression. Second, they were pro-

<hr>

[48] MPC, *History and Organization of the Hukbalahap;* Taruc, *Born of the People,* p. 60; and interview with Peregrino Taruc, Camp Crame, Quezon City, 13 July 1970.

American in that they wanted American forces to help drive out the Japanese and were willing to cooperate with American officials to do that. And third, they agreed that they needed to organize a large, broad resistance movement that might have to last for months, perhaps years, before American forces could return to help them defeat the Japanese. Because armed peasant groups in Central Luzon had already appeared, because the peasant movement had been strong in Central Luzon prior to the invasion, and because important leaders in Central Luzon and in the country's leftist groups knew one another, the Front's leadership hoped that villagers in Central Luzon would be the backbone of the resistance army.

One might suppose, when looking at an organizational diagram of the resistance movement as a whole, that the United Front ran the Hukbalahap. This certainly was how it was supposed to be. More precisely, the PKP, being the most prominent group in the Filipino left, theoretically controlled the Hukbalahap. "Cold war" logic, too, would lead one to conclude that once a movement included a Communist Party it was not a popular organization but one manipulated by power-hungry communists. This, however, does not follow. Even if the Communist Party had played a major role, the resistance still would have been spontaneous and grounded firmly in Central Luzon's villages. A relatively more important communist component would not have detracted from the evidence that the Hukbalahap had overwhelming popular support. But the Communist Party lacked deep roots in Central Luzon and could add little to the resistance. Consequently, the PKP did not control the Hukbalahap, although individual communists participated actively in it.

After the United Front's founding conference, most national committee members returned to Manila determined to organize against the Japanese government. They and others in the League, Civil Liberties Union, PKP, and other groups went underground. These people established a mobile radio station called "Free Philippines," which broadcast anti-Japanese programs; they published newspapers and leaflets; and some tried to sabotage the regime, which by that time had taken firm control of metropolitan Manila and had the cooperation of numerous Filipino officials.

As the new government took hold, it clamped down on all opposition, nearly squeezing to death the resistance in Manila. The Japanese military and the Manila police located and destroyed the "Free Philippines" in early 1943. They arrested people suspected of subversion and threw them into Fort Santiago prison where some languished or died, including Pedro Abad Santos and Crisanto Evangelista.[49]

Among those who escaped arrest, some gave up political work completely; others left Manila either to help guerrilla groups or to hide. Some helped the Hukbalahap, particularly its publications and its training

---

[49] Peregrino Taruc interview, 13 July 1970; and Casto Alejandrino interview, 12 November 1970.

sessions for guerrillas and Hukbalahap government leaders. Still others in United Front groups stayed in Manila, despite the dangers, to continue resistance work. Through precarious and intricate means, they smuggled information to guerrillas, including the Hukbalahap. One underground group was the "League for National Liberation," composed of businessmen and professionals, incuding Jesus Lava, a physician who was a younger brother of Vicente Lava and a PKP member.[50] But the national committee of the United Front never had time to develop. Although some committee members continued to work in the resistance, others had been arrested or had gone into hiding. Nor did the United Front have authoritative leaders who made policy acceptable to the resistance movement as a whole. The United Front remained basically a spirit or sense of unity shared by people who were resisting. Consequently, even though Hukbalahap squadrons, barrio governments, and general headquarters may well have looked on groups such as the League for National Liberation in a united front spirit and appreciated whatever supplies they contributed, these groups were in no position to run the Hukbalahap movement.

As for the PKP, it was more organized than the United Front but it was not a mass-based party. The Japanese occupation reduced its membership still further, confused its supporters, and seriously damaged its organization. As these difficulties were compounded by the tenuous relations the party leadership had with the peasant movement in Central Luzon in the first place, it is understandable why major policies that the PKP leaders made and asked the Hukbalahap to follow were, in large measure, ignored.

The Japanese occupation immediately hurt the PKP when the military imprisoned Pedro Abad Santos, Crisanto Evangelista, and other prominent members in early 1942. These arrests and the general disorder at the time caused many PKP members to panic. One PKP report said later, for example, that members in the small party organization in Laguna "withdrew under their shells like turtles."[51] Another PKP branch reported afterward that a majority of its members "stayed home" and "refused to act."[52] A PKP appraisal of the party organization in Manila found, reluctantly, that its membership decreased rather than increased during the war. This was particularly disturbing, the report added, because meanwhile the numbers in the Hukbalahap and other anti-Japanese groups increased.[53] Attempts between 1942 and late 1944 to recruit new members

---

[50] Interview with Jesus Lava, Camp Crame, Quezon City, 19 August 1970; and Taruc, *Born of the People*, p. 173.

[51] "Malakanang Oportunismo" [Rightist Opportunism in the Southern Luzon Bureau], circa 1944.

[52] "Pangkalahatang Ulat ng PKP sa Timog Luzon" [General Report of the PKP in Southern Luzon], 15 September 1945.

[53] "Pangkalahatang Ulat ng Marrcom mula ng Mayo hanggang Agosto 1945 na iniharap sa Kombensio Septiembre 15, 1945" [General Report of Marrcom (Manila-Rizal Regional Committee) from May until August 1945, presented to the Convention of 15 September 1945] (Hernandez Exh. M 2-43; CFI, Manila).

and reorganize were unsuccessful. A PKP leader after the war criticized the party for not having organized Manila workers during the occupation, but Jesus Lava, who was in Manila for part of that time, explained that the PKP found organizational work in Manila nearly impossible because "it had only a limited number of cadres among the labor movement even before the war, and, because of the Japanese, it was too difficult and dangerous for any kind of labor movement or communist education. . . ."[54] When individuals in the party tried to revise the party's organization in order to cope with what they hoped were only temporary setbacks, they ran into other problems. Leaders gave assignments to cadres who were unqualified for the jobs, many members had lost contact with the party, "discipline was loose," many older party members were "uncooperative," there was "practically no work on propaganda and education among members," members "lacked confidence and had a defeatist attitude," members received "no supervision from the few leaders" who remained, and the party had "no unity on political matters."[55]

The lack of agreement on political issues was partly a consequence of honest difference among party leaders, but it was also because the meaning of "party membership" itself was too broad. Whereas top PKP leaders like Vicente Lava and Mateo del Castillo had studied theories of communism and party building, most "members" had not. PKP documents written during the occupation bemoaned this; so did Mateo del Castillo, who was the main link between the PKP and the Hukbalahap. Near the end of the occupation, for instance, he complained that lower level party leaders in Pampanga and Tarlac were not versed in the theoretical and practical knowledge of the party's doctrines.[56] He was further upset because meetings of supposed party members discussed "personal problems" and how to get more food to the guerrillas, rather than issues related to the "political struggle" and other party matters, and he said people did not understand the difference between being a member of the party and a

[54] Jesus Lava interview, 19 August 1970. Jose Lava, brother of Jesus Lava and secretary-general of the PKP at the time, was the one who criticized the party for having failed to organize workers during the Japanese occupation: "Milestones," pp. 23-24.

[55] "Ang Pakikibaka ukol sa Mabilis na Ikapagbabagong-tatag ng PKP" [The Struggle for a Rapid Reestablishment of the PKP] and "Sampung Pinakamababang Kahilingan sa Ikapagbabagong-tatag ng PKP" [The Ten Most Basic Needs for the Reconstruction of the PKP] in Ang Patnugot: Pahayagang ukol sa Kaalamang pangpolitika [The Leader: Periodical for Political Education], vol. 1, no. 1, 15 May 1944 (CapDoc, Ag.); A. Mirazol, "Report of Reco 3," 23 June 1944 (CapDoc, Ag.); MRB [Manila-Rizal Bureau], "Pahayag—Pampasinaya ng MRB sa Lahat ng mga Kasapi ng Partido" [Announcement—Decisions of MRB for Party Members], 14 October 1944 (CapDoc, Ag.); C. Villapando [Mateo del Castillo], Organization Department, to Reco 3, 4 December 1944 (CapDoc, Ag.); "Pangkalahatang Ulat ng PKP sa Timog Luzon" [General Report of the PKP in Southern Luzon], 15 September 1945.

[56] Villapando [Mateo del Castillo] to Reco 3, 4 December 1944. Other documents citing this problem include the following: "Ang Pakikibaka" [Struggle for Re-establishment] and "Sampung Pinakamababang" [Ten Basic Needs. . .], Ang Patnugot, 15 May 1944; and Mirazol, "Reports of Reco 3," 23 June 1944.

member of a peasant or other "mass organization." Consequently, among the few resistance activists who may have considered themselves PKP "members," most probably had a broad interpretation similar to Silvestre Liwanag's. Liwanag said he considered himself a party member during the Japanese occupation "because communism was the spokesman for the poor, fighting for the poor against exploiters, and seeking true independence for the Philippines."[57]

The overall effect of these difficulties confronting the PKP was that in Manila, according to PKP documents, "party work did not progress" and the party became weaker. In the country as a whole, according to another PKP document, the party was not at the forefront of the masses.[58] Also reflecting these problems was the inability of top leaders in the PKP to get most Hukbalahap activists to adhere to several major party polices.

One central policy of the PKP during the occupation was the united front idea itself, which, according to the PKP, should allow even landlords to join the resistance if they were anti-Japanese. But many villagers in the Hukbalahap disagreed. "It was difficult during the Japanese occupation," said Peregrino Taruc, "to convince peasants of the necessity that the United Front could include landlords who were sometimes their enemies."[59] Peasants in Central Luzon, wrote one PKP leader after the war, had been "just waiting for such a situation as the war to liquidate their landlord enemies" and consequently were reluctant to listen to the party's view about the landlords in the United Front.[60] Indeed, some peasants took advantage of the confusion, especially during the early months of the occupation, to attack and even kill landlords and their type. For example, early in 1942 Bernardo Poblete, who became a Hukbalahap leader, and other AMT activists in Pampanga murdered a manager of the large PASUDECO sugar central.[61] Villagers in Nueva Ecija told me of similar cases, including one landlord in Cabiao whom local Hukbalahap guerrillas killed in 1942 even though his family had contributed money to the resistance. As one man explained, "He was a bastard. He and his armed guards had screwed many tenants before." Despite the PKP's efforts during the occupation, del Castillo reluctantly reported in late 1944 that "anti-landlord thinking among the masses is still strong," and many peasants in Pampanga and Tarlac thought that landlords should not be given their share of the harvests even if they had contributed to the resistance.[62]

According to the PKP's policy, peasants in Central Luzon were also supposed to abandon their peasant organizations, such as AMT and

[57] Liwanag interview, 21 July 1970.
[58] MRB, "Pahayag—Pampasinaya" [Decisions of MRB], 14 October 1944; Jose Lava, "Milestones," p. 23; and "Sampung Pinakamababang Kahilingan" [Ten Basic Needs], *Ang Patnugot*, 15 May 1944.
[59] Interview with Peregrino Taruc, Camp Crame, Quezon City, 9 July 1970.
[60] Jose Lava, "Milestones," p. 23.
[61] Ibid.; Taruc, *Born of the People*, p. 58.
[62] Villapando [Mateo del Castillo], to Reco 3, 4 December 1944.

KPMP, and instead form BUDCs (Barrio United Defense Corps) in order to show those in the United Front who were not peasants that the resistance movement was not "a class organization." The PKP official policy also said that peasants should form BUDCs rather than the Japanese-imposed neighborhood associations.[63] But many in the Hukbalahap movement either did not hear or paid no heed. Local peasant organizations continued in many places and overlapped with barrio Hukbalahap governments, which villagers rarely called BUDCs and which sometimes hid behind the cover of neighborhood associations formed in order to satisfy the Japanese. Eventually, according to a PKP analysis written later, "it was the refusal of our rank and file, arising from the refusal of the masses themselves to follow our rank and file, which forced the Party leadership to change its instructions" and "permit" neighborhood associations as a screen behind which to conduct resistance work.[64]

A final example of a major PKP order that Hukbalahap activists ignored was the "retreat-for-defense policy." In mid-1943, after Hukbalahap guerrillas had suffered several serious setbacks, those top leaders of the PKP who were still active and who could attend a meeting decided that all Hukbalahap guerrillas should retreat to the mountains or lie low and that they should engage in no battles unless absolutely necessary for defense. Furthermore, this policy instructed Hukbalahap political organizations to go deeply underground.[65] The actions of Hukbalahap squadrons and their reputation among villagers for being aggressive showed that they did not adhere to the PKP's policy. Hilario Felipe, a Hukbalahap leader in Talavera, said that although he "heard of the idea [of retreat for defense], I didn't know all that it was supposed to do. But I do know that we here in Talavera didn't retreat. And we took the offensive against PC and Japanese many times in the war." The PKP's policy apparently was similarly unimpressive to other Hukbalahap squadrons because Luis Taruc and Casto Alejandrino, top commanders of the guerrilla army, said that most Hukbalahap squadrons never followed the retreat policy.[66] Taruc also said that the leaders who made this policy were "those who had had the least contact with the mass movements of the people" and hence had the least understanding of what people wanted. They included, for example, Vicente Lava and the few PKP leaders who had studied communism in Moscow prior to the war. Not only Hukbalahap squadrons ignored the policy; such PKP members as Taruc, Alejandrino,

---

[63] Jose Lava, "Milestones," p. 23; Taruc, *Born of the People*, p. 61.

[64] "Coordinate Revolutionary Activities in the Cities and Towns with the Armed Struggle in the Field," 9 May 1950 (CapDoc, Ag.).

[65] Sources concerning the PKP's "retreat-for-defense policy" include "Political Resolution Adopted at the National Conference of the Communist Party of the Philippines held 28 September-3 October 1944" (CapDoc, Ag.); "Ang Opportunismo" [Opportunism], 3 September 1945 (CapDoc, Ag.); Jose Lava, "Milestones," pp. 28-29; Alejandrino interview, 12 November 1970; Bulaong interview, 20 July 1970; Cunanan interview, 11 August 1970; and Taruc, *Born of the People*, pp. 142, 144.

[66] Alejandrino interview, 12 November 1970; Luis Taruc interview, 27 January 1970.

and others close to the peasantry rejected the official PKP position on this and related matters. Eventually, near the end of the war, the PKP reversed its policy and recognized that "the rank and file [of the party] and the masses had not followed" the retreat policy and the party "finally accepted the incorrectness of the tactics of 'retreat for defense.' " PKP leaders who made the policy, according to later party documents, had been more concerned with their own personal safety than with the welfare of the party or the country; the policy had suited the low morale among many in the PKP.[67]

To say, however, that the PKP as a party or its top leaders could not control the Hukbalahap does not deny that individual members of the PKP had important and influential roles in the Hukbalahap resistance. In addition to Taruc, Alejandrino, Feleo, and del Castillo, other PKP members also devoted themselves to the Hukbalahap. Undoubtedly, some of them helped the Hukbalahap to become what it did. But it would be incorrect to say that these persons controlled the resistance in Central Luzon, as so much of its origins can be traced to local organizations and far more numerous were leaders who were not in the PKP. It would also be inaccurate to say that the actions of these Hukbalahap-PKP leaders constituted PKP policy. Many of their actions in fact violated official PKP policy and coincided with what people who were not party members were doing.

Liberation from the Japanese

The Japanese occupation ended for most people in Central Luzon in late 1944 or early 1945. Although people were relieved, those last months were among the war's most bloody and destructive.

"The last year of the occupation was the worst," said Carlos Rivera of San Ricardo, Talavera. "There was so much fighting, so many dead, so many bombs and burning fields." The year began with major battles between Hukbalahap squadrons and Japanese and PC troops. The Japanese military had apparently decided to launch an intensive drive, hoping to destroy the Hukbalahap. "Maybe the Japanese figured this was their last chance to stop the resistance before the Americans returned," said Hilario Felipe, a Hukbalahap leader in Talavera. "The fewer guerrillas they had to worry about, the better they could fight the Americans." In February 1944, Japanese and PC troops made zona raids on several barrios of Talavera, rounded up over a hundred people suspected of being in the Hukbalahap, and took them to a chapel in barrio Sibul for interrogation. There the soldiers beat up several and killed those who resisted. Among the dead was

<hr />

[67] "Coordinate Revolutionary Activities," 9 May 1950; "Political Resolution ... 28 September-3 October 1944"; "Ang Opportunism," 3 September 1945; "Pangkalahatang Ulat ng PKP sa Timog Luzon" [General Report of the PKP in Southern Luzon], 15 September 1945.

a Huk leader. After threatening the others with harsh punishment, the soldiers released them.[68]

One month later, a battle lasting three days involved squadrons from Talavera and nearby municipalities. "It was the worst fight of the war for me, I think," said a tenant farmer who was only twenty years old at the time. "We killed some Japanese and PC, alright, but they killed some of us, too." Among the dead was Amando Santa Ana. The long-time peasant activist died in battle as commander of a squadron from Talavera. Japanese soldiers found his body, and the next day they displayed his head in the bayan of Talavera as a warning to all others.[69] "I felt so terrible," recalled Hilario Felipe, "when I heard that Santa Ana had been killed. And the way the soldiers mocked him by decapitating him made me furious. I felt sick for days. He was a close friend from years before. Many good men died during the Japanese occupation, but I'll always remember Santa Ana." Many others in Talavera did too.

By mid-1944, reports said that the Americans were on their way to the Philippines. "Our hopes kept rising as the rumors got stronger," said a wife of a tenant in San Ricardo. Then sometime in October, another man recalled, "I heard that American soldiers had landed in the south. A relative who had been in Cabanatuan the day before told me. He said the news was being whispered all over the market there." Optimism among Hukbalahap squadron 8 guerrillas soared. "We sort of celebrated by attacking a PC outpost in barrio Sibul," said Religio Felipe of Talavera. During the following weeks, in fact, the Hukbalahap guerrillas there "became overconfident; we took chances in November that we shouldn't have," according to a former guerrilla in San Ricardo. "We were anxious, I guess, and expected the Americans to be in Talavera long before they came." During one battle in November, Hilario Felipe was wounded and two of his cousins were killed.

On the eve of the American forces' arrival in Nueva Ecija, the PC commander in Talavera, Captain Burgosino Fausto, and his soldiers deserted the Japanese. They fled from the bayan and joined USAFFE squadron 311. Then in the presence of an American officer in another USAFFE squadron, Fausto pledged allegiance to the United States. Several months earlier, the acting mayor in Talavera had also abandoned the Japanese and hid; some said he then helped the Hukbalahap.[70]

The PC's switch to USAFFE groups may have prompted more friction between the Hukbalahap and USAFFE in Talavera and other parts of Nueva Ecija. "For a while there, it seemed like we were fighting against USAFFE more than against Japanese," one former guerrilla in San Ricardo said. During one such battle in December 1944 near barrio Murcon not far from San Ricardo, half the USAFFE men involved and several Hukbalahap guerrillas were reportedly killed.[71] Because the PC and the Hukbalahap

[68] *HDP, Talavera;* and interviews in San Ricardo.
[69] *HDP, Talavera.*
[70] Ibid.
[71] Ibid.

had been enemies throughout the occupation and because USAFFE and Hukbalahap groups either had been at odds or had endured uneasy truces, the PC and USAFFE together may have increased the hostilities. And the Hukbalahap guerrillas' distrust for USAFFE groups deepened. As one tenant farmer in San Ricardo said, "Why did the USAFFE accept the PC? The PC had fought for the Japanese. And why did they continue to oppose us when we were against the Japanese? They encouraged the PC, now their companions, to fight us as the war ended so they could take the credit for what we had done to resist the Japanese."

Meanwhile, the Hukbalahap movement in Talavera continued its resistance and made plans to help the American forces when they arrived for the final push against the Japanese military. Patricio del Rosario, who had been an officer in the Hukbalahap command for Nueva Ecija (Reco 9) since early 1944, came to San Ricardo to discuss with Hukbalahap leaders in that part of Talavera what to do when the Americans returned. According to Ramon Tapang, a Hukbalahap government official in the barrio, del Rosario told them that "the American soldiers were coming from the north. They had landed near Dagupan [in Pangasinan]. We talked about what we could do to help liberate Talavera. We had been waiting a long time for the Americans to return; I remember how relieved I was." Already some Japanese soldiers had retreated from Talavera, Tapang continued, "but we knew they were only hiding and that the last days would be difficult ones."

In late January 1945, the Americans came. "Their planes flew over and dropped bombs," said a peasant in San Ricardo. "God, were we scared. It was like the beginning of war again." "My carabao was killed," said another man, "and I remember hearing guns and mortars all day." A report from an American USAFFE officer recorded some of the action in the vicinity:

> Jap line on east side of Licab [west of Talavera] . . . to barrio Palusapis, Guimba, still holding. Shelling on Baloc, Malayantoc, and Maligaya (8 miles east of Guimba) caused some Jap casualties. During night Jap troops continue to pass thru . . . Maligaya to Muñoz. Barrio Bantug near Muñoz [bordering Talavera on the north] heavily occupied by Japs in foxholes, by-passed during bombing on Muñoz on 28 January.[72]

The fighting went on intermittently for several days. Together the Hukbalahap, USAFFE guerrillas, and the American army fought the Japanese army as it retreated to the distant mountains.

In the first week of February, American soldiers finally marched into the plaza of Talavera to a hero's welcome. "It was like a big fiesta," remembered one elderly resident. "We had been hoping that the Americans would

---

[72] "Message from Lapham regarding Jap Line from Licab River," 30 January 1945, in "M-1 Operation, G-2 Journal and File #2," folder no. 1, entry no. 457 (RG 94, WW II Operations Reports, 1940-1948, 6th Army 106-2.2; Federal Records Center, Suitland, Md.).

return." While everybody ate that day, a band played and leading citizens boomed ceremonious speeches.

Within days, the senior American officer in charge, following orders from General Douglas MacArthur, appointed local Filipinos to perform governmental duties. Among those appointed were individuals with reputations of being pro-Japanese and prominent USAFFE personalities, including Carlos Nocum and one other leader of USAFFE squadron 311. No Hukbalahap leaders were included, much to the disappointment of some. Other Hukbalahap leaders, however, like Alfredo Buwan, said, "I was too relieved at the time to think too much about who was appointed." "I wanted to settle back to a normal life and farm," said the son of Patricio del Rosario, "and was glad the worst was over with no more deaths and destruction than there were." When Patricio del Rosario returned to his home in San Ricardo, "we had a big celebration—a fiesta—because the war was over and our leader was back," Ramon Tapang said. Despite the sense of victory that he and other Hukbalahap supporters felt, del Rosario was troubled. Why, he wondered, had the American soldiers excluded Hukbalahap members from the municipal offices while appointing not only USAFFE people like Nocum but others who had worked openly with the Japanese? The question bothered others in the Hukbalahap too, like Hilario Felipe. "For the moment, though," said Felipe, "I just enjoyed the liberation from the Japanese."

Elsewhere in Central Luzon, too, Hukbalahap supporters joined American soldiers to push out the Japanese forces. Earlier, in September 1944, the Hukbalahap leadership and the PKP had called for an "all-out offensive" against the Japanese regime to be coordinated with the approaching American forces. In late October, when reports reached the Hukbalahap general headquarters that American soldiers had landed on Leyte Island, "we were jubilant," said commander Luis Taruc. A special edition of the movement's publication *Katubusan,* Taruc said, announced that "victory was approaching, that the days of the enemy were numbered, and once more [we called] upon all guerrillas, regardless of affiliation, to join together in the final effort to throw off the . . . Japanese-puppet regime."[73] From December 1944 into February 1945 Hukbalahap squadrons pressed the Japanese, liberated towns, and fought, in the words of one United States military report written later, "side by side with American forces" as the Americans moved down from Tarlac, Nueva Ecija, Pampanga, and Bulacan, and then into Rizal and Manila.[74] Luis Taruc claimed that the Hukbalahap "paced the American army all the way to Manila."[75] The Americans also accepted the Hukbalahap guerrillas' assistance. Silvestre Liwanag described, for instance, the help given to the Americans by the squadrons he led in western Pampanga:

[73] Taruc, *Born of the People,* p. 183.
[74] MPC, *History and Organization of the Hukbalahap.*
[75] Taruc, *Born of the People,* p. 188.

When the American army returned [to Central Luzon], my group joined forces with the United States army under the command of Colonel Leonard. I provided territorial information to the US forces since my men were familiar with the terrain. We helped build bridges and prepare the way for the drive to Manila from the Bataan side. Together we also fought the Japanese. Before the Americans arrived, we had captured an air base near Floridablanca that the Japanese had been using. It had over one hundred planes. This and other intelligence information we gave to the Americans; we also turned the base over to them. All together, I guess, our squadrons worked with Colonel Leonard and his men for about one month.[76]

Many other Hukbalahap squadrons did the same. Squadron 87, for example, fought alongside American soldiers to liberate the municipalities of Polo and Ubando, Bulacan, and Hukbalahap squadrons in Nueva Ecija under Jose de Leon's command fought with the United States Sixth Army from Tarlac to Cabanatuan, Nueva Ecija, where their combined forces captured a Japanese prison and released American and Filipino prisoners.

Several American sources, too, praised the Hukbalahap guerrillas for their skills and assistance. The conclusion of one United States military study of the Hukbalahap said, "considering only the military activities, its services were of value in routing the enemy from Central Luzon. In terms of value in dollars and cents and American lives saved, the work of the Hukbalahap compares favorably with that of any other guerrilla unit throughout the Philippine Islands."[77] American officers also found on arrival that Hukbalahap squadrons had already freed several towns from Japanese control and had established temporary municipal governments. Among them were the provincial capitals of San Fernando, Pampanga, Tarlac, Tarlac, and Santa Cruz, Laguna. The Hukbalahap had also appointed "liberation governors" for three provinces: Juan Feleo in Nueva Ecija, Casto Alejandrino in Pampanga, and Jesus Lava in Laguna. Because Hukbalahap leaders had never planned to hang on indefinitely to these towns and because they regarded the Americans as allies, the Hukbalahap welcomed the American troops when they arrived in these towns and, as two United States military sources reported, cooperated with those American officers responsible for providing a transitional government until the Philippine government in Manila was secure again.[78] "Once liberation was under way," Peregrino Taruc explained, "the Hukbalahap planned to disband because there was no longer any reason to fight."[79] Symbolic of the Hukbalahap's intentions were the American and Filipino flags that fluttered over the municipal buildings as American soldiers walked into the towns which Hukbalahap guerrillas had liberated.

[76] Liwanag interview, 21 July 1970.

[77] MPC, *History and Organization of the Hukbalahap.*

[78] 441st CIC Detachment, "Monthly Information Report," February 1945, p. 43; and MPC, *History and Organization of the Hukbalahap.*

[79] Peregrino Taruc interview, 9 July 1970. Several other leaders and documents confirm his statement.

The Hukbalahap rightfully took some of the credit for ending the Japanese occupation. Besides killing Japanese soldiers and Filipino collaborators, wrote Luis Taruc to President Sergio Osmeña and General MacArthur, the Hukbalahap "strengthened the feeling of self-respect among the Filipino people. It has helped the people to preserve their harvest from Jap and Puppet banditry, and to establish institutions of their own to fight against the Jap bandits."[80] Villagers in Central Luzon had also fed, clothed, and manned a guerrilla army for three years. In many barrios and towns, they had established and managed their own governments. And the feeling of unity permeated the countryside far more than before. Finally, the expulsion of the Japanese left a heady air of victory, which those in the Hukbalahap resistance movement breathed with satisfaction. They expected recognition for their achievements from other Filipinos in general and from the returning Philippine—American government. Some Hukbalahap guerrillas even expected American or Filipino officials to honor them with medals and money.

Peasants in Central Luzon now looked forward to a more stable and less dangerous life. Most people in the Hukbalahap wanted to live peacefully in their barrios with their families. Some Hukbalahap guerrillas wanted to leave agrarian life and become soldiers in the country's army, which the returning government would have to reconstruct. They believed that they had the experience to be government soldiers and, they informed the government, if they were "assigned as Military Police in Central Luzon to work with all lawful authorities . . . law and order would be more easily maintained."[81] Some Hukbalahap leaders such as Luis and Peregrino Taruc, Casto Alejandrino, and Juan Feleo and several PKP leaders discussed how to influence the returning Philippine government so that it would take a progressive stance on the social, political, and economic issues confronting the battered nation. "We figured," explained Peregrino Taruc, "that because of the Hukbalahap's achievements and its political strength at least in Central Luzon, the Osmeña government would have to take us into account."[82] Hukbalahap participants and leaders knew, however, that the end of the Japanese occupation would not mean an end to other problems. "I knew that we'd have to have our peasant groups," Alfredo Buwan of San Ricardo said solemnly, "because landlords would be coming back. Life was still difficult, and there was much to do after the Japanese left—there had been so much destruction. But I think people were hopeful. I know I was. And we little people had become stronger; we were more organized."

[80] Luis Taruc, to MacArthur and Osmeña, circa February 1945, enclosure 10 in MPC, *History and Organization of the Hukbalahap.*

[81] MPC, *History and Organization of the Hukbalahap.*

[82] Peregrino Taruc interview, 9 July 1970.

Chapter 4
PRELUDE TO REBELLION

"AT FIRST, the end of the Japanese occupation was like a sunrise on a clear, warm morning," recalled an elderly tenant in San Ricardo in 1970. "It felt good. It promised things would get better." His eyes followed a long shadow of a mango tree across a rice field. "But the sun wasn't coming up after all. It was going down. Things got worse, really, not better."

During the closing months of liberation in 1945, the Americans turned against the Hukbalahap. Then government troops began arresting Hukbalahap participants. Landlords and police victimized villagers who joined peasant organizations or who petitioned for larger shares of the harvest. Government soldiers armed with machine guns confronted peaceful peasant demonstrators in Cabanatuan and other towns of Central Luzon. "We had no choice," explained another tenant in San Ricardo. "We had to defend ourselves and families." Unresolved problems and tensions that had accumulated over the years, coupled with the immediate troubles during 1945-1946, fueled Central Luzon as if it were a steam boiler without a safety valve. By mid-1946, the peasant movement in Central Luzon became a peasant rebellion.

The Americans and the Hukbalahap

San Ricardo, Talavera
Roberto Aspia had been in the Hukbalahap for nearly three years when he returned to his family in San Ricardo in February 1945. He had been away for several days with Hukbalahap squadrons that had helped American troops to liberate the Bulacan-Nueva Ecija border area from retreating Japanese forces. "Now that the war was over, we thought things would be more normal. I planned to farm our parcel of land so my father could rest. He was pretty old. He had tenant-farmed all his life." But Aspia only stayed in his village for a few days. USAFFE guerrillas, now attached to American army troops headquartered in Cabanatuan and to those Talavera government officials appointed by American officers, "began to hunt

down us Hukbalahap like wanted men," he said. "So was the constabulary. It was unbelievable. If I hadn't left San Ricardo, I might have been killed." Aspia fled to San Jose, a municipality north of Talavera. He figured the USAFFE and constabulary there would not know he had been in the Hukbalahap. He returned in late 1945 because his ailing father needed help with the harvest. Within days after returning, he said, a constabulary officer charged him with "crimes he said I committed during the Japanese occupation."

Central Luzon

Roberto Aspia's troubles were typical among Hukbalahap veterans in 1945, and the American military's hostility toward the Hukbalahap was a major cause. After they had used the Hukbalahap guerrillas to defeat the Japanese in Central Luzon and had complimented them for their dedication, American commanders ordered that the Hukbalahap guerrillas be disarmed. "Utilize those guerrillas which can be profitably employed," ordered one United States Sixth Army command in early February 1945. And another near the same time added, "Avoid making them [the Hukbalahap] feel discriminated against. . . . [But] disarm them as their areas of activity come within our sphere of control. . . ."[1] Discrimination, however, was inevitable. Most, if not all, USAFFE guerrillas could remain armed because they were technically under the command of American officers such as McKenzie, Lapham, and Anderson in Central Luzon. Unlike the Hukbalahap, they had been officially recognized during the occupation by the U.S. commander-in-chief of the Southwest Pacific, General Douglas MacArthur. So while USAFFE groups in Central Luzon were allowed to keep their arms and, in many cases, absorbed into the American liberation forces, Americans wanted the Hukbalahap forces to disarm.

After cooperating with Hukbalahap soldiers in western Pampanga for nearly a month, Silvestre Liwanag said, the Americans suddenly "disarmed eight of my squadrons" in late January 1945. "The method was sneaky. They first told my men that if they turned in their old arms, they would replace them with newer models. But, they never did." Instead, Liwanag explained, American officers told the Hukbalahap guerrillas to "go back home. They arrested me and some of my officers. They took us to Pangasinan, put us in jail, and interrogated us."[2] These Americans were in the U.S. Counter Intelligence Corps (CIC), part of whose mission was to "detect and investigate all matters pertaining to espionage, sabotage, treason, sedition, disaffection, and subversive activity."[3] After two weeks of

[1] *Sixth Army on Luzon,* circa 1946, p. 60 (RG 94, WW II Operations Reports, 1940-1948, 6th Army 106.0.3; Federal Records Center, Suitland, Md.).

[2] Interview with Silvestre Liwanag, Camp Crame, Quezon City, 21 July 1970.

[3] AFPAC Regulations, GHQ, AFPAC, "Counter Intelligence Corps: General Provisions," 1 August 1945, p. 1 (RG 94, WW II Operations Reports, 1940-1948, 32nd Infantry Division, Counter-Intelligence Reports, 332-2.25, December 1945; Federal Records Center, Suitland, Md.).

incarceration, the CIC officers told Liwanag that he and other arrested
Hukbalahap companions were accused of subversion, kidnapping, murder,
and communism. "I told them," recalled Liwanag, " 'I'm not a communist,
just a guerrilla.' " Paying no heed, however, the Americans transferred
their prisoners back to San Fernando, Pampanga, to await final imprisonment on a distant island. Fortunately for Liwanag and his companions,
friends helped them to escape the first night. They ran west to the
Zambales mountains and hid.

When American officers ordered those Hukbalahap squadrons which
had been fighting with U.S. troops in Manila to disarm, the astonished
guerrillas refused. As they started back to Central Luzon, American
military police stopped them and forced them at gunpoint to turn over
their weapons. Armed civilians, they were told, would not be allowed
behind American lines. But what about the USAFFE units behind the lines?,
the Hukbalahap men asked. They are not civilians, the American police
reportedly answered; they are soldiers attached to the United States forces.[4]
Tomas Calma, a Hukbalahap squadron leader, was leading three Hukbalahap units back to Pampanga after the battle for Manila when American
officers asked them to drop their guns. Some refused and were promptly
arrested. Calma was confused. He concluded that there had been some
mistake. So did Agaton Bulaong, a Hukbalahap leader from Bulacan,
when he and his men were forced to hand over their guns in February
1945. The same thing happened to numerous Hukbalahap participants in
Nueva Ecija and other parts of Central Luzon.[5]

Besides disarming the guerrillas, American-appointed Filipino officials
also arrested Hukbalahap participants. Charges ranged from refusing to
surrender weapons and thievery to "communist subversion" and pro-
Japanese collaboration. Frequently, the accusers and sources of "intelligence information" fed to investigating CIC detachments were USAFFE
leaders who had been appointed to local government positions. Among the
major Hukbalahap leaders imprisoned in early 1945 were Silvestre
Liwanag, Jose de Leon of Nueva Ecija, Bernardo Poblete of Pampanga,
and the top two commanders, Luis Taruc and Casto Alejandrino. American soldiers arrested the latter two men, together with fourteen "prominent
Huk leaders," according to a CIC report, the last week of February 1945 in
San Fernando, Pampanga. Arresting these leaders, the CIC decided, was
the only way of ending the "Huk domination in the area." Even though
Hukbalahap leaders there had been cooperating with the Americans, the

---

[4] Taruc, *Born of the People*, p. 190.

[5] Tomas Calma, Biographical Information (PF, CapDoc, Ag.); interview with Agaton
Bulaong, Camp Crame, Quezon City, 20 July 1970; interview with Cenon Bungay, Camp Crame,
Quezon City, 15 July 1970; interview with Peregrino Taruc, Camp Crame, Quezon City, 9 July
1970; Taruc, *Born of the People*, pp. 190-201; "Pangkalahatang Ulat ng Lupong Panglalawigan
ng Nueva Ecija" [Genral Report of the Nueva Ecija Provinical Committee], 8 June 1945
(CapDoc, Ag.); and Narding [Mamerto Baniaga], "Ikatlong Ulat ng P'Com ng Nueva Ecija"
[Third Report of the Nueva Ecija Provincial Committee], 6-15 September 1945 (CapDoc, Ag.).

CIC complained that the Hukbalahap had "hindered the entire area from returning to a normal way of life."[6]

"The single worst thing that the USAFFE and Americans did to the Hukbalahap," said Cenon Bungay, a tenant farmer and Hukbalahap squadron leader in Pampanga, "was the massacre of 109 Hukbalahap guerrillas in Malolos [a municipality in Bulacan]."[7] According to Bungay and other Hukbalahap sources, guerrillas in squadron 77 were walking through Malolos on their way home to Pampanga. Like most of Central Luzon by early February 1945, Malolos had been liberated from the Japanese. Policing the area were American and Filipino soldiers. Suddenly several of these soldiers surrounded the Hukbalahap guerrillas, disarmed them at gunpoint, and took them to the officer in charge, a USAFFE colonel named Adonias Maclang. Maclang was well-known among Hukbalahap guerrillas as a "tulisaffe"—a dishonorable guerrilla. He accused the Hukbalahap guerrillas of raiding and looting Malolos. Squadron 77 commanders denied this. Without a trial, Maclang forced all the detained Hukbalahap guerrillas to dig a mass grave, then ordered soldiers to shoot them. He did this with the knowledge and consent of American CIC officers present at the time. The Americans later appointed Maclang the mayor of Malolos.[8]

Many Hukbalahap participants denounced the Malolos killings and other abuses. Taruc, Alejandrino, and other Hukbalahap spokesmen, for example, protested to General MacArthur and President Osmeña. Others demonstrated in the town plazas of Central Luzon and Manila and petitioned government officials to release arrested Hukbalahap veterans and order USAFFE soldiers and police to stop abusing Hukbalahap veterans. Several thousand persons demonstrating in Manila in late September 1945 probably influenced President Osmeña to free Taruc, Alejandrino, and several other resistance leaders from prison.[9] Former Hukbalahap guerrillas also formed a Veterans League and asked the government to recognize the Hukbalahap as a bona fide guerrilla movement whose members would be entitled to veterans benefits. Some former Hukbalahap also went underground in order to escape harassment.

Meanwhile, many Hukbalahap participants continued to cooperate with

---

[6] 441st CIC Detachment, "Monthly Information Report of Activities in SWPA," February 1945, p. 43-44 (RG 94, WW II Operations Reports, 1940-1948, CIDT-441-0.2, CIC; Federal Records Center, Suitland, Md.).

[7] Bungay interview, 15 July 1970.

[8] Abraham I. Felipe, Armed Forces of the Philippines, "A Case of Voluntary Defection: Iluminada A. Calonge," undated (PF-Calonge, CapDoc, Ag.). This is a biographical account, based on interrogations and other sources, of a Huk participant who was captured in 1950. "History of Squadron 77" and "Hukbalahap, Seventh Regional Command, Record of Casualties (Deaths)," both with enclosure 13 in MPC, History and Organization of the Hukbalahap; B. Entenberg, "Agrarian Reform and the Hukbalahap," Far Eastern Survey 15 (14 August 1946):245-248; Taruc, Born of the People, p. 191.

[9] Manila Times, 24 September 1945, p. 1; Manila Chronicle, 25 September 1945, pp. 1 and 3, and 28 September 1945, p. 1; and Taruc, Born of the People, p. 211.

American officials. Many disbanded peacefully and surrendered their arms on request. In September 1945, when the top leaders of the resistance movement formally announced the end of the Hukbalahap, they prepared at the request of the American military headquarters a roster of all Hukbalahap guerrillas. "We did this in good faith," explained Luis Taruc. "We gave the lists to the CIC people as one of the requirements in order to get formal recognition for the Hukbalahap."[10] Even though leaders such as Luis and Peregrino Taruc, Casto Alejandrino, and Juan Feleo had been imprisoned and mistreated, they still hoped that either American officials or Filipino leaders such as President Osmeña would right the wrongs that had been done against the Hukbalahaps, stop local officials and USAFFE units from mistreating them, and acknowledge the Hukbalahap's contribution in the war against the Japanese.

Eventually American officials did recognize four Hukbalahap units—about two thousand persons. But Peregrino and Luis Taruc and other leaders later viewed this as a divide-and-rule tactic by Americans to turn fellow Hukbalahaps against one another.[11] A United States military study in December agreed. Recognizing a few Hukbalahaps but excluding the rest, this study said, was "an attempt to divide and conquer and to make it appear to outside observers that there was dissension and diversity in the Hukbalahap, which would cause the organization to lose the support and trust of the people backing it."[12] But the tactic did not succeed; and many recognized Hukbalahaps turned down their veterans' benefits once they realized that others had been excluded.

Why Americans Turned Against the Hukbalahap

The explanation for the American and Filipino authorities' behavior is not that the United States Pacific Command never officially approved the Hukbalahap. Such a technicality could easily have been fixed, as the Hukbalahap forces had assisted so admirably the returning American forces. The explanation lies with the merging of several groups who disliked or distrusted the Hukbalahap.

One group was the USAFFE in Central Luzon. Not all of them, of course, opposed the Hukbalahap, but many USAFFE officers, both Americans and Filipinos, did. Early in the Japanese occupation, the Hukbalahap leadership had angered American USAFFE officers in Central Luzon by refusing, in the words of one USAFFE record, to turn over "complete military authority of all your [Hukbalahap] men" to the chief commander of USAFFE guerrillas, Lt. Col. Thorpe and his appointed officers.[13] Later in

[10] Interview with Luis Taruc, Quezon City, 27 January 1970.

[11] Ibid.; Peregrino Taruc interview, 9 July 1970.

[12] MPC, *History and Organization of the Hukbalahap.*

[13] "Minutes of the Conference Held at a Barrio of San Luis, Pampanga, 5 and 7 July 1942, between Representatives of the Military Committee of the National Anti-Japanese United Front and the Representatives of Lt. Col. Thorpe, U.S. Army," [signed] Capt. Joseph Barker, Capt. B. L. Anderson, Lt. B. L. Pettit, Luis Taruc, and Casto Alejandrino, enclosure 9 with MPC, *History and Organization of the Hukbalahap.*

1942, after USAFFE officers had lost patience with the Hukbalahap, Thorpe issued a general order that all guerrillas who were not members of USAFFE units were enemies of the American government.[14] From then on, USAFFE and Hukbalahap relations deteriorated. Leaders in the Hukbalahap general headquarters had wanted to cooperate with USAFFE units and made several attempts to do so, but they refused to be under USAFFE's command.[15]

The Hukbalahap and the USAFFE had two important differences, which made their merger impossible while also making their relationship more hostile. As noted in the previous chapter, Hukbalahap forces aggressively resisted the Japanese, whereas USAFFE forces consciously followed a more retiring strategy of collecting intelligence information and waiting for the American army to return. Second, the Hukbalahap was a popular-based guerrilla movement with political organizations in the villages. USAFFE officers opposed the Hukbalahap for creating these extragovernmental units. These differences, together with other disputes such as the Hukbalahap claiming that USAFFE units abused villagers in order to get food and money, resulted in several armed clashes between them even during liberation.

USAFFE guerrillas told the U.S. army what they thought of the Hukbalahap. Even in 1943-1944 they had direct radio and courier contact with U.S. Pacific Command stations outside the Philippines. "The Hukbalahap," wrote Major Robert Lapham of the Central Luzon USAFFE in January 1945 to the CIC, "is subversive, . . . a radical organization. . . . Its major operations and activities of carnage, revenge, banditry and highjacking . . . never [have been] equalled in any page of history of the Philippines." Another report based on assessments from USAFFE contacts in mid-1944 said the Hukbalahap "is reported to be modelled after the communistic organizations in China and is motivated by purely personal and political objectives. Pedro Abad Santos, a known communist and rabid anti-Jap, is believed to be the brains of the unit. This group is very active in sabotage work and is ruthless and undisciplined." The USAFFE Marking's unit in September 1944 reported that the Hukbalahap "is Anti-Democratic and Anti-Nippon; Communist by party affiliation, and Bolshevist in its tendency." It then went on to applaud in glowing terms what other guerrilla units had been doing.[16] Some USAFFE accounts even claimed

---

[14] 443rd CIC Detachment, USAFFE, Interrogation Report No. 348: Subject—Wilbur J. Lage, Captain, Infantry, to Officer in Charge, 9 January 1945 (miscellaneous records on guerrillas in the Philippines, ID No. 14 and 42; Federal Records Center, Suitland, Md.).

[15] For more detail concerning Hukbalahap and USAFFE efforts to reach agreements for cooperation, see Kerkvliet, "Peasant Rebellion," pp. 238-242.

[16] 441st CIC Detachment, "Monthly Information Report," February 1945, exhibit 3; GHQ, Southwest Pacific Area, G-2, "Luzon Guerrilla Organizations," 20 June 1944, p. 23 (PI Guerrilla War Forces box, folder ID 322.24; Federal Records Center, Suitland, Md.); The Command, Marking's Fil-American Troops, through the Chief, Guerrilla Intelligence Division, Luzon, Philippines, "Answers to Circular No. 5, Questionnaire," 8 September 1944 (miscellaneous records on guerrillas in the Philippines; Federal Records Center, Suitland, Md.).

that Hukbalahap forces aided the Japanese and received many of their weapons from the Japanese.[17]

When the United States Sixth Army came to Central Luzon during liberation, its officers concluded, based largely on information from USAFFE units, that the hostile relationship between the Hukbalahap and USAFFE was unreconcilable. The Americans then decided to "prevent trouble [between the two guerrilla groups] by refusing to recognize the Hukbalahaps and disarming them forcibly. In those areas where the Hukbalahap was particularly strong, the American-sponsored civil authorities were provided with armed guards."[18] Those "armed guards" included the very USAFFEs who opposed the Hukbalahap. The Americans even used USAFFE veterans to form Military Police (MP) units in Central Luzon, which were supposed to replace the Philippine Constabulary (PC). And because many in the PC had abandoned the Japanese regime at the eleventh hour and then joined USAFFE units, former PC, too, became Military Police. Consequently, the MP force that the returning Americans established to keep law and order specifically excluded Hukbalahap participants while including USAFFE participants and former PC soldiers, both of whom were anti-Hukbalahap.

Another group who disliked the Hukbalahap included landlords and political elites in Central Luzon. Even though most of them had not resisted the Japanese regime and many had collaborated with it, they quickly switched to the Americans' side during liberation. Persons such as collaborationist governor Jose David, a Pampangan politician from a large landed family, easily got the Americans' attention. David's claims that the Japanese had ordered him to surrender his provincial government to the Hukbalahap helped to confirm American military officers' belief that the Hukbalahap was anti-American.[19] In numerous municipalities of Central Luzon, American officers in 1945 appointed persons from the local elites to be mayors, chiefs of police, and councillors until elections could be held in 1947. CIC detachments, too, listened to persons from the same upper-class families who earlier had been alarmed at the overlap between the Hukbalahap and the 1930s peasant movement. They were also people whom the Hukbalahap had criticized and attacked during the war.

"With the landing of the American forces," Vicente Lava of the PKP and United Front wrote after liberation in 1945, these "puppets and

---

[17] "Msg fr. Guerr (Anderson) re. Recommen. no Hukbalahaps Units Be Given Arms or Ammo," in M-1 Operation, G-2 Journal and File No. 2, Folder No. 1, 29 January-10 February 1945, entry 480 (RG 94, WW II Operations Reports, 1940-1948, 6th Army 106-2.2; Federal Records Center, Suitland, Md.); and Col. S. V. Constant, Security and Intelligence Division, HQ, Second Service Command, "List of Four Organizations in the Philippine Islands," 5 October 1945 (I.G. File No. 3144, Report No. 1441, OSS File ID No. XL 21979; Military Records, National Archives, Washington, D.C.).

[18] *Sixth Army on Luzon,* circa 1946, p. 59.

[19] "Msg fr. Cabangbang re. Nips Leaving Spies in Manila, etc., re. Guerra Reports," in M-1 Operation, G-2 Journal and File No. 2, Folder No. 1, 29 January-10February 1945, entry 585.

collaborators" who maintained "their subservience to the Japanese . . . to save their necks" were now "bowers and scrapers" who

> have lost no time in beginning their diabolic campaign of systematically destroying the Huk and the United Front with lies and provocations. Characteristic of their pernicious activities are the rumors that they have spread that the Huk is anti-American. Daily rumors are circulated of pending raids on American camps by the Huk. False news that an American soldier here or there has been killed by the Huk . . . creates suspicion, distrust, and hostile feelings . . . [and fears] that the Huk is setting up a government against the Osmeña government and that the Huk will kill all landowners and capitalists and distribute their land and properties. . . . Lately these counter-revolutionaries through their hirelings have resorted to all sorts of provocations, such as killing Huk soldiers, civilian organizers, and members of village and municipal councils. . . . From the results of the investigations and attitudes of the CIC . . . of the American army, it is apparent that evidence, testimony, reasoning, when they come from our side, make no impression. Testimony and evidence from our opponents, seemingly without regard for their past performances, are . . . final.[20]

Americans and Filipino elites who feared any movement tainted with communism also ignored the Hukbalahap's accomplishments and believed allegations about its criminal acts, murders, and anti-Americanism. Perhaps they simply feared the Hukbalahap movement's potential political strength in the postwar years and used "communism" as a convenient way to discredit it. After all, the Hukbalahap had not been just another guerrilla group. It was a popular guerrilla army with a mass organization spread across Central Luzon and parts of Southern Luzon. To Filipino elites and American officials, any popular organization with determined leaders, many of whom were peasants themselves, threatened the established order. The political system in the country had never experienced such a phenomenon. It ran contrary to elitist politics, which had tolerated only a moderate amount of nonelite participation. Moreover, the villagers in the Hukbalahap had guns, and they had learned guerrilla warfare. Probably none of its leaders' assurances—that Hukbalahap participants were loyal to the American government, that they accepted the returning Filipino Commonwealth government and President Osmeña, and that they would turn over their guns after the occupation was over and when other guerrilla forces did the same—could dissuade the Americans and the landed Filipinos. They imagined that the worst would happen unless they took direct action against the Hukbalahap. So much the better if they could also argue that this was a communist movement. The CIC and other

[20] V. G. Lava, "Whither the United Front Movement in the Philippine Islands?" circa 1945, appendix 7 of "Hukbalahap" by the San Fernando CIC Field Office, Richard M. Snethen, 2nd Lt. Infantry, Commanding, 1135th CIC Detachment, AFWESPAC, 24 October 1946 (ID No. 924310; Federal Records Center, Suitland, Md.).

officials made just that point in reports, speeches, and high-level meetings.[21]

Taken together, these interests—the anti-Hukbalahap USAFFE leaders, the collaborators, the PC, the landed elites in Central Luzon, American and Filipino officials protecting the status quo, and those who believed or wanted to believe that the Hukbalahap was dangerous and communistic— were heavy strikes against Hukbalahap veterans. Vicente Lava was right. It was difficult for Hukbalahap spokesmen and defenders to get their side heard. Authorities tended to exclude or downplay what did not fit their view of the Hukbalahap—including official statements and reports that the Hukbalahap had vigorously resisted the Japanese and admissions by high-ranking Philippine army officials in late 1945 that there was no proof against the Hukbalahap for criminal acts. Officials also tended to interpret information in such a way as to confirm their distrust or dislike of the Hukbalahap. Some argued, for example, that the reason so many people in Central Luzon supported the Hukbalahap during the war was that the guerrillas forced them to do so.[22]

Unrest in San Ricardo, Talavera: 1945-1946

The denial of the Hukbalahap movement's contribution was the backdrop for the main drama in San Ricardo and other villages of Central Luzon in 1945 and 1946. The peasantry renewed its efforts to reform the tenancy system and to get social justice. People picked up where they had left off before the Japanese came, although things were not exactly the same. Now they possessed the experience of their resistance movement and the memories of the Japanese occupation itself. But they had to contend with the conditions of those first postwar years.

"Conditions after the war were terrible," recalled Ramon Tapang, the small landowner who had been a leader in the Hukbalahap government in San Ricardo. "For one thing, there was a bad rice shortage because fighting and everything had destroyed so many fields or had made harvesting too dangerous. The bombing and fighting also destroyed irrigation canals and dikes. The land my brother and I farmed, for example, was a

[21] Headquarters, 1135th CIC Detachment, AFWESPAC, "Staff Study on Communism in the Philippines," 24 October 1946, p. 2 (miscellaneous records on guerrillas in the Philippines; Federal Records Center, Suitland, Md.); San Fernando CIC Field Office, 1135th CIC Detachment, "Hukbalahap," 24 October 1946, pp. 3, 5, 6; and Capt. George B. Hamner, G-2 Liaison officer, Headquarters, Military Police Command, AFWESPAC, Cabanatuan, "Survey of Hukbalahap Activities, Nueva Ecija," 12 November 1945, p. 1 (Office of AC of S, G-2, Headquarters Seventh Army, ID No. 285993; Federal Records Center, Suitland, Md.).

[22] MPC, *History and Organization of the Hukbalahap;* Capt. Hamner, Headquarters, MPC, Cabanatuan, "Survey of Hukbalahap Activities, Nueva Ecija," 12 November 1945, p. 3; 441st CIC Detachment, "Monthly Information Report," February 1945, pp. 35-43; and San Fernando CIC Field Office, 1135th CIC Detachment, "Hukbalahap," 24 October 1946, p. 6.

mess. Our carabaos were also killed."[23] Another villager, who was a tenant at the time for Manolo Tinio, added, "One of my carabaos was killed in the fighting. The other one was practically worked to death that first year after the war because I was always lending her out to neighbors who had lost theirs." Leonardo Basa, a tenant with 3 hectares in San Ricardo, said, "My family and I returned to San Ricardo in 1945. We had lived with my wife's relatives in San Isidro [in Nueva Ecija] during the occupation. When we came back, our house was practically demolished and the land was filled with weeds and grass." San Ricardo residents had to work hard from May through July 1945 to prepare their fields and plant. The shortage of carabaos, farm implements, and other necessities made the work even more difficult than usual. "People who had been in the Hukbalahap, like myself," Eugenio Gomez said bitterly, "also kept getting interrupted while we tried to farm. We had to keep our eyes and ears open all the time for those damn USAFFE who worked with the Military Police. Or were they the PC? I forget. Anyway they would pick up former Hukbalahap for no reason at all. I remember the day I was seeding my seed bed that year. I had to drop everything and scoot like a rat to a hiding place because some USAFFE rode into San Ricardo. I could see them from the field, and I was scared they might pick me up. I lay low for several days after that. I did that several times." Gomez's brother had to finish the seeding and tended his fields when he was in hiding. Some former Hukbalahap participants left San Ricardo because they feared arrest or other abuses.

Returning landlords caused further problems. "Not all of them came back right after the war," said Gomez. "Maybe some were too afraid." But most in the Talavera area did return—if not they themselves then their representative, such as a relative or hacienda manager or a katiwala. Manolo Tinio, for example, came back briefly, then dealt with his tenants through one of his loyal katiwala for the next few years. His brother, Vivencio Tinio, who had inherited in 1940 about 450 hectares of their father's land in San Ricardo, also returned. Troubles between tenants and landlords began almost immediately. "My landlord wanted back rent," complained one man. "He said he hadn't gotten his full rent during the occupation. I told him he was wrong." Another tenant said, "My land-owner refused to help with planting expenses. He said he didn't have to because he didn't have enough cash. But he still wanted half the harvest. Now, that was just unfair!" "Manolo Tinio wouldn't help either," said Eugenio Gomez. "Tinio claimed I owed him rent for 1943 and 1944. But I told his katiwala that wasn't so, because Tinio had cheated me out of rice before then. I had just made up for it since he hadn't been around during the Japanese occupation." Other bones of contention were loans and interest rates, which went up immediately after liberation. "Four cavans of palay for interest for every 100 pesos borrowed was common after the

---

[23] My account of the situation in San Ricardo and elsewhere in Talavera during 1945-1946 is based mainly on conversations with people who had lived there during that time. In addition, I have used the following sources: Pagaduan, "Kasaysayan ng Talavera"; and *HDP, Talavera*.

war," one man recalled. "One hundred percent interest for rice was high before the Japanese occupation. But it was common afterward. Landlords and moneylenders even were charging 150 and 200 percent," said Hilario Felipe. And interest-free loans, which had become increasingly rare in the late 1930s, all but disappeared after 1945. "Even small landlords, with only three or four tenants, became stingy with interest-free loans after the occupation," said Leonardo Basa. Many landlords simply allowed no loans. Perhaps they had no rice or cash to lend, or perhaps they felt that whatever rice reserves they had could be more profitably sold at high market prices in rice-starved Manila. From the peasants' viewpoint, however, the landlords just made things tough for them.

Disputes in 1945 and 1946 over high interest rates, loans, sharing agricultural expenses, and rent payments sometimes led to evictions. "Landlords seemed to think we were dogs tethered on a rope who would have to do whatever they ordered. If you refused to obey, they could come and kick you off the land. Manolo Tinio's armed guards did it to some tenants here after the war," said Alfredo Buwan. On the nearby Hacienda Jacinto, the hacendero's armed guards evicted several tenants just before harvest late in 1945 because, according to people in San Ricardo, the tenants had started to harvest before the manager had given permission. "Guards came, tore down those tenants' homes, and then Jacinto's manager hired harvesters from someplace else to cut their palay," said one man. The tenants took the case to court in Cabanatuan, this man continued, "but they didn't get anywhere with it. My wife's brother was one of those evicted. We had to take in him and his family after that. He never did find another parcel to tenant farm. From then until he died in the 1950s, he had to scrape along by doing seasonal work."

Landlord-tenant disputes that first year after the Japanese occupation culminated during the 1945/46 harvest. Tenants in San Ricardo and other barrios had asked for 60 percent of the harvest rather than only 50 or 55 percent. "We brought this up long before harvest time," said Eugenio Gomez. "I remember," said Leonardo Basa, "that Patricio del Rosario called a meeting in August or September and told us that Juan Feleo and other spokesmen were negotiating with President Osmeña in Manila for us to get 60 percent." In November, del Rosario brought Juan Feleo to San Ricardo. "People came with their lunches and listened to him speak. He was such a pleasant, warm man," recalled Eugenio Gomez who was there that day. "He told us to keep together, like fingers pressed together in a fist, and we'd get the 60 percent share. He also said the president [Osmeña] was listening to us and would persuade the landlords to agree to our demands." By December 1945, just as harvest reached its peak, representatives of the landlords and tenants did agree to a 60-40 share system in which landlords and tenants were to share agricultural expenses equally.[24] But many landlords in Talavera failed to

[24] *Star Reporter*, Manila, 12 and 28 December 1945; and a copy of the agreement found among CapDoc, Ag., with the following heading and title: Komonwels ng Pilipinas, Kawanihan ng Paggawa, Maynila [Commonwealth of the Philippines, Department of Labor, Manila], Marcelo Adduri, Kalihim ng Paggawa [Secretary of Labor], "Kasunduan" [Agreement], 18 January 1946.

abide by it. "My landlord," reported one tenant, "said 50-50 was the deal he had with me. If I want 60 percent, I'd have to pay all expenses." Eugenio Gomez recalled that "Manolo Tinio's katiwala came out to the fields, while we harvested, with armed guards. They took Tinio's share—50 percent. There was nothing we could do. 'Go to court if you don't like it,' the leader of the guards shouted to us. But that was a joke. By the time the court could make a decision, it would be too late. Besides, the judges were just pawns of the landlords anyway." Other landlords told their tenants that the 60-40 agreement negotiated in Manila applied to the next harvest, not to this one.

During these disputes over the harvest, "a group of Hukbalahap veterans from Talavera," according to several people in San Ricardo, ambushed the armed guards of a large landowner in the municipality. Two or three guards died. Benito Santos, a tenant who had seen relations between landlords and tenants deteriorate sharply over the years, recalled that shooting: "I wouldn't have done such a thing myself. But I understand why those Hukbalahap did it. It seemed like it was one thing after another. Landlords were just getting worse and using force more and more to get what they wanted. I didn't think we should use violence in turn, but many of my barrio mates disagreed."

An important organization in Central Luzon pushing for the 60-40 share was the "PKM." This was the peasant movement that inherited the vestiges of the Hukbalahap, the KPMP, and the other peasant groups that had preceded it. PKM stood for Pambansang Kaisahan ng mga Magbubukid or National Peasants Union. The principal PKM leader in San Ricardo was Patricio del Rosario, the former Hukbalahap and KPMP leader from the barrio who, at sixty-four years of age, had seen the peasant movement in Central Luzon grow from the small groups he had known as a young tenant farmer in Bulacan to the PKM that encompassed all of Central Luzon. Many persons active in the PKM of San Ricardo had been in the Hukbalahap. Some of the older ones also had participated in peasant groups preceding it. One life-long resident of San Ricardo asserted, "The PKM was a continuation of the KPMP." Another man described the PKM as "practically the same thing as the Hukbalahap movement we had here during the Japanese occupation. Most of the people in the Hukbalahap were in the PKM. The difference was that the PKM was for agrarian reforms. The Japanese weren't here any longer." Some people in San Ricardo could not keep the names of these groups straight, as if to say, "KPMP, Hukbalahap, PKM—what's the difference? They're basically all the same anyway." Eugenio Gomez, who tenant-farmed 3 hectares at that time near San Ricardo, said he had been too young to be much involved with the KPMP, although he had been in the Hukbalahap. But he was in the PKM and, he said with a smile, "I remember older people telling me that one distinction between the PKM and the KPMP was the PKM's flag. The KPMP in San Ricardo never had its own flag, I was told. But we had one for the PKM. It was a red flag like other PKM chapters in Nueva Ecija had. Except ours had 'San Ricardo, Talavera' spelled across the bottom." It was red, explained Alfredo Buwan, because that was the color of the Filipinos' flag when they fought for independence from Spain.

A typical PKM activist in San Ricardo was Roberto Aspia, the Hukbalahap veteran who had stayed away from the barrio for fear of being
arrested. He joined the PKM after returning to San Ricardo in late 1945.
He was only twenty-one years old then and a tenant farmer on 2.5 hectares,
which his father had been farming. Their landowner, who lived in Cabanatuan, owned 75 hectares in San Ricardo and more land elsewhere. Aspia's
father had been a tenant on Manolo Tinio's land until the early 1930s.

> My father didn't like doing odd jobs for Tinio—he didn't want to be like a
> servant for Tinio. One day he told Tinio that. Tinio got real angry and told my
> father either to do as he asked or leave his land. My father was a mild-mannered
> guy; he didn't like trouble. So he left and found this other landlord to plant for.
> But he was always bitter towards Tinio. So was I. I was old enough at the time
> to know what was happening.

Later in the 1930s, Aspia's father supported the strikes of fellow tenants
against their landlords. "I used to help these men," said Aspia, "and once I
attended a demonstration with my father." When the Japanese invaded, "I
joined the Hukbalahap. I hated the way the Japanese treated people. Two
soldiers beat up one of my cousins." After the occupation and after
returning to San Ricardo in late 1945, the Talavera Military Police accused
him of crimes allegedly committed while in the Hukbalahap. "I wasn't put
in jail, although I don't know why. Lots of Hukbalahap veterans were."
But he did suffer a prolonged investigation. Meanwhile, he farmed his
father's parcel and joined the PKM because, he explained, "we tenants had
to protect ourselves against the bad practices of the big landowners.
Standing alone, a peasant cannot do much. But together, peasants could
stand up to the landlords." Also, he said, he was active in PKM because
many persons from the Hukbalahap were involved.

"I'd say that maybe 70 or 75 percent of the peasants in Talavera were in
the PKM," estimated Hilario Felipe, a former Hukbalahap activist who
was an elected officer in the PKM Talavera chapter. "That kind of unity
was greater than any other peasant union before or since." And, he added
after I had asked specifically about San Ricardo, "that barrio had one of
the strongest PKM groups in the area." According to provincial PKM
reports in 1945 and 1946, Talavera had one of the earliest and most
energetic PKM chapters in Nueva Ecija. It was one of five municipal PKM
chapters in September 1945 that helped organize and staff the provincial
PKM headquarters located in Cabanatuan.[25] Patricio del Rosario, among
other leaders from Talavera, served on the PKM committee for Nueva

[25] Narding [Mamerto Baniaga], "Ikatlong Ulat ng P'Com" [Third Report of the Nueva Ecija
Provincial Committee], 6-15 September 1945; Pambansang Lupong Tagapagpatupad [National
Committee of PKM], to Lupong Panlalawigan PKM sa Nueva Ecija [PKM Provincial
Committee in Nueva Ecija], 30 October 1945 (CapDoc, Ag.); and Narding [Mamerto Baniaga],
"Ika-V Ulat ng P'Com ng Nueva Ecija sa mga Kasama sa PB" [Fifth Report of the Nueva Ecija
Provincial Committee to Comrades in the Politburo], 15 January 1946 (CapDoc, Cr.).

Ecija and sometimes represented Talavera or the province at meetings and demonstrations elsewhere in Central Luzon and in Manila.

The objectives of the PKM, according to people in San Ricardo, were simple. Roberto Aspia spelled them out one day as a group of men squatted on a shady path and discussed those years. He said somewhat angrily,

> First, the PKM wanted better relations with landlords. Second, we were against high interest rates on loans. We wanted landlords to give low interest loans and the government to set up banks where we could borrow easily. Third, we wanted the existing laws implemented, like laws to protect peasants against landlords and protect small landowners from losing their land to a big landowner. Fourth, we wanted justice for everyone, no matter what a person's social standing. Government officials were pawns of the big landowners. They helped the landowners, but not us little people. The PKM wanted to change that.

Aspia paused to light a cigarette. Another man spoke: "The PKM wasn't against landlords. We wanted the landlords, but we wanted them to be just. We opposed the *policies* of the landlords. Getting a larger share was important. But also, we wanted landlords to stop treating us as their slaves." If the policies had changed, another villager explained to me later, "relations between tenants and landlords would have been nice again." "The PKM didn't want to redistribute land," said Alfredo Buwan, a long-time peasant activist in the village. "Sometimes there was talk about having the government purchase lands of those hacenderos who refused to change their ways according to the law," Buwan continued, "but that wasn't really a main part of the PKM. Loans and bigger shares—those were the main concerns."

More specifically, people in San Ricardo recalled, the PKM advocated that all tenants should get at least 60 percent of the harvest and preferably 70 percent. If the share was 60 percent, landlords and tenants would share expenses equally. If the share was 70 percent, tenants might have to pay more than half, perhaps all the agricultural expenses. Regarding loans, peasants wanted landlords to guarantee them rice rations with either no interest or, at the most, a small fee. They also wanted landlords to recognize their right to borrow additional rice at modest interest rates—not the 100 or 200 percent rates that were then common. And they wanted the government to sponsor rural banks that would lend money to peasants at low interest rates without requiring collateral.

The PKM's activities in San Ricardo and other barrios of Talavera were similar to what the movement did in the 1930s. Peasants demonstrated and paraded in the bayan of Talavera and in Cabanatuan, their delegations went to other demonstrations in Central Luzon, their representatives negotiated with landlords and landlord organizations in Nueva Ecija, and they petitioned local, provincial, and national government officials. PKM actions also overlapped with Hukbalahap veterans' attempts to get recognition as legitimate guerrillas and to stop the Military Police from harassing them. As many in the PKM were former Hukbalahap, the overlap was natural enough. For instance, a contingent from San Ricardo marched in a demonstration in Cabanatuan the afternoon of 7 November 1945. About seven thousand people from the province marched first through the streets, then stopped at a park in the center of town to listen to several speakers, including Juan Feleo. They chanted slogans and carried placards such as "60-40 Harvest Share," "Recognition for the Hukbalahap," "Get Japanese Collaborators Out of Government," and "We Want Feleo for Governor." A Military Police commander reported afterward to headquarters in Manila that the demonstration "was at all times peaceful and orderly, which is very unusual for such a large gathering."[26] Eugenio Gomez from San Ricardo attended; he recalled the event as "a parade of thousands of peasants from all over. We were there to protest against government troops illegally arresting former Hukbalahap and to ask that the government make landlords share the harvest 60-40. I remember being a little frightened because there were lots of police and MPs there with guns. Those of us parading had no guns."

Because of repression, PKM members could not be as active as they would have liked. Harassment and abuses against peasant activists had been common for years, but, according to villagers, by late 1945 and 1946, local police, Military Police, and "civilian guards" intimidated, arrested, and even killed Hukbalahap veterans and PKM supporters. Talavera, according to a provincial PKM leader's report in late 1945, was one of several municipalities whose PKM members were arrested and where government troops burned houses and destroyed personal property with no apparent cause.[27] "They picked on people they thought had been in the Hukbalahap or active in the PKM," explained Eugenio Gomez. "They'd come into the barrios, arrest somebody, and take him to jail. People sat in jails in Talavera and Cabanatuan for months without knowing why and without a trial." "The people behind these abuses," explained Hilario Felipe of Talavera, "were those former USAFFE, who hated the Hukbalahap, and the landlords, who hated the PKM."

"Civilian guards" were especially important to landlords. In Talavera civilian guards made their appearance in late 1945 or early 1946. Many had been private guards on haciendas in Talavera or nearby municipalities; others had been members of Carlos Nocum's USAFFE guerrillas, squadron 311. Nocum was an intimate of Talavera authorities. He was also an appointed member of the municipal council. And he was close to landlords. As many of his USAFFE men needed work after the Japanese occupation, Nocum used his connections to get them jobs as local "peace officers," who later became known as civilian guards. Landlords were the ones who wanted these peace officers or civilian guards to restore peace

[26] Capt. Hamner, Headquarters, MPC, Cabanatuan, "Survey of Hukbalahap Activities, Nueva Ecija," 12 November 1945, p. 11.

[27] Narding [Mamerto Baniaga], untitled document from the Nueva Ecija PKM secretary, circa late 1945 (CapDoc, Cr.).

and order after liberation. But they had in mind more than cracking down on thieves and highway bandits. They were especially anxious about the growing peasant movement. Civilian guards, therefore, became basically armed groups that landlords used and that the local government and Military Police sanctioned. Illustrative of this arrangement was that landlords and the Military Police paid the civilian guards' wages.

The unfortunate part, residents of Talavera quickly pointed out, was that men who were civilian guards frequently had no quarrel with the peasants they abused. Of course, some USAFFE veterans had grudges against particular individuals from the Hukbalahap, and some civilian guards may have had other reasons for their vengeance. But most civilian guards were unemployed or landless "little people" who needed work and took whatever employment they could find. "They were used by hacenderos," said Hilario Felipe, "against other little people—us—who were really like them."

Illustrating the accounts of repression in San Ricardo was the experience of Ruben Sanchez. In 1946, he was in his early twenties, a former Hukbalahap, a member of the PKM, and a tenant farmer. His father, also a tenant farmer and PKM member, had been active in the KPMP before the war. One evening in February, several civilian guards and a half dozen MP soldiers stormed into San Ricardo. They demanded food from several people, including the Sanchez family. Although Sanchez's father gave what they could not spare, several civilian guards accused Sanchez and one of his brothers of being in the Hukbalahap. They also demanded to know if he and others were PKM members. If they were, said one soldier, that would be still another crime. By this time, several armed men had drawn their guns. Sanchez's older brother instinctively ducked down behind a tree, but the soldiers shot him. He died instantly. Then the armed men left. While his mother wailed, Sanchez and others tried to care for his brother. Before leaving, the armed men had warned that other PKM and Hukbalahap could expect the same treatment if they did not change their ways. "I had no choice," Sanchez explained, "but to avenge my brother's death. My family and I had taken too much from those bastards already. I got a gun and went more or less underground. I joined the *hukbo ng mga magbubukid* [the peasants' army]."

It was in this context of the PKM's efforts and the growing repression that people in San Ricardo discussed the importance of the Democratic Alliance (DA). "The DA was sort of a branch or army of the PKM," Leonardo Basa explained. "If you were in the PKM, you were part of the DA too." Illustrative of the overlap was that Patricio del Rosario and Hilario Felipe, both of whom were PKM officers in Talavera, were also officers in the DA. "The purpose of the DA," said Eugenio Gomez, "was to run candidates for office. That was in [April] 1946." As villagers explained it, the rationale for the PKM putting so much effort and hope in that election was to reform the government—or at least to begin doing so. "Since so many government officials were pawns of the landlords," said Hilaro Felipe, "we had to get persons who believed as we did elected to congress and other offices. If we did this, then we'd get better laws—laws that would benefit everybody, not just the landlords." Roberto Aspia put it in a slightly different way: "The government was filled with collaborators who hated the Hukbalahap and landlords who hated the PKM. So the DA and PKM wanted to get the collaborators and landlords out of office and replace them with people like Juan Feleo—people who defended the peasants and the Hukbalahap."

The local elite, according to the villagers, were extremely angry about the DA and even more unhappy about its strength in Talavera and elsewhere in Nueva Ecija. "The landlords' civilian guards were even more active during that election campaign than they had been before," recalled Hilario Felipe. They made campaigning difficult for DA candidates, and they intimidated villagers who attended DA- and PKM-sponsored events.

The repression climaxed in February 1946. Landlords ordered civilian guards to kill Patricio del Rosario. "They didn't have the guts to shoot him outright," his son said. "They kidnapped him one night as he was making the rounds of peasant leaders in the barrios. We never found his body. No one in the government tried to find his murderers." Hilario Felipe believed as many residents did that landowners killed del Rosario, "because they were really afraid of losing at the polls that year. Killing him was supposed to be the ultimate threat to everybody to stop supporting DA candidates." But, he added, "Patricio wouldn't have wanted people to panic and quit. He once told me that if anything happened to him, the other leaders should not give up the struggle against the landlords."

For villagers in San Ricardo, the April 1946 election turned out to be the most meaningful one up to that time—and maybe ever since. When thinking back, many proudly referred to that election as the one in which candidates won because they had the backing and votes of their movement, the PKM. The only offices up for election were seats in congress and the presidency and vice-presidency. Local and provincial elections had been put off until a year later. Nueva Ecija had two congressional seats, and for each one the DA had its own candidate. Talavera was in the First Congressional District. The DA's candidate was an attorney named Jose Cando, who had been involved with peasant groups for years. For president and vice-president, the DA endorsed the candidates of the Nacionalista Party (NP), incumbent president Osmeña and vice-presidential candidate Eulogio Rodriguez. Osmeña had not been a collaborator during the Japanese occupation and, because of his support for the PKM's 60-40 sharing proposal, peasants in San Ricardo preferred him. Those candidates that the DA supported received the majority of votes in Talavera (Table 13). It was, indeed, a victory for the PKM and DA there. Moverover, DA candidates won decisive victories elsewhere in Central Luzon too.

The Peasant Movement in Central Luzon

The experiences of people in San Ricardo illustrate two major themes in Central Luzon's history following the Japanese occupation. First, peasant

Table 13

1946 ELECTION RESULTS FOR TALAVERA, NUEVA ECIJA

Congress (1st District)	Cando[a]	Carlos	Corpuz	Galindez	Jose	Romero	Totals[c]
	2,837	0	597	258	13	15	3,720
President	Osmeña[b]	Roxas	Moncado				
	3,176	911	2				4,089
Vice-president	Rodriguez[b]	Quirino	Salvador				
	3,069	761	4				3,834

Sources: Philippines, Commission on Elections, "Tabulation of Votes by District and Municipality for Congress, 1946" and "Tabulation of Votes by District and Municipality for President and Vice-President, 1946" (Manila: Office of Commission on Elections, mimeo).

[a]DA ticket candidate.

[b]DA-endorsed candidate.

[c]According to official records for 1947, Talavera had 4,552 registered voters.

unrest was widespread and had important continuities with earlier unrest and the Hukbalahap. These continuities combined with poor social and economic conditions to create a more unified peasant movement. Second, the movement emphasized political action aimed directly at the national government, hoping thereby to influence policy. These observations must be elaborated in order to understand more completely why government officials and landed elites became so repressive and why this period was a prelude to rebellion.

Agrarian Unrest and the PKM

Agrarian conditions in Central Luzon in the late 1930s had been bad, but after the Japanese occupation they were worse. They may have been even more grave than during the occupation. Rice production, crucial to the economy, was only 9.2 million cavans in Central Luzon in 1946, or less than 73 percent of 1942 production (the last year for which figures are available). Figures for the Philippines as a whole were even less. Not until 1950 did rice production in Central Luzon exceed what it had been in 1942. And sugar cane, the other important crop in the region, practically vanished after the war. The amount of cane grown did not approach prewar levels until 1952. Large landowners saw no reason to plant cane, because the sugar centrals had been destroyed during the war. Unemployment and low wages in the towns and barrios of Central Luzon were additional problems in the 1940s. Not until the 1950s did agricultural workers get paid what they had received prior to the war. And their real wages remained smaller because inflation was high. Population, too, continued to rise. Between the 1939 and 1948 censuses, the number of souls in the four Central Luzon provinces increased from 1.4 million to 1.6 million, or more than 14 percent. For the Philippines as a whole, population jumped 20 percent.

Furthermore, the tenancy system remained. The percentage of tenant farmers in the 1940s was larger than it had been a decade before, and landlord-tenant relations were worse. When the landed elites returned to Central Luzon after the war, they too were hurting financially. They demanded more from their tenants but gave less in return. A major dispute, for example, was over who would pay for the planting and other agricultural expenses. During the 1930s, landlords and tenants generally shared expenses equally. Now more landlords wanted tenants to pay most, sometimes all, of those expenses but continue to share the crop on a 50-50 basis. As one tenant in Cabiao, Nueva Ecija, explained, "After the Japanese left, the landlords came back. But they wouldn't give loans and they wouldn't share expenses for harvesting, planting, and so on. If you didn't like it, landlords would say you can leave because there are others who will farm the parcel. But there wasn't any place to go."[28] Added to these conflicts were animosities as a consequence of tenants and landlords often having been on opposite sides during the Japanese occupation. The social and economic conditions and anti-Hukbalahap behavior of American and Filipino officials provided the environment in which the peasant movement in Central Luzon grew more forceful.

Even before the war's end, people in numerous villages of Central Luzon had begun to organize peasant associations. When Cenon Bungay's Hukbalahap squadron disbanded in yearly 1945, he returned to his home barrio in San Simon, Pampanga, and found that already his brothers and other tenants there had negotiated with their landlord about rents, loans, and payment of agricultural expenses.[29] When Benjamin Cunanan returned to his family in Concepcion, Tarlac, after his Hukbalahap squadron had fought beside an American unit against straggling Japanese soldiers, he and fellow tenant farmers formed a union that had the same purposes as those of their AMT chapter in the 1930s.[30] Peasants in several municipalities of Nueva Ecija began to organize in February and March 1945, and in April representatives from these groups established a Nueva Ecija peasant association. Then in May or June, numerous peasant leaders, former Hukbalahap leaders, and some officers in the Communist Party (PKP) met in a barrio of San Fernando, Pampanga, to form the PKM. During the months that followed, the organization grew to more than 500,000 souls—nearly four times the

[28] Interview, barrio Sinipit, Cabiao, 11 March 1970.
[29] Bungay interview, 15 July 1970.
[30] Interview with Benjamin Cunanan, Camp Crame, Quezon City, 11 August 1970.

combined membership of the two largest prewar peasant associations, the KPMP and AMT.[31]

PKM leaders at the provincial and national levels of the organization included persons active in the Hukbalahap and earlier peasant groups such as Jose de Leon.[32] In the 1930s, de Leon had given so much of his time to the KPMP that he once wrote that his wife and ten children were an "unfortunate family [who] suffered greatly" because of his activism. He had no steady income. He was also imprisoned once for alleged political crimes resulting from his KPMP work and from his association with the Communist Party. One of de Leon's closest friends was Juan Feleo. Like Feleo, de Leon had had more than the typical amount of formal education, having graduated from high school in 1928 in Aliaga, Nueva Ecija, and he was from a small landowning family. His father had been a local leader in the revolution against Spain at the turn of the century. Early in the Japanese occupation, de Leon became a local leader in the Hukbalahap resistance. He proved to be an astute guerrilla and became a regional commander for his home province. After the war, the American government officially recognized some of those Hukbalahap under his command, but it did not recognize de Leon himself. Instead, American CIC soldiers put him in prison. In late September 1945, the government decided to release him, probably in part because of numerous public demonstrations demanding the release of all Hukbalahap leaders. De Leon returned to Nueva Ecija and joined the PKM and the Hukbalahap's Veterans League. In March 1946, the PKM's second national conference, held in a barrio in Hagonoy, Bulacan, elected de Leon to its national committee.

Several national committee members had been active in the peasant movement since the 1930s (see Table 14). Were biographical information available for all twenty members who were elected in 1945 and the twenty-one members elected in 1946 (a total of thirty-six different persons), probably more individuals with experience in the movement could be identified. Indicative, too, of the PKM's continuity with earlier organizations were its two vice-presidents, Luis Taruc and Juan Feleo, and its president, Mateo del Castillo.

Like the peasant unrest of the 1930s and the Hukbalahap, the PKM was strongest in Bulacan, Nueva Ecija, Pampanga, and, to a lesser extent, Tarlac. Most of the national leadership came from these first three provinces. They were also the first to have provincial committees, which overarched the PKM groups or "chapters" in the municipalities. In Nueva Ecija, for example, the number of PKM chapters grew from a handful in mid-1945 to eighteen by October 1945. By January, 1946, nearly all of the

---

[31] Executive Committee of the PKM, to the Third Regular Session, Congress of the Philippines, 26 January 1948 (Hernandez Exh. W 435-440; CFI, Manila).

[32] This account of Jose de Leon comes mainly from the following sources: Dimasalang [Jose de Leon], "Pagtaya sa Sarili" [Self-Appraisal], undated (PF, CapDoc, Ag.); Taruc, *Born of the People*, pp. 100-101; and Kerkvliet, "Peasant Rebellion," pp. 269-270.

Table 14

PKM NATIONAL COMMITTEE MEMBERS WHOSE PREVIOUS ACTIVISM IS KNOWN

National committee member	*Activism prior to PKM leadership*
Casto Alejandrino	AMT, Socialist mayor (Pampanga, 1940), PKP, Hukbalahap
Mateo del Castillo	Labor and peasant organizations, PKP, Hukbalahap
Vivencio Cuyugan	AMT, Socialist mayor (Pampanga, 1940)
Juan Feleo	KPMP, PKP, Hukbalahap
Mariano Franco	Peasant organizations, Hukbalahap
Ben Layug	AMT, Socialist mayor (Pampanga, 1940)
Jose de Leon	KPMP, PKP, Hukbalahap
Federico Maclang	PKP
Fernancio Sampang	AMT, Socialist mayor (Pampanga, 1940)
Luis Taruc	AMT, PKP, Hukbalahap
Peregrino Taruc	Leftist groups (Manila), PKP, Hukbalahap
Pedro Villegas	Peasant and labor organizations, Hukbalahap

Sources: "Kasaysayan ng Kilusang Magbubukid sa Pilipinas" [History of the Peasant Movement in the Philippines], circa 1946 (Hernandez Exh. W 411-429; CFI, Manila); and Benedict J. Kerkvliet, "Peasant Rebellion in the Philippines: The Origins and Growth of the HMB" (Ph.D. dissertation, University of Wisconsin, Madison, 1972), pp. 448-450.

province's twenty-seven municipalities had PKM groups. Support for the PKM was so "overwhelming," according to a PKM document, that its Nueva Ecija provincial committee could not keep abreast of requests for speakers, literature, and other assistance.[33] In Central Luzon as a whole, Luis Taruc wrote later,

[33] "Mabilis na Lumalaganap ang PKM sa Nueva Ecija" [PKM Spreads Rapidly in Nueva Ecija], *Magbubukid,* January 1946 (CapDoc, Ag.); "General Rules and Regulations of the National Peasants Union," approved at a meeting of the National Governing Body, San Fernando, Pampanga, September 1945 (CapDoc, Ag.); Narding [Mamerto Baniaga], "Ulat ng P'Com sa Nueva Ecija" [Report of the Provincial Committee in Nueva Ecija], 2 October 1945 (PF, CapDoc, Ag.); Pambansang Lupon [National Committee of PKM], to Lupong Panlala-

It was extremely easy to organize among the people, due to the work of the Hukbalahap. When a demonstration became necessary, the barrios could be swiftly circularized and in three days we could have a demonstration of 50,000 in any of the provincial capitals of Nueva Ecija, Pampanga, Tarlac, and Bulacan—and many more in Manila.[34]

PKM groups also started in other areas—for example, in parts of Bataan, Pangasinan, Laguna, Quezon, and Camarines Norte. But these provinces were secondary to Central Luzon in terms of unrest and numbers of PKM chapters. The national committee of the PKM had planned in 1945 to extend the organization beyond what it described as the PKM's *baliwarte* (bailiwick) of Central Luzon. A year later, however, it recognized that only "20 percent of the plan was carried out."[35] The major reason why the PKM was confined to one region was that villagers elsewhere were not visibly discontented, or if they were, they showed their frustration in other ways. Central Luzon was the region with widespread peasant unrest.

As an organization, the PKM was more advanced than earlier peasant associations. "The contrast," wrote Luis Taruc,

between the prewar and postwar forms of mass organization was a good indication of how the metal of our movement had been tempered in the heat of war. The haphazard and rather uncoordinated methods of the AMT were replaced by smooth-running committees which had division of labor and which sought to involve their memberships.[36]

Municipal chapters and committees linked together PKM groups in the barrios. Peasant leaders, many of them experienced, worked in PKM activities at local, provincial, and national levels of the organization. Several leaders from peasant and nonpeasant backgrounds devoted their lives to this work, living on subsistence allowances drawn from PKM members' contributions and fund-raising projects. From time to time, provincial PKM leaders organized day-long "school" sessions where as many as one hundred villagers discussed agrarian problems and PKM activities and took courses designed for future peasant leaders. The PKM had at least three provincial offices—in San Fernando, Pampanga; Malolos, Bulacan; and Cabanatuan, Nueva Ecija—and a national office in Manila. Running these offices were full-time staffs and volunteers. Among other tasks, these offices prepared and circulated memoranda, leaflets, other literature, and the PKM's monthly newspaper called *Magbubukid* (Peasant). The PKM had lawyers in order to fight numerous court battles on behalf of evicted tenants, illegally detained villagers, and abused Hukbalahap veterans. Also important were the PKM's symbols of peasant

wigan [PKM Provincial Committee in Nueva Ecija], 30 October 1945; Narding [Mamerto Baniaga], "Kalahatang Kilusan" [Movement in General], 21 October 1945 (CapDoc, Ag.).

[34] Taruc, *Born of the People*, p. 218.

[35] PKM National Committee, "Palawakin ang Kilusang Magbubukid" [Expand the Peasant Movement], October 1946 (CapDoc, Ag.).

[36] Taruc, *Born of the People*, p. 218.

unity: its major spokesmen, particularly Feleo and Luis Taruc, who were known throughout the region; its slogans; its flags and banners; its political skits, which PKM "cultural troupes" performed in barrios across Central Luzon; and its songs, such as the one below.

"We Are Peasants"

We are what they call mere peasants;
Who were created by God in sincere love;
We who live by our own toil,
We are those peasants, always in poverty, always sacrificing;
No rest from work, suffer more and more,
While others depend on us.

We are peasants who always wear shorts,
We work in rain or shine without resting;
We are the planters who show no fear,
Who prepare the land with carabao, plow, and rake;
We are those planting with bended bodies,
Mud to our knees on rainy days.

When we peasants quit working,
All will go hungry and the nation will cry;
Those who are selfish and usurpers,
Only pretend they know poor people's feelings;
That is why we peasants and all workers,
All act together to DRAG DOWN THE DEMON!

The PKM was far from being a tightly integrated organization. Nor could its leaders dominate it from the top. Local PKM groups still had a good deal of autonomy. They based most of their actions on how they themselves saw the situation rather than on how top leaders saw it or on prescriptions from above. Peasants also defined membership loosely. For example, despite the strict definition spelled out in circulars from the PKM national office that members should pay an annual dues of 1.20 pesos, many who considered themselves PKM members did not and often could not pay.

What is significant, however, is that thousands of villagers in Central Luzon identified themselves with PKM rather than just with a local group set apart from groups in other barrios and municipalities. Villagers participating in local PKM chapters saw that their groups were part of a larger whole. In this important sense, the PKM was a peasant union. Through it a majority of rural folks in the region did unify.

Given the peasant unity and organization that the PKM represented, the landed elites of Central Luzon did, indeed, have cause to be worried—even afraid—of what might happen to their society. They had never had to cope with such a peasant movement before. The peasantry's organization at the end of the previous decade had been bothersome enough from the land-lords' viewpoint. But already in 1945-46, the movement had surpassed that.

To make matters even worse for the elites, the PKM became strong enough to threaten elite political power.

The PKM and the 1946 Election

The explanation for why the peasant movement had its own candidates for Congress in the 23 April 1946 election is a combination of at least two things. First, the development of the movement itself had led PKM participants and leaders to the conclusion that one avenue for seeking justice and reforms was to elect their own candidates to public office. Peasant groups had begun to do this, at least for local offices, in the 1930s. The Hukbalahap resistance pushed this further, for numerous villages had their own governments and the Hukbalahap governed several municipalities and provincial capitals during liberation until American soldiers arrived.

Second, the situation after the Japanese occupation encouraged the PKM to run its own candidates. Because so many of the local officials appointed by Americans 1945 disliked Hukbalahap veterans and opposed peasant organizations, the obvious thing for peasants to do was either persuade the national government to replace these officials or try to elect representatives more to their liking. Their efforts to get new appointments failed in several instances. Then the PKM, through its national leaders, joined the newly formed Democratic Alliance (DA), a loose association of groups and individuals who advocated political reforms, opposed having Japanese collaborators in government, and planned to run candidates for office. (The next section explains more about the DA.) As the PKM represented the largest number of people among the DA affiliates, it was the backbone of the party in Central Luzon. The first election following the Japanese occupation was not for local offices but for national ones in April 1946, so the peasant movement pushed for congressional candidates it had nominated on the DA ticket.

Prior to that election, the peasantry in Central Luzon demonstrated its potential political strength on several occasions. Two were illustrative.

The first was the attempt to get Juan Feleo appointed governor.[37] Between April 1945 and November 1945, Nueva Ecija had two governors; by the following May, it had three more. The turnover was rapid because governors either resigned or the national government replaced them as a

---

[37] This account is based on the following sources: *Star Reporter,* 11, 12, 14, and 19 November 1945, and 11, 12, and 28 December 1945; *Manila Chronicle,* 13 December 1945, p. 3, 3 March 1946, p. 1, 1 May 1946, p. 1, and 9 May 1946, p. 1; *Manila Times,* 14 December 1945, p. 7; Narding [Mamerto Baniaga], "Paliwanag ukol sa paglapit ni Tomacruz sa DA" [Explanation concerning Tomacruz's Advances toward the DA], circa January 1946 (PF, CapDoc, Ag.), "Ikatlong Ulat ng P'Com" [Third Report of the Nueva Ecija Provincial Committee], 6-15 September 1945, and untitled document from the Nueva Ecija PKM secretary, circa late 1945; and Capt. Hamner, Headquarters, MPC, Cabanatuan, "Survey of Hukbalahap Activities, Nueva Ecija," 12 November 1945. I am grateful to Professor Ronald K. Edgerton for clarifications regarding Nueva Ecija's governors in 1945-1946.

result of intense public pressure against them. Probably all these governors were from the province's landed elite, and at least the first two, Juan Chioco and Herminio Algas, had served the provincial government during the Japanese occupation. Besides that, Chioco and Algas used "peace-keeping forces" to abuse unionized peasants and former Hukbalahap guerrillas. On numerous occasions, Hukbalahap veterans, the PKM, the DA, and other groups protested against these men. People said Chioco was responsible for "merciless punishment of sick and undernourished [Fili-pino] war prisoners," and his behavior during the Japanese occupation earned him the nickname "Number One Guillotine Man." By mid-November, people had forced the national government to investigate him and request his resignation. The government then appointed Algas. But demonstrations continued, including a sit-down strike in Cabanatuan in December and a parade that same month by a thousand representatives from the PKM, Hukbalahap veterans, and DA in front of the presidential palace in Manila. People opposed Algas because he had been on the provincial board during the Japanese occupation and he was helping landlords to subvert the 60-40 crop sharing plan that the PKM and landlord associations had agreed to.

Many placards at these demonstrations read "Feleo for Governor." This was also the PKM, DA, and Hukbalahap veterans' joint proposal to President Osmeña. They believed Feleo could restore peace in the province. Some elite politicians recommended the same thing. Attesting to Feleo's popularity, for example, was an MP report dated November 1945:

> He [has] campaigned vigorously throughout the province of Nueva Ecija and into the legislature for improved living and working conditions for peasants and laborers. . . . Feleo is an experienced leader, well acquainted with a great many people and widely known. . . . With his experience in teaching and his ability as an orator, Feleo has become an idol of the tenant farmers or poor working-class Filipinos. He is certainly a man to be feared by his political opponents in Nueva Ecija. . . . Should Gov. Chioco . . . leave his post, the general opinion is that Feleo will be a likely candidate for governor of Nueva Ecija with a very good possibility of winning.[38]

Osmeña, however, never did appoint Feleo. Nor was Feleo ever elected. He probably would have been, as the Nueva Ecija DA convention in December nominated him, but no gubernatorial election was held in 1946.

The second illustration of the peasantry showing its growing political strength was the negotiation for a harvest-sharing agreement.[39] In October

[38] Capt. Hamner, Headquarters, MPC, Cabanatuan, "Survey of Hukbalahap Activities, Nueva Ecija," 12 November 1945, p. 2.

[39] *Manila Chronicle,* 27 October 1945, p. 1, 30 October 1945, p. 1, 11 November 1945, p. 1, 13 November 1945, p. 1, 20 November 1945, p. 1, 28 November 1945, p. 3, and 30 November 1945, p. 1; *Manila Times,* 24 September 1945, p. 1; Bataan Provincial Committee, "Instruction No. 5, to PKM," 19 June 1947 (CapDoc, Ag.); and Luis Taruc interview, 27 January 1970. Also see footnote 24.

1945, the PKM leadership went directly to President Osmeña and U.S. High Commissioner Paul McNutt with the peasantry's demands for a larger share of the crop. Because of the growing unrest in Central Luzon resulting from agrarian problems and abuses against Hukbalahap veterans and because of the PKM's size and organization, the Osmeña government listened. Eventually it forced landlords to negotiate in earnest. By the end of December, both sides signed a 60-40 sharing agreement. The PKM celebrated it as an example of what peasant unity could do.

"We thought that [sharing] agreement was just the beginning," Cenon Bungay said.[40] "Our PKM chapter in San Simon worked hard on the 1946 election. We wanted to get DA candidates elected, because they were our candidates and would work for what we wanted." But, he added, it was also an election "against collaborators like Roxas and against the brutality and other injustices by the landlords and MPs." Peregrino Taruc, who was the coordinator of the DA campaign in Pampanga, said, "The DA was basically against fascism. By that I mean the use of brute force, suppression by the elite class. This was a central issue in the 1946 election—the repression by collaborators, landlords, and the government. Repression went right on during the campaign. The reason people in the barrios became so involved in that election is because of the agrarian situation, the repression, and the appeal DA candidates had."[41]

PKM groups in Central Luzon, according to Luis Taruc, were "crucial to the campaign."[42] Luis Taruc was the DA's nominee for Congress from Pampanga's Second District. "Most barrios [in Pampanga] had PKM councils," Taruc said. "There were usually seven to twelve persons per council. Each PKM council divided up the families in its barrio, and then each council member took the responsibility to talk to certain family heads. They urged people to vote for the DA candidates, talked about the issues, passed out leaflets, and accepted contributions for the DA campaign if people could give. For leaflets we used a ratio of one to fifty—one leaflet for fifty persons." Taruc added that he himself did not need to campaign much in his own district. Instead, he campaigned for DA candidates elsewhere.

The issues, the serious problems in Central Luzon, the PKM, the DA, the candidates—these must have been the correct combination for success because DA candidates in Central Luzon did well. The DA ticket had twenty-three candidates for Congress in several parts of the country. Six of them won; all were in Central Luzon: two seats each in Pampanga and Nueva Ecija, and one seat each in Bulacan and Tarlac (see Table 15).

For the office of president and vice-president, voters in Central Luzon gave a healthy majority to incumbent President Osmeña and his running mate Eulogio Rodriguez, the Nacionalista Party's candidates whom the DA had decided to endorse rather than run its own candidates. Stated

---

[40] Bungay interview, 15 July 1970.
[41] Peregrino Taruc interview, 9 July 1970.
[42] Luis Taruc interview, 27 January 1970.

Table 15
DEMOCRATIC ALLIANCE CANDIDATES FOR CONGRESS, APRIL 1946

Province[a]	Candidate	Votes Received	Placed	Winning vote	Votes for closest rival of DA winner
Bataan	Jose Simpao	4,281	3/5[b]	5,613	
**Bulacan (1)	Jesus Lava	16,968	1/2	16,968	14,398
Cebu (7)	Angel Y. Ancajas	2	6/6	12,538	
Ilocos Norte (1)	Jose Llanes	22	4/4	10,847	
Iloilo (1)	Valentina Carmarines	3	3/5	12,736	
Iloilo (1)	Nicolas Nonato	0	4/5	12,736	
Iloilo (1)	Espeleta	0	5/5	12,736	
Iloilo (3)	Agripino Soquena	211	5/5	9,491	
Iloilo (4)	Maximino Jimenea	0	4/5	8,664	
Iloilo (5)	Nicolas B. Centino	311	5/6	12,768	
Laguna (2)	Pedro Villegas	2,675	5/16	7,132	
Negros Occidental (3)	Serafin Nava	16	6/8	12,479	
**Nueva Ecija (1)	Jose Cando	19,302	1/6	19,302	10,474
**Nueva Ecija (2)	Constancio Padilla	17,598	1/11	17,598	12,849
Nueva Ecija (2)	Enrique Jimenez	5	10/11	17,598	

Table 15 (continued)

DEMOCRATIC ALLIANCE CANDIDATES FOR CONGRESS, APRIL 1946

Province[a]	Candidate	Votes Received	Placed	Winning vote	Votes for closest rival of DA winner
Palawan	Jesus Roces	6	4/5	6,577	
**Pampanga (1)	Amado M. Yuzon	26,322	1/5	26,322	5,317
**Pampanga (2)	Luis Taruc	39,289	1/3	39,289	1,312
Quezon (1)	Cirilo Lavadia	485	4/6	16,851	
Rizal (1)	Gualberto Cruz	1,850	6/8	20,652	
**Tarlac (2)	Alejandro Simpauco	18,578	1/2	18,578	5,611
Manila (N)	Manuel M. Crudo	2,979	4/6	20,089	
Manila (S)	Severino P. Izon	1,458	8/16	22,345	

Source: Philippines, Commission on Elections, "Election Returns for House of Representatives by Province for 1946-1965" (Manila: Office of Commission on Elections, mimeo).

**DA winners.

[a]The number in parentheses after the province's name indicates the congressional district. No number means a lone district. In the case of Manila, (N) is North District, (S) is South District.

[b]Read as "placed third out of five contenders."

another way—the way that those in the peasant movement sometimes put it—the PKM and DA voted against Manuel Roxas and his running mate Elpidio Quirino, who ran on the new Liberal Party (LP) ticket. "The biggest issue against Roxas," explained Peregrino Taruc, "was that he had been a collaborator with the Japanese, and he violently disliked the Hukbalahap and peasant organizations because they kept pointing out that he was a collaborator."[43]

The April 1946 election in Central Luzon, in short was a unique victory for the peasant movement. Now the region's villagers would have six representatives in the House of Representatives—not a majority, by any means, but a start. And they had demonstrated that their political power was still increasing. Now the landed elites and established politicians realized, PKM leader Mateo del Castillo wrote a few months later, "that their domination in the countryside will come to an end if they must depend on the democratic procedure. To gain political power through democratically conducted elections is now impossible for them to do. This is because of the existence of a strong peasant organization [that is] conscious of its economic and political rights."[44]

The Democratic Alliance

When pushing for reforms, the peasant movement in Central Luzon was never entirely alone. Helping it was the Democratic Alliance. The DA represented another attempt to converge two streams in Philippine politics —the peasant movement in Central Luzon and the predominantly urban left. The United Front had been a previous effort. A possible third tributary, which I can only mention, was the labor union movement, particularly a new federation called the Congress of Labor Organizations (CLO). Largely because groups in the CLO represented fewer people than the peasant movement's PKM and Hukbalahap veterans did and because they were generally less active, the CLO's role apparently remained minor.

During the last months of the Japanese occupation, some of those individuals and groups who had been active in leftist causes prior to the war and who had been part of the United Front began to think seriously about what they would do after the Japanese had surrendered. They knew that the Philippine Commonwealth government, led by President Sergio Osmeña and overseen by the Americans, would return. And they knew that the United States still intended to give the Philippines its independence. They doubted, however, that leaders like Osmeña and the dominating political party, the Nacionalista (NP), could satisfactorily address such pressing problems as poverty, agrarian unrest, reconstruction after a

[43] Peregrino Taruc interview, 9 July 1970.
[44] Mateo del Castillo, "Del Castillo Explains Central Luzon Muddle, Hits Landlords," *Katubusan*, 23 September 1946, vol. 2, no. 37 (CapDoc, Ag.).

devastating war, and a weak economy heavily dependent on the United States. They worried that the government, even after independence, would have the same kinds of policies it had in the 1930s and continue to cater to landed elites and corrupt politicians.

The Communist Party in the Philippines (PKP) was one of these groups. In September 1944, as the demise of Japanese became increasingly apparent, the PKP convened a conference to discuss plans for the remainder of the occupation and the party's role afterward.[45] In addition to PKP leaders, several top Hukbalahap leaders also attended. The conference decided that the PKP, as it worked to rebuild its own organization, would also help after liberation to transform the anti-Japanese resistance movement into a broad-based political movement for political and economic reforms. This political movement, agreed the people attending this conference, should be in the same spirit as the United Front, that is, all individuals and groups who had opposed the Japanese occupation and who supported the movement's broad goals should be welcomed. The three major goals were (1) to prevent Filipinos who had collaborated with the Japanese from holding political office, (2) to campaign for immediate independence from the United States, and (3) to push the returning Osmeña administration to endorse reforms that would benefit lower- and middle-class Filipinos rather than rich Filipinos and foreigners.

After the PKP conference had accepted these guidelines, it had to resolve a disagreement over implementation. Vicente Lava, who was still the PKP's president going into the meeting but who was replaced by a three-man general secretariat during this meeting, urged that the resistance movement should immediately form its own government. The resistance movement, argued Vicente Lava, must have its own national United Front Government to confront Osmeña when he returns. This way, Lava said, the resistance movement could compel the Osmeña government to be progressive and bring some of the movement's representatives into his administration's cabinet.[46] Although the outgoing PKP president had supporters for this position, a majority at the conference rejected it, in part, according to a PKP leader's analysis written later, because "the advocates of such [a]

[45] "Political Resolutions Adopted at the National Conference of the CPP, held September 28–October 3, 1944" (CapDoc, Ag.): *Ang Bolsibik* [The Bolshevik], November 1944, vol. 1, no. 8 (CapDoc, Ag.); VY [Vicente Lava], "Comments on the Secretariat's Answer to P-G's Thesis on the United Front and the National Government," 6 January 1945 (PF, CapDoc, Ag.); interview with Peregrino Taruc, Camp Crame, Quezon City, 13 July 1970; interview with Luis Taruc, Quezon City, 25 February 1970; interview with Casto Alejandrino, Camp Crame, Quezon City, 5 November 1970; Jose Lava, "Milestones," pp. 28-29.

[46] The following documents by VY [Vicente Lava] elaborate Lava's argument as of late 1944 and early 1945: "Our Agrarian Policy," 1 September 1944 (PF, CapDoc, Ag.); "The People's State and Government," 2 September 1944 (PF, CapDoc, Ag.); "Comments on P-G's Thesis on United Front and the National Government," 2 January 1945 (PF, CapDoc, Ag.); "Comments on Secretariat's Answer to P-G's Thesis," 6 January 1945; and "Thesis on the Urgent Need for the Establishment of a Provisional National Revolutionary United Front Government," 9 January 1945 (PF, CapDoc, Ag.).

. . . government were responsible for the wrong tactical policy of retreat [for defense during the occupation]. . . ."[47] The majority decided instead to accept, at least initially, Osmeña and his administration because he was anti-Japanese and simultaneously to "mobilize the masses" to pressure Osmeña to be progressive.

The results of that 1944 conference were the basis on which PKP leaders during the first half of 1945 planned "a new political party" with other anti-Japanese groups and individuals. In July 1945 this coalition formed the Democratic Alliance. Its program, which its founding document outlined and which DA spokesmen and candidates espoused during the following months, specified several reforms. The central themes were to give immediate relief to the homeless and other victims of war, including "legitimate guerrillas"; to unite all anti-Japanese groups and elect representatives from them to local and national offices; to remove collaborators from "positions of political and economic control or influence"; to revamp the national economy; to give workers and peasants a fair share; to guarantee civil liberties; and to support a free and independent Philippines. It was in short, a moderate program reflecting the diversity of the allied groups. The DA, wrote Luis Taruc, was not

> revolutionary. It believed in the ballot and the peaceful petition as the instruments through which the people's will should be expressed and achieved. It did not propose even the mildest socialization or change in the system of society as we knew it. The path it proposed would have led no further than the development of a healthy industrialized capitalist country out of the feudal agricultural colonial condition that we had.[48]

The DA's national spokesmen and the groups represented at DA-sponsored events also reflected the kind of alliance it was. Jesus Barrera was its president. Prior to the Japanese occupation he had been a leader in the country's Civil Liberties Union; during the occupation, he had refused to serve the government. In addition to Barrera, the DA's national executive committee had six persons, all from prominent families, well-educated, and active in the Filipino left.[49] Included in this executive committee was Vicente Lava, who represented the PKP's presence in the alliance. Among the groups affiliated with the DA were the Philippine Lawyers' Guild, the PKM, the Hukbalahap's Veterans League, Democratic

---

[47] Jose Lava, "Milestones," p. 28.

[48] Taruc, *Born of the People,* p. 214. Also see Democratic Alliance, National Executive Committee, "Program of the Democratic Alliance," 16 July 1945, app. 8, in San Fernando CIC Field Office, 1135th CIC Detachment, "Hukbalahap," 24 October 1946.

[49] The seven members of the DA's National Executive Committee were Jesus Barrera (president), Antonio Araneta, Manuel M. Crudo, Jose Hilario, Vicente Lava, Rafael Ledesma, and Jose B. L. Reyes. Democratic Alliance, "Program of the Democratic Alliance," 16 July 1945, p. 8, app. 8, in San Fernando CIC Field Office, 1135th CIC Detachment, "Hukbalahap," 24 October 1946.

Youth League, League for the Defense of Democracy, Llanes Guerrilla Veterans, Blue Eagle Guerrilla Veterans, Congress of Labor Organizations, Fishermans Union, Manila Railroad Company Employee and Workers Union, Rural Transit Employees Union, and the Shoemakers' Union.

Although the Democratic Alliance originally intended to counter the Nacionalista Party, it later decided to endorse the NP's candidates for president (the incumbent Sergio Osmeña) and vice-president (Eulogio Rodriguez) for the 1946 election. This was a difficult decision for the DA, as its previous criticism against Osmeña had been so sharp. The PKP's position, for example, was that the DA under no circumstances should endorse Osmeña because he was a "reactionary and counterrevolutionary" like other "compradore-bourgeois" politicians. Instead, the PKP proposed, the DA should have its own candidates for the country's two highest offices. A decisive majority of the DA's leadership, however, rejected this, as did a minority within the PKP itself (including Vicente Lava). The DA decided that, above all else, Senator Manuel Roxas, the presidential nominee of the new Liberal Party that had previously been a faction within the Nacionalista Party, must be defeated. Not only had he been a top-ranking collaborator in the Japanese regime, but he was also a fascist and he opposed immediate independence for the Philippines. They feared that if Roxas became president, economic conditions in the country would worsen and repression would increase. At least Osmeña, concluded a majority of DA leaders, was receptive to some progressive ideas and was neither a fascist nor a Japanese collaborator. A majority of the DA's leadership also believed at the time of the party's nomination convention in February 1946 that DA supporters would hold the balance in the election. DA leaders estimated that Roxas and Osmeña were running neck and neck.[50] As it turned out, Central Luzon did vote overwhelmingly for Osmeña, but it was not enough to prevent Roxas's election.

Democratic Alliance organizations in the provinces nominated their own candidates for the House of Representatives. In Central Luzon, the peasant movement's local and provincial leaders determined the party's choices. The DA served a purpose similar to that of the Popular Front Party in Pampanga in the late 1930s. The DA, however, was a more coherent party than the Popular Front had been. The Democratic Alliance, said Luis Taruc, "was the best channel through which the people [in Central Luzon] could flow away from the parties that were dominated by landlords and compradores."[51]

The DA also assisted the PKM and Hukbalahap veterans. Its national office helped to organize several large parades and rallies in Manila that brought to the country's attention the seriousness of agrarian problems in

[50] VY [Vicente Lava], "UF Against Fascism and the Role of Osmeña," 6 September 1945 (PF, CapDoc, Ag.), and "Criticism of the Majority PB [Politburo] Resolution, Our Policy Towards Osmeña, and Its Supplementary Material," 20 October 1945 (PF, CapDoc, Ag.); Hoeksema, "Communism in the Philippines," pp. 280, 309.

[51] Taruc, *Born of the People,* p. 215.

Central Luzon and the gravity of the repression against PKM members and former Hukbalahap. And the DA's national program included the peasant movement's major demands. For example, it wanted to "give tenants an equitable share of the harvest"; "recognize all trade unions and peasant associations and their right of collective bargaining"; "outlaw company unions"; "grant loans to tenants and small proprietors and eliminate the usurious practices of landlords and merchants"; "prevent landgrabbing and arbitrary evictions of tenants and small proprietors."

The major bridge between the peasant movement in Central Luzon and the Democratic Alliance as a national political party were those provincial and other leading spokesmen for the PKM and Hukbalahap veterans who were also prominent DA leaders. In Nueva Ecija, for example, Mamerto Baniaga was provincial secretary of the PKM, a member of the PKP, and a provincial leader for the DA. He knew well many of those in the DA's national office in Manila. Juan Feleo was both a national spokesman for the PKM and Hukbalahap veterans as well as active in the DA at the national level. Such individuals helped to guide the peasant movement into electoral politics and to speak on behalf of the peasantry among leftists in Manila.

Mateo del Castillo was a good example of those who linked the peasant movement and the DA at the national level.[52] At the age of 49, this mild-mannered man who was known for his honesty was elected president of the PKM in 1945. Before that he had been a political advisor in the Hukbalahap's general headquarters, and in the 1930s he had worked on behalf of the KPMP and other peasant groups in Central Luzon. He was also an officer in the Communist Party. Born the son of a Spanish landowner in the Southern Luzon province of Batangas, del Castillo was well educated and rather well-to-do. After selling land inherited from his father, he invested in a restaurant, rooming houses, and other real estate in Manila. The earnings from these properties supported himself, his wife, and their children. Partly through his own study and partly through the influence of boarders in his rooming houses who were active in labor unions in the 1930s, del Castillo became increasingly involved with labor organizations and the peasant movement. Soon his political life overshadowed everything else. He neglected his properties and eventually sold most of them in order to repay accumulating debts and contribute to peasant groups and the Communist Party. This left his family in a poor financial state. During the 1930s, the police and Philippine Constabulary arrested him several times for making allegedly seditious speeches in Central Luzon. As president of the PKM after the Japanese occupation, del Castillo was in charge of the organization's national office in Manila, was responsible for publishing the

---

[52] In addition to several PKM documents written by Mateo del Castillo which I have cited earlier, sources for this man's biography come from the following: Taruc, *Born of the People*, pp. 88-89; and Philippines, Armed Forces of the Philippines, "Case Studies of 11 Top Filipino Communists" (Camp Aguinaldo, mimeo, 1958). Also see Kerkvliet, "Peasant Rebellion," pp. 819-822.

PKM's *Magbubukid*, was a frequent PKM envoy to government officials, and spoke widely throughout Central Luzon at parades and demonstrations of Hukbalahap veterans and PKM supporters. He also represented the PKM in meetings of the DA national leadership and enthusiastically campaigned in 1946 for the party's congressional candidates.

Repression Yields Rebellion

For rural folks in Central Luzon, the results of the April 1946 election marked a high point of the peasant movement. In the context of conflicts between tenants and landlords, harassment against Hukbalahap veterans, and poor economic conditions, the election of their six DA candidates to Congress permitted at least the hope that things could improve. To their disappointment, however, the situation grew worse. Many who in April had expected things to improve were rebelling by the next September. Why?

Typical reasons were, "We were forced to because of what the landlords and constabulary were doing," "civilian guards and the PC had me on their wanted list," "government soldiers tried to arrest me because I was in the PKM," "the landlords' armed guards killed my brother." The reason, in short, was repression. Repression by itself did not cause the rebellion, but it pushed many people to believe they had no choice but to fight back with guns.

The repression grew, according to villagers' descriptions, in three stages. Other evidence also conforms to this pattern. The first period extended from early 1945 to late 1945. The second was from late 1945 until just after the April 1946 election. The third was from May 1946 until August or September 1946, the time that marked the beginning of the rebellion. As one individual in San Ricardo, Talavera, characterized it, the repression became worse as time went on, "like rice cooking in a pot—it first got hot, then began to boil, and then it bubbled over."

From liberation until late 1945, harassment by landlord guards and government authorities was a problem for Hukbalahap veterans and peasant union participants. "The Hukbalahap disbanded after liberation, just as we had always planned," said Peregrino Taruc as he began to explain what happened later in 1945.[53] "Americans disarmed some squadrons; other Hukbalahaps put aside their weapons voluntarily and returned to their barrios. But American and Filipino soldiers continued to torment Hukbalahap veterans." This was one reason why Hukbalahap leaders decided in September or October 1945 to turn over rosters of Hukbalahap participants to the United States military. "We hoped," Peregrino Taruc continued, "that the rosters would show our sincerity, so that the Hukbalahap would be recognized as a legitimate resistance movement and so that the harassment of Hukbalahap veterans would stop. Instead American and

---

[53] Peregrino Taruc interview, 9 July 1970.

Filipino soldiers used the lists to hunt down Hukbalahap veterans. They arrested them in meetings and demonstrations, in their homes, and wherever else they could. They even circulated the lists among landlords and employers. Many people were turned down for jobs because their names were on the lists. Landlords evicted tenants who had been in the Hukbalahap." Agaton Bulaong, who had been a Hukbalahap commander in Bulacan, said, "It was as though Hukbalahap veterans were wanted criminals. That's how landlords and the police treated us."[54] Government sources confirm this. An American military report, for example, told government officials in October 1945 that Hukbalahap veterans were "being traced and killed by both [USAFFE] guerrillas and Puppet Constabulary and . . . they are being rounded up by U.S. Armed Forces."[55]

Villagers in peasant organizations, too, were often victimized. For example, by mid-1945, according to reports from the PKM provincial committee in Nueva Ecija, USAFFE veterans and Military Police detachments had teamed up to intimidate villagers who were trying to organize. The abuses increased, reported the PKM provincial secretary late that year, until "MP raids against peaceful farmers and other citizens occurred on nearly a daily basis." PKM leaders and the PKM headquarters in Cabanatuan were especially vulnerable. In September alone, MPs in Nueva Ecija reportedly raided the house of Juan Feleo, ransacked the PKM headquarters twice, and arrested one PKM provincial officer whom they later released.[56] In Pampanga, Cenon Bungay said, landlords "told tenants that if they held any meetings, they'd be evicted. Their guards broke up lots of meetings, too."[57]

Although the landlords, MP officers, police, and government officials sometimes denied that these abuses happened, they usually tried to justify them. One common justification was that "radical elements," "agitators," and "communists and socialists" were responsible for the disruption of "peace and order," which the police and authorities only tried to restore. For example, a Labor Department report explained trouble in Tarlac in 1945 this way: "Radical elements inspired by unscrupulous leaders, who are in fact only aiming at having a cut from the tenants, are becoming more aggressive and are formulating new demands to landlords."[58] Another justification was that Hukbalahap veterans and PKM participants were

---

[54] Bulaong interview, 20 July 1970.

[55] Col. S. V. Constant, Security and Intelligence Division, "List of Four Organizations in the Philippine Islands," 5 October 1945. "Puppet Constabulary" refers to Filipinos who had been in the constabulary during the Japanese occupation, many of whom afterward joined the Military Police.

[56] "Pangkalahatang Ulat" [General Report of the Nueva Ecija Provincial Committee], 8 June 1945; Narding [Mamerto Baniaga], "Ikatlong Ulat ng P'Com" [Third Report of the Nueva Ecija Provincial Committee], 6-15 September 1945, "Ulat ng P'Com" [Report of the Provincial Committee in Nueva Ecija], 2 October 1945, and untitled document from the Nueva Ecija PKM secretary, circa late 1945.

[57] Bungay interview, 15 July 1970.

[58] Philippines, Department of Labor, *Labor Bulletin* 1 (January 1946): 176-177.

"criminals," "bandits," and "lawless." For example, several MP patrols and offices in Central Luzon reported from June through mid-December that Hukbalahap groups had attacked them. (Later investigations, according to Military Police records, proved these accusations to be false.)[59] Local government officials also complained to MP commanders and to the national government that PKM groups had broken laws and thus deserved punishment.

Undoubtedly, villagers, including PKM participants, did break laws. As one tenant in San Ricardo said, "We weren't angels." But many laws were directed specifically against peasant organizations and Hukbalahap veterans. The municipal council in Concepcion, Tarlac, for example, passed ordinances during 1945 that helped make Tarlac, in the words of one American observer, "the center of agrarian repression and unbridled reaction." For instance, this observer went on, the effect of one ordinance regulating meetings in public places was that peasants

> cannot hold meetings on their own lands since a meeting is defined as anything "within public view" without prior sanction by the powers in Tarlac. Furthermore, a public place is defined as anything "to which the public generally has access." Thus halls, buildings, cafes, etc., fall into this category. In effect, ANY gathering in Tarlac is a "Public Meeting" under this neat legislation and requires registration.[60]

Landlords, mayors, and other officials also frequently blamed the Hukbalahap veterans for murders, robberies, and other crimes in Central Luzon. Hukbalahap spokesmen like Luis Taruc and Juan Feleo repeatedly denied these, although they did admit that the Hukbalahap had had some "bad people" who had committed crimes. At least two Military Police reports corroborated this defense. As one of them said in November 1945, part of the reason why the Hukbalahap had a bad name was that

> all crimes not definitely proven otherwise are laid to the activities of the Hukbalahaps, when in reality only a small percentage of these crimes [2 out of 475 cases in Nueva Ecija between July and November] were actually committed by members of the organization and even then it is doubtful that the organization sanctioned or sponsored their actions.[61]

[59] Pampanga Province, MPC, AFWESPAC, *Daily Log,* 25 June-13 December 1945 (RG 94, WW II Operations Reports, 1940-1948 Pacific Theater, 98-USF6-MPCD-0.3.0; Federal Records Center, Suitland, Md.).

[60] Sidney Reitman, to Mr. Ickes, 19 November 1945, with Copies of Five Ordinances and Resolutions, Concepcion, Tarlac, dated from 28 June 1945 to 3 November 1945 (RG 126, File No. 9-7-30, Division of Territories and Island Possessions; National Archives, Washington, D.C.). Mr. Reitman was writing from Manila but had been stationed, while in the United States Army, in Tarlac.

[61] Capt. Hamner, Headquarters, MPC, Cabanatuan, "Survey of Hukbalahap Activities, Nueva Ecija," 12 November 1945, pp. 3, 11.

A third contention against the Hukbalahap and to some extent the PKM was that they possessed guns illegally. Although many Hukbalahap veterans had surrendered their firearms, willingly or unwillingly, others had hidden theirs. The guns belonged to them, they said, and they might need them to protect themselves against enemies; besides, why should they give up their guns when USAFFE guerrillas kept theirs. Several officials, however, dismissed these explanations as "feeble justifications."[62] Mayors, police chiefs, and landlords demanded that the peasant "outlaws" be disarmed, and claimed armed Hukbalahap veterans were terrorizing the countryside. A MP investigation in Nueva Ecija in November, however, found that "there appears to be no foundation to recent reports that members of the Hukbalahap openly carry arms in . . . Nueva Ecija."[63]

Unfortunately for the peasantry, even those government reports that included evidence countering accusations against the PKM and Hukbalahap often turned right around to state that the Hukbalahap and PKM were "communistic" and the Hukbalahap had shown its "true intentions" by refusing to surrender all weapons. On balance, consequently, such reports strengthened the indictments by landlords and others.

The tempo of repression definitely quickened in December 1945 and January 1946. It continued to escalate through the election in April. The added fuel to the fire was the landlords' resistance to the 60-40 crop-sharing plan that the Osmeña government had approved and the election campaign. The PKM office in Nueva Ecija reported in January and February that MPs, equipped with machine guns and radio transmitters, frequently traveled now to the barrios, breaking up meetings and picking up anyone suspected of being in the PKM or DA or a Hukbalahap veteran. At the same time, the authorities paid little attention to landlords who flagrantly violated agrarian laws. One report exclaimed, "the reactionary Filipinos and Americans are mobilizing the MPs in order to stop all activities of the progressive movement"; another predicted that martial law was imminent.[64] From Bulacan came reports that large landowners did "whatever they could to obstruct the implementation of 60-40 and equal sharing of expenses," including hiring armed men to intimidate tenants. In some cases, as these guards tried to take forcefully a larger share for landlords than they deserved, the tenants raised flags and blew their *tambuli* to call other peasants to help them resist the guards.[65] As the election campaign heated up, newspapers printed many accounts of abuses such as the day MP troops raided a barrio of Pulilan, Bulacan, searched the homes of Hukbalahap veterans, and machine-gunned several men and

---

[62] MPC, *History and Organization of the Hukbalahap.*

[63] Capt. Hamner, Headquarters, MPC, Cabanatuan, "Survey of Hukbalahap Activities, Nueva Ecija," 12 November 1945, p. 4.

[64] Narding [Mamerto Baniaga], "Ika-V Ulat," [Fifth Report of the Nueva Ecija Provincial Committee], 15 January 1946; and Nueva Ecija Lupong Panglalawigan [Provincial Committee], "Ulat Pampolitika No. 3" [Political Report No. 3], 5 February 1946 (CapDoc, Ag.).

[65] "Bulacan," *Magbubukid,* January 1946.

a woman. DA Congressional candidate Jesus Lava then demanded that the Secretary of Interior Alfredo Montelibano withdraw all MPs from Central Luzon.[66]

In Pampanga, according to Peregrino Taruc who was the DA campaign coordinator there, "DA workers and organizers had to be wary of civilian guards, MPs and other 'armies.' The MPs even used armored cars to break up political rallies, driving the cars straight at people standing in the plaza with guns aimed and ready to shoot." Just before election day, armed men "ransacked and destroyed the DA headquarters in San Fernando, Pampanga, arrested several people in the office, and killed some of them. I managed to escape," Peregrino Taruc said, "and I ran to a far away barrio. It was then that I began to go underground."[67] Several DA leaders were murdered during the campaign, including the president of the party in Pampanga.[68]

By May the repression's severity prompted a report in a Communist Party publication to conclude that the landlords had decided to destroy the movement completely, first by eliminating its leaders and then its following.[69] Neither carefully prepared appeals by leaders such as Luis Taruc to the Manila Rotary Club and other respectable forums nor angry cablegrams from Mateo del Castillo and others to officials as high as President Harry Truman seemed to bring any relief for the peasantry.

Government officials, meanwhile, became more militant and frequently justified their actions as blows against communism and terrorism. Major Edward Lansdale, who was the chief of the United States military's intelligence branch in the country, alleged to his superiors in March 1946 that Hukbalahap leaders were "Communist-inspired" and "like all true disciples of Karl Marx" believed

> fully in revolution instead of evolution. They have made their boast that once their membership reaches 500,000 their revolution will start. Meanwhile, in the provinces of Pampanga, Nueva Ecija, Tarlac, Bulacan, and Pangasinan, they are establishing or have established a reign of terror. So ironclad is their grip and so feared is their power that the peasants dare not oppose them in many localities. Upon liberation, their members were about 50,000; sources now report some 150,000 tribute-paying members. . . . [The Hukbalahap is now organized] into trigger men, castor oil boys, and just big strong . . . ruffians to keep the more meek in line.[70]

---

[66] *Manila Chronicle,* 8 March 1946, p. 1.

[67] Pergrino Taruc interview, 9 July 1970.

[68] *Manila Chronicle,* 25 April 1946, p. 1.

[69] Leon Gomez, "Laganapang Pananakot ng mga MP sa Kalagitnang Luson" [Widespread Terrorism of MP in Central Luzon], *Ang Organisador,* 30 April 1946, vol. 1, no. 3 (CapDoc, Ag.).

[70] Major Edward G. Lansdale, Chief, Intelligence Branch, Office of AC of S for Int., G-2, Headquarters, AFWESPAC, "The Philippine Presidential Campaign, II," 14 March 1946, p. 10 (Philippine Guerrilla Movements, folder marked Philippines 8000; Federal Records Center, Suitland, Md.).

The government in Manila stationed more Military Police in Central Luzon. In Nueva Ecija, for example, the MPs in February began to double their number, from six companies to twelve companies (two thousand men).[71] In December the United States Army had offered machine guns to police forces in Central Luzon, but Secretary of Interior Montelibano declined. He said the police were supposed to keep peace and order, not kill people. A month later Montelibano changed his mind. He had five thousand machine guns distributed to municipal and provincial police forces in Central Luzon.[72] Despite this increased use of force, presidential candidate Manuel Roxas still campaigned on the issue that the Osmeña administration was friend and protector of "lawless elements" in Central Luzon.[73]

Also during this period, landlords and the government became even more intimate than before. First, jurisdiction over the MPs changed in January from the United States Army to the Commonwealth government's Interior Department. It, in turn, specifically approved what until then had been only informal cooperation between MP detachments and local police forces. The Interior Department requested that local government officials use MPs to maintain "peace and order."[74] As local governments in most cases were in the hands of the landed elites, this arrangement allowed landlords even easier access to the national police than they had known previously. Second, landlords and local governments throughout Central Luzon recruited men, most of whom were USAFFE guerrilla veterans and hacienda guards, to be "civilian guards," who supplemented local police and MP forces. The landlords and government agencies, including the MP headquarters and Department of Interior, paid the civilian guards' salaries and supplied them with weapons.[75]

In late 1945 some villagers in Central Luzon had begun to fight back in order to protect their homes and take retribution against those who abused their families and friends. During the first months of 1946, more people joined them. They became known loosely as the "peasant army." As the number of clashes increased between MP patrols, local police, and USAFFE guerrilla veterans, on the one side, and "armed peasants" and "Huks," on the other, authorities and landlords argued more emphatically that military force was the only way to stop the lawless villagers.

After the April election, repression became worse, resulting in more armed peasants and clashes between them and government forces. In late

[71] *Manila Chronicle,* 26 February 1946, p. 1.

[72] *Manila Chronicle,* 15 December 1945, p. 1, 8 January 1946, p. 3, and 19 January 1946, p. 1.

[73] Ibid., 9 April 1946, p. 2, and 21 April 1946, p. 1.

[74] Ibid., 15 December 1945, p. 1, and 8 January 1946, p. 3.

[75] Macario Peralta, Jr., Lt. Col., to President Roxas, "Subject: Capability of MPC [Military Police Command] to Deal with Huk Problem," 19 August 1946 (Roxas Papers, Bundle 59; National Library, Manila); interview with Jose Crisol, former secretary of defense (President Ramon Magsaysay's administration), Civic Action Program Office, Camp Aguinaldo, Quezon City, 15 December 1969; *Manila Chronicle,* 23 May 1946, p. 1, 13 July 1946, p. 1; *Manila Times,* 7 October 1946, p. 5, and 30 March 1947, p. 24.

April, Governor Mariano Santa Romana of Nueva Ecija resigned from office in despair, saying that the feuds between the Hukbalahap and the USAFFE guerrilla veterans were beyond control. The USAFFE veterans, he said, were "now terrorizing the Huks."[76] By early May, according to one newspaper account, the numerous government troops and their arsenals made Central Luzon look more like an occupied country than a part of the Philippines. Armored cars and jeeps with machine guns patrolled the highways, and MP squads traveled the side roads.[77] The congressmen-elect on the DA ticket cited instance after instance of MPs and civilian guards abusing villagers and warned that unless these forces were removed, bloodshed and civil strife would continue to get worse.

In early May these congressmen-elect submitted a five-point proposal to the government and to representatives of the landlords and USAFFE guerrilla veterans: (1) remove the present MP commanders in Central Luzon; (2) enforce the existing executive order to disband and disarm the civilian guards; (3) remove MPs who served in the government and constabulary during the Japanese occupation; (4) confine MPs in Central Luzon to their barracks long enough to work out a truce between them and Hukbalahap veterans; and (5) prohibit USAFFE veterans and civilian guards from trying to enforce law and order.[78] The lame-duck Osmeña administration accepted parts of this and ordered a "truce." Juan Feleo, del Castillo, the six DA congressmen-elect, and other leaders in the peasant movement then appealed to armed villagers to abide by the truce. Now, they said, the situation would improve. But actually there was no truce. Clashes between government troops and armed peasants, MP raids of barrios, and arrests of peasant leaders continued. According to DA president Jesus Barrera, Secretary Montelibano admitted he had no control over the MPs and was helpless.[79] Senator-elect Tomas Confesor from Iloilo tried, as various peasant spokesmen had, to remind everyone what the basic problem was:

> It is certainly revolting to read that MPs raid barrios and shoot peasants at random. If it is true that armed peasants resort to terroristic practices, the MPs have no certification to resort to the same methods. We could never cure the problems that have produced agrarian rages in Central Luzon by the use of machine guns. The root of the evil that besets Central Luzon lies in the fact that the average peasant under normal conditions does not produce adequate goods from the soil that he tills that would give a decent livelihood. What an average man wants is to produce from his labors adequate income to sustain decently a family.[80]

A big blow for the peasant movement came the last week of May. President Manuel Roxas was sworn into office and the new Congress

[76] *Manila Chronicle,* 1 May 1946, p. 1.
[77] Ibid., 9 May 1946, p. 1.
[78] Ibid.
[79] Ibid., 19 May 1946, p. 1.
[80] Ibid., 14 May 1946, p. 3.

began its first session. The six Central Luzon congressmen-elect on the DA ticket, however, were prohibited from taking their seats. So was another congressman-elect from Bulacan who was known to be sympathetic to the peasant movement. People in San Ricardo, Talavera, were bitter. "Put simply," tenant Eugenio Gomez said, "they threw our congressmen out." Roberto Aspia's explanation was that "Roxas and other collaborators and politicians who were against the PKM threw the DA congressmen out because they saw that little people were getting too much power." Many others in Central Luzon agreed. Cenon Bungay of Pampanga recalled, "People in my municipality were furious after Taruc and Yuson were unseated. It was completely and totally unjust."[81] Benjamin Cunanan in Tarlac said, "After we heard that the DA congressmen were thrown out, our PKM chapter had an emergency meeting. Everybody was angry. Some said this was the last straw. Others were afraid that now Roxas would just turn the MPs completely loose on us."[82]

The House of Representatives and President Roxas alleged that these congressmen had used terror and other illegal means to win. Yet the House never did vote a resolution to suspend these men. A year later, the House committee assigned to study the proposed resolution to suspend was still deliberating. Meanwhile, the Speaker of the House continued to refuse to let these congressmen take their seats. The congressmen from Central Luzon could only protest and deny the charges.

The real reasons for refusing to seat these congressmen, along with three senators who had similar views, were apparently two. First, the Roxas administration and most congressmen and senators simply wanted DA representatives out of their way. As Luis Taruc explained, "The election of six Democratic Alliance congressmen . . . had prevented Roxas from having a two-thirds majority in the lower house, and gave promise of even greater accomplishments for the democratic movement in future elections. The opposition, therefore, became the immediate target of Roxas."[83]

Second, these congressmen, together with the three unseated senators, strongly opposed a controversial proposed treaty between the United States and the Philippines. This was the Philippine Trade Act of 1946, commonly known as the Bell Trade Act. The United States had said, by law, that it would give large amounts of postwar reconstruction money to the Philippines only if its government approved, once the country had become independent, the Bell Trade Act. The major effects of the act would be to open Philippine markets to American manufacturers and grant Americans equal rights with Filipinos—"parity"—to exploit the country's natural resources. The act, in short, would extend for twenty-eight years after the Philippines had political independence all the free trade agreements that had existed between the Philippines and the United States since 1909. In order for the Philippines to give Americans such a favored status,

[81] Bungay interview, 15 July 1970.
[82] Cunanan interview, 11 August 1970.
[83] Taruc, *Born of the People,* pp. 226-227.

however, the country had to amend its brand-new constitution. In order to do that, Congress had to approve such an amendment. Shortly after independence in July 1946, the Congress did just that. The amendment to allow parity passed by one vote. The unseated congressmen and senators, however, could not vote. But, as the Philippine Supreme Court said a year later (by which time it was too late to change what had been done), "If these [ousted] members of Congress had been counted, the affirmative votes in favor of the proposed [parity] amendment [to the Constitution] would have been short the necessary three-fourths vote in either branch of Congress."[84]

The refusal to seat the six DA congressmen, coupled with the Roxas administration's zeal for military force, resulted in more violence and more peasants going underground. There seemed to be no stopping either the MPs, police, and civilian guards or the armed peasant groups. In June, for example, unidentified persons kidnapped two PKM leaders from Central Luzon as they traveled to Manila, where they had planned to meet with other PKM spokesmen and then try to negotiate with President Roxas. They were never heard from again. In a letter sent to Roxas to protest continued abuses, the PKM said that in two months alone, MPs and civilian guards had killed over five hundred peasants and peasant leaders. Three times that number had been imprisoned, tortured, or were missing.[85]

In Malolos, Bulacan, in July, the local MP detachment "raided and demolished our Veterans League office," said Agaton Bulaong, who was the chairman of the Hukbalahap's Veterans League for that province. "Luckily for me, I wasn't there at the time. I was out visiting a barrio. But the soldiers were looking for me and other leaders. After this, I went underground. I joined some other old Huks."[86]

Villagers in San Ricardo blamed most of the escalated violence on the new government. "The MPs and civilian guards just got worse and worse after that [April 1946 election]," said Alfredo Buwan. "Roxas took revenge against people in Central Luzon because they had voted against him." As the situation grew worse, others joined Ruben Sanchez in the "peasant army." Benito Santos, the elderly tenant who had been so discouraged because landlord-tenant relations had continued to deteriorate recalled, "After that [1946] election, more PKM and Hukbalahap began to fight back. I couldn't do it myself, maybe because I was already too old or maybe because I didn't agree. But I sure couldn't blame them. They had to defend themselves."

During June, July, and August, leaders of the PKM, Hukbalahap, DA and PKP met numerous times with Roxas, members of his cabinet such as the new Secretary of Interior Jose C. Zulueta, MP commanders, provincial governors, and representatives of Central Luzon landlords. Juan Feleo,

[84] Alejo Mabanag et al. vs. Jose Lopez Vito et al., Supreme Court Case No. L 1123, 5 March 1947, Philippines, Official Gazette 43 (June 1947): 2081.

[85] Taruc, Born of the People, p. 227.

[86] Bulaong interview, 20 July 1970.

Jesus Lava, Luis Taruc, Mateo del Castillo, Casto Alejandrino, and other spokesmen for the peasant movement tried to negotiate a settlement or at least a truce. "We thought there was still a chance to stop the fighting," recalled Luis Taruc. "From there we hoped a permanent settlement could be discussed seriously."[87] Jesus Lava recalled that the Communist Party's position was that "Parliamentary struggle was still possible. So it agreed to participate in what Roxas called the 'pacification program' to get peace restored in Central Luzon, where things were getting hot with encounters between peasants and the constabulary-civilian guard alliance. The program was aimed, on the one hand, at calming down the peasants, while on the other, at getting the constabulary [meaning MPs] and civilian guards to quit harassing the peasants."[88] Between mid-June and late August, in an on-again, off-again fashion, PKM and Hukbalahap spokesmen traveled in Central Luzon with Military Police officers and government officials. While peasant spokesmen encouraged villagers to set aside their weapons, government officials urged mayors, landlords, and MP commanders to abide by the truce and disband the civilian guards.

Meanwhile, government officials also negotiated with leaders of some of the armed peasant groups. In mid-July, for example, Jose de Leon of Nueva Ecija met with Secretary Zulueta in Talavera. The unseated congressman Jose Cando had arranged the meeting. De Leon had been underground for several weeks and reportedly represented 5,000 armed peasants in the province.[89] Hilario Felipe of Talavera knew about the meeting and learned soon afterward what happened. "De Leon told Zulueta that armed peasants would be willing to register their guns," recalled Felipe. "But he also said that they would do this only if Roxas helped the Hukbalahap be [officially] recognized [as an anti-Japanese guerrilla army] and if Roxas would get rid of the civilian guards."[90]

The "pacification program" and negotiations with leaders of armed peasants, however, failed. Roxas reportedly agreed to abolish the civilian guards, but he had promised this before, too. Within days after the "pacification program" had begun, Juan Feleo, Luis Taruc, and others protested that civilian guard and MP terrorism had already resumed. And it continued through July and August. In mid-August, Juan Feleo, Mateo del Castillo, and Luis Taruc stated in Manila that civilian guards and local government officials were "sabotaging the pacification program."[91]

Meanwhile, government officials and landlords countered that armed peasants continued to attack and refused to abide by the terms of the "pacification program's" truce. President Roxas's office even announced in

---

[87] Luis Taruc interview, 25 February 1970.

[88] Interview with Jesus Lava, Camp Crame, Quezon City, 19 August 1970.

[89] *Manila Chronicle,* 11 July 1946, p. 1.

[90] Hilario Felipe's account is close to what the *Manila Chronicle* reported (11 July 1946, p. 1). The newspaper, however, said that de Leon had agreed to "surrender" and "yield" firearms, rather than just register them, as Felipe said.

[91] *Manila Chronicle,* 17 August 1946, p. 1.

late July that soon the government would start arresting leaders of the Hukbalahap and hold them responsible for the "lawlessness in Central Luzon." That same day, the police detained Casto Alejandrino for questioning. What particularly angered the government and landlords was that the number of armed peasants seemed to be increasing and they refused to surrender their weapons. Although perhaps exaggerated, a military police report to President Roxas in mid-August 1946 estimated that Central Luzon had ten thousand armed "Huks."[92]

Juan Feleo and other spokesmen for the peasant movement countered, however, that "the Huks are cooperating with the administration of President Roxas, but regard surrender of firearms as not included in our agreement with Secretary Zulueta."[93] That agreement, according to spokesmen for the peasantry, included registration of guns, not surrender. The spokesmen also defended the peasants who fought with MPs and civilian guards. If they did this, Taruc said in mid-July, they did so only in self-defense, for they were the ones the MPs and civilian guards were chasing and harrassing. If let alone, he said, the peasants would disband in accordance with the government's policy.[94] In short, to the extent any truce existed during June, July, and August, it was, as Luis Taruc wrote later, "in effect only at the top level, between the government representatives and the peasant leaders. On the level of the fields there was open conflict."[95]

The end of even this weak truce came in late August. It came amid more government threats to escalate the violence. On 24 August 1946, for example, Colonel Mariano N. Castañeda, chief of the Military Police, threatened to use bombs and artillery "against the Huks if they don't behave." "The government," he said, "is not bluffing, and we mean business. We are coming to knock them out quick. The stability of the Republic is being threatened."[96]

On this same day, August 24, Juan Feleo rode with his wife and five other persons through Nueva Ecija toward Manila. They were scheduled to meet Luis Taruc and Casto Alejandrino and then confer with Secretary Zulueta. As Feleo had been in the province on a mission for the "pacification program," several MPs escorted him. When they came to barrio Baluarte in Gapan, very near the Bulacan-Nueva Ecija boundary line, armed men in MP uniforms and riding a command car kidnapped Juan Feleo. He was never seen again alive. In September a newspaper reported that a decapitated body found floating in the Pampanga river was positively identified as Juan Feleo's. Four other bodies found nearby were those of Feleo's companions, who also had been kidnapped. Although no one has ever proved who kidnapped and killed Feleo, it was widely suspected, with supporting circumstantial evidence, that civilian guards,

[92] Lt. Col. Macario Peralta, Jr., to President Roxas, "Capability of the MPC to Deal with the Huk Problem," 19 August 1946.
[93] *Manila Chronicle,* 16 August 1946, p. 1.
[94] *Manila Chronicle,* 20 July 1946, p. 1.
[95] Taruc, *Born of the People,* p. 231.
[96] *Manila Chronicle,* 25 August 1946, p. 1.

under orders from Nueva Ecija and Bulacan landlords and possibly Roxas himself, did it.[97] Thousands of Hukbalahap veterans and PKM participants were sure that these were Feleo's murderers. As one tenant in San Ricardo said, "They killed Feleo like they killed del Rosario and others. Landlords and the soldiers did anything to get their way." Feleo's murder was also the time peasants often cited to mark the beginning of rebellion in Central Luzon.

Feleo's murder ended the "pacification program" even at the top level. Several leading peasant spokesmen, including Luis Taruc and Casto Alejandrino, knew that no peaceful settlement could be achieved now. On 29 August 1946, Taruc sent a letter to President Roxas to say that he was joining the armed peasants:

Dear Mr. President:

The supreme test of your power has come. In your hands rests the destiny of our miserable people and our motherland. . . .

. . . [A]s I write this, your blood-thirsty subordinates are already making an all-out punitive campaign against the peasants. The MPs are shelling barrios and shooting civilians. They are even threatening to use bombs. Suspects they catch (and they just pick up anybody) are subjected to all despicable tortures. Together with the civilian guards, they are virtually in control of all government machinery, conducting a reign of terror worse than the Japs.

The latest report is the kidnapping of Feleo—topping the long list of well-known peasant leaders lost in the same manner, because they clung to the hope that your government would intervene and make democracy survive. Feleo's loss is the most serious sabotage your subordinates have done so far. . . .

The peasants of Central Luzon are loyal to our country and to our Constitution. You know that. They are humble, peaceful, and law-abiding. They do not entertain even the slightest idea of resisting the duly constituted authorities. . . . Now under the guise of crushing lawlessness, the MPs, civilian guards, and some of your provincial and municipal officials have trampled in the dust our Constitution and suppressed every democratic right of the peasants, to crush not lawlessness and banditry, but the vanguard of the patriotic peasant movement, the Hukbalahap veterans and the PKM.

From our three conferences and from your public commitments you gave us sufficient reason to start an earnest campaign of persuading the peasants to have faith and confidence in you. Our demands were very reasonable. And you approved them:

1. Temporary right of the people to keep their firearms in view of their present insecurity. Registration of those firearms to enable the govenment and the community concerned to check up and control their proper handling.

2. Stop MP raids. Civilian guards must be controlled. . . . The constitutional rights of the people must be protected.

[97] *Manila Times,* 26 August 1946, p. 1, 27 August 1946, p. 1, 28 August 1946, p. 1; *Manila Chronicle,* 12 September 1946, p. 1; Juan Feleo, Biographical Information (PF, CapDoc, Ag.); Crisol interview, 15 December 1969; interview with Lazaro Francisco, Cabanatuan, Nueva Ecija, 4 June 1970; and Taruc, *Born of the People,* pp. 236-237.

3. Removal of Governor David of Pampanga, fascist municipal officials and MP officers like Lieutenant Reyes, Captain Bausen of Mexico, Captain Sandang of Magalang, Captain Escalena of Nueva Ecija, Lieutenant Erginio of Bulacan.

4. Put into effect badly needed social welfare projects and agrarian reforms.

But actually before the people could see the concrete and full realization of our understanding, your reactionary subordinates, blood-thirsty MP officers and mercenary guards, sabotaged our efforts. . . . Confused, overwhelmed, and finally giving in to enemies of democracy and progress, you are now reportedly determined to use the mailed fist, the imperialist-fascist method instead . . . .

I respectfully inform you that I believe I will be of more service to our country and to our people and their government if I stay now with the peasants. In spite of every harm and provocation done to them I am still confident I can help guide them in their struggle for democracy. . . .

You have your choice, Mr. President—be a real liberal and a true leader of Filipinos and rest assured of our cooperation. But be an imperialist fascist agent and you will find that there are enough Filipinos who have learned a lot in the last war and who will not give up in peace social gains acquired during that war. . . .

Mr. President, extremists may want you to order the bombing and cannonading of the poor—to kill them by the thousands. They may want hand to dip and feet to wallow in blood to their heartless satisfaction. But they should know that they can never bomb out the people's new-found hopes and convictions— that democracy, freedom and a lasting peace are for all, including the common men who feed the nation when it is starving and fight for it when it is in danger. . . .[98]

[98] Taruc, *Born of the People,* pp. 238-240.

Chapter 5
REBELLION: 1946 - 1948

ROBERTO ASPIA swayed at one end of the long two-man saw. He and his partner were busy cutting a large hardwood log into boards for an addition to the house of Aspia's neighbor. As they pushed and pulled the heavy saw, the men discussed plans for the addition with the house's owner. Walking by, I said, "Good morning." "*Halika*," Aspia called out, smiling broadly and motioning me to come over. "This is how us Huks help each other out." The others laughed as they continued working. Another man, sharpening a saw blade, added, "In the mountains in those days we cut bigger logs than this." Alfredo Buwan, who was the oldest of the five men working there, finished marking the next cut, then took Aspia's place at the saw. Buwan was sixty-five years old, but worked just as vigorously as Aspia and the others, who were all in their early fifties. Aspia took a glass of heavily sweetened coffee and a biscuit that his neighbor's daughter offered to the men. "Our American friend here and I talked about the Huks and other things last week," he informed the others as he squatted down beside me to rest. "One thing I told him was that Huks had to help each other in order to survive."

While I watched the men work, it was hard to imagine them as rebels—as men who joined armed groups and fought battles against government troops. Battles had even been fought near this Talavera barrio of San Ricardo. Now in 1970, men worked peacefully. Down the dusty street women carried laundry to the creek. In the stubble field behind the small house, boys tended several carabaos. A soft breeze rustled the bamboo in the front of the house. Next door a woman tended a fire outside to cook rice for the midday meal, while keeping an eye on her naked two-year-old toddling around the barren yard.

Life had not always been so tranquil in San Ricardo. Even this peaceful appearance was deceptive, for life was hard and far from satisfying for most people. Still, physical danger in 1970 was clearly less than it had been some twenty years before. The Japanese occupation had been upsetting enough. The years that immediately followed seemed equally bad, if not worse. Consequently, reform-oriented peasants in San Ricardo, other barrios in Talavera, and elsewhere in Central Luzon rebelled.

Although some villagers had resorted to guns in late 1945, rebellion did not become widespread in Central Luzon until the second half of 1946— within weeks after the Philippines had become an independent republic. As the government's armed forces and the landlords' civilian guards intensified their campaign against the peasant movement from 1946 through 1948, the revolt grew stronger.

At first it had many names: "the peasants' army," "the army," "the Huks," "People's Army for Democracy," "Hukbo ng Bayang Api ukol sa Demokrasia, Kapayapaan, at Kasaganaan" (Oppressed People's Army for Democracy, Peace, and Prosperity). The one that eventually stuck appeared as early as June 1947 among the rebellion's surviving documents: "Hukbong Mapagpalaya ng Bayan" (HMB; People's Liberation Army).[1] Frequently participants referred to themselves simply as "Huks."

Some villagers joined the HMB's military squadrons. Others fed, clothed, and otherwise supported the guerrilla army through the HMB's underground network of couriers and informants reconstructed from the days of the Hukbalahap resistance. It was a people's army, composed of and supported by villagers in Central Luzon and, to a lesser extent, Southern Luzon. These people believed the HMB expressed what the peasant movement had been demanding for a long time: agrarian reform, justice for those who had been in groups like the PKM and Hukbalahap, and an end to government and landlord repression.

The Rebellion in San Ricardo and Talavera

The turning point for many villagers in San Ricardo was the murder of Juan Feleo in late August 1946.[2] "This was, I'd say, the real beginning of the rebellion," said Roberto Aspia. Alfredo Buwan agreed, then added, "The thinking of lots of people here was, well, if they can kill Feleo, who was so well-known, then there's no hope for others of us in the PKM. The civilian guards can easily bump us off." Before Feleo was kidnapped, five hundred Hukbalahap veterans who had been hiding in the Sierra Madre mountains planned to meet him in Bongabon, a municipality east of Talavera. "They were going to register their weapons, just as Commander [Jose] de Leon had agreed," explained Hilario Felipe, a PKM leader in Talavera. Feleo was to represent them when they met with Military Police (MP) officers. That registration of weapons never took place once people learned about Feleo being kidnapped and killed. "It was certainly bad timing on the government's part," added Felipe. "What it showed us even more than I had believed before was that the soldiers were out of hand. Not even the president [Roxas]

[1] Central Luzon Command (CLC), "Instruction No. _ [illegible] sa Panahon ng Tagulan" [Instruction No. — for the Rainy Season], 15 June 1947 (CapDoc, Ag.).

[2] This account of events and conditions in San Ricardo and elsewhere in Talavera relies heavily on my interviews with residents there in 1970.

could control the soldiers." Felipe said he went "more or less underground" after this in order to hide from government troops and civilian guards. So did many others in Talavera during the next two years.

Battles, Repression, and Economic Hardship
Conditions in San Ricardo between mid-1946 and 1950 were, in the words of one lifelong resident, "just as bad, and in some ways worse, than the Japanese occupation." One serious problem was the fighting between government soldiers and peasant rebels. Jose Cando, the Democratic Alliance (DA) congressman from Nueva Ecija who had been denied his place in Congress, had been trying to resolve the differences between the landlords and tenants when he telegraphed President Roxas on 2 September 1946, one week after Feleo's kidnapping. His message reported the effects of the military on villagers near Talavera:

> I have met responsible Huk leaders. They are, like Feleo, behind you in your pacification campaigns and willing to surrender and register firearms. They deplore recent MP and civilian guard raids. If possible please order those stopped. After Feleo's [kidnapping] incident, Huks who were for surrender and registration numbering thousands left the poblacions and barrios. Leaders need some time to contact and bring them [to] your fold. Shelling and machine gunning of many barrios in Cabanatuan, Aliaga, and San Isidro have dispersed Huks who were for surrender and for registration. Statement from you to allay fears may work wonders. . . .[3]

Roxas's reply to Cando was, "You may assure lawless elements that all activities of MPs may be stopped as soon as they are ready to respect the law and surrender their arms."[4] Around San Ricardo, the military intensified its campaign against Roxas's "lawless elements." Carlos Rivera, the elderly tenant who had once farmed for General Manuel Tinio, said what many San Ricardo residents did: "There were battles around 1946 and 1947 that were as bad as the ones during liberation from the Japanese."
     Soldiers on the government's side included the Military Police (MP), civilian guards, and Philippine army units. They used mortars, machine guns, heavy artillery bombs, and airplanes.
     "There weren't always battles," said one woman in San Ricardo as she recalled those years. "But when they occurred, I took my children and hid. Sometimes we hid for days." The battles in the Talavera vicinity came intermittently. They would occur several days in a row, and then there would be none for weeks or months. In October 1946, for example, a couple of Philippine army infantry units attacked what were reported to be two thousand armed peasants in an area extending from San Jose (north of

---

[3] Cando, to President Roxas, 2 September 1946 (Roxas Papers Bundle 59; National Library, Manila).

[4] President Roxas, to Jose Cando, 2 September 1946 (Roxas Papers, Bundle 59; National Library, Manila).

Talavera) to Laur (east of Talavera). Next, there were a few battles near San Ricardo in November. Then none until January. One tenant farmer remembered particularly well the fighting in January: "My brother was killed. He was in the peasants' army. He was killed in Rizal [a municipality next to Talavera]." In January that year, a Manila newspaper reported four MP companies had fought armed peasants in barrios in and around Cabanatuan. For the remainder of 1947 and 1948, people in San Ricardo remembered several sizable battles. Most of them were in the middle of 1947, late 1947, and early 1948. In May 1947, for example, twenty-one companies began what one newspaper termed "new operations" against armed peasants in Nueva Ecija's southern and central municipalities, including Talavera. The MPs reportedly had surrounded one thousand Huks.[5]

Worse than the battles, from the point of view of people in San Ricardo, was the continuous repression and abuse. "In 1946, 1947, actually the rest of the forties," recalled Ramon Tapang, "civilian guards and the constabulary arrested anyone they wanted, burned houses, took food, and raped. These men were absolutely the worst." Many from Talavera, according to several residents, sat in jail for months, even more than a year, because MPs had accused them of being "communists." A newspaper report, in September 1946, for example, said that jails in Cabiao, San Isidro, Licab, Cabanatuan, and Talavera were overcrowded because three hundred "Huks" had been arrested.[6] "Once in 1947," recalled a villager in San Ricardo, "ten or fifteen civilian guards came to my house when I was out in the fields plowing. They took my chickens, a large bag of rice, and other things. One neighbor tried to stop them. They just beat him up." Several villagers remembered the day in 1947 when civilian guards, with a MP officer in charge, came to San Ricardo and started destroying houses. "They burned nearly all the houses in Kasili [a sitio of San Ricardo]," said the wife of Eugenio Gomez. "They did it because they said we were all PKM, Huk, and communists," said another person.

"People in barrios like San Ricardo were favorite targets of the constabulary and civilian guards," explained Hilario Felipe, "because they had been strong Hukbalahap barrios, had many people in the PKM, and so had the most 'wanted men'." People who had been in these organizations were "wanted," villagers in San Ricardo explained, because the government had declared that the PKM and Hukbalahap were illegal. Although villagers did not agree on the year that the government had declared these groups illegal, most were sure it was 1946 or early 1947. So even though President Roxas did not formally declare these two groups illegal until March 1948, the military and provincial governments had long considered them as such.

[5] *Manila Chronicle,* 11 October 1946, p. 1, 18 October 1946, p. 1, 26 January 1947, p. 1, 23 May 1947, p. 12, 29 May 1947, p. 16.
[6] *Manila Times,* 4 September 1946, p. 1.

Repression was so intense between 1946 and 1950 that many people in San Ricardo swore that the area was under martial law. The enforcers of martial law, peasants explained, were the soldiers and the civilian guards. The leader of the civilian guards in Talavera by this time was Carlos Nocum, the former USAFFE guerrilla who, as Roberto Aspia described him, "wanted to stomp on all us Hukbalahap veterans like you'd stomp on a cockroach."[7]

Civilian guards had an infamous reputation in San Ricardo. So did the Military Police or, as the government renamed this group in 1948, the Philippine Constabulary (PC). [In order to avoid unnecessary confusion, I shall use, from here on, Philippine Constabulary or PC.] People in San Ricardo and other Talavera barrios remembered especially well one particular PC unit. Its name was "Nenita." Its leader was an officer named Napoleon Valeriano. Its symbol was a skull and crossbones. Soldiers wore this insignia on their shirt sleeves and carried flags with it. "It was," said Andres Franco, a tenant during the 1940s, "an accurate badge. The Nenita unit broke bones, killed, and cut off people's heads." Some residents even called Nenita groups the "skull squadrons."

A common description for the Nenita unit was "fierce." "Nenita soldiers were, indeed, fierce," said a man who had been a tenant all his life in San Ricardo. "And I was afraid of them too. My God, they were capable of doing anything!" "Their reputation for being cut-throats was known far and wide," said another person. "When they arrested somebody, they'd take him back to their headquarters and torture him for information about the Huks," said one man. "My brother-in-law, who lived in San Jose, was forced to drink water until his belly was like a ball," said an elderly woman. "Then the soldiers jumped on him! He didn't even know anything to tell." Residents in San Ricardo had numerous accounts of things they had seen or heard about Nenita detachments. Corroborating them was a Talavera historian who cited many occasions on which Nenita soldiers opened fire on barrios thought to have armed peasants, burned houses of suspected rebels or residents helping the rebels, and abused villagers.[8]

Civil war aggravated economic hardship, the third major problem in San Ricardo. Several families left the barrio to find safer places to live—in the bayan of Talavera, in Cabanatuan, even in distant provinces and Manila. "I took my wife and children," explained one man who had been a tenant in San Ricardo until 1947, "and we moved to Manila. We lived with relatives. I worked as a laborer for a construction company. We didn't come back to San Ricardo until about 1955." Those who moved only a short distance, such as to the bayan, often tried to continue their farming by going back and forth between their new homes and their lands in San Ricardo. "It was hard to do this for months and years," said one villager. "Travel wasn't safe in those days. You never knew when the PC or police would stop you, ask for money, even arrest you."

[7] One newspaper report, too, cites "Captain Carlos Nocum" as the leader of the civilian guards in Talavera. *Manila Chronicle,* 2 April 1947, p. 1.

[8] Pagaduan, "Kasaysayan ng Talavera."

The Castro family from San Ricardo, for example, decided they had to leave the barrio in 1947. The family consisted of three households—a father and mother, who still had small children, and two sons and their wives and children. Together they had farmed 10 hectares of fair rice land that the elder Castro had homesteaded in 1917. The land was a few kilometers east of San Ricardo. "The situation here was really bad after the war," the elderly mother, Mrs. Castro, recalled to me. "By 1947 it was unbearable. We couldn't take it anymore." "The worse part," she went on, "was the civilian guards and soldiers. They brought nothing but terror. They'd come and demand maybe five cavans of bigas from each family here," she said as she pointed out the window of the family's three-room wooden house in San Ricardo. "If you didn't give, they'd say you were a Huk and arrest you, take you to the garrison." "They could even beat you or kill you," one of her sons added. All three households moved to a barrio along the national highway and next to the bayan. Mrs. Castro explained, "We figured we'd be safer there." They stayed until 1950. For three years—1947-1949—they planted no crops because they thought it was too dangerous and difficult to go back and forth between the bayan and their land. Nor did they have any steady work. They eked out a living from things like "selling clothes, part-time work, or whatever we could do." They subsisted on a diet of wild grass and rice. "There were eighteen of us altogether," said one son. "We had to watch every grain we had." The family ended up borrowing both cash and rice, "some from rich people in Talavera, some from a government bank" in Cabanatuan.

When they finally could return to San Ricardo to live and plant their land, they had a bad crop the first year. This not only prevented them from starting to repay their debts but forced them to borrow some more. Between 1950 and 1956, they said, "We worked hard to pay off the big debt. We could never get enough ahead." In 1956 they sold their 10 hectares to a large landowner from Batangas for 10,000 pesos. This covered their debt, "with a little left over." The two sons then became tenant farmers. Their father died in the 1960s.

The majority of villagers stayed most of the time in San Ricardo. Rebellion, battles, repression, and fear, however, did disrupt village life and make farming more difficult. One man said, for example, "I couldn't take care of my land so well because sometimes it was very dangerous to go out into the fields." Others told about the difficulties of harvesting crops at precisely the right time for maximum yield. Certainly these years were less fruitful in terms of harvest yields and amount of rice that stayed in the barrio than some years of the Japanese occupation had been.

Landlord-tenant relations also remained bad: disputes over paying agricultural expenses, high interest rates on loans, landlords refusing to give loans, and no enforcement of agrarian laws. Several of the large landlords from Talavera stayed away, although they left behind katiwala and managers to watch the land and collect their share of the harvests. Some of them asked their tenants to pay only 30 percent of the crop for rent, similar to what they had asked during the Japanese occupation while they lived in Manila. This is what Manolo Tinio said he asked of his tenants. When I talked to him one day in 1970, Tinio pointed out the large window of his San Ricardo rest house and said, "This was Huk land; this whole area was controlled by the Huks. There was no way I could stay here to be sure I'd get my 45 percent of the crop." He did not pay any agricultural expenses during this time; thus, he said, "I was only entitled to 30 percent." Some people in San Ricardo who had tenant-farmed for Manolo Tinio during those years confirmed this was so. Others did not; they said that they paid 45 and 50 percent of their crops to Tinio. Still others said that Manolo Tinio had begun to eject tenants and to use tractors and wage laborers instead. Manolo Tinio, however, said that he did not begin using machinery and wage laborers until 1952, after things had "quieted down here."

Vivencio Tinio, Manolo's younger brother, however, acknowledged, as several people in San Ricardo had told me, that he began to use machinery and wage laborers in the late 1940s. Part of the 450 hectares in San Ricardo Vivencio Tinio had inherited from his father, General Manuel Tinio, included about 150 hectares which were not yet planted in palay after World War II. One chunk of this land was 100 hectares, which twenty *buwisan* (leasehold) tenants and their families used. They paid Vivencio Tinio about 60 pesos per year; in return they kept all the vegetables and fruits they could grow. But Vivencio Tinio decided to convert that land into a "mechanized farm." "I wanted to put the land to good use," explained Tinio, "and I figured mechanized farming was the best way."[9] Hilario Felipe of Talavera recalled that Vivencio Tinio was "one of the first landlords in this area to mechanize. But I know there were others in Nueva Ecija about this time, too." Using bulldozers and wage laborers, Vivencio Tinio had the land cleared of shrubs, trees, and gardens, and then turned into irrigated palay fields. One result was that twenty tenant families had to find someplace else to farm. Another result was the permanent reduction of the amount of land that villagers could farm. This aggravated the already serious problem of insufficient land for the number of families who wanted to farm.

Many tenants objected to things that landlords or the katiwala and managers did which violated, in their view, their contracts or were otherwise unjust. They even protested against the mechanization of farming. But repression and inaccessible government officials made dissent in the late 1940s and early 1950s even more difficult than before. The PKM and other peasant organizations, which before had acted in the open, now were "illegal" in the government eyes. Peasants had to protest in less obvious ways. The main way to voice discontent and to reinforce others who were similarly angry was to join or support the HMB.

Rebellion: The HMB

Perhaps above everything else, the explosion of the agrarian unrest into rebellion in and around San Ricardo during the second half of the 1940s

---

[9] Interview with Vivencio Tinio, Quezon City, 15 November 1970.

demonstrated the degree to which landlord-tenant relations had deteriorated. As in the past the large landowners in Talavera called on their armed
men—civilian guards—and the Philippine Constabulary to enforce their
rules. But unlike the 1930s, now peasants, too, had an army: the HMB
guerrillas. The sides were therefore a little more even.

As Manolo Tinio said, there were times between late 1946 and the early
1950s when landlords could not safely venture into many parts of Talavera
unless they brought a small army with them. One tenant in San Ricardo
said about those years, "The HMB did protect people against terrorism
and unscrupulous landlords—at least as best they could." Several people
credited armed peasants from San Ricardo and surrounding villages with
helping them to plant and harvest their rice in 1947 and 1948. "They helped
with the actual planting," said one elderly tenant farmer, "and others stood
guard, watching out for any civilian guards and PC who might be looking
for PKM people." Other people cited 1949 as a year the peasant army
helped them harvest their rice before landlords took it all; still others said
1950.

Partly because of the rebellious situation and the peasants' army, many
tenants in San Ricardo were also able to keep a little more of what they did
grow than they otherwise would have been able to. Just as villagers had to
be wary of civilian guards and the PC, so, too, landlords, their katiwala,
and their managers had to be wary of peasants who were armed. This
meant less supervision and scrutiny, thus sometimes allowing tenants to
take more of the crop. Manolo Tinio complained, for example, that his
katiwala, who was supposed to supervise and collect the rent in his absence
during these years, was "a 'yes' man for the tenants." "He was scared of
them," Tinio explained. "He did whatever they wanted. That's one reason I
got only 10 or 20 percent of the harvest instead of 30." One tenant said that
Tinio's katiwala was actually part of the rebellion's underground government. Villagers in San Ricardo did not consider it cheating to take more
rice. As one person told me: "I took only what I was entitled to." Another
tenant, whose landlord had 100 hectares in San Ricardo and an adjoining
barrio, said that he was able to keep 60 percent of his harvest "because of
the HMB." This, he went on, "was actually the law. But before, my
landowner didn't follow the law; he took 50 percent, sometimes more."

The HMB's control in San Ricardo and the protection the guerrilla army
could provide, however, was limited. The barrio was not a "liberated area"
of the sort found in Vietnam and China during their peasant-based
revolutions in the 1940s. The peasant army in Talavera was unable to
prevent all civilian guards and PC detachments from coming into San
Ricardo. Nor could it stop Vivencio Tinio from ejecting several peasant
families from his land and commencing to turn the land into a mechanized
farm. It did force him, however, to hire armed guards from another
province to watch over his workers, and the rebellious conditions did slow
down the conversion of his land to mechanization. Nor could the peasant
army prevent all landlords in the area from taking more than their share of
the annual harvests. In short, peasants could prevent the intrusions of

landlords or their representatives sometimes and in some places but not all the time in all places.

During the height of the revolt in Talavera, between 1946 and 1950, threats, counterthreats, fears, and apprehensions frequently led to tacit understandings between tenants and landlords and kept their respective armed groups from fighting over harvests. Tenants also usually gave landlords what they considered a fair share even when they had the opportunity to take the entire harvest. When tacit understanding failed, however, showdowns occurred. In a sitio of San Ricardo, for example, a newspaper account said that two Huks and one civilian guard were killed in December 1946 during a fight over newly harvested palay on Manolo Tinio's land.[10] Such clashes often punctuated the harvest season.

To San Ricardo residents, the HMB also meant "Huk justice." As one tenant described this, "The Huks caught, tried, and punished carabao thieves, rapists, and murderers. This made San Ricardo a safer place for people to farm their fields and live. The government wasn't able to stop these things." Another man said in this connection, "The Huks caught those criminal civilian guards, even PC soldiers." And people recalled at least one occasion when Huk justice fell on a landlord in Talavera. HMB soldiers killed him, not so much because of his bad practices with his tenants, but because he employed the meanest civilian guards in the area. No one else protected them against banditry and injustices, so villagers protected themselves.

Stated in terms of issues, peasants in San Ricardo said that the HMB "fought on the side of the little people, the poor people, and against the big people and the soldiers"; it wanted "better conditions for the peasants, a larger share of the harvest for them"; it wanted "landlords to be fair"; it wanted "peasants to have their own organizations"; it wanted "the Hukbalahap to be recognized for what it did against the Japanese." In addition, the HMB wanted to "reform the government." This had various meanings among residents in San Ricardo, but generally it meant to make people more equal. Although this would not have required abolishing the tenancy system and redistributing land, it would have meant having a government that assured peasants free elections and economic and social security. "We wanted the landlords or the government to guarantee us enough to eat and a roof over our heads," said one tenant who aptly summarized what many others had stated. To "reform the government" also meant to "stop the civilian guards and PC from beating up my family" and "let the DA congressmen hold office." All these were the foremost issues that gave meaning to the name "People's Liberation Army"—liberation from opression and repression.

As far as residents of San Ricardo were concerned, the rebellion did not advocate radical changes. The issues and problems involved were as recent as the PKM and Democratic Alliance election campaign of 1946 and as old as tenants' strikes in the 1930s. Nor was rebellion the means that even those in the guerrilla army itself would have preferred. "I didn't want to fight for

[10] *Manila Chronicle,* 13 December 1946, p. 5.

my life and my share of the harvest," said Andres Franco. "These bastards—landlords, civilian guards, soldiers—they all made me take up a gun." His sentiments echoed those of other villagers who joined or supported the rebellion. Peasants wanted justice and at least the security of a subsistence living. They wanted what many thought the traditional landlord-tenant relationship had guaranteed years ago.

What is more, according to former HMB guerrillas like Franco, Aspia, Felipe, and Sanchez, peasants thought the revolt would last only a short time. They expected the authorities to reconsider the major issues, get rid of the civilian guards, and make landlords treat tenants fairly. Roberto Aspia said, for example, "I went underground in 1946. The next year I was in the guerrillas again. But it wasn't like during the Japanese occupation. We weren't against the government. We wanted reforms, true. But so did the PKM. We were fighting to save our lives. I didn't figure I'd have to do this for years and years. Just until the government understood this."

The HMB's organization in San Ricardo was similar to the Hukbalahap's. It was both an underground government and a guerrilla army. The underground government, like the Hukbalahap resistance, included villagers who were responsible for gathering food, clothing, and intelligence information for the guerilla army and who kept in contact with other underground governments in the municipality. And there was a leadership group for Talavera as a whole.

The HMB guerrilla army in the vicinity of Talavera included men and a few women from San Ricardo and other barrios. Between 1946 and late 1948, the area supported two squadrons, each divided into several squads, just as the Hukbalahap resistance army had been. For a while, one squadron was known as "squadron 8," the same as the Hukbalahap squadron in Talavera during the Japanese occupation. According to Roberto Aspia, the number of HMB guerrillas during these years in the Talavera area was "maybe two hundred to three hundred." Aspia and other former HMB guerrillas in San Ricardo also made clear that they were not always "in the field or in the mountains." "We went back and forth, between our work and families in the barrio and our duties as guerrillas in the field." said Ruben Sanchez, who had joined the peasants' army in February 1946, one of the first in San Ricardo to do so. HMB guerrillas, said another former rebel, were "sometimes here in San Ricardo, maybe working or helping their neighbors, and sometimes on operations against government soldiers, and sometimes at a mountain camp" in the Sierra Madres to the east.

The guerrillas from San Ricardo and other parts of Nueva Ecija started to build mountain camps in 1947. "They were places to run to for hideouts when it was too 'hot' in the barrio or when operations were too dangerous," explained Roberto Aspia. "Ours wasn't in the same place all those years. We moved it around." The camps included makeshift buildings and "sometimes vegetable gardens," said Sanchez.

The HMB guerrillas' reputation was good. People in San Ricardo recalled the guerrillas as "decent men," "they were polite," "they helped us." No one complained that the HMB in the Talavera area forced others to join them or forced residents to contribute food. Several specifically said that the guerrillas did not do this because, as one tenant explained, "the guerrillas were the same as us—peasants, little people." Some residents, however, did say that there were villagers who gave food when guerrillas asked, less out of support for the guerrillas and more out of fear that the guerrillas might hurt them or conclude they were against the HMB. But, as one elderly tenant said, "I never heard of Huks actually forcing people to give or threatening them."

Judging from villagers' conversations, nearly everyone in San Ricardo was implicated in the HMB, if only by virtue of having relatives who were either in the underground or in the guerrilla army itself. And no one in San Ricardo openly supported the landlords, civilian guards, or PC. Not even Manolo Tinio's katiwala did that. If there were any residents who sided with the local elites, they probably moved to Talavera's bayan or Cabanatuan or kept their sentiments private. The village was too intimate with the rebellion to tolerate much internal opposition to it. There were, however, different degrees of support for the HMB.

First, some people participated directly in the underground government or the guerrilla army. Those in this category frequently had been Hukbalahap veterans or PKM members. In many cases, too, they joined the HMB to avenge the death or mistreatment of a relative or close friend by the PC or civilian guards. People in the guerrilla army tended to be younger than activists in the underground; they were generally in their twenties and thirties, such as Roberto Aspia, Ruben Sanchez, and Hilario Felipe. But there were exceptions, such as Alfredo Buwan, a Hukbalahap veteran who joined the peasant army in late 1946 when he was in his fifties.

Two additional men illustrate the type of person active in the HMB. Jose Sulit joined the HMB guerrilla army in 1947. At the time he was a twenty-four-year-old tenant farmer for a landowner who had 60 hectares in San Ricardo and another barrio. Sulit said he had been active "a little" in the Hukbalahap before. When asked why he had joined the HMB, he replied: "What would you do if someone killed your brother and there was no way to get justice done? And if the murderers were government soldiers—the PC? This is what happened to me. That's when I joined. After all, if the law is killing people, especially your relatives, where else can you turn?" Andres Santiago was in his late thirties when he took the job that Ramon Tapang had had during the Hukbalahap resistance. Although Tapang helped Santiago, he did not want to be responsible again for arranging supplies for the guerrillas. Like Tapang, Santiago also had been in the Hukbalahap underground. He wanted to be in the HMB, he explained, "because so many Hukbalahap veterans were being killed and going underground. Another thing, the HMB was like the PKM, which I was in. It wanted to get decent ways so peasants could borrow without paying interest rates that were so damn high. And it wanted other things so peasants could live better."

A second type of supporter was those villagers who did not participate directly in the HMB but helped it by contributing food and supplies that the underground network collected for the HMB. An illustration here is Tomas Basa, who was an agricultural laborer during the 1940s. He had relatives who were in the HMB, he said, "but I never was, actually. I gave food and things to the Huks, and didn't mind doing it when my wife and I had some to spare. But I didn't want to get deeply involved. Maybe I was just scared of getting killed or being arrested."

A third category was people who felt, in the words of one tenant in San Ricardo, "caught in the middle between the Huk guerrillas and the PC. I just tried to keep a balance between the two. I gave rice to guerrillas when I was asked. But when the PC came asking questions, I answered as truthfully as I could without getting in trouble with either them or the guerrillas." This man was a tenant for a small landowner with whom, he said, "I had good relations. He was a good man." And he had not been active in the Hukbalahap or other peasant organizations. Consequently, he had no strong motivation to join or enthusiastically support the rebellion. Another individual in this category was Carlos Rivera, the man who had been a tenant for General Manuel Tinio many years before. He had nothing bad to say about the HMB during the first years of the rebellion, but neither did he have anything strong to say on its behalf. "I was just praying for the day everyone would quit killing each other," he said. "I know the Huks were little people, like me, but I just didn't want to become entangled in it all." He had managed to avoid becoming involved in previous peasant movement activities, and by the late 1940s he had even less reason to be part of the rebellion. He was sixty-seven years old, he was no longer a tenant, and had begun to purchase half a hectare of land not far from the bridge in San Ricardo. "I was buying it from the bank in Cabanatuan," he said, and then added, "I'm still paying for it." He grew vegetables and bananas, some of which he and his wife ate. They sold the remainder in the bayan and in Cabanatuan. Most people in this category had never been active in the peasant movement partly because their relations with landlords were still tolerable or they had no strong grievances against civilian guards, the PC, or government. Some may have wanted to refuse any help to the HMB even when asked but felt too intimidated by the village's general support to be candid. They went along when they had to.

Exactly how large each of these three categories of HMB was is unknown. From 1946 through 1948, the majority in San Ricardo were in the first two. The situation did change, however, during the years discussed in the next chapter.

The HMB in Central Luzon

While the rebellion grew in San Ricardo, it also grew in Central Luzon. Its development showed that the peasant rebellion was one more phase in the Central Luzon peasantry's prolonged struggle. Peasants resorted to organized violence to pursue basically the same objectives that had been at issue for years and to defend themselves against government and landlord soldiers. But even as they rebelled, Huk participants and leaders sought legal recourse.

Reluctant Rebels

After Silvestre Liwanag, the Hukbalahap guerrilla commander in western Pampanga, had escaped from the San Fernando prison in March 1945, he stayed on the run. The American Counter-Intelligence Corps (CIC), he explained, "was scouting the provinces for me. I had to keep going from town to town, from barrio to barrio."[11] By early 1946, Liwanag said, "I was back again in the mountains along the Zambales-Pampanga border." With him were "more than three hundred other Hukbalahap companions." As Liwanag had been their commander during the Japanese occupation, he assumed the same role again. He thought that he and these men were the first Hukbalahap veterans to reassemble in order to defend themselves against what he called "the repressive measures of the American-Philippine government."

Liwanag and his companions, however, were not alone. For example, Benjamin Cunanan said that he and several other Hukbalahap veterans from his home barrio in Concepcion, Tarlac, regrouped after "the CIC and the MPs burned down our barrio in revenge against the people there for having had anything to do with the Hukbalahap."[12] By mid-1946, Cunanan's group numbered about forty men. They appointed him their commander. In eastern Laguna, in the vicinity of Longos, Hukbalahap veterans had been regrouping in mountain hideouts since late 1945. Among them was Pedro Villegas, even though he and other Hukbalahap veterans there had been granted official recognition. That recognition failed to spare them from the constabulary's abuses. By mid-1946, Villegas was the leader of two hundred men who hid in the mountains of Laguna and Quezon provinces.[13]

As a consequence of the intense repression prior to and after the April 1946 national election, several other bands of armed peasants, frequently led by Hukbalahap veteran commanders, dotted Central Luzon and parts of Southern Luzon by mid-1946. "Our very lives were at stake," said Cenon Bungay of San Simon, Pampanga, when he explained why he and eight other Hukbalahap veterans and PKM members from his area resorted to guns. "What would you do? We had no choice but to go underground."[14] Alejandro Briones, a Hukbalahap veteran commander in Nueva Ecija,

---

[11] Interview with Silvestre Liwanag, Camp Crame, Quezon City, 21 July 1970.

[12] Interview with Benjamin Cunanan, Camp Crame, Quezon City, 11 August 1970.

[13] "Ulat ng SLRC sa PB ng PKP" [Report of the Southern Luzon Regional Committee to the Politburo of the PKP], 13 August 1945 (CapDoc, Ag.); Jose Magsikap, "Maikling Kasaysayan ng HMB sa Timog Luson" [A Short History of the HMB in Southern Luzon], *Mapagpalaya*, 29 March 1950, vol. 2, no. 22 (Politburo Exh. C2; CFI, Manila); and "History of Reco 4," circa 1953 (CapDoc, Ag.). *Mapagpalaya* [Liberator], was a HMB publication in the 1950s.

[14] Interview with Cenon Bungay, Camp Crame, Quezon City, 15 July 1970.

wrote that after the April elections, "President Roxas's attacks" drove him and other PKM and Democratic Alliance members "into the hills."[15] A "spontaneous peasant uprising" was growing rapidly, said Peregrino Taruc about this period.[16] What the uprising needed was a degree of coordination and central leadership.

In June 1946, several men met in barrio Mandili in Candaba, Pampanga to make a contingency plan. Casto Alejandrino, the former vice-commander of the Hukbalahap's general headquarters, said, "Government repression was forcing some kind of organization for self-defense."[17] The prevailing mood at the meeting was that government and landed elite assaults would continue and that the "pacification program" would fail, as it already was beginning to do. All twenty men who attended the meeting were Hukbalahap veterans. Some, said Alejandrino, were also "[Communist] Party members"; others, he said, "were not, but they were military men." Those attending who are known to me were Agaton Bulaong (from Bulacan), Tomas Calma (Pampanga), Jose de Leon (Nueva Ecija), Silvestre Liwanag (Pampanga), Peregrino Taruc (Pampanga), Pedro Villegas (Laguna), Mariano Franco (Nueva Ecija), Sergio Cayanan (Pampanga), Juan Feleo (Nueva Ecija), Luis Taruc (Pampanga), and Casto Alejandrino (Pampanga). At least the first six were already underground and leading armed groups by this time.

The plan resulting from the June meeting divided the area with armed peasant groups into two zones, each with its own command—the Central Luzon Command (CLC) for the region where the rebellion was concentrated and the Southern Luzon Command (SLC) for the region where the number of armed peasants was small but where the mountainous terrain was excellent for guerrilla hideouts. The meeting also selected Luis Taruc to be the commander-in-chief and Casto Alejandrino to be the vice-commander-in-chief, the same positions these two men held in the Hukbalahap resistance army. Taruc, Alejandrino, and several others at the meeting did not join the armed peasants, however, until after Feleo's murder and the collapse of the "pacification program."

Taruc and Alejandrino exemplified the continuity between the rebellion and earlier years of the peasant movement. Another example was Tomas Calma. In 1942, Calma had joined the Hukbalahap guerrillas, he said, "for the purpose of fighting the Japanese."[18] He was twenty-three years old then, one of seven children of a poor family in San Luis, Pampanga. One of his sisters had also been in the Hukbalahap; she was killed in battle. In the Hukbalahap, Calma was first a squadron member, then a squadron commander, and eventually a commander of several squadrons in Pam-

[15] Alejandro Briones, "My Biography Since 1945—September 17, 1951" (PF, CapDoc, Ag.).

[16] Interview with Peregrino Taruc, Camp Crame, Quezon City, 9 July 1970.

[17] Interview with Casto Alejandrino, Camp Crame, Quezon City, 16 July 1970. Also see Taruc, *Born of the People*, pp. 228-231.

[18] Tomas Calma, Sworn Statement to the Philippine Constabulary, 26 April 1948 (PF, CapDoc, Ag.). Other information in this account of Calma's background comes from documents found in a folder on him: Biographical Information (PF, CapDoc, Ag.).

panga. When the United States Sixth Army arrived in Central Luzon, Calma and his squadrons helped it liberate Manila. Afterward, the Americans disarmed and arrested many of his men, despite Calma's protests. After the Japanese occupation, he worked as a mechanic for a bus company in San Luis. He joined a labor union that was affiliated with the Congress of Labor Organizations (CLO) and apparently was active in the Democratic Alliance during the 1946 election campaign. Meanwhile, the harassment of Hukbalahap veterans had been increasing. It finally forced many veterans in the area, including Calma, to hide. Eventually, Calma explained, the "Huks had to start up again . . . to fight for the rights and justices of the masses."

Certainly not all PKM participants or Hukbalahap veterans joined the rebellion or even enthusiastically supported it. Some, according to one Central Luzon Command report in June 1947, were too frightened. Others even became "puppets" of the constabulary and civilian guards. Still others, reported Jose de Leon from Nueva Ecija in December 1946, simply abandoned the movement in order to avoid being implicated.[19] Repression took its toll. It prompted many who had been active in the peasant movement to quit and stay away from the HMB.

More numerous, however, were the PKM members and Hukbalahap veterans who did support and join the revolt. A report from the movement in Nueva Ecija in October 1947, for example, claimed that even though civilian guard and police attacks had caused despair and fear among PKM members and others, 95 percent of them believed in the peasant movement's objectives and helped the HMB. And Agaton Bulaong spoke for several Huk leaders when he said, as he described how the HMB grew between 1946 and 1948: "Joining us all the time were members of the PKM and other progressive groups being suppressed."[20]

In order to join or enthusiastically support the rebellion, however, people had to have, as Luis Taruc said, "a purpose. They had to have reasons, something to fight for."[21] Taruc then summarized those purposes: "People in the barrios, the nonintellectual type of Huk, joined because they had causes—like agrarian reform, government reform, anti-repression, recognition of the Hukbalahap—and, frequently, because they simply had to defend themselves, their very lives against repression." Important to many in the guerrilla army, said Peregrino Taruc about this period, "were personal reasons." Most people who joined, he said, wanted revenge "for the killing or bad treatment or abuses of a relative or close friend."[22] Some joined, he said, because of personal attachments to others in the HMB, such

[19] CLC, "Instruction," 15 June 1947; and Leon [Jose de Leon], to Mga Kasama [Companions], 28 December 1946 (CapDoc, Ag.).

[20] Nueva Ecija Provincial Committee, "Ulat Pang-Politika Bilang 7" [Political Report Number 7], 10 October 1947 (CapDoc, Ag.); and interview with Agaton Bulaong, Camp Crame, Quezon City, 20 July 1970.

[21] Interview with Luis Taruc, Quezon City, 27 January 1970.

[22] Interview with Peregrino Taruc, Camp Crame, Quezon City, 8 July 1970.

as former companions in peasant organizations and the Hukbalahap or their former Hukbalahap commanders. But, said Agaton Bulaong, "agrarian reform and getting rid of the civilian guards were all mixed together with other reasons, like revenge or some other personal thing. It's hard to separate them out. After all, most of the people had been in the peasant movement for a long time."[23]

Indicative of the major concerns of the HMB were the five "minimum terms of peace" that Luis Taruc outlined for a journalist in February 1947:

1. The immediate enforcement of the bill of rights, especially the right to assemble, freedom from arbitrary arrest, ending of cruel and unjust punishment, trial by unprejudiced judges.

2. Dismissal of all charges against Huks, MPs, and civilian guards alike growing out of the past five months. All that happened during those hot days should be forgotten. Release all political prisoners.

3. Replacement of fascist-minded officials in municipal and provincial governments and [the] Municipal Police Command in the provinces affected by the agrarian unrest.

4. Restoration of all Democratic Alliance congressmen to their seats.

5. Implementation of President Roxas's land reform program beginning with a foolproof 70-30 crop distribution law and leading toward eventual abolition of tenancy.[24]

In short, the rebels sought the objectives that the peasant movement had wanted before. The immediate goal was to stop the repression. Only then could the peasant movement, through its leaders at local and national levels, work with landlords and government officials to resolve agrarian problems. These problems covered the range of long-standing peasant complaints— from landlords who took too much of the harvests and failed to pay their share of the expenses, to landlords who evicted tenants without just cause and government officials who were partial to the landed elites' interests. Because these problems were so persistent and seemed to some people unresolvable, a few leaders in the peasant movement, in Congress, and even in the Roxas administration began to talk about ending the tenancy system altogether. Taruc noted this in his peace proposal. The HMB did not emphasize, however, the abolition of tenancy. Taruc himself said, "Land redistribution and ending tenancy were not central for most people [in the rebellion]. People just wanted small changes—a bigger share of the crop and fair treatment so they and their families could live easier."[25]

HMB guerrillas believed that their military actions were mainly defensive. "We formed the HMB in order to defend ourselves against the government's forces," explained Silvestre Liwanag.[26] Persons attending the

[23] Bulaong interview, 20 July 1970.
[24] *Manila Chronicle*, 7 February 1947, p. 1.
[25] Luis Taruc interview, 27 January 1970.
[26] Liwanag interview, 21 July 1970.

meeting in Candaba, Pampanga, in June 1946 agreed that the military policy of the reconstituted guerrilla army would be defensive rather than offensive. Writing later about this decision, Luis Taruc said, "We decided that if assaults on the people continued, we would reassemble on a purely defensive basis, avoid encounters and fight only when cornered and attacked, or when the people were being persecuted to the point where they would ask protection from the squadrons."[27] For over two years, between 1946 and 1949, Agaton Bulaong said, "We [in the guerrilla army] sort of lay low, had a wait-and-see outlook, seeking only self-defense."[28] "We never had an overall plan or strategy regarding military action in those years, between 1946 and 1949 or '50," Luis Taruc said. "It was mostly a matter of self-defense."[29] Cenon Bungay, who had become an HMB squadron leader, explained that the Huks maintained a defensive stance because "armed overthrow of the government wasn't our objective."[30]

The leadership of the rebellion also continued to use legal channels. As early as September 1946, only a few weeks after Juan Feleo had been killed, Jose de Leon, Casto Alejandrino, and other leaders queried government officials about a peace proposal based on the peasants' demands of May and June when the "pacification program" had begun. Between then and mid-1948, HMB leaders continued to put out feelers and make suggestions for a negotiated peace.

This desire to bargain rather than fight with the government prompted the HMB's "expansion program." Cenon Bungay from San Simon, Pampanga, described its purpose:

In September or October 1946, I went to a meeting in Bulacan. Luis Taruc was in charge. The purpose was to discuss this expansion program and make assignments. The decision, I think, to have an expansion had already been made by the top leaders before the meeting. Anyway, I was assigned to lead an expansion group to Batangas in 1947. . . . The objective was to build the movement, to increase its strength so it could bargain with the government from a better position. . . . Guns were for self-defense.[31]

Luis Taruc stated, "We wanted to be on the offensive politically, but also have a military defense in order to protect ourselves while doing political organizing."[32] Although this organizing focused on Central Luzon, HMB leaders anticipated that the movement could enjoy support in Southern Luzon and perhaps elsewhere. They reasoned that the peasant movement in Central Luzon could expand now, even though it had not been able to before, because social and economic conditions elsewhere were also bad, because

[27] Taruc, *Born of the People*, p. 229.
[28] Bulaong interview, 20 July 1970.
[29] Luis Taruc interview, 27 January 1970.
[30] Bungay interview, 15 July 1970.
[31] Ibid.
[32] Interview with Luis Taruc, Quezon City, 25 February 1970.

villagers in Southern Luzon also disliked President Roxas and the Liberal Party government, and because guerrillas from Central Luzon could help to protect those who wanted to organize.[33] If the rebellion had popular support beyond Central Luzon, its leaders believed, the government surely could no longer ignore the need for reforms and the HMB could bargain from a position of greater political strength than even the PKM had known.

Also indicative of the peasant movement's desire to settle disputes peaceably was the resurgence of PKM chapters in Central Luzon whenever repression let up long enough for peasants to feel sufficiently free. According to the few surviving peasant movement documents from this period, both local PKM leaders and the national PKM president, Mateo del Castillo, encouraged local chapters to rebuild and attempt to use legal channels.[34] Similarly, the HMB leaders in the municipalities and barrios of Central Luzon tried, as Cenon Bungay said about his work in Pampanga, "to help tenants by talking to their landlords who weren't following the tenancy agreements, who weren't implementing the 60-40 or 70-30 share systems. We Huks talked to the landlords and asked that tenants be given what was due them. Sometimes we threatened the landlords, too, but usually not because terror usually doesn't work."[35]

Finally, the HMB supported candidates for mayor and governor in the November 1947 local elections. Some of the candidates with HMB support ran on a Democratic Alliance ticket; others were on the Nacionalista ticket. None was specifically nominated by the HMB. The Democratic Alliance organization by this time was far weaker than it had been in 1946. And campaigning by local peasant leaders on behalf of favored candidates was even more difficult than in 1946. Moreover, according to Alfredo Saulo, who ran for—and lost—a seat on the Provincial Board in Nueva Ecija as a Democratic Alliance nominee, there was "so much ballot-box stuffing and other cheating by the opposition" that even if the movement's candidates could "win the vote, they still lost the election."[36] Few peasant movement candidates in Central Luzon won that year.

HMB leaders also endorsed a "no" vote on the March 1947 plebiscite that would amend the Philippine Constitution to allow "parity rights" for

---

[33] Lupong Pambansa ng PKM [National Committee of the PKM], "Palawakin ang Kilusang Magbubukid" [Expand the Peasant Movement], October 1946 (CapDoc, Ag.); Felipe [Luis Taruc], to Eureku, circa late 1946 or early 1947 (PF-Luis Taruc, CapDoc, Ag.); and interview with Jesus Lava, Camp Crame, Quezon City, 12 August 1970.

[34] Madrigal, "PKM, Ulat Para sa Kalagayan nang Distrito No. 1" [PKM, Report on the Situation in District No. 1], Nueva Ecija, 29 December 1947 (CapDoc, Ag.); Conrado Villapando [Mateo del Castillo], Lupong Pamunuang Pambansa [National Executive Committee of the PKM], to Lupong Pang-Lalawigan [Provincial Committee of PKM], Tarlac, 7 January 1947 (CapDoc, Ag.); and Pambansang Kaisahan ng mga Magbubukid [PKM], Manila, "Kapasiyahang Pinagtibay ng Bagong Lupong Tagapagpaganap ng LPP ngayong ika-4 ng Enero 1948" [Resolutions Passed by the New Executive Committee of the National Committee on 4 January 1948] (CapDoc, Ag.).

[35] Bungay interview, 15 July 1970.

[36] Interview with Alfredo Saulo, Quezon City, 20 January 1970.

Americans. The DA congressmen-elect's opposition to "parity" in 1946 had been one reason why they were not permitted into Congress. Now, a year later, these unseated DA congressmen and several prominent nationalists in Philippine politics urged voters to reject the proposed amendment. It apparently aroused little interest, however, among most villagers in Central Luzon. The issues of imperialism and nationalism alone were not salient for them. Moreover, repression and other inequalities made an effective campaign against the amendment impossible. It therefore passed easily. According to official totals, only 11 percent of all Filipino voters voted "no." In Central Luzon provinces, the percentages opposed ranged from 10 percent in Pampanga to 34 in Bulacan.[37]

The Growth of the Rebellion

In both size and organizational strength, the peasant rebellion grew between 1946 and late 1948. The number of guerrilla soldiers in Silvestre Liwanag's command, for example, increased from three hundred in mid-1946 to one thousand later that year.[38] Benjamin Cunanan in Concepcion, Tarlac, led forty men in mid-1946; two years later his command had grown to four hundred and fifty guerrillas. Cenon Bungay had one hundred men in his squadron in the San Simon, Pampanga, area by 1947. Ninety of them went with him on the expansion mission to Batangas, where their number increased to two hundred by 1949. The small number he had left behind in San Simon, meanwhile, grew again to one hundred and twenty-five. Agaton Bulaong's command in Bulacan began with a small number and increased to "between eight hundred and nine hundred" by early 1949. In Laguna, according to a report from a Huk commander there, the number of rebel guerrillas increased from two hundred to four hundred in 1946. Two years later, another HMB document said, the number was greater by "several-fold."

The two top leaders of the rebellion's army agreed that the number did increase rapidly, although they disagreed on the figure. Casto Alejandrino said there were about five thousand armed persons by 1948; Luis Taruc said about ten thousand.[39] Leaders had difficulty estimating the number partly because members went back and forth between underground barrio organizations and armed guerrilla groups.

Following the contours of the Hukbalahap that had preceded it, the HMB established methods to gather intelligence information, pass com-

---

[37] Plebiscite returns, by province and city, are in Kerkvliet, "Peasant Rebellion," pp. 427-428.

[38] The examples cited in this paragraph come from the following: Liwanag interview, 21 July 1970; Melencio Guevara, Sworn Statement to the Philippine Constabulary, 18 July 1960 (CapDoc, Cr.); Cunanan interview, 11 August 1970; Bungay interview, 15 July 1970; Bulaong interview, 20 July 1970; Commander Albert Ross, Hukbo Bating "B," "Kalagayan pang-Politika" [The Political Situation], 3 November 1946 (CapDoc, Ag.); and Magsikap, "Maikling Kasaysayan" [Short History of the HMB in Southern Luzon], *Mapagpalaya*, 29 March 1950.

[39] Alejandrino interview, 16 July 1970; and Luis Taruc, *He Who Rides the Tiger* (London: Geoffrey Chapman, 1967), p. 27.

munications, and otherwise assist the guerrillas.[40] In many cases, barrio residents who had been leaders in the Hukbalahap's barrio governments were also leaders in the HMB's underground. Barrio and municipality organizations collected information about government forces and civilian guards through channels that sometimes reached into the offices of mayors, police chiefs, and constabulary detachment headquarters. Frequently, this network stymied the government's forces. In January 1948, for example, PC officers told a Manila newspaper that their military campaign in Central Luzon had failed, at least temporarily, because of two problems. First, the peasant rebels had a superior intelligence system that kept them well posted on PC movements so they could disperse easily. And second, barrio residents would cooperate with the PC only reluctantly or under pressure. People commonly used government-sanctioned barrio councils and organizations such as parent-teacher associations to "cover" their partisan work for the rebel army. An underground communication network, which included couriers in each barrio group and prearranged places to leave and pick up messages, laced much of Central Luzon. By 1948, the network also linked parts of Southern Luzon to the Central Luzon strongholds. The houses of sympathetic persons in Manila served as communication "posts" between the two regions. Through this communication system, sympathizers also carried supplies and food to guerrilla squads hiding in mountains or distant barrios, or to camps where veteran guerrillas were training recruits.

The peasant rebels formed squads and squadrons similar to those in the Hukbalahap. In many cases they used squadron numbers from Hukbalahap days. The main work of the rebel groups was political—"to build and sustain the support of the people," as Luis Taruc put it.[41] "In the barrios," explained Silvestre Liwanag, "Huks told people all about what had happened to the Hukbalahap, about how the Americans had 'rewarded' them for their good, anti-Japanese fighting. We told them, too, why people had to carry guns again just to get simple justice."[42] Cenon Bungay said that he and other HMB guerrillas and underground members in San Simon, Pampanga, "did much the same kind of work we had done as PKM

---

[40] This paragraph is based on several sources, especially the following: interviews with Casto Alejandrino, Camp Crame, Quezon City, 14 and 16 July 1970; Luis Taruc interviews, 27 January and 25 February 1970; Peregrino Taruc interview, 9 July 1970; OB [Organization Bureau of the PKP], "Ang Ating Gawain ukol sa Pahatiran: Sa Lahat ng Organo ng Partido" [Our Tasks Concerning Communications: To All Party Organs], 15 December 1948 (CapDoc, Ag.); CLRC [Central Luzon Regional Committee], "Mga Alituntunin at Taktika ukol sa Gawaing 'Factional' sa Sinapupunan ng mga Org. ng Kaaway" [Steps and Tactics for Factional Work Inside Enemy Organizations], 27 November 1946 (CapDoc, Ag.); Anci, Ingat-Yaman, PKM Lupong Pang Bayan No. 7 [Treasurer, PKM Municipal Chapter No. 7], Talavera, circa 1948 (CapDoc, Ag.); Lupong Pang Bayan [Municipal Chapter], PKP, "Ulat ng Seccom No. 3 (San Antonio, Nueva Ecija) sa P'Com" [Report of Sectional Committee No. 3 (San Antonio) to the Provincial Committee], 25 May 1948 (CapDoc, Ag.); and *Manila Chronicle,* 18 January 1948, p. 1.

[41] Luis Taruc interview, 27 January 1970.

[42] Liwanag interview, 21 July 1970.

members, before taking up guns: talking to people, organizing, helping them with problems when we could." Of course, he added, "we couldn't move around quite so freely, and we had to hide sometimes. Only when forced by the civilian guards or PC, though, did we fight."[43] Small squads of armed peasants made the rounds of the barrios in their areas, said Luis Taruc. They held meetings and sometimes performed theatrical presentations with villagers and sang songs to dramatize the issues and "build up the morale of the Huks and barrio people."[44]

The guerrilla forces that remained in the barrios, circulated among barrios, or traveled between the barrios and their camps in the mountains were also responsible for policing their "mass base" areas and protecting residents as best they could against government and landlord armies. These guerrilla groups, according to HMB documents, were the "people's security police."[45] Their military actions included fighting intruding police and civilian guards, ambushing PC patrols, destroying the property of landlords who violated the contracts with their tenants, and kidnapping or killing municipal officials. Distinct from these forces were the "regular forces." They led the expansion missions to a few areas outside of Central Luzon and helped peasant leaders in these places to form new organizations and win support for the HMB.

The guerrillas' weapons—mainly rifles—came from several sources. Many were those acquired by the Hukbalahap during the Japanese occupation. Others, according to Benjamin Cunanan, "were M-1 rifles and other weapons that American soldiers had discarded" after the Japanese occupation. "We collected them, then repaired and reassembled them."[46] Another source was the civilian guards. Luis Taruc explained that because landlords and mayors sometimes neglected to pay their civilian guards or paid them very little, the guards defected from time to time to the HMB, "bringing their guns and ammo with them. Others secretly sold, even gave guns and bullets to us."[47] Finally, rebels managed to get weapons and other supplies from the Filipino and American military bases in Central Luzon. Civilians working on these bases helped them steal and purchase guns and bullets. Sometimes American servicemen themselves sold guns and other materials to the HMB.[48]

[43] Bungay interview, 15 July 1970.

[44] Luis Taruc interview, 27 January 1970.

[45] CLC, "Instruction," 15 June 1947; Sagasa, "Report, Instructions," 16 October 1947 (CapDoc, Ag.). Also see Taruc, *Born of the People*, p. 252.

[46] Cunanan interview, 11 August 1970.

[47] Luis Taruc interview, 27 January 1970. Also, Lava interview, 12 August 1970; "Ayaw na ng Guwardia Sibil" [Civilian Guards Don't Like It Anymore], *Katubusan* [Redemption; a Communist Party (PKP) publication], 23 June 1947, vol. 3, no. 23 (CapDoc, Ag.); and *Manila Chronicle*, 13 July 1946, p. 1.

[48] San Fernando CIC Field Office, Richard M. Snethen, 2nd Lt. Infantry, Commanding, 1135th CIC Detachment, AFWESPAC, "Hukbalahap," 24 October 1946, p. 11 (ID No. 924310; Federal Records Center, Suitland, Md.); and Leon O. Ty, "The Hunt for Huks," *Philippines Free Press*, 10 April 1948. Ty bases his report on interviews with former Huks.

Although the rebellion became stronger, it had numerous problems as well. Its least successful efforts were the expansion missions. HMB forces from Central Luzon that went north and south frequently had problems getting food and supplies from villagers in new, unorganized areas. And underground supply lines back to their Central Luzon bases were too long and tenuous. The main problems afflicting the expansion forces, wrote Luis Taruc in late 1946 or early 1947, were too little food and medicine and insufficient political understanding among rank and file soldiers.[49] Alejandro Briones from Nueva Ecija, who was on an expansion mission to Pangasinan with one hundred other guerrillas in 1946-1947, reported that government forces continually chased them, and the peasants there helped the soldiers "because they feared us much at that time because it was their first sight of Huks." Briones and his companions never reached their destination, and government soldiers forced them into unfamiliar mountains. Eventually, Briones wrote, "due to lack of supplies, almost all of us were attacked by malaria fever. Many died and I suffered due to lack of medicine."[50] After he and other survivors had recovered, they returned to the safety of Central Luzon. Similar difficulties confronted a contingent of PKM members from Central Luzon that went to Negros and Iloilo (in the Bisayas region) in 1946. Even though peasants in Negros lived miserably, said one PKM report, the PKM group failed to spark interest in organizing. The PKM members themselves went hungry, because villagers would not feed them.[51] Only in parts of Southern Luzon, near areas where the Hukbalahap's Southern Luzon squadrons had been, did peasant activists from Central Luzon have some success. Even there, the movement never had the degree of support that it enjoyed in Central Luzon.

The rebellion also had problems in Central Luzon. The underground communication network, for example, lacked sufficient numbers of trained couriers. Rebels who were hiding frequently had too little food and money. And HMB guerrillas often had too few weapons and ammunition to go around. More serious were discipline problems. Although the guerrillas were generally "a well-disciplined fighting force," wrote Luis Taruc, leaders admitted there were abuses.[52] Because the revolt grew rapidly, some persons who joined were, in Agaton Bulaong's words, "bad people."[53] HMB squadron leaders later learned to recruit more selectively. But still the guerrillas did things that damaged their reputation. For example, Luis Taruc cited instances when guerrillas repaid government atrocities with atrocities of their own. And they killed people whom they thought were spies or enemies but were later shown not to be.[54] The Huks, in short,

[49] Felipe [Luis Taruc], to Eureku, circa late 1946, early 1947.
[50] Briones, "My Biography since 1945."
[51] B. Serrano, to Leon Gomez and Pando [Mateo del Castillo], "Ulat ukol sa Negros Occidental" [Report Concerning Negros Occidental], 26 August 1946 (CapDoc, Ag.).
[52] Taruc, He Who Rides the Tiger, p. 30.
[53] Bulaong interview, 20 July 1970.
[54] Taruc, He Who Rides the Tiger, p. 30; Taruc interview, 25 February 1970.

sometimes violated their own standards and wronged the very people they claimed to be defending.

A letter from a HMB squadron commander in Bocaue, Bulacan, depicted both the commitment and the difficulties of the peasant rebels. It was found on the commander's body. The constabulary had killed him and twenty-one others during one of the government's drives into the area. The HMB commander had intended the letter for the mayor of Bocaue:

> Dear Mayor:
> Being a commander of Unit No. 4 we are here now in your territory for some investigation. I am writing you this letter to ask for some help to put our municipality in peace and order. And I think you know already our standard of living. That night and day we are sacrificing to make another form of government that we can see today. We cannot taste even a little Democracy. Democracy [exists now] only for those who are on the highest line. . . . We have many comrades that are sick and wounded and [do not] have a cent to buy medicine. We are here waiting for your answer. And your kindness is highly appreciated.[55]

Despite the problems and setbacks, the peasant movement survived. By 1949, wrote Luis Taruc,

> the Huks had solidly organized the people in practically all the barrios in the areas of the Zambales, Arayat, Sierra Madre, and Caraballo mountains [encircling Central Luzon] and along the swamps which cover over 40,000 square kilometers and extend across the borders of four provinces [Nueva Ecija, Bulacan, Pampanga, and Tarlac]. The barrios along the Pampanga River were also organized. Throughout the many phases of their struggle, the rebels were aided by the peasants living there.[56]

National Level: The PKP and Other Allies Leave the Movement

As repression intensified and the rebellion grew, the peasant movement's alliance with other groups fell apart. Particularly because of the Democratic Alliance's fate, Peregrino Taruc argued, "the movement [of peasants, progressives, and nationalists], which was becoming centralized through the DA, became decentralized—at least for a time."[57] This promising political party had virtually collapsed by the time of the November 1947 elections. One reason was that the collaboration issue faded. It had been a central pillar around which many diverse groups had rallied to form the DA. Without it, they had too little in common. Another reason was repression. Members of the PKM, which had been the DA's main strength at the polls, dissolved their chapters, went underground, or abandoned the movement altogether. DA groups themselves were victimized, forcing local party workers to go underground or forsake further association with the DA. Most individuals or

---

55 *Manila Chronicle,* 9 January 1948, p. 1.
56 Taruc, *He Who Rides the Tiger,* p. 43.
57 Peregrino Taruc interview, 9 July 1970.

groups who had joined the Democratic Alliance had not bargained for such a storm of harassment. "They didn't want to be arrested and so on," said Peregrino Taruc, who had been a DA organizer in Pampanga. Consequently, he said, "as things became hot, many in the DA backed out." Or they tried to save the DA by disassociating it from the PKM and Hukbalahap. For example, Taruc said, "Jesus Barrera [president of the DA] didn't want my brother Meliton to come to his house anymore for fear of being linked to the PKM or Huks." This was after President Roxas had formally proclaimed in 1948 that the PKM and Hukbalahap were subversive, illegal organizations. Agaton Bulaong explained that because of the growing rebellion in Bulacan, "middle-class people who had been enthusiastic about the DA simply abandoned the struggle and the peasants."[58]

The Communist Party (PKP) dramatically illustrated the splintering of the united front that leaders of the peasant movement and leftist groups had been trying to form. The PKP opposed the rebellion. It admonished those peasants and PKP members in Central Luzon who rebelled and urged them instead to use elections and other legal means to pursue reforms. The party's highest policy-making bodies—the politburo and central committee—wanted to reconstitute the alliance with other political groups in order to challenge the country's political elites in the following elections. And in the 1947 election, by which time the Democratic Alliance was too disorganized to have its own nominees for the country's Senate, the PKP even endorsed four senatorial candidates running on the Liberal Party (LP) ticket, the party of President Roxas.

The rebellion in Central Luzon precipitated disagreements within the PKP itself, making it unable to lead either a peaceful political movement or an armed uprising. Not until mid-1948, after new leaders had ousted the previous ones, did the PKP change its position and endorse "armed struggle." Meanwhile, however, the peasants' revolt in Central Luzon raged on. William Pomeroy, an American Communist Party member who studied and later joined the HMB, wrote that while Hukbalahap veterans "regrouped and fought spontaneously," the Communist Party was

> disorganized, without unity on strategy and tactics, and with no clear perspective for the period ahead. At best, provincial organizations of the Communist Party, of the Democratic Alliance, of the PKM and of the CLO, largely on their own, were giving direction to peasants arming themselves and fighting back against suppression. This condition, in fact, prevailed from mid-1946 until mid-1948, a period of constant and spreading fighting, during which time the leaders of the movement called merely for a democratic peace and the restoration of the former state of democratic rights. . . . Only the heroism and the fighting capacity of the people, with leaders who fought largely on their own initiative, frustrated and turned this phase of the imperialist-ordered suppression into a failure.[59]

[58] Bulaong interview, 20 July 1970.

[59] William J. Pomeroy, *Guerrilla and Counter-Guerrilla Warfare* (New York: International Publishers, 1964), pp. 62-63.

Leaders of the PKP later looked back on this period and criticized their policies and actions. From these criticisms one can learn what happened. Between 1944 and 1948, the PKP's leadership emphasized two tasks: engage in "legal and parliamentary struggle" for political change and strengthen the party. To achieve the first, the PKP joined the Democratic Alliance and campaigned for DA candidates in the 1946 election. To achieve the second, the party's leadership concentrated on recruiting members and trying to construct a hierarchical organization from the politburo down to committees, sections, and cells. Because the PKP believed that the urban working class would provide the leadership for a future revolution, it emphasized recruitment and organizational work among workers in metropolitan Manila. A later PKP document, which criticized this emphasis, said that in addition to the "election struggle," the PKP between 1945 and 1948 had given its "greatest concentration" to the "economic struggle of the trade unions" and thereby had neglected the peasant movement.[60] The PKP, however, did not entirely ignore the peasantry. Some Central Luzon peasants joined the party, although the number is unclear because documentation is incomplete. According to available PKP records, the party in Nueva Ecija in October 1945 had 955 members (this was a smaller figure than a June 1945 report had cited). In the Southern Luzon province of Laguna, PKP leaders reported 500 members in March or April 1945, but 300 in late 1945. Laguna PKP leaders added, however, that the second figure was still double what membership had been in 1941. In the Manila-Rizal area, the number of PKP members in early 1946 was between 180 and 266.[61]

Although leaders wanted to increase the party's membership, they never

[60] PKP, Politburo, "Purge Opportunism and Opportunist Elements from the Party," 1 September 1948 (CapDoc, Ag.). Among additional PKP records that document the party's emphasis on the working class, particularly the trade unions in the greater Manila area, are the following: PKP, "Resolution of the Fifth Congress," 24 February–1 March 1946 (CapDoc, Ag.); PKP, Maralva, "Patnubay ng Guro sa Magaang Pagtuturo" [Teacher's Guide for Easy Instruction], 15 January 1946 (CapDoc, Ag.); "Ano ang Ibinubunga ng Matatag na Pakikibaka?" [What's the Result of Steady Struggle?] and "Ang Panloob na mga Kalagayang Pampolitika" [The Internal Political Situation], both in a PKP publication called *Ang Organisador* [The Organizer], 31 July 1946, vol. 1, no. 7 (CapDoc, Ag.).

[61] "Pangkalahatang Ulat ng Lupong Panglalawigan ng Nueva Ecija" [General Report of the Nueva Ecija Provincial Committee], 8 June 1945 (CapDoc, Ag.); Narding [Mamerto Baniaga], "Ulat ng P'Com sa Nueva Ecija" [Report of the Provincial Committee in Nueva Ecija], 2 October 1945 (PF, CapDoc, Ag.); "Pangkalahatang Ulat ng PKP sa Timog Luson (SLRC) Simula sa Kaniyang Pagkakatatag Hanggang Ngayon" [General Report of the PKP in Southern Luzon (Southern Luzon Regional Committee) from its Beginning until the Present], 15 September 1945 (CapDoc, Ag.); "Kabuuang Ulat ng Kagawaran ng OD ng Marrcom Buhat nang Magkombensyon noong Septembre 15, 1945" [Complete Report of the Organization Department of the Manila-Rizal Regional Committee Dating from the Convention of 15 September 1945], 13 January 1946 (CapDoc, Ag.); "Ulat ng OD" [Report of the Organization Department (of Manila-Rizal Regional Committee, or Marrcom)], circa early 1946 (CapDoc, Ag.); and "Ulat ng Marrcom Buhat ng Idaos ang Plenum noong Ika-21 ng Marso, 1946 hanggang sa Kasalukuyan" [Marrcom Report from the Plenum Meeting of 21 March 1946 until the Present], circa June or July 1946 (Hernandez Exh. M 66-70; CFI, Manila).

intended to build a large "mass party." They felt such an effort would be unwise, partly because of the uncertain legal status of the PKP after the war. The PKP could operate in the open like any other organization, but leaders worried that the government might suddenly reverse the laws and make communism and membership in the PKP illegal. Besides, there already existed groups and organizations that PKP members could help to lead. PKP policy also urged members to encourage "unorganized masses" to organize and join leftist groups.

From these ongoing organizations and from organizations that PKP members had helped to form came new party members. Many recruits in metropolitan Manila, therefore, were workers active in various labor unions, most of which had no attachment to the PKP although some individual union members did. One criticism that party leaders in Manila made about themselves in 1945-1946 was that they had failed to recruit many people from labor unions. As a result, party leaders said, the PKP "lagged behind" the trade union movement.[62] In Central Luzon, too, PKP members frequently were active in the other organizations, particularly the PKM and Hukbalahap veterans' associations. In Nueva Ecija, for example, surviving documents said that small PKP groups in some municipalities consisted of people already active in PKM chapters. Some of Nueva Ecija's PKM provincial leaders, including its secretary Mamerto Baniaga and president Juan Feleo, were also in the PKP. PKP organizers in Nueva Ecija also depended, at least initially, on the PKM's organization in other ways. In October 1945, for instance, Baniaga reported that although the PKP organization did not yet have its own provincial committee, it could temporarily use the PKM's provincial committee and office.[63]

Partly because the PKP did expand by working through other organizations and because it emphasized open electoral struggle in which votes were the key, its membership was not homogeneous nor was it a tightly disciplined organization. PKP top leaders realized this and even expected it to some extent. Nevertheless, they frequently complained in party documents about too little discipline and commitment among members.

Roughly, there were three types of PKP members. The first and largest was the rank and file in metropolitan Manila, Central Luzon, and a few other

[62] "Pangkalahatang Ulat ng Marrcom Mula sa Mayo Hanggang Agosto 1945 na iniharap sa Kombension Septembre 15, 1945" [General Report of Marrcom (Manila-Rizal Regional Committee) from May until August 1945, presented to the Convention of 15 September 1945], (Hernandez Exh. M 2-43; CFI, Manila); "Ang Pagbabagong Tatag ng Marrcom" [The Reorganization of Marrcom], 3 August 1946 (Hernandez Exh. M 62-63; CFI, Manila); OD [Organization Department] Marrcom, to PB [Politburo], "Ulat Bilang 2" [Report No. 2], 5 December 1946 (Hernandez Exh. M 53-61; CFI, Manila).

[63] Narding [Mamerto Baniaga], "Ulat ng P'Com [Report of the Provincial Committee of Nueva Ecija], 2 October 1945; and Lupong Panglalawigan [Provincial Committee], Nueva Ecija, "Ulat Pampolitika No. 3: Itulak ang mga Lakas na Progresibo na Tumulong sa Pagtataguyod sa Pinakamababang Hangarin ng Partido ukol sa Mabilis na Ikababagsak ng Reaksion" [Press the Progressive Forces to Help Advance the Party's Minimum Aim Concerning the Immediate Defeat of Reactionaries], 5 February 1946 (CapDoc, Ag.).

provinces. Many, if not most, were persons already active in peasant and labor associations who later joined the PKP. In fact, one criticism top PKP leaders had about membership recruitment after World War II was that the rank and file members were scarcely distinguishable from nonparty members. A 1950 party document, for instance, criticized poor recruitment practices during previous years. Party recruiters, the document said, rarely discussed the party's principles, rules of discipline, and required dues. Instead, recruiters brought people into the party with intentions of explaining everything later. This gave members the impression that discipline in the party was loose. Furthermore, the document went on, nearly anybody could join the PKP. As long as a person "said any progressive idea, joined demonstrations," expressed some sympathy with ideas that the PKP supported, and gave contributions, he could be a member. Some recruiters simply considered persons as members of the party, and reported them as such to higher party officers, without actually bringing them into the party.[64]

Despite several training schools for members and numerous educational materials that the party's top leaders prepared, its reports complained that the party's central problems during the 1940s were "loose party discipline" and "low political understanding" among the rank and file and even many long-time party leaders. Mamerto Baniaga from Nueva Ecija wrote in May 1946, for example, that only some of those in the party's central committee knew communist political theory. And, he said, most members in "lower organs do not understand the significance of politics, what is Marxist-Leninism. . . , what is reactionary, what is progressive, what is the class struggle." Thus, Baniaga concluded, cadres and typical party members were almost "on an equal plane in terms of political theory as average members in the mass organizations."[65] Similarly, a report from one local PKP leader in 1946 said that many members did not study the literature sent from the PKP's national headquarters in Manila, and those who did read, for example, the party's *Katubusan* (Redemption) "don't like it anyway."[66] Even in Manila, where the PKP focused its attention, party leaders complained that despite efforts to educate members, their "political consciousness" and commitment remained low.[67] The situation may have improved later, but apparently not sufficiently. In 1950 a new PKP official publication hoped to educate the party's membership because, its editorial said, "we must recognize the fact that the politicalization of the great

[64] PKP, "Guide for Recruiting New Members to the Party," circa 1950 (CapDoc, Ag.).

[65] Kas. Narding [Mamerto Baniaga], "Papaano Mapalalakas ang Liderato ng Partido" [How to Strengthen the Party's Leadership], *Ang Organisador,* 31 May 1946, vol. 1, no. 5 (CapDoc, Ag.).

[66] "Ulat sa Buwan ng Dec. ng Sec. V" [December Report from Section 5], 8 January 1946 (CapDoc, Ag.). This was from a PKP group in an unidentified part of the country.

[67] Arong, OD ng Secom [Organization Department of the Section Committee], "Ulat ng Sec. VII" [Report of Section 7], 30 November 1945 (Hernandez Exh. AAAA 17-18; CFI, Manila); "Ulat ng Marrcom" [Report of the Manila-Rizal Regional Committee], circa June or July 1946; OD Marrcom, to Politburo, "Ulat Bilang 2" [Report No. 2], 5 December 1946.

majority of our Party members remains at a comparatively low level."[68]
Most "Party members," consequently, probably looked on their "membership" in the broadest sense of the term. Top PKP leaders, in contrast, frequently had a different notion of what a "party member" was or at least should be. Understandably, therefore, they were disappointed when they realized how "undisciplined" the rank and file members were and how difficult it was to change them.

The second category of PKP members was much smaller in number but still included a broad range of persons. They were between the rank and file and the party's top leaders. They might be called middle-level or subprovincial PKP leaders, including people whom PKP records called "cadres." Some members in this category were not firmly attached to such "mass organizations" as labor unions or the PKM. Many, however, were. Judging from specific individuals in this category who were active in the peasant movement in Central Luzon, most had been leaders among peasants longer than they had been members or leaders in the PKP. They were, in short, closely identified and involved with the PKM and earlier peasant organizations. Compared to most village activists, however, they had more formal education. Examples were Luis Taruc and Silvestre Liwanag of Pampanga; Juan Feleo, Jose de Leon, and Mamerto Baniaga of Nueva Ecija; and Agaton Bulaong of Bulacan. Although some were more knowledgeable than others about communist theory, they all probably shared a view about what the movement was about and a vision that was more long-range than most rank and file members or others in the peasant movement had. In this respect they were closer to the third type of PKP members.

In the third category were the party's top leaders and theoreticians. They were responsible for setting PKP policies or proposing policies for the approval of the party's central committee and congress. Many of these leaders had lived in Manila most of their lives and were highly educated, whether self-tutored or university graduates. In many cases they were also deeply involved with the party's labor union work. Principal examples of top PKP leaders were Pedro Castro, Jorge Frianeza, and Geruncio Lacuesta, all of whom served as the party's general secretaries between 1945 and 1948; Vicenta Lava, the general secretary prior to 1945; Mateo del Castillo; Jose Lava; and Federico Maclang. Men like Balgos had come into the PKP through their personal hardships, poverty, and the labor union affiliations. Others, such as Vicente and Jose Lava and Mateo del Castillo, were from wealthy or at least very comfortable economic backgrounds, but joined leftist political groups and the PKP because of their political and intellectual convictions.

---

[68] *Ang Komunista* [The Communist], August 1950, vol. 1, no. 1 (CapDoc, Ag.). This publication identifies itself as the "Organ of Theory and Practice of the Communist Party of the Philippines."

Partly because of their top positions in the PKP or because they had joined the PKP through labor unions or personal convictions, these top leaders were not closely involved with the peasant movement between 1945 and 1948. Some never had been. The possible exception was Mateo del Castillo, for he was the national president of the PKM. Even he, however, had entered the peasant movement in the 1930s as a national spokesman rather than as a local or provincial peasant leader. Similarly, he had entered the PKP itself at its national level. Consequently, he had no peasant constituency or following the way Juan Feleo, Luis Taruc, or similar PKM leaders had. And because he was so busy in Manila running PKM's national office, he could not be close to the PKM's local levels or to the peasantry itself.

The three categories of PKP members are by no means exclusive. Some individuals, for example, might fit into two categories. Casto Alejandrino, Luis Taruc, and Peregrino Taruc, for example, were in the party's central committee—practically at the top of the party's hierarchy. At the same time, they resided in Central Luzon, not Manila, and worked directly in the peasant movement, particularly in Pampanga. Moreover, they bucked official PKP policy in support of the peasantry. In February 1946, for example, Luis Taruc was among several Pampangan delegates to a PKP convention who walked out because the top leadership decided not to support Amado Yuson for Congress. Even though Yuson was the nominee of the Democratic Alliance in Pampanga, the PKP leadership argued that the party could not endorse him because he reportedly had collaborated with the Japanese during the occupation. As the allegation was disputed, the overriding consideration, in the opinion of Taruc and others, was that Yuson had the peasantry's support in Pampanga because he had participated in the peasant movement.[69] Casto Alejandrino, Luis Taruc, and Peregrino Taruc also contradicted PKP policy in 1946 by going underground and joining the peasantry's rebellion.

This analysis of the PKP can illuminate what happened to the party during the first years of the rebellion. Because "membership" was loosely defined and because the party tried to rest its organization largely on "mass organizations" that did not necessarily share common interests, reactions among party members to the growing peasant rebellion varied considerably. Stated briefly, PKP members most likely to have joined or supported the rebellion were those close to the peasant movement, whereas the members least likely to have done so were those in Manila involved with the urban labor movement. This was roughly the pattern among rank and file members and PKP provincial leaders and cadres.

In Manila, government repression against labor unions and suspected communists increased in 1946 and the following years. This was an important reason, according to PKP documents, why the number of party

[69] Jose Lava, "Milestones," p. 33. Lava names only two of the Pampangan delegates who walked out in disgust. The one other than Luis Taruc is a "Com. Linda," who probably is Silvestre Liwanag. Liwanag was often known as "Linda" or "Linda Bie."

members there decreased in 1946, why most party groups in the area were "paralyzed and inactive," why party leaders and cadres were "demoralized," and why party leaders were "ineffective." Despite the repression, party members in metropolitan Manila did not join the rebellion in Central Luzon, at least not in significant numbers. Instead, remaining PKP members and leaders there began to reorganize in order to protect themselves while at the same time continuing to work, albeit more cautiously, among workers and labor unions. In late 1946, the PKP in metropolitan Manila still had not made satisfactory headway with the labor movement. As two reports from the PKP in Manila put it, the party was still too "aloof" and "isolated" from the "masses and proletariat." Consequently, party leaders there wanted to try again to become more effective within the labor movement.[70] They could not do that and support the rebellion in Central Luzon, too. In the first place, workers were not inclined to rebellion. Second, as PKP recorded accounts stated, trade union members and the "working class" offered little or no support to the peasant movement in general.[71]

In the countryside, meanwhile, some PKP members joined the rebellion, but others did not. As repression increased in Laguna, for example, party leaders painfully reported that many PKP members "lost their courage" before those in the peasant movement did. PKP members denied their membership in the Hukbalahap for fear of government reprisals, and they refused to sign petitions on behalf of persecuted Hukbalahap veterans lest they themselves be harassed. The number of party members in the province also decreased; and the number of party groups decreased in 1946 from nine to four. Among some of those party members who "disappeared," to use the description of one Laguna PKP report, some may have joined the rebels. Many probably did not, because a report noted that "many cadres and members are weak-hearted" in the face of suffering and hardship.[72]

In Central Luzon, too, repression and the growing revolt resulted in some PKP members staying with the peasant movement while others left it. When Luis Taruc reported in late 1946 or early 1947 about the situation in the region, he said barrio people generally supported the struggle but "most [party] members are either overwhelmed and [have] temporarily lost their wits and forget for a time their revolutionary roles and status—or are simply misfits." Party leadership, he added, would have to be reconstructed. Jose de Leon, who was a commander of rebel guerrillas in Nueva Ecija, wondered in late December 1946 why the party's provincial com-

[70] "Ulat ng Marrcom [Report of the Manila-Rizal Regional Committee], circa June or July 1946; "Ang Pagbabagong Tatag ng Marrcom" [Reorganization of Marrcom], 3 August 1946; OD Marrcom, to Politburo, "Ulat Bilang 2" [Report No. 2], 5 December 1946.

[71] Jose Lava, "Analysis of Party Leadership since Roxas's Victory," circa 1949 (PF, CapDoc, Ag.); PKP, Central Committee, "Resolusyong Pampolitika" [Political Resolution], May 1948 (CapDoc, Ag.).

[72] "Pangkalahatang Ulat ng PKP sa Timog Luson" [General Report of the PKP in Southern Luzon], 15 September 1945; Tanggol, SLRC [Southern Luzon Regional Committee], "OD Reports from 5 October-31 October 1946" (CapDoc, Ag.).

mittees had not been providing any guidance.[73] Both de Leon and Taruc, however, were PKP members, as were several other individuals who went underground and joined the HMB, including Mamerto Baniaga, Agaton Bulaong, Silvestre Liwanag, Casto Alejandrino, and Peregrino Taruc. Probably many rank and file members, too, joined the guerrilla army or participated in the HMB underground—not because they were in the PKP, but rather because they were part of the peasant movement as PKM members or Hukbalahap veterans or because they had no other way to escape the government and landlord armies.

The top leadership of the PKP, which was responsible for the party's policies, opposed rebellion. While it watched the government and landlords become more repressive in 1946, it had remained, according to a later account by Jose Lava, "vague in its objectives and tactics." It provided little guidance to help peasants cope with the situation in Central Luzon. When it did take a position in mid-1946 during the "pacification campaign," it "favored partial arms surrender . . . entertaining the illusion that by so doing the forces of reaction will be appeased." And when Vicente Lava recommended in June 1946 that the party begin going underground and prepare for "armed struggle" because he believed that "forces of reaction would immediately and ruthlessly proceed to destroy the democratic movement," the PKP's top leaders rejected the proposal as "alarming." During the following months, more people in the peasant movement went underground and formed guerrilla groups. Still the PKP leadership, said Jose Lava, "instructed the lower organs [of the party] to hold their ground in the open and not to retreat underground." According to a May 1950 PKP document, these instructions were "completely ignored" and many of the party's "lower organs and rank-and-filers" went underground, formed armed groups, and "refused to be arrested and tortured." And according to Jose Lava, the party leaders' action was responsible for "the partial destruction" of the PKP and peasant organizations in Central Luzon.[74]

Among the several reasons for the PKP leadership position regarding rebellion, two were most important. Jesus Lava, who was in the PKP during the 1940s and who became its general secretary in the 1950s, was among those former PKP leaders who discussed one of them. "The party's view, simply, at that time was that the peasants were fighting out of self-defense. This wasn't a strong enough basis for launching an armed struggle."[75] There had to be stronger motives, he said, before the PKP could justify abandoning "legal, parliamentary struggle" or making parliamentary struggle secondary to armed struggle.

---

[73] Felipe [Luis Taruc], to Eureku, circa late 1946 or early 1947; Leon [Jose de Leon], to Mga Kasama [Companions], 28 December 1946.

[74] Jose Lava, "Analysis of Party Leadership," circa 1949; Jose Lava, "Milestones," p. 33; "Coordinate Revolutionary Activities in the Cities and Towns with the Armed Struggle in the Field," 9 May 1950 (Politburo Exh. M 204-211; CFI, Manila).

[75] Interview with Jesus Lava, Camp Crame, Quezon City, 19 August 1970.

The second reason was that the working class and labor movement did not support rebellion. Because the workers were "the proletariat" who would be at the forefront of real revolution, the 1940s were not the right time for the party to support armed struggle. Such top PKP leaders as Pedro Castro, Geruncio Lacuesta, and Jorge Frianeza were among those who argued this position within the PKP's policy-making circles. They and others who had been helping the labor movement said that if the PKP supported the peasants' revolt, the workers in unions with PKP members would desert those unions. Furthermore, they said, the government would increase its harassment of those unions and their members.[76]

According to Peregrino Taruc, both of these reasons were symptomatic of a more fundamental difficulty within the party between 1946 and 1948. The party lacked "a theory or theoretical understanding" that would justify such a rebellion, he said. Consequently, "there was indecision on the part of the party while armed struggle was actually going on in the provinces." Peregrino Taruc then quipped, with a smile, "armed struggle was in practice before it was in theory."[77]

As the rebellion continued, however, it forced some of the top leaders to reassess the party's position and draw different conclusions. They believed that the party should at least make "armed struggle," rather than "legal, parliamentary struggle," the "principal form of struggle." Gradually the number of top PKP leaders with this position grew, although they remained a minority until 1948.

In the meantime, disagreements over rebellion and several other issues caused serious splits within the party's leadership. Conflicts grew, for example, within the politburo, between the politburo and other parts of the PKP's top leadership (such as the party's organization department), and between party leaders who were publicly known and others who were less visible because they were the party's "second front." Jose Lava wrote, for instance, "the record of the regular PB [politburo] and the SF [second front] from September 1946 to January 1947 is one of continuous conflicts and contradictions, with mutal accusations of demoralization; inefficiency, etc., resulting in their failure to give political and organizational guidance to the lower Party organs." In another analysis, Jose Lava wrote that this "crisis within the Party leadership . . . continued for more than a year and a half. . . . The sharpening ideological struggles within the Party leadership was but the reflection of the qualitative development necessarily attendant to the transition from the [party's] period of youth to the period of adolescence."[78]

---

[76] PKP, Politburo, "Pakikibaka ukol sa Kapayapaang Pandaigdig, Tunay na Kalayaan ng Pilipinas, at Demokrasiya ng Bayan" [Struggle for World Peace, True Philippine Independence, and People's Democracy], 1 February 1947 (CapDoc, Ag.); PKP, Central Committee, "Resolusyong Pampolitika" [Political Resolution], May 1948; Jose Lava, "Analysis of Party Leadership," circa 1949; PKP, Politburo, "Purge Opportunism," 1 September 1948.

[77] Peregrino Taruc interview, 9 July 1970.

[78] Jose Lava, "Analysis of Party Leadership," circa 1949, and "Milestones," p. 38.

The PKP's top leadership became so seriously divided in 1947 that some of those leaders who believed the party should support the peasants, Jesus Lava said, "began to provide under-the-table leadership, so to speak, to the peasants' armed struggle."[79] Peregrino Taruc, who was with the peasants' guerrilla army at the time, said that persons in the minority of the PKP leadership in Manila helped to arrange paper, stencils, and other supplies for the HMB.[80] Some individuals who disagreed with the politburo and the majority position on the question of rebellion even ceased to recognize the politburo's authority.[81]

In January 1947, the PKP's central committee reaffirmed the party's 1946 stance and said, "The Communist Party does not believe in the use of force and violence or in conspiracy as its methods to achieve its programs," and that it would pursue its goals through constitutional means, "relying upon the soundness of its program to rally the people to support and carry it out."[82] At the next central committee meeting in May 1948, however, the PKP reversed its position. The majority decided that the "main form of struggle" should be "armed struggle," with all other methods subordinate to it. The meeting went on to remove General Secretary Jorge Frianeza from office, suspend him, Geruncio Lacuesta, and Pedro Castro from the party, and hold all three responsible for the "errors" of previous policies, including that of opposing rebellion. The new PKP leadership later expelled Castro and Lacuesta because, according to PKP documents, they would not recognize their errors and refused to reform.[83] Among those elected to hold top offices in the PKP's new leadership were Jose Lava, Jesus Lava, and Mariano Balgos.

Government and Landlord Responses to the Huks

Violence had pushed peasants to rebel. More violence compelled them to continue the rebellion and in turn become more violent themselves. The way to end the revolt, according to the Roxas administration and most governors, mayors, and landlords in Central Luzon, was to crush it. President Roxas relied on his "iron fist" policy. Because the young republic could not support its own military, it needed—and received—aid from the United States. For every three swings the government took at the peasantry with its iron fist, however, it opened its other hand to offer an "attraction policy," which included promises to implement land reform, disband the civilian guards, and grant amnesty to rebels who surrendered.

[79] Jesus Lava interview, 19 August 1970.
[80] Peregrino Taruc interview, 9 July 1970.
[81] Jose Lava, "Milestones," p. 37.
[82] PKP, Politburo, "Pakikibaka ukol sa Kapayapaang Pandaigdig" [Struggle for World Peace], 1 February 1947; and Jose Lava, "Analysis of Party Leadership," circa 1949.
[83] PKP, Central Committee, "Resolusyong Pampolitika" [Political Resolution], May 1948; and Jose Lava, "Milestones," pp. 40-44.

Iron Fist Policy

Shortly after the murder of Juan Feleo in late August 1946, President Roxas and the government's military leaders announced that they would crush the revolt in sixty days. What followed, according to rebel leaders, was a "terror campaign, aimed not merely at annihilating us but at smashing our mass base."[84] And it lasted not sixty days but most of the next two years. Companies of Philippine Constabulary troops, civilian guards, and municipal policemen used heavy artillery, armored cars, tanks, and airplanes against bands of rifle-toting peasants in the barrios and fields of Central Luzon. In the process, they destroyed villages and killed many people not directly involved with the rebellion. Fortunately, the military operations usually affected only a few parts of the region at any one time and lasted only a short time in any one area.

Big operations were like one in late January 1947: four constabulary companies from Nueva Ecija; a field artillery company, a chemical company, and mortar company of the Philippine army; another constabulary company from Tarlac; and Piper Cub airplanes—all bombarded barrios in western Nueva Ecija where six hundred Huks reportedly had been staying. Two months later the government used spotter planes to direct the artillery fire of twenty-five hundred troops chasing rebels camped on the slopes of Mount Arayat and in the fields and swamps of municipalities nearby. The government claimed that HMB casualties were heavy, although rebel leaders said only four guerrillas died. Many civilians were killed and arrested. Another large battle occurred in February 1948 between civilian guards and 150 rebels. After four hours of fighting, according to a newspaper account, PC and Philippine army units reinforced the civilian guards and silenced the rebels' guns.[85]

Government authorities also took strong measures against the public. The PC took control of many municipal police forces in Central and Southern Luzon. Several municipal mayors and some provincial governors required residents to purchase passes before traveling beyond their home barrios and towns. People in Tarlac had to pay fifteen centavos each month for their passes. Citizens in Nueva Ecija and Laguna had to pay forty centavos and sometimes had to renew the passes each week. Mayors and governors in Nueva Ecija and Laguna reportedly used the money to equip civilian guards and special agents. Persons without valid passes risked imprisonment, a beating, and even death. In 1948, Secretary of Interior Jose Zulueta announced that the national government itself would begin such a pass system for Central Luzon and parts of Southern Luzon.[86]

Local governments and PC detachment commanders imposed curfews to inhibit those who aided guerrilla rebels in the middle of the night. They

[84] Taruc, *Born of the People*, p. 241.

[85] *Manila Chronicle*, 29 January 1947, p. 1, 28 March 1947, p. 1, and 29 March 1947, p. 1; Taruc, *Born of the People*, pp. 255-257; and *Manila Chronicle*, 3 February 1948, p. 28.

[86] *Manila Times*, 30 August 1947, p. 1; *Manila Chronicle*, 3 July 1947, p. 1, 11 September 1947, p. 16, 20 March 1948, p. 2.

forced residents of entire barrios to evacuate and, reported Luis Taruc, "herded them like goats" into the bayan of municipalities. They did this sometimes to protect villagers from approaching battles but other times because they suspected the residents were hiding the HMB. Authorities also arrested anyone suspected of being a rebel or supporting the rebellion. Despite the writ of habeas corpus in Philippine law, many people sat in jails for months and years without trial. Rumors spread that President Roxas would impose martial law.[87]

Although he never declared martial law, Roxas did vow in August 1946 that the government would use any measure to force peasants to surrender their guns. In January 1948, he said that his government would accept no conditions from any rebels who wanted to negotiate or surrender. A week later he told a governors' convention that "soft glove" efforts to deal with villagers had failed. "The only way to fight force," he said, "is to meet it with superior force."[88] Among the other government officials holding similar views was Secretary of Interior Zulueta, who was responsible for the Philippine Constabulary. The Huks, he said in April 1947, had only two choices: unconditional surrender or annihilation. He was confident that with a continued supply of guns and ammunition from the United States, the Philippine military would successfully crush the rebellion within a matter of weeks. In July, when it was clear that the rebellion had not yet been crushed, Zulueta gave PC chief Mariano Castañeda "carte blanche authority" in all operations against the "dissidents."[89]

Central Luzon mayors, governors, and landlords generally supported this military policy. When one hundred mayors from Central Luzon met with Zulueta in March 1947, for example, they advocated "war to the death" for all Huks. "The only good Huk is a dead one," was the consensus among these mayors. In the following December, eighteen out of twenty-seven Nueva Ecija mayors voted against a moderate peace proposal made by the Nueva Ecija governor Juan Chioco. They believed that "Huk annihilation is the only solution." Mayors, governors, and landlords alike opposed any efforts to disarm the civilian guards, even though Secretary Zulueta came under intense pressure from a minority of mayors and from others to do so. One of the staunchest defenders of the guards was the governor of Pampanga, Jose Lingad, who was also the leader of the province's civilian guards.[90]

Government officials and large landowners justified the use of force in several ways. The armed peasants, they said, were "dissidents" and "terrorists" who kidnapped municipal mayors and attacked guards whom land-

[87] *Manila Chronicle,* 6 December 1946, p. 1, and 10 August 1948, p. 1; "Patuloy na Nambubugbog ang mga MP" [MPs Continue Brutality], *Katubusan* [Redemption], 13 January 1947, vol. 2, no. 53 (CapDoc, Ag.); Felipe [Luis Taruc], to Eureku, circa late 1946 or early 1947; Pagaduan, "Kasaysayan ng Talavera"; and *HDP,* volumes for Central Luzon provinces.

[88] *Manila Chronicle,* 24 August 1946, p. 1, 13 January 1948, p. 1, and 23 January 1948, p. 1.

[89] *Manila Chronicle,* 2 April 1947, p. 1, and 12 July 1947, p. 1.

[90] *Manila Chronicle,* 30 March 1947, p. 1, 17 December 1947, p. 1, 30 December 1947, p. 28, and 24 June 1948, p. 1.

lords hired to protect their crops. Such people, they said, only understood violence. The HMB also disrupted "peace and order" to such an extent that the landlord association in Nueva Ecija, for example, complained to Roxas that they were at "the mercy of the tenants" to get a share of the crop. Moreover, they said, what the tenants did not take illegally, the guerrilla soldiers did. Finally, opponents of the peasant movement said that the rebels were "communists." Some officials allowed that only the leaders were communists but that they forced other barrio residents to join the movement by threatening to kill anyone who refused. Other officials and military officers equated all Huks with communists. Some claimed that the Russians shipped ammunition and food to the Huks by submarine. When President Roxas declared in March 1948 that the Hukbalahap and the PKM were illegal organizations and all members were subject to arrest, his justification was that both organizations sought "to overthrow by forceful means the present government" and "establish their own government with the help of force and fear."[91]

American government officials reinforced the views that the rebels were communists and that communism was the cause of rebellion. In October 1946, for example, the U.S. Army Counter-Intelligence Corps in the Philippines prepared two reports for other U.S. agencies and the Philppine government. One was on communism in the Philippines; the other was on the Hukbalahap. According to these documents, the PKM and the Hukbalahap—meaning the Hukbalahap veterans—were "undoubtedly the largest Communist groups in the Philippines." Furthermore, the PKM's "Communistically inclined leaders . . . created the agrarian unrest in Central Luzon." These groups now had been "forced underground," said the report on the Hukbalahap, "but [they] have retained the necessary arms and a large group of devoted followers. The Hukbalahap is firmly holding out with high anticipation of further Russian aid in the form of money and reinforcements. . . . [T]hen they will completely overthrow the Government and set up the Communist Government in the Philippines."[92] A year later, intelligence reports to the United States War Department still portrayed the unrest in Central Luzon as communistic and said the "chief subversive organizations" in the country, including the PKM, received money from American Communists and the U.S.S.R. One report

[91] *Manila Chronicle,* 13 February 1947, p. 1, 16 March 1947, p. 1, 3 May 1947, p. 12, 17 December 1947, p. 1, 20 December 1947, p. 28, 23 January 1948, p. 1, and 7 March 1948, p. 1; Dominador Tombo, Agent, Department of Interior, to the Secretary of Interior [Jose Zulueta], 9 January 1947 (Roxas Papers, Bundle 45; National Library, Manila); "Excerpt from the Minutes of the Meeting of the Nueva Ecija Landowners Association Held in Cabanatuan," 21 September 1947 (Roxas Papers, Bundle 48; National Library, Manila); and Manuel Roxas, President of the Philippines, "Pahayag ukol sa Hukbalahap at sa Pambansang Kaisahan ng mga Magbubukid" [Proclamation Concerning the Hukbalahap and the National Peasants Union], 6 March 1948, p. 1 (Roxas Papers, Bundle 57; National Library, Manila).

[92] San Fernando CIC Field Office, 1135th CIC Detachment, "Hukbalahap," 24 October 1946, pp. 8, 12; Headquarters, 1135th CIC Detachment, AFWESPAC, "Staff Study on Communism in the Philippines," 24 October 1946, p. 3 (miscellaneous records on guerrillas in the Philippines; Federal Records Center, Suitland, Md.).

was pleased to note, however, that the Philippine government "is showing increasing awareness of Communist activity . . . and has indicated its intention of halting the spread of subversive activity."[93]

Generally, the authors of these documents offered no evidence to substantiate their view of the peasant organizations. When they did, the evidence usually was that some "Communist documents" had been captured from the peasant guerrillas or that the PKM, Hukbalahap, and DA, like other "Communist groups," opposed parity rights for American businessmen and opposed permanent American military bases in the Philippines. They also exaggerated the influence on the peasant movement of those participants who were allegedly PKP members.

Opposition to communism in its former colony was one reason why the United States assisted the Philippine military efforts to squash the rebellion. But even before, in the second half of 1945, its State Department and War Department had decided to give military aid to the Philippines after the country's independence the following July. The major reasons concerned protection for American business opportunities in that part of Asia and for American military bases in the Philippines.[94] Later, the "Communist" rebellion in Central Luzon, too, influenced the amount of aid.

The rebellion made United States assistance imperative from the Philippine government's point of view. Philippine officials estimated in 1946 that the rebellion's guerrilla army numbered between 9,500 and 10,000.[95] Both Filipino and American officials worried whether the Philippine military had sufficient men, supplies, training, and discipline to fight this large number of rebels. For example, Colonel Macario Peralta, an

[93] Intelligence Division, War Department General Staff, "Current Situation in the Philippines," 1 October 1947, p. 5 (RG 319, Planning and Operations, 1946-1948, P&O 350.05, case 232; Military Records, National Archives, Washington, D.C.).

[94] An adequate elaboration of this important point cannot be made here, but among the primary sources I have seen that support this are the following: Strategy Section, Operations Division, War Department General Staff, "Post-War Base Requirements in the Philippines," 23 April 1945, appendix to Tab E (RG 165, Operations and Planning, OPD 336 TS, case 81; Military Records, National Archives, Washington, D.C.); Robert P. Patterson, Undersecretary of War, to William L. Clayton, Assistant Secretary of State for Economic Affairs, "Trade Relations and U.S. Military Interests in the Philippines," 4 June 1945 (RG 165, Operations and Planning, OPD 093.15 PI, case 18; Military Records, National Achives, Washington, D.C.); Lt. Gen. J. E. Hull, Assistant Chief of Staff, OPD, War Department, to Commander in Chief, USAF, Pacific, "U.S. Military Assistance to Philippines in Post-Surrender Period," 16 October 1945 (RG 165, Operations and Planning, OPD 093.5 PI, case 44; Military Records, National Archives, Washington, D.C.); and Brig. Gen. G. A. Lincoln, Chief, Strategy and Policy Group, OPD, to Budget Officer, War Department, "U.S. Military Assistance to Philippines Subsequent to 1 July 1946," 28 December 1945 (RG 165, Operations and Planning, OPD 093.5 PI, case 51; Military Records, National Archives, Washington, D.C.).

[95] Lt. Col. Macario Peralta, Jr., Office of the President, to the President [Manuel Roxas], "Capability of the MPC to Deal with Huk Problem," 19 August 1946 (Roxas Papers, Bundle 59; National Library, Manila); and Headquarters, MPC, Philippine Army, Office of AC of S for Intelligence, "Secret Intelligence Trend Report, Week Ending November 5, 1946" (Roxas Papers, Bundle 26; National Library, Manila).

advisor to President Roxas, wrote to the president in August 1946 that even though municipal police, civilian guards, and Philippine army units would supplement the country's 22,000 constabulary troops, he still had to conclude that unless the PC "is strengthened considerably . . . it cannot 'solve' the [Huk] question."[96] The previous month the Philippine government had requested the United States to give food, fuel, clothing, training, and ammunition for its Filipino soldiers. After studying the request, the War Department recommended over $19 million in military aid and wrote,

> It is represented by the Philippine Delegation that the budget of the Philippine Republic for fiscal year 1947 is totally inadequate to support the Philippine Army in these respects. Such examination of the financial and economic position of the Philippines as the committee has been able to make leads to the conclusion that such aid is essential to prevent disintegration of the Philippine Army, with the attendant danger of lawless elements in the Island becoming completely out of hand.[97]

For numerous reasons, including the burden of helping the country to rebuild from the ruins of World War II and its small tax revenues, the Philippine government continued to depend on American military aid during the following years. The total amount of military assistance to the Philippines between the end of World War II and mid-1948 was $72.6 million. This included, among other expenditures, $36 million to equip 33,000 soldiers, the replacement and maintenance of military equipment that the United States government purchased, and annual supplementary aid for additional military and civilian equipment.[98]

[96] Lt. Col. Peralta, to the President, "Capability of the MPC," 19 August 1946. At the time Peralta wrote, the Philippine Constabulary was called the Military Police (or Military Police Command).

[97] Gen. George J. Richards, Chief, Budget Division, War Department, "Military Assistance to the Philippine Islands," 11 July 1946 (RG 319, Office of Chief of Staff, OCS 093 PI, 1946, case 29; Military Records, National Archives, Washington, D.C.).

[98] U.S. Department of State, Agency for International Development, *U.S. Overseas Loans and Grants and Assistance from International Organizations, July 1, 1945-June 30, 1972* (Washington: 1973), p. 77; Maj. Gen. George J. Richards, Chairman, War Department Committee on Assistance to the Philippines, "Military Assistance to the Republic of the Philippines," 20 March 1947 (RG 319, Plans and Operations, 1946-1948, P&O 381 TS, section II-A, case 32; Military Records, National Archives, Washington, D.C.); Memo for the Record, "United States Military Assistance to the Philippines," 21 April 1947 (RG 319, Plans and Operations, 1946-1948, P&O 381 TS, section II-A, case 32; Military Records, National Archives, Washington, D.C.); Moore, Manila, COMGENPHILRYCOM, to War Department, "Cost of Military Assistance to the Philippine Republic," 30 April 1947 (RG 319, Plans and Operations, 1946-1948, P&O 091 PI, section I, case 11; Military Records, National Archives, Washington, D.C.); and Lt. Gen. LeR. Lutes, Director of Service, Supply and Procurement, War Department, "Program for Retaining Arms and Equipment: Philippine Army Program," 8 May 1947 (RG 319, Plans and Operations, 1946-1948, P&O 400 TS, section IV, case 56; Military Records, National Archives, Washington, D.C.).

Despite the military assistance from the United States, the Roxas government's iron fist policy failed to stop the rebellion. The government reported in 1947 that it had forced 3,400 rebels to surrender and had captured 500 more.[99] President Roxas, Secretary Zulueta, and other government officials continued to predict that peace and order would be restored shortly. The Philippine military's intelligence claimed in November 1947, for example, that "the internal unrest . . . will very likely subside in approximately four to six weeks."[100] But two months later, Representative Topacio Nueno summarized the situation well when he stated that the peasants were still fighting and the government's iron fist policy had "totally failed." Instead of stopping the rebellion, Senator Tomas Confesor said in July 1947, the government's planes and tanks were making it worse.[101]

Confesor and Nueno were among a growing minority of congressmen and provincial government officials who opposed the government's policies in Central Luzon. Military force, they contended, was the wrong way to handle a problem that stemmed from the landlords' injustices and oppressive economic conditions. Representative Felixberto Serrano, for example, said in December 1947 that the Huks were not communists but peasants "thrown to despair" because the United States refused to recognize officially the Hukbalahap, because of what happened after the 1946 election, and because of the government's policies on agrarian unrest. He described the Roxas government's suppression of the Huks as a "policy of madness" motivated "by a spirit of revenge."[102]

Furthermore, critics argued, the iron fist approach was prolonging the rebellion. Not only did artillery shells and bombs hit innocent people, but the PC, civilian guards, and police burned houses, destroyed crops, looted property, and shot innocent people. This behavior compelled more peasants to support or join the guerrillas. By February 1947, Senator Confesor had become so angry about military abuses that he called Secretary Zulueta a "Hitlerian general" and demanded the resignation of both Zulueta and General Castañeda.[103]

The military abuses were extensive. Cenon Bungay of Pampanga recalled, "The mailed fist policy meant open season on all suspected Huk and PKM. And, of course, this also meant trouble for people who were not directly involved."[104] A peasant guerrilla leader in Laguna wrote in November 1946:

[99] Philippines, Department of Defense, *Annual Report to the President, July 1946-June 1947*, p. 11.

[100] Gen. A. M. Jones, Chief, United States Military Advisory Group to the Republic of the Philippines, to Commander-in-Chief, Far East Command, "Weekly Summary of Activities," 3 December 1947, p. 1 (RG 319, Plans and Operations, 1946-1948, P&O 091.711 PI, section V-A, case 46/22; Military Records, National Archives, Washington, D.C.).

[101] *Manila Chronicle*, 22 January 1948, p. 1, and 10 July 1947, p. 1.

[102] *Manila Chronicle*, 18 February 1947, p. 1, 22 April 1947, p. 1, and 22 December 1947, p. 24.

[103] *Manila Chronicle*, 19 February 1947, p. 1. Also see *Manila Chronicle*, 12 February 1947, p. 1.

[104] Bungay interview, 15 July 1970.

Democratic freedoms are completely smashed; farmers and other citizens are attacked, arrested, shot, jailed, and even killed. The enemy is like the fascists during the Japanese occupation. MPs are waging wars on peasants and others. The people are really fed up . . . and hence are giving support to the Huks. They give food, especially, as contributions.[105]

Luis Taruc reported from Central Luzon after the first several months of the revolt that "MPs shoot at anybody in the fields." Later he wrote that soldiers, civilian guards, and police burned to the ground numerous Central Luzon barrios and arrested and killed people at whim. The soldiers also "zoned" barrios by rounding up all residents, and then masked informers pointed to supposed HMB supporters. In the jails, Taruc said,

the arrested men were beaten and tortured. . . . Repeatedly they were given the water-cure, that torture . . . in which water is poured into a man until his stomach is swollen and the water runs from his nose and ears, and then he is beaten. Bullets were placed between their fingers, and they were given electric shocks. Our most active comrades were killed, and then reported "shot while trying to escape."[106]

Mateo del Castillo summarized the continuing repression in the country-side when he wrote in January 1948 on behalf of the PKM to the Philippine Congress. Shortly before, President Roxas had vowed to a governors' convention to wage "all-out war on the armed peasants." After disagreeing with Roxas's position and reminding the Congress that the peasants were only trying to defend their rights, del Castillo said,

The PKM also begs to disagree with the President when he claimed the people are already enjoying "democratic peace." The truth is that there is neither peace nor real democracy in our country today. Many innocent lives of peasants and their wives and children have been and are being killed in a disastrous fratricidal strife. The picture of our farms in Central and Southern Luzon is one of grief and desolation. A virtual reign of military terror grips the countryside. You cannot say peace has returned when hundreds of peasants are being herded like animals in jails and military camps, a majority of them without due process of law. Democracy is a misnomer when tens of thousands go about in rags, racked by disease and hunger, while a few influential people wallow in surplus riches and wear out their lives in bacchanalian orgies.[107]

Among the infamous military groups of the government and landlords were the civilian guards and the PC's "Nenita" units. Jose Crisol, who was

[105] Commander Ross, Hukbo Bating "B," "Kalagayan pang-Politika" [The Political Situation], 3 November 1946.
[106] Felipe [Luis Taruc], to Eureku, circa late 1946 or early 1947, and Taruc, *Born of the People,* pp. 241, 242-245.
[107] Executive Committee, PKM, to the Third Regular Session, Congress of the Philippines, 26 January 1948 (Hernandez Exh. W 435-440; CFI, Manila).

an officer in the Philippine army in the 1940s and secretary of defense in the 1950s, said that the civilian guards were "one of the most undisciplined groups you could possibly imagine. They contributed greatly to the rise of the Huk movement, what with all the injustices they aided in and carried out."[108] Another army officer who was stationed in Central Luzon from 1946 until 1950 recalled that men in the civilian guards were "local gangsters, goons, people of bad reputations out to make good with the law, avoid punishment, and make a living besides. Sometimes they were even former Huks, from the Japanese occupation days." Although civilian guards worked with government soldiers, he said, they were more attached to municipal mayors and local landlords, who used them to "pick up or fight Huks. Many [civilian guards], however, used this opportunity to take out personal grudges against innocent people by pointing them out as HMB or HMB sympathizers whether they were or not. And they took advantage of people in other ways, too, using terror tactics which local PC could not stop even had they wanted to."[109]

The "Nenita" or "skull squadrons" were under the command of Napoleon Valeriano. These PC units, said the Filipino army officer, "aroused the fear of God in people. The mere mention of his [Valeriano's] name was enough to frighten people." The special tactic of these squadrons was to cordon off areas; anyone they caught inside the cordon was considered an enemy. "Naturally," said this army officer, "many were innocent people. And many of these were killed. When I was stationed in the Candaba area [in Pampanga], almost daily you could find bodies floating in the river, many of them victims of Valeriano's Nenita Unit."[110]

The military's behavior was so bad in San Antonio, Nueva Ecija, for example, that even the municipal council unanimously passed a resolution to condemn the PC:

> Whereas, the frequent military operations conducted by members of the Philippine Constabulary against the Huks have caused untold suffering and deprivation among the peaceful and law-abiding citizens, especially to the peasant elements who were mostly the victims of a series of atrocities committed by members of the Philippine Constabulary;
>
> Whereas, during the military operation conducted by members of the armed forces of the Philippines in the barrio of Lawang Cuyang, this municipality, on May 21, 1947, seven (7) peaceful and law-abiding citizens were wantonly killed without question, while others were brutally tortured and one was maimed for life;
>
> Whereas, a military operation was again conducted by different units of the Philippine Constabulary within the jurisdiction of this municipality in the early morning of January 31, 1948, wherein peaceful and law-abiding inhabitants of the outlying barrios evacuating to Poblacion proper because of fear and apprehension were unjustly intercepted on the way, unlawfully herded together during the whole

[108] Interview with Jose Crisol, Civic Action Program Office, Camp Aguinaldo, Quezon City, 15 December 1969.
[109] Interview with Col. Florentino Villacrusis, Talavera, Nueva Ecija, 28 June 1970.
[110] Ibid.

day in a secluded place about two hundred meters away from the municipal government building, brutally manhandled in a manner so reminiscent of that savage and brutal chapter of the Japanese reign of terror, and wherein the Municipal Mayor in his sincere desire to intercede in behalf of these unfortunate victims, was openly rebuked and grossly disregarded by the Commanding Officer of a unit of the Philippine Constabulary known as the Skull Squadron;

Whereas, simultaneous with this tragic drama, another unit of the Philippine Constabulary operating in the barrio of Papaya of this municipality, unlawfully and criminally burned seventeen (17) houses therein to the great damage and prejudice of the poor owners who are now completely bewildered as to whether we are still living under the Japanese reign of terror and greed;

Whereas, during the baptismal party held in the house of Councilor Robinson Panlilio on February 1, 1948, several soldiers of the same Skull Squadron unlawfully and illegally entered the said house, ordered the invited guests among whom were Dr. Numeriano Lustre, likewise a Municipal Councilor, Judge Daniel V. Domingo and several others, to go down and who were subsequently screened without any justifiable reason or motive other than to assert their despotism;

Whereas, on the same date another unit of the Philippine Constabulary operating in the barrio of San Francisco, this municipality, entered the premises of one Angel Linsangan and forcibly took away P86.00 in cash, two chickens and two cartons of Piedmont cigarettes without the consent of the owner;

Whereas, as sequel to those atrocities the Municipal Mayor, the Municipal Secretary and members of the Police forces were subjected to a series of investigations, subsequently ordered disarmed by the Provincial Commander of this province, while two policemen, Basilio Bicos and Bartolome Larote, were badly manhandled on alleged complicity with the Huks, a rotten strategy so often resorted to by some members of the Philippine Constabulary when dealing with peaceful and law-abiding citizens within their zone of operation;

Whereas, this unholy state of things if not properly checked on time will only be fruitful of undesirable results;

Now, therefore, on motion of Councilor Estanislao Ortis, duly seconded by Councilor Gregorio Lustre;

Resolved, as it is hereby resolved, that the Municipal Council in special session assembled, hereby condemns the arbitrary acts of the members of the Philippine Constabulary who, in one way or another, participated in the said atrocities committed in the guise of a noble mission of preserving law and order, but who, on the contrary, sowed the seeds of dissension and contempt in the hearts of those peaceful and law-abiding citizens of the Republic, and be it,

Resolved, finally, that the Municipal Secretary be, as he is hereby, authorized to send a copy of this resolution to his Excellency, the President of the Philippines; to Hon. Jose Zulueta, Secretary of the Interior; to Hon. Juan O. Chioco, Provincial Governor, this province, and to the two Nueva Ecija solons, Hon. Jose A. Cando and Hon. Constancio Padilla, for their information and consideration.[111]

[111] Juan Cando, Municipal Secretary, "Excerpt from the Minutes of the Special Meeting of the Municipal Council of San Antonio, Nueva Ecija, Held on February 9, 1948; Resolution No. 11" (Roxas Papers, Bundle 48; National Library, Manila).

Two weeks after the San Antonio municipal council had passed this resolution, Senator Pablo David urged President Roxas to keep Major Napoleon Valeriano out of Pampanga. The senator wrote that too many people complained about Valeriano "for having committed many atrocities, not only against dissident elements but against law-abiding people."[112]

Valeriano, however, remained. He was even promoted to colonel. By 1949, he had become a chief strategist for the government's campaign to counter the rebellion.

In March 1948, an event occurred that reminded many people in the peasant movement of Juan Feleo's death a year and a half earlier. Manuel Joven, the executive secretary of the Congress of Labor Organizations (CLO), was murdered. He was thirty-nine years old. He had been active in the trade union movement since the 1930s, a member of various peasant organizations, and a resistance leader in Laguna during the Japanese occupation. Available evidence showed that the Philippine Constabulary soldiers killed him. Even a memorandum that President Roxas wrote to Secretary Zulueta indicated this:

> I have been informed that the investigations conducted thus far about the death of Manuel Joven show that special agents of the Philippine Constabulary participated in the commission of the crime. The evidence also reveals that the murder car had been hired by constabulary agents and the rental was paid by constabulary headquarters.[113]

As far as I could determine, no one in the PC was ever charged with the crime.

Agrarian Reform and Negotiations

Secondary to the iron fist approach to stop the rebellion were agrarian reforms and negotiations. The Roxas government and some landlords did consider plans to increase the tenants' share of the harvests. Congress also passed more legislation, which Roxas signed into law in September 1946, to govern landlord-tenant relationships. But little came of the plans for agrarian reform. And the new tenancy law was not enforced in most areas of the country, including Central Luzon. Even if it had been, the law provided tenants with a smaller share of the rice harvest than the 60-40 system, which was approved in late 1945.[114]

The Roxas government also began to purchase a few landed estates, some of which were in Central Luzon, that were to be resold to tenants.

---

[112] Senator Pablo Angeles David, to President Roxas, 25 February 1948 (Roxas Papers, Bundle 55; National Library, Manila).

[113] Manuel Roxas, President of the Philippines, to Jose C. Zulueta, Secretary of Interior, 4 March 1948 (Roxas Papers, Bundle 45; National Library, Manila). For a newspaper account of Joven's background and death, see *Manila Times,* 26 February 1948, p. 1.

[114] For more about the September 1946 law (Republic Act 34), see Kerkvliet, "Peasant Rebellion," pp. 497-500.

This was nothing new, however. President Quezon's administration had begun similar purchases in the late 1930s. The purchases never could have solved agrarian problems in Central Luzon. The total acreage involved was infinitesimal. Furthermore, high prices for the land prohibited most tenants from paying for the land later. Beyond that, improprieties and corruption plagued the government agencies responsible for the administration of these lands.[115]

In Central Luzon, meanwhile, both government and landlords agravated the agrarian difficulties in other ways. For example, the government and the United States army evicted over two thousand families, most of them poor laborers and tenant farmers, in order to expand Clark Air Base in Pampanga. Although the government promised to compensate the families for their houses and lands, many of the victims protested against eviction and complained about low and tardy payments.[116] An unknown number of other tenants in Central Luzon also lost their rights to use land, according to surviving PKM documents, because more landlords introduced machinery to replace them.[117]

Concerning negotiations, the Roxas administration stated that it would discuss a settlement if HMB leaders stipulated no prior conditions. The administration also made clear that it opposed amnesty for rebels, a suggestion favored by a vocal minority in Congress. The reason, according to the Roxas government, was that the Huks were "lawless," "criminals," and "subversives." The government's stance, in short, suggested that it could not seriously consider rebel offers to negotiate because HMB leaders stipulated that they would reject attempts to characterize them as outlaws, criminals, or subversives. Meanwhile, within days after he had strongly reaffirmed that the armed peasants must surrender unconditionally, President Roxas proclaimed amnesty for Filipinos who had collaborated with the Japanese during World War II.[118] Whatever merits this decision might

[115] Newspapers reported some of these problems as they surfaced when tenants on estates near Manila began trying to buy land from the government: *Manila Chronicle,* 5 February 1948, p. 1, and 13 February 1948, p. 1. More detailed evidence is found in the following: Philippines, Committee to Look into the Conditions of the Buenavista Estate in San Ildefonso, Bulacan, *Report of the Presidential Committee* (Manila: 20 August 1954); Philippines, Presidential Investigating Committee on Bahay Pare, "Memorandum for the President: Bahay Pare Estate Report" (Manila: 29 August 1955), and "Memo for the Chairman, Land Tenure Administration; Bahay Pare Estate," undated; James P. Emerson, *Land Reform Progress in the Philippines, 1951-1955* (Manila: International Cooperation Administration, 1956), pp. 13-14; and David O. D. Wurfel, "The Bell Report and After: A Study of the Political Problems of Social Reform Stimulated by Foreign Aid" (Ph.D. dissertation, Cornell University, 1960), pp. 434-435.

[116] *Manila Times,* 15 December 1947, p. 8; *Manila Chronicle,* 18 January 1948, p. 1; *Central Luzon Chronicle (Manila Chronicle* supplement), 11 January 1948 and 15 February 1948.

[117] Executive Committee, PKM, to the Third Regular Session, Congress of the Philippines, 26 January 1948; and "Memorandum ng PKM sa Ikatlong Kongreso ng Pilipinas" [Memorandum of the PKM to the Third Congress of the Philippines], March 1948 (Hernandez Exh. W 669-671; CFI, Manila).

[118] *Manila Chronicle,* 28 January 1948, p. 1.

have had, it certainly added insult to injury for many in the HMB who had resisted the Japanese occupation and had been denied any official recognition for Hukbalahap accomplishments.

On 15 April 1948, President Roxas died unexpectedly while visiting Clark Air Base in Pampanga. Succeeding him was Vice-President Elpidio Quirino. Although the republic grieved the death of its first president, there was also a sigh of relief. Critics of Roxas's policies toward the rebellion had grown more numerous. So had those who worried that Roxas had assumed so much power that his administration verged on dictatorship. Particularly alarming to many who previously had said little publicly about the administration's policy in Central Luzon was Roxas's proclamation that the PKM and Hukbalahap were illegal, subversive organizations. Senator Alejo Mabanag, for example, stated,

> If there's still any doubt as to the fascistic character of our government, that doubt should be dispelled by the declaration. In no democratic government can such an order be issued. Crimes and illegal associations are defined by law, and it is up to the courts whether certain associations have violated the laws. I'm afraid that under this policy even the Nacionalista Party might be declared an illegal association.[119]

While others may have chosen softer words, many in governmental circles agreed with Mabanag's point.

The mounting controversy, coupled with the fact that HMB leaders had indicated their willingness to negotiate, must have helped the new president to try that route. Through intermediaries, President Quirino and HMB representatives had several weeks of constant communication. The result was an agreement to meet in order to negotiate at length.

As part of that agreement, President Quirino granted amnesty on 21 June 1948 to "leaders and members of the . . . Hukbalahap and . . . PKM who have committed crimes of rebellion, sedition, illegal association, assault upon, resistance and disobediance to persons in authority and/or illegal possession of firearms," provided they "have presented themselves with their arms and ammunition" to government authorities.[120] Although undefined in the president's statement, "present arms" meant registering, rather than surrendering, the guns. This at least was the HMB's understanding and the way newspaper accounts reported it.[121] Huk leaders, therefore, came to Manila to settle the details of the registration procedure and to discuss issues underlying the agrarian unrest.

The period for amnesty and negotiations lasted from June 21 to August 15. During that time, three significant things happened. First, many HMB guerrilla soldiers, looking forward to peace, registered their weapons. For

---

[119] *Manila Chronicle,* 9 March 1948, p. 28.

[120] President E. Quirino, Proclamation #76, 21 June 1948 (reprinted in Agoncillo and Alfonso, *History of the Filipino People,* pp. 546-547).

[121] See, for example, *Manila Chronicle,* 26 June 1948, p. 1, 28 June 1948, p. 1, and 15 July 1948, p. 24.

example, Jose de Leon, the HMB's highest ranking guerrilla leader in Nueva Ecija, registered his guns in Cabanatuan. With him were other Huks. In Santa Cruz, Laguna, over 150 armed peasants in one day registered their weapons. Among them was HMB commander Pedro Villegas, who said that he expected many more Huks to do the same.[122] Alejandro Briones, who had been in the HMB from the beginning, wrote that during amnesty he lived with his family in Victoria, Tarlac, visited other friends in other towns, registered with the PC, and talked with the mayor in his home municipality.[123] Huk leaders who came to Manila met several times with Quirino and his representatives, and they spoke to businessmen's clubs, on radio, and to universities. Congress even decided to seat Luis Taruc as the congressman from Pampanga's second district, and gave him the salary he would have received had he been seated in May 1946.

Second, the PC and other authorities in the provinces violated, from the point of view of peasants in the HMB, the conditions of the truce and amnesty. In several places, peasants who came to register their weapons were surpised when PC officers demanded that they surrender the guns. And many who refused were arrested. Similarly, civilian guards and PC soldiers searched barrios for those people who had signed registration lists a few days before. If found, the soldiers beat up these people and demanded their guns.[124]

People in San Ricardo, Talavera, only vaguely recalled this amnesty, because the period did not differ significantly from the months before or after it. Roberto Aspia, for example, remembered there were some Huks who "surrendered," but "there were still lots of civilian guards and PC stealing our food and arresting people they thought were with the movement. It wasn't any different." Andres Franco, another guerrilla in San Ricardo during the 1940s, remembered the amnesty but said, "it would have been foolish of me to go to the PC and say I was a Huk." Even if President Quirino meant what he said, it was too dangerous, according to Franco, because "the Nenita soldiers were still around and they'd pick me up, kill me even, once they knew I was a Huk."

In short, whatever the intention of government officials in Manila might have been, provincial officials, especially the military, continued to do as they had before—to disarm the peasants and squash the revolt. Furthermore, the civilian guards still had their weapons and remained on the payrolls of landlords, mayors, and PC.

Third, not all—maybe not even most—of the armed peasants registered. Whether they would have, had the enforcement of amnesty been as HMB leaders expected, is unanswerable. But certainly once they heard that the PC in one place had beaten up somebody after he had registered, they took

[122] *Manila Chronicle,* 1 August 1948, p. 1, and 27 July 1948, p. 1.
[123] Briones, "My Biography since 1945."
[124] Agoncillo and Alfonso, *History of the Filipino People,* pp. 522-523; Taruc, *Born of the People,* pp. 260-261.

no chances. Groups of Huks also ambushed PC patrols and civilian guards during July and August, just as soldiers continued to attack villages and search for people in the movement.

This confusion in the countryside made negotiations in Manila between the Quirino administration and HMB leaders even more difficult than they would have been otherwise. As it was, discussions hit serious snags almost immediately. The rebel leaders wanted assurance that the government would immediately implement agrarian reforms and resell landed estates. They wanted Quirino to remove General Castañeda, chief of the PC, and several other officials who had been especially hostile to the peasant movement. And they demanded that the government discontinue the special privileges that Americans had in the Philippines, including the parity arrangement for American businessmen. But the Quirino government's responses disappointed the HMB representatives, because their preliminary discussions with Quirino in May and June had led them to believe that the government would be more sympathetic.[125]

The truce and amnesty period ended sooner in the countryside than it did in Manila, where government and HMB representatives talked. The situation was a repeat of the "pacification program" of mid-1946, which had never really taken hold in Central Luzon although government officials and PKM leaders continued to talk to each other and to act as if it was working.

On August 14, the day before the amnesty period would have officially ended, the negotiations in Manila fell apart. That evening, Luis Taruc later wrote, "our intelligence unearthed a scheme to kidnap me. My brother-in-law was mauled by thugs gunning for me. The ghost of Feleo hovered over the fruitless negotiations. I left the city and went back to the field early the next dawn. The following day the PCs and civilian guards made simultaneous raids throughout Central Luzon."[126]

[125] For further discussion of the negotiations from the point of view of HMB representatives, see the following: Taruc, *Born of the People*, pp. 259-263, and Kerkvliet, "Peasant Rebellion," pp. 615-624.

[126] Taruc, *Born of the People*, p. 261.

Chapter 6
THE RISE AND FALL

AS THOSE HMB leaders who had been in Manila for negotiations fled to Central Luzon, the government's soldiers followed close behind. Another wave of military operations began. The Quirino government vowed that the peasant "insurgents" would be brought to their knees. In order to elude their pursuers, Luis and Peregrino Taruc, other Huk leaders, and several HMB "security forces" lived for weeks at a time in the Sierra Madre mountains. Only couriers connected them to the barrios of Central Luzon. Mateo del Castillo, president of the PKM, was one of these rebels. Because the PKM had been declared a subversive organization and negotiations had collapsed, he joined the HMB. "We had a hard time," recalled Luis Taruc. "We were terribly hungry."[1] Once after going for days without food, the band of guerrillas spotted a carabao on a hillside. They did not know who it belonged to, but they shot and killed it anyway. Then they feasted. Del Castillo and several others ate so fast that they became sick. The last weeks of 1948 were not auspicious times for these HMB leaders.

Meanwhile, in the lowlands of Central Luzon, villagers harvested their palay crops and tried to make the best of difficult times. They also continued to rebel.

The rebellion reached its peak during 1951. After that it followed the course of most peasant revolts in history—it waned, then faded away. Many rebels simply left their HMB squads. Others surrendered or were captured. Others were killed in the battles that became more numerous during the 1950s. Villagers grew weary of the fighting. Many who before had supported the HMB now became ambivalent toward it. Those men and women who continued to resist had to retreat farther into the mountains—farther away from the people who were their source of strength.

[1] Interview with Luis Taruc, Quezon City, 25 February 1970.

203

San Ricardo and Talavera

The situation in San Ricardo, Talavera, according to people there, was much the same in 1949-1951 as it had been the preceding two years.[2] Some people left the barrio and then returned, depending on the severity of the fighting and the behavior of the civilian guards and Philippine Constabulary. Most stayed in San Ricardo and continued to farm, although that became increasingly difficult and dangerous as the number of soldiers in the area increased. Consequently rice production decreased. Most peasants still feared and hated the PC and civilian guards, who continued to take whatever they wanted—chickens, money, rice, women. As for the landlords, more of them moved, leaving their lands under the protection of their hired guards and the government troops. This undoubtedly contributed to the hostilities and tensions between those who were supposed to restore "law and order" and the barrio residents.

San Ricardo may have suffered less than most other barrios in Talavera, because it was one of the strongest HMB barrios. The PC and civilian guards thought twice or thrice before venturing there. They knew that HMB participants in the barrio were alert and could call on HMB squadrons elsewhere in the province. Nevertheless, villagers were never immune from outside encroachments.

The HMB organization in San Ricardo—and apparently in Talavera as a whole—became somewhat stronger between 1949 and 1951. Residents continued to outfit and feed armed peasants who moved among the barrios and between barrios and their mountain hideouts. The Philippine government tried unsuccessfully to impose its own barrio organization on San Ricardo, just as it tried to do in other barrios in Central Luzon. Andres Santiago, one leader in the barrio's HMB organization, explained that "these things the government set up had nothing inside them. We [in the HMB of San Ricardo] used them to cover our own movement."

Overarching the underground organization in San Ricardo and other barrios was the HMB leadership for Talavera. "It was the same set-up we had for the PKM," Hilario Felipe explained. He knew well. He had been a leader in both the PKM and HMB for Talavera. The number of leaders varied, according to Felipe, but usually it was "about ten people." According to HMB documents, a group such as this was called a "section committee" or "seccom." Some of the leaders lived and worked in the bayan itself; others lived in barrios; and still others stayed much of the time "in the field" with HMB guerrilla groups. In this manner Talavera's leaders kept in touch with both parts of the HMB movement—the underground organization and the armed guerrillas. They also communicated, usually through letters sent by courier or through the regular mail system, with leaders in other municipalities and the "regional committee" or "Reco" that incorporated Nueva Ecija and parts of adjacent provinces. Felipe described

[2] This section is based primarily on conversations with people in San Ricardo and elsewhere in Talavera in 1970.

Talavera's leaders as peasants who previously had been in the PKM, Democratic Alliance, or Hukbalahap. When I inquired whether these persons also belonged to the Communist Party (PKP), Felipe said, "No, unless you mean 'belong' in the way the PC said. To them almost any Huk was a Communist Party member."

People from San Ricardo, particularly young men, continued to join the HMB guerrillas. "Sometimes we recruited men to join us guerrillas," said Roberto Aspia, who had been an HMB soldier. "Huks especially asked close relatives to join—brothers, first cousins, people like that," said Andres Franco, another former HMB soldier, who had relatives in both the HMB underground and the guerrilla forces. Apparently most joiners needed little prodding; as before, they became rebels not through the urgings of others but out of anger, revenge, and a desire to protect themselves against the PC and civilian guards.

The November 1949 national election campaign, especially, swelled the HMB's numbers. According to Tomas Basa, for example, who had been sympathetic but had not been deeply involved with the rebellion, "It was the most vicious campaign I can remember. It was so bloody." Hilario Felipe elaborated by saying, "Quirino's men would even kill people who had only spoken against him or in favor of [Nacionalista Party presidential candidate] Laurel." Religio Felipe said, pointing in the direction of the Talavera River, "You could find people's heads bobbing in the water there—people who had been killed by the PC because they opposed Quirino." So in self-defense, many joined the rebellion. The widely shared opinion among villagers in Talavera was that Quirino and his supporters also stole that election. They stuffed ballot boxes and used other illegal means to a degree that surpassed even the 1946 election. This was more evidence for peasants that resistance and rebellion were the only options they had.

The HMB's official position in the 1949 election, according to documents and statements its national leaders prepared, was to support Senator Jose Laurel for the presidency. Several people who had been in the HMB in San Ricardo, however, did not want him to be president. Because he had been president during the Japanese occupation, they regarded him as a "collaborator" and "against the Hukbalahap." Others, however, favored Laurel simply because Quirino's government was so oppressive. As one woman who had been a supporter of the HMB underground said as she lit a slender cigar, "There was too much trouble, too much fighting. The Huks didn't want to keep this up. Lots of people figured if they got another government elected, we could all go back to peaceful lives."

HMB guerrillas, too, were violent, even though they claimed their actions were for self-defense. They ambushed PC patrols and civilian guards, hijacked trucks and cars, stole money, and once tried to destroy the PC provincial command post in Cabanatuan. A few former HMB guerrillas also said that some of their companions were unnecessarily abusive. For instance, an HMB squadron in another municipality held up a passenger bus and then, with no apparent motive, shot some passengers.

"They were what you'd call 'hot-heads' in the movement," Hilario Felipe said. "You could never get rid of all of them. But we tried to be disciplined. Treating people well was our first principle."

As was true during the Hukbalahap, most persons in the HMB learned guerrilla tactics from experience and their companions, not through formal training. Only a small number in Talavera, according to Hilario Felipe and Roberto Aspia, attended schools in the Sierra Madre mountains that the HMB's provincial and national leaders organized. Few schools actually convened, as far as they knew, and the class sessions lasted just a couple weeks each.

In 1950, Felipe attended an HMB school, which, he said, "was mainly on politics and history." The twenty-five people there were HMB leaders from several municipalities in Nueva Ecija and Bulacan. The two instructors, said Felipe, "were Huks, too. I think they were also in the Communist Party. One at least said he was. Sometimes they talked about us joining the party in order to be better leaders." One thing the instructors did that Felipe remembered well was criticize HMB guerrillas who used *anting-anting* and were superstitious. Anting-anting are amulets; many guerrillas had them. At the school, Felipe said, "we were told anting-anting were bad and that guerrillas who wore them lacked discipline." Several documents from the Communist Party (PKP) did rebuke such practices. One said, for instance, "One of the worst effects of this [belief in anting-anting] is the abandonment by comrades carrying charms of those comrades who get hit" because believers in anting-anting must avoid the sight of blood.[3] When Felipe told fellow HMB rebels in Talavera that they were not supposed to use anting-anting, he recalled, "they didn't agree." He himself never understood why such practices were wrong, for some of the best guerrillas wore anting-anting and were very superstitious.

The school ended early, Felipe said, because PC soldiers discovered the Huks' camp and "nearly caught all of us right then and there." All managed to escape. Felipe rejoined his squadron in Talavera. That was the last of his formal education in the HMB.

One important development for the HMB in Talavera in the late 1940s was the contacts—and a certain degree of sympathy—it nurtured inside the municipal government. The mayor was Leopoldo Diaz, a respected physician. He also owned land farmed by tenants. He had been elected in November 1947 on the Liberal Party ticket, the same as the Roxas-Quirino government. Yet his reputation among HMB participants and supporters was far better than either President Roxas's or President Quirino's. Although Diaz and some others in his municipal administration were not members of the HMB, they tried to moderate the excesses of the military. Diaz himself was opposed to civilian guards, as were a number of local government officials in Nueva Ecija by that time. How much Diaz did on behalf of the peasants' rebellion was unclear. Some people, for example, said he simply straddled the line between the PC and the HMB in order to

---

[3] PKP, "Organizer's Guide No. 7," July 1955 (CapDoc, Ag.).

avoid repercussions from either one. Others said he actually defended the HMB's objectives and even silently approved the giving of food and supplies to guerrillas. However, Diaz was definitely an improvement, in the eyes of rebel sympathizers, over previous mayors. Many Huks considered him their friend.[4] Diaz chose not to run again in November 1951, although this had little consequence for the movement. By then the HMB had lost considerable ground.

There are several reasons why the rebellion in San Ricardo and other parts of Talavera died down, then all but disappeared by 1953-1954. Some lie with the nature of the Huk movement itself.

Most peasants who joined or supported the HMB wanted to protect themselves and their families against repression and abuses, and they favored agrarian reforms. Their objectives did not become more radical during the rebellion itself, despite the efforts and desires of some HMB leaders. A middle-aged woman in Talavera made this point well. She was the daughter of a peasant leader in Talavera who died fighting against repression, and she was married to a rebel leader who was still in prison when I talked to her in 1970. She had been close to the peasant movement and the HMB. "There were many reasons why the HMB wasn't victorious," she began. "But the most important one was that many peasants weren't against the Philippine government. I mean both peasants in the HMB itself and others who just supported it. It was one thing to be against the Japanese, who were outside invaders, during the war, as the Hukbalahap was. But it was another thing for people here [in Nueva Ecija] to be opposed to the government of their country." She shook her head as if to say she wished the situation would have been different. Alfredo Buwan of San Ricardo clarified this further when he said, "Once the landlords and government showed they would stop abusing us, we [in the rebellion] were ready to put aside our guns, too."

Another important reason was expressed by Ruben Sanchez. In 1952 he "retired from guerrilla life," as he put it. He had been in the rebellion since 1946. "People were really just tired," he explained. "They just wanted the turmoil and fighting to stop. The HMB lost many supporters because of this feeling. Pretty soon HMB squadrons and underground organizations didn't have many people left either. That's when I quit." This feeling resulted partly from little hope that the revolt could make any more headway. As Roberto Aspia put it, "It had reached a point where we [in the HMB] couldn't go any further."

The limited goals of the movement plus this weariness were the context in which peasants detected changes in the government—especially the

---

[4] In addition to conversations with people in San Ricardo and the bayan of Talavera, my information about Diaz's role comes from an interview with Luis Taruc (25 February 1970) and a document written by Jesus Lava in 1950: NMT [Jesus Lava], to O Beria [Federico Maclang], 25 June 1950 (Politburo Exh. N 399-401; CFI, Manila). In 1950, Jesus Lava was the PKP's politburo supervisor for Regional Committee (Reco) 1, which included Nueva Ecija. Maclang was head of the PKP's organization bureau in Manila and also a politburo member.

military—which in turn, further undermined the rebellion. The individual whom people in San Ricardo commonly associated with the improvements was Ramon Magsaysay. Most of the things attributed to him occurred while he was secretary of defense (1950-1953) in President Quirino's administration. Former rebels and nonrebels alike claimed that Magsaysay "cleaned up the PC and Philippine army" so that soldiers no longer stole from peasants, "got rid of the civilian guards," "promised amnesty to Huks and kept his word about it," and "understood that we weren't criminals and that we wanted only what was rightfully ours."[5] The government— again, Magsaysay was the man given the credit—also began to implement some agrarian reforms. Peasants believed that Magsaysay, especially after he became president, would force landlords to allow tenants to keep 55, 60 some even said 70 percent of the harvests. Less important, but still cited, was that the government purchased the de Leon hacienda in Talavera and promised tenants there the opportunity to rebuy the land for their own.

These improvements attracted to the government those people who before had felt caught in the middle between the HMB and PC and civilian guards. They now were more willing to give information to the military and less willing to help the HMB. The improvements even whittled away HMB support among those sympathetic to the movement. They became hopeful again that peace could come, that their families would be safe from landlord armies and soldiers, and that generally things would improve a little. Finally, the changes appealed to a sizable number of HMB participants and guerrillas. For example, in 1952 Roberto Aspia "surrendered because Magsaysay guaranteed amnesty and had eliminated all the civilian guards." He returned to full-time tenant farming.

Also contributing to the HMB's decline was that government forces pursued Huks where they had not before and did so with fewer abuses against villagers. Hilaro Felipe attributed this to Magsaysay "making the soldiers disciplined." This increased military pressure made guerrilla life more difficult. Andres Franco complained, for example, "We [Huks] spent more and more of our time just trying to elude the soldiers" in the mountains and across the fields of Nueva Ecija and "trying to get enough food and ammunition to stay alive." Many rebels were killed, surrendered, or were captured. By 1953, only scattered bands of armed rebels remained in the vicinity of Talavera. Most were frequently cut off from the barrios that had previously supported them. A document taken by government soldiers from the body of a dead Huk soldier illustrated this. It chronicled the activities of this man and his companions during his last days. He wrote that they were constantly on the move, that they spent most of their time arranging to get food and supplies from people in San Ricardo and other barrios in Talavera and a nearby municipality, and that they lacked communication with their contacts in the barrios. They apparently had no time for anything other than trying to survive.[6]

---

[5] Sentiments like this are also expressed in Pagaduan's "Kasaysayan ng Talavera."
[6] "1952 Daily Record," 12 January-19 March 1952, author's name unknown (CapDoc, Ag.).

Some Huks retreated far away from Talavera. Hilario Felipe, for example, said, "My cousin said he was going to the Ilocos region and get support from people there for the HMB." That was in 1952. "We never heard from him again," Felipe added.

Most of the HMB rebels who survived simply slipped back into the rhythm of village life once they were sure the authorities would not harass and abuse them or their families because they had been in the HMB, the PKM, or the Hukbalahap. One example was Ignacio Diaz, a tenant farmer who in 1970 also worked part time for the government's irrigation bureau in Talavera "cutting grass along the dikes." He was no relation to the former mayor of Talavera, but he was the son of a man who had given his life to the peasant movement in Talavera. Ignacio Diaz had watched the peasant movement in the 1930s, he had joined the Hukbalahap as a young man after the Japanese had killed one of his brothers, and he had joined the PKM after the war. He joined the peasant army in 1946 before it was known as the HMB. From then until late 1952 he led a guerilla squad composed of men from San Ricardo and nearby barrios. He spent most of 1952, however, "away from San Ricardo, hiding because government troops were too many," Diaz said, then paused and carefully ground a cigarette butt into the dirt floor of his house. He had begun to build the house in 1968, but it remained incomplete in 1970 because he could afford no more materials. "We heard about the amnesty Magsaysay promised. At first we didn't believe it because there were lots of 'amnesties' before, too." "Yes," added Diaz's neighbor, joining in the discussion. "I had to leave the Huks in 1948 because I had malaria so bad. There was supposed to be amnesty then, too, but I had to move completely away in order to recover because otherwise the PC would have arrested, maybe killed me."

I asked Diaz how he had felt about giving up, especially as some Huks still continued to stay in the hills and rove Central Luzon. "We didn't give up," he said somewhat indignantly. "I didn't, anyway. I still wanted the same things the PKM had wanted. We've still got a peasant union today—the MASAKA.[7] It's a continuation of the PKM. To have our own peasant organization was one thing we fought for as Huks. So we won some things out of it." His neighbor nodded in agreement. Diaz then added that the Huks would have been foolish not to recognize that the situation had changed by the early 1950s. There was nothing more to be gained by using guns, according to Diaz. The Huks could never defeat the government's soldiers even if that had been their aim. And with Magsaysay's reforms, his election to president, and promises of more agrarian reforms, Diaz explained, "we could farm again and reorganize our peasant movement to use our strength in numbers, not guns, to get reforms." Besides that, other peasants had become less sympathetic to the Huks. Diaz then explained, "We little people have to be like a cluster of bamboo: close together with

[7] MASAKA is an acronym for Malayang Samahang Magsasaka (Free Farmers Union).

strong roots so we are firm in our purpose, but bend a little with the changing winds."

The Peak: 1949-1951

Elsewhere in Central Luzon, too, the winds were changing and peasants in the movement were bending. Two themes were most pronounced. The first, which this and the following section will develop, was that the movement reached its zenith in 1949-1951, partly as a consequence of an alliance between the HMB and the PKP. It was a precarious alliance at best; leaders never adequately resolved numerous problems. Second, because the military tried to be more selective about whom they shot at and government officials began to appear concerned about the peasants' plight, support for the movement dwindled and more rebels could lay aside their guns with less fear of repression. These changes exacerbated weaknesses within the rebellion, including tensions between the communist-oriented leaders and the other people in the movement.

The rebellion was strongest from about 1949 until early 1951. According to the HMB and PKP records, armed Huks numbered between eleven thousand and fifteen thousand, a notable increase over the 1946-1948 period and roughly equal to the armed strength of the earlier Hukbalahap resistance army. According to former Huk leaders, the problem during these years was not too few people—either in the guerrilla army or in the barrio support groups—but insufficient ammunition, guns, money, and supplies for all who wanted to join.

The government's and landlords' inhumane behavior, more than anything else, drove villagers to join the rebels. Carlos Fernando's experience was an illustration. He joined the HMB in 1950. At the time he was a twenty-two-year-old tenant farmer in barrio Santo Domingo in Lubao, Pampanga. His elderly father, too, had been a tenant and so were most of his relatives. He joined the HMB, he said,

> because the civilian guards were so bad, so brutal. For example, they burned down our house and the houses of many others in our barrio and elsewhere in Lubao. Besides that, the civilian guards and soldiers chased me because two of my brothers were Huks. You see, civilian guards were especially brutal to people who had relatives in the movement. So, I went into the mountains of Bataan and joined the Huks there. Most of these Huks were from Lubao; my brothers were there, and so were other relatives, like Commander [Silvestre] Liwanag, who is my cousin. This is why I joined this particular Huk group.[8]

The approach of President Quirino's administration was basically the same as Roxas's: use military force and terror to crush these "Communist rebels." Undoubtedly some people in the PC, army, and other government agencies tried to offset the excesses of their colleagues. They must have

---

[8] Interview with Carlos Fernando, Camp Crame, Quezon City, 10 August 1970.

been frustrated, however. Military commanders such as Colonel Valeriano continued to lead "Operation Supercharge" or similarly named attacks that had infantry men charging through villages, tanks rumbling across rice fields, and planes dropping bombs (including napalm) on "Huk hideouts" or "Huk concentrations." The secretary of the interior, whose department included the Philippine Constabulary until 1951 and who helped make policies regarding the rebellion, was Sotero Baluyut—an enemy of the peasant movement from as far back as the 1930s when he was governor of Pampanga. Secretary Baluyut vehemently defended the civilian guards, wanted to increase the PC's forces, believed all Huks were communists, and advocated that they be "annihilated."[9]

License to abuse, arrest, and kill in the name of peace and order was particularly rampant during and after the November 1949 election campaign. The HMB and PKP top leadership had announced its highly qualified endorsement of Jose Laurel, the Nacionalista Party nominee for president. The primary reasons were that he was the lesser of two evils and the leadership believed their support would strengthen the movement's bargaining power with him. Probably the only effect the endorsement had, however, was give supporters of the Liberal Party and Quirino further reason to use police and the army against not only suspected Huks but also Nacionalista Party and Laurel backers. Consequently, explained Alfredo Saulo, who in 1949 had closely observed the Huk movement and a year later joined his friend Luis Taruc, "the masses in Central Luzon became Huks so fast. . . . People were so fed up with the government and afraid of repression that they joined the Huks even knowing they couldn't get a rifle until they could take one from a dead army or PC soldier."[10] Cenon Bungay, who in 1949 commanded about two hundred Huk guerrillas in Batangas in Southern Luzon, recalled that the number of new recruits "swelled after that election. Batangas was Laurel's home province, and many of his supporters joined and helped the HMB. They were so angry about Laurel being cheated out of the election because of ballot stuffing and every other kind of corrupt practice."[11] The Huks were numerous enough by 1950 for Bungay to form three "field commands," each with about three hundred people.

Besides becoming more numerous, the Huks also became better organized. The HMB's revamped organization, which leaders had begun in late 1948, was most nearly intact between 1949 and 1951. The guerrilla army was divided into field commands (FC). "They were similar in size and organization to battalions," explained Benjamin Cunanan, who had been the commander of field command #21.[12] During the height of rebellion, FCs ranged from one hundred armed peasants to over seven hundred. FC 21, for example, had 650 armed people in 1951. Each had a commander,

[9] See stories from the *Manila Chronicle* such as these: 28 September 1948, p. 1, 14 October 1948, p. 1, 4 December 1949, p. 1.

[10] Interview with Alfredo Saulo, Quezon City, 4 February 1970.

[11] Interview with Cenon Bungay, Camp Crame, Quezon City, 15 July 1970.

[12] Interview with Benjamin Cunanan, Camp Crame, Quezon City, 11 August 1970.

vice-commander, and three or four other officers who, together with a "security force" of ten to twenty guerrillas, composed the FC's headquarters. Each field command encompassed several squadrons and squads, each with its own leaders. The FCs generally stayed in one vicinity and their headquarters often had camps in remote areas. Cunanan said, for example, that FC 21's forces "operated on the Pampanga-Tarlac side of Mount Arayat." Cenon Bungay explained that the FC he commanded in Batangas province "stayed mainly in one municipality. Small squads would go out every day and talk with barrio folks, explaining the Huk's program, picking up any new men who wanted to join, arranging for supplies, or ambushing enemy soldiers."[13]

"A group of Huk guerrillas never could, not even at the rebellion's peak, stay in a barrio for long periods of time," said Casto Alejandrino, who was still one of the movement's top military leaders in the 1950s.[14] "Only individual Huks or a small number of guerrillas could stay in a barrio for several days or even weeks." Of course, Alejandrino continued, "there were other Huks in the broad sense of the word—not limited just to armed guerrillas—who lived in the barrios. They lived in their home barrios and were political educators, in charge of supplies, or some other kind of cadre. We called these people 'OD cadre' "—shorthand for "organization department cadre." Other Huk leaders referred to these individuals as "barrio organizers." Whatever the name, they were the contact people for HMB guerrillas in the vicinity. They collected, as Luis Taruc explained, "food, clothing, and other things for the Huks and left these supplies in prearranged places. Some of these places," Taruc grinned, "were the same ones we had devised during the Hukbalahap days."[15]

Barrio supporters were included in "section organizing committees," which in turn were units within "district organizing committees." Roughly, there was one district committee for each field command, and at least one section committee for each Huk squadron. Encompassing several district committees and their field commands were "regional committees" (Recos), whose leadership tried to oversee and coordinate both military and non-military sides of the movement. Reco 2, for example, incorporated the Huks in Pampanga and Tarlac plus the scattered few in Bataan, Zambales, and Pangasinan provinces. In mid-1951, it had seven field commands and six district committees. Each district committee had from three to six section committees and from one thousand to six thousand members.[16]

The HMB rebellion's geographical center—"Huklandia" according to Manila newspapers—included Nueva Ecija, Pampanga and Tarlac, and

[13] Bungay interview, 15 July 1970.
[14] Interview with Casto Alejandrino, Camp Crame, Quezon City, 14 July 1970.
[15] Interview with Luis Taruc, Quezon City, 27 January 1970.
[16] District Organizing Committee #A, "Political Report," to Reco 2, March 1951 (CapDoc, Ag.); Reco 2, "Enlarged Conference Report," 26 May-15 June 1951 (CapDoc, Ag.); and Reco 2, "Summary of Annual Political Report," January to December 1952 and "Summary of Annual Organizational Report," 1952 (CapDoc, Ag.).

Bulacan. They were the core provinces for Recos 1, 2, and 3, respectively. Their neighboring, more mountainous provinces had some Huks and hence were fringe areas for Recos 1, 2, and 3. The heart of Reco 1, for example, was Nueva Ecija; its periphery included Nueva Viscaya, eastern Pangasinan, and northern Quezon. Another fairly strong Reco in terms of organization and numbers of members was Reco 4. Its core was Laguna and Batangas and its periphery included Cavite and southern Quezon. The provinces in these Recos were "the most decisive ones," wrote Luis Taruc in 1950, "as they have been in the past" for the peasant movement.[17]

In addition to these four, the movement had five others: the Bicol region (Reco 5), the Bisayas region (Reco 6), Mindanao (Reco 7), and Northern Luzon (Recos 8 and 9). All, however, were far weaker than the first four, and they relied on Huks in Central Luzon for supplies and recruits. Even at the peak of the Huk rebellion, each of these five Recos had only a few hundred armed guerrillas, many of whom had traveled to these areas from Central Luzon on "expansion missions" that the HMB-PKP leadership had initiated. Moreover, the Huk guerrillas in these areas never enjoyed close ties with local peasant organizations nor strong support within the barrios.[18]

"These Recos and field commands were not something entirely new," said Cenon Bungay as he explained the significance of the HMB's organization during the early 1950s. "They grew out of the previous organization. What this reorganization did was to bring closer together those HMB guerrillas and barrio supporters in an area, and that area closer to other Recos." It improved communication and coordination. Bungay gave an example. "Our communications among FCs in Reco 4 through couriers, contacts in the barrios, and district leaders were good enough so that squads, squadrons, companies, and FCs [in Reco 4] knew pretty well what each other was doing. It was efficient enough so that all three FCs in Batangas could come together or participate in a coordinated attack within twenty-four hours if needed."[19] Casto Alejandrino, who was the commander of Reco 4 in 1949-1951, illustrated this point by saying, "We could assemble over eight hundred men for a military operation if I wanted, although we never did this because we mainly fought guerrilla-style."

To illustrate this coordination, Alejandrino described a large raid in Santa Cruz, Laguna, in August 1950.

[17] Enteng [Luis Taruc], to SEC [Secretariat of the PKP], 9 September 1950 (Politburo Exh. 0 278; CFI, Manila).

[18] This brief comparison of the nine Recos is based on several interviews and captured documents. Among the more important ones are these: interviews with Jesus Lava, Camp Crame, Quezon City, 12 and 19 August 1970; interviews with Casto Alejandrino, Camp Crame, Quezon City, 14 and 16 July and 5 and 12 November 1970; PKP, Organization Bureau, "Pangkalahatang Ulat Pang-Organisasyon" [General Organizational Report], May 1950 (Politburo Exh. 0 1049; CFI, Manila); and National Organization Department, "Pangkalahatang Ulat Pang-Organisasion" [General Organizational Report], 15 August 1951 (CapDoc, Ag.).

[19] Bungay interview, 15 July 1970.

We had a few hundred men. The purpose of that attack was mainly political—a display of force for propaganda purposes. The purpose was also economic—raid the municipal treasury. We got 86,000 pesos. We should have had more, but we couldn't open some safes inside the building. The purpose was also military—to damage enemy forces. Here Bungay, for example, made a good showing. He and his men were brave and efficient against Philippine ground forces."[20]

The Santa Cruz attack was one of several simultaneous ones by HMB groups on 26 August 1950, the anniversary of the Philippine Revolution of 1896. The previous March 29 the Huks had assaulted several other targets to commemorate the eighth anniversary of the founding of the Hukbalahap. Although not all field commands in Recos 1-4 could participate, many did. In Pampanga, for example, the Reco 2 leadership reported ambushing a PC patrol and killing its commander and four soldiers; assaulting a camp of PC and civilian guards after which "the enemy fled, leaving a thousand rounds of ammo, some guns, blankets, food"; raiding a PC-civilian guard garrison and causing "heavy losses on the enemy side"; briefly seizing the municipal center of Mabalacat during which time "two spies were liquidated" and twelve houses burned as a result of fighting between HMB and government soldiers.[21] Elsewhere—particularly in Nueva Ecija, Bulacan and Tarlac—Huk actions were similarly diverse that day.

HMB and PKP leaders were pleased with the March 29 raids. These and the ones on August 26 turned out to be the rebellion's largest demonstrations of military and organizational strength. They also caused the Quirino government its greatest fright. Several officials predicted that the Huks would strike Manila next.

Another indication of the HMB's strength was its financial situation. Rebel leaders never felt they had enough cash and supplies. Nevertheless, Luis Taruc recalled, "we were financially better off between about the time amnesty collapsed [August 1948] and the [November] 1951 elections than we had been before then or when I came down to Manila [in May 1954]."[22] Those Huk groups who were somewhat better off shared their supplies and money with weaker groups. Specifically, Recos 1 and 2, which the HMB general headquarters considered "self-sufficient," sent money and supplies to the rebellion's "national finance department." It in turn distributed these to weaker districts and guerrilla units in Recos 3 and 4 as well as to "expansion forces." Reco 2's leaders, for instance, sent 3,000 pesos to the national finance department in August 1950. Huk squadrons had taken the money from the post office in Arayat, Pampanga.[23] Reco 4 in Southern

[20] Alejandrino interview, 16 July 1970.

[21] Enteng [Luis Taruc], to SEC [Secretariat of the PKP], 1 April 1950 (Politburo Exh. 0 652-657; CFI, Manila).

[22] Luis Taruc interview, 25 February 1970.

[23] Enteng [Luis Taruc], to O Beria [Federico Maclang], 31 August 1950 (Politburo Exh. N 349-352; CFI, Manila); and Enteng, to NFC, Com. F, and OB [Organization Bureau], 31 August 1950 (PF—Luis Taruc, CapDoc, Ag.).

Luzon, too, could sometimes assist other Huk groups. In June 1950, for example, thirty-two Huks from Laguna carried extra guns and supplies to the small contingent of guerrillas who were trying to establish Reco 5 farther south in the Bicol region.[24] Even more frequently, Huks within the same Recos shared supplies with one another. In July 1950, for example, a Huk squadron in Nueva Ecija gave bullets and guns to another squadron in that province.[25]

"Confiscation," to use the Huks' term for what the Philippine government called "stealing," was the rebels' most lucrative source of cash. Certain Huk squadrons specialized in robbing payroll offices, holding up trains, and intercepting cargo trucks traveling between Manila and Central Luzon. Manuel Caiyod was a leader of one of these squadrons. Its largest confiscation, he said, was 76,000 pesos taken from the payroll car of the Manila Railroad Company in October 1950. Half the money went to the HMB-PKP's national headquarters, which distributed it among other Recos; the other half stayed with Reco 4.[26]

Cash covered only a portion of the Huks' needs. Cenon Bungay expressed well what was apparent from other leaders' recollections and from documents: "The FCs existed on contributions people gave—rice, vegetables, cigarettes, clothing. Cash contributions were very few, maybe 500 to 1,000 pesos a year for an entire FC. And only about 20 percent of that cash stayed with the FC; the rest we sent up to the Reco. We never had enough cash, so that was a major problem for the movement." The villagers' contributions "from their meager earnings really kept us going. Most of us also got help from our families. Even though my brothers and mother in Pampanga were very poor, they still sent me things to Batangas whenever they could."[27]

Supplementing confiscations and contributions a little were "production bases" in mountains bordering Central Luzon and in the Laguna-Quezon area. Noncombatant Huks cleared patches of land—the largest was about the size of two football fields side by side—and planted cassava, kamote, and other root crops. A handful of people tended these patches year around. They provided subsistence to Huks who were hiding in the mountains or hiking to another area.

Casto Alejandrino once tried to estimate how many pesos the Huk rebellion needed each year to survive. "I figured it this way: For each armed Huk, we needed 15 pesos per month for basic food, 5 pesos per month for other expenses like cigarettes and such, 30 pesos each year for clothing, 10 pesos a year for shoes. This is about 300 pesos per man." This would mean 1.5 million pesos each year for five thousand armed Huks; and

---

[24] "Minutes of Reco 4 Conference," 21-27 June 1950 (Politburo Exh. N 137-147; CFI, Manila).

[25] "Mga Dagliang Gawain ng RC 1 Mula sa Junio 15 sa Julio 10, 1950" [Immediate Tasks of Reco 1 for period 15 June to 10 July 1950] (CapDoc, Ag.).

[26] Filemon V. Tutay, " 'I Almost Killed Quirino'—Huk Commander Amat," *Philippines Free Press,* 10 May 1952, pp. 6-7.

[27] Bungay interview, 15 July 1970.

3 million pesos for ten thousand Huks. "In addition," Alejandrino went on, "you'd have to add other expenses that varied more, like medicine, guns, ammunition, books, paper, stencils, mimeograph machines, and so on."[28]

The PKP's national finance department, too, tried to calculate the rebellion's total requirements. For 1952, the only year for which I found such information, it anticipated expenditures of 9.2 million pesos. (It is doubtful that the movement ever actually had this much, particularly after its peak strength had passed.) This amount, according to the projected budget, would cover the minimum needs of all districts, field commands, Recos, and national departments. The major anticipated expenditures were "maintenance, arms and ammunition, clothing and allowances, in that order." The budget expected about half the amount would come from "contributions and taxes" (whether in kind or in cash), about a third from confiscations, and the remainder through production bases.[29]

While former Huk leaders and available documents described the rebellion's strengths, they also detailed its weaknesses during this 1949-1951 period. Insufficient money and supplies were major problems. They handicapped everything the movement did, from convening small training sessions for squadron commanders to buying weapons from smugglers and American GIs. The Huk's communications network, despite being an impressive web of couriers and secret messages, never had enough people to make it work as well as Reco leaders wished. Moreover, it never included radios. In 1948, a few Huk leaders managed to purchase in Manila "wireless communications equipment" worth several thousand pesos. They sent it to Central Luzon. All of the equipment, however, was either lost or captured by government forces before the Huks could use it. Never again did the movement have enough cash that was not desperately needed for something else in order to buy radio equipment once more.[30]

Another problem was dishonesty. PKP leaders called it "financial opportunism." All Recos, Luis Taruc reported from Central Luzon in September 1950 to the PKP secretariat, "are dangerously far behind the [desired] standard of devotion, honesty, integrity, and selflessness in matters of material opportunities."[31] The next month in Pampanga, for instance, a "new soldier escaped with the money and jewels" worth over 600 pesos that a Huk squadron had confiscated. He had been entrusted to deliver these valuables to the national finance department. Besides being a financial loss, it demoralized, or as one document said, "made groggy"

---

[28] Alejandrino interview, 16 July 1970.

[29] "Finance: Key to All Our Tasks," *The Communist*, vol. 2, no. 2, August 1951 (CapDoc, Ag.). This publication was one of the principal, although irregular, ones from the PKP's national offices. The "tax" referred to was essentially another term the PKP used for contribution. Neither the HMB nor the PKP collected a tax in the usual sense of the word.

[30] Magusig, to Military Committee through the C.D. [Communication Department] Supervisor, 24 August 1950 (CapDoc, Ag.); and PKP, National Communication Department, "Detailed Plan," 30 August 1950 (CapDoc, Ag.).

[31] Enteng [Luis Taruc], to Coms. of SEC [PKP Secretariat], 26 September 1950 (Politburo Exh. 0 518; CFI, Manila).

other Huks.[32] Such behavior also jeopardized the Huks' support among villagers. "The misuse of finances turns away the masses' trust in our organization," reported the Reco in Southern Luzon in August 1950. For example, it went on, many cadres, contact men, and army leaders wore clothes and shoes and smoked cigarettes "that are more high class than those of the people. When people see this, they begin to suspect that the things they give to help the movement are being used improperly."[33] Confiscations and contributions, Casto Alejandrino said, "were not always used and distributed as they were supposed to be. The distribution system was like a bunch of pipes connected together but with holes in them. Money and goods leaked out because of financial opportunism, bad management, and bad accounting practices. Sometimes, for example, Reco headquarters would get only 20 percent of what they were supposed to receive. We tried to correct these errors, of course. The Huks had its own anti-graft-and-corruption laws long before the Philippine government did."[34]

"We were always weak in military training, too," said Agaton Bulaong, who had been a Huk commander in Bulacan from 1946 until the rebellion's end. "We never really took training seriously enough. God knows it was damn difficult. Even in 1950-1951, when we were strongest, we had lots of problems holding training schools. But if we'd been more serious about it, we could have done better."[35] Insufficient training and guidance were among the major reasons Huk spokesmen frequently cited to explain mistakes and abuses that guerrillas occasionally committed. In Pampanga in August 1950, for example, HMB soldiers criticized themselves for killing and beating captured government soldiers.[36] Casto Alejandrino complained that "Huks from Reco 1 who were crazy killed Mrs. Quezon [wife of the deceased president Manuel Quezon] and others in her car" in April 1949. "They had no orders to do that. It was another case of poorly trained cadres and poor control over the movement by the leadership."[37] Jesus Lava, who was the PKP politburo's "supervisor" for Reco 1 in 1950, said, "Just before I came to Nueva Ecija in May, several Huks had stolen one hundred carabao from several farmers and then sold them and kept the money for their own. This kind of corruption was too common. All Recos had problems like this, but Reco 1 was the worst." Part of the reason was that "government terrorism was so severe there." The Huks were hungry and "terrorism forced them to do bad things in turn. My main job as supervisor was to clean up the Reco, to make reforms."[38]

[32] Enteng [Luis Taruc], to Com. P, 5 October 1950 (Politburo Exh. 0 493; CFI, Manila), and to F, 9 October 1950 (Politburo Exh. 0 645-648; CFI, Manila).

[33] Reco 4, "Palakasin ang Pananalapi ng Kilusan at Bakahin ang Financial Opportunism" [Strengthen the Movement's Finances and Curb Financial Opportunism], August 1950 (CapDoc, Ag.).

[34] Alejandrino interview, 16 July 1970.

[35] Interview with Agaton Bulaong, Camp Crame, Quezon City, 20 July 1970.

[36] "Sagot sa Questionnaire" [Answers to a Questionnaire], 6 August 1950 (CapDoc, Ag.).

[37] Alejandrino interview, 16 July 1970.

[38] Jesus Lava interview, 12 August 1970.

Finally, the rebellion, despite its strengths, could not stop the government's military actions. The rebels could only blunt them. Nor could the movement prevent spies from infiltrating its ranks or protect itself sufficiently against government surveillance. The most injurious example occurred in October 1950. The government's intelligence units simultaneously raided twenty-two Manila homes and apartments and captured six officers in the HMB-PKP's national leadership. Among them was PKP general secretary Jose Lava. Government soldiers also arrested over a hundred others and took hundreds of documents that later assisted their anti-Huk campaign. When other Reco and national leaders at the general headquarters camp in the mountains of Laguna heard about the arrests, their feeling was the one "that divers have when their air hoses are cut deep down in the jagged caverned coral reefs, or that men have in mines when the tunnel behind them caves in. . . ."[39]

Communist Party "Projects Its Leadership"

In 1948, as noted in the previous chapter, the Communist Party (PKP) decided to support the revolt in Central Luzon. Soon thereafter, the party went even further. It stated that the PKP should lead the HMB at all levels: village, municipal, provincial, and national. The party's national leaders knew, however, that real leadership of the rebellion required more than an alliance between top PKP leaders and key HMB leaders. Nor was it enough that some important HMB leaders were also party members. In order to lead the movement, the party needed, in the words of one of its appraisals in 1948, to "establish and make the PKP's leadership felt" within the HMB.[40] Its leaders realized this was not a task easily or quickly done, for the PKP had never been a "mass-based" party, it had had weak ties with the peasant movement in Central Luzon, and as a party memorandum stated in late 1949, even many supporters of the "armed struggle" had a "deep prejudice against communism and communists."[41] Nevertheless, party leaders believed it imperative to "capture the people's uprising in the provinces."[42]

The main reasons, according to the PKP, were these: First, the HMB

---

[39] William J. Pomeroy, *The Forest* (New York: International Publishers, 1963), p. 88. At that time, October 1950, Pomeroy and his Filipina wife, Celia Mariano Pomeroy, were in charge of the HMB-PKP's national education department and were with several other leaders in the Laguna mountain camp.

[40] "Pagpapalawak, Pagpapalakas, at Pagpapatatag ng Hukbo" [How to Expand, Strengthen, and Stabilize the Army], circa 1948 (CapDoc, Ag.).

[41] To PB-Out [Politburo outside of Manila], unsigned, 10 November 1949 (Politburo Exh. 0 310-311; CFI, Manila).

[42] Gaston [Jose Lava], to Comrades of PB[Politburo] Out, 10 December 1949 (Politburo Exh. 0 86; CFI, Manila).

guerrillas were too "undisciplined," too "untrained and uneducated in military and political matters," and too loosely connected. Left in this condition, the armed peasants would surely fail. On the other hand, with proper tutelage and leadership from the PKP, the armed struggle would become an effective, tightly organized "revolutionary movement." Second, the party's role, as prescribed in Marxist-Lennist thought, was to lead the revolution for which the Philippines was now ready. For instance, a PKP document dated April 1950 argued,

> It is axiomatic in Marxist strategy that unless the Communist vanguard succeeds in projecting its hegemony (political and organizational) over the struggle against the enemy, the danger exists that some other political party or group, taking advantage of the revolutionary situation, may launch a counterrevolution to stop the revolution from taking its full course. Under our present situation, considering the fast tempo of development of the revolutionary situation and the present subjective strength of the Communist vanguard, such a danger is very real, making it imperative that we multiply our subjective strength manyfold, to enable us to carry on the revolution against the present enemy as well as against the counter-revolution. Aggressively Project the Party Leadership Over the Struggle for National Liberation![43]

This statement followed the PKP's decision, made during its January 1950 "Enlarged Conference of the Politburo," that the "objective situation" showed convincingly that a "revolution situation" existed, "requiring only the *total mobilization of the entire Party membership* and mass movements it is leading, to render irreversible the tendencies and processes now at work, to make the QLP [Quirino-Liberal Party] administration more unstable" and thereby creating a "revolutionary crisis."[44]

The HMB was no longer just a peasant rebellion, according to the PKP. It was the "military arm" of a revolution led by the Communist Party. That revolution would overthrow the government and establish a new one based on "Bagong Demokrasia" (New Democracy), which would require major changes in the country's politics and economy.

The PKP's military and political resolutions of January 1950 left many members with the impression that Quirino's government would be overthrown by 1952. The party's secretariat later corrected this, however, by saying that the period 1950-1952 was a "crucial" one that could, but not necessarily would, result in the overthrow. The party's top leadership was certain, however, that they had only a few years in which to accomplish the deed. "Rather than a long period of military struggle in which the enemy would be slowly bested through superior tactics and maneuver," stated a

---

[43] This statement is from a document dated April 1950 and reprinted in the PKP's *Ang Komunista* [The Communist], vol. 1, no. 1, August 1950 (CapDoc, Ag.), emphasis in the original.

[44] PKP, Politburo, "Resolution Adopted by the Enlarged Conference of the Politburo," January 1950 (CapDoc, Ag.), emphasis in the original. Also, Alejandrino interview, 14 July 1970; Saulo interview, 4 February 1970; Jose Lava, "Milestones," p. 49.

party document used as a text in PKP training schools, "our military
strategic offensive must be relatively short and speedily victorious. It must,
in other words, have an insurrectionary character." Seizure of power would
climax a combination of guerrilla, insurrectionary, and even "regular
warfare in which HMB forces would meet imperialist-puppet forces in
positional warfare."[45]

Among those PKP leaders most influential in shaping these policies were
Jose and Jesus Lava.[46] They were younger brothers of the deceased Vicente
Lava, the PKP's general secretary during the Japanese occupation. Jose
and Jesus, too, held this office in the party—first Jose from 1948 until his
capture during the October 1950 "politburo arrests" in Manila, and then
Jesus from 1950 until his own capture in 1964. Sons of the prominent and
rather well-to-do Lava family of Bulacan, Jose and Jesus had graduated
from the University of the Philippines in the 1930s—Jose as a lawyer and
Jesus as a doctor. They practiced their respective professions prior to the
Japanese occupation, while also active in such leftist groups as the League
for the Defense of Democracy. During the Japanese occupation they joined
the Hukbalahap resistance movement. Before that Jesus had already joined
the PKP. Jose later joined the PKP because, in his words, of a "deep
feeling for humanity," an awareness of class conflict, and his "desire to do
something for the underdogs."

After the Japanese had been driven out, Jose and Jesus Lava participated in the Democratic Alliance in Manila and in Bulacan province,
where Jesus was one of two DA nominees for Congress in the 1946
election. He won, although like the other DA winners, he was not allowed
to take his seat. Soon thereafter he went underground in order to elude
political enemies connected to Manuel Roxas's Liberal Party. However, he
did not immediately join the peasant rebellion. He stayed mainly in the
greater Manila area with his brother Jose and other theoreticians of the
PKP. He was still in Manila in late 1947, by which time, he recalled, "a
vocal minority in the party argued that peasant rebels in the province
should be helped." He and brother Jose were in this minority. They were
also among those leaders responsible for the PKP's decision in mid-1948 to
reverse previous policy and support the rebellion. Jose and Jesus Lava had
carefully studied Marxist-Leninist thought and were generally regarded by
their peers as the party's best theoreticians. For this reason, they were
exceptionally persuasive during politburo and central committee meetings
when discussing what the party's policies should be.

[45] PKP, Politburo, "Additional Political-Military Strategic Conceptions: Clarifications of the
Enlarged PB Conference Resolution," circa 1950 (CapDoc, Ag.); and PKP, "Military Strategy
and Tactics," circa 1950 (CapDoc, Ag.).

[46] Information about Jose and Jesus Lava comes from the following: Jose Lava, Biographical
Information (PF, CapDoc, Ag.); Jesus Lava, Biographical Information (PF, CapDoc, Ag.);
interviews with Jesus Lava, 12 and 19 August 1970; Noli Me Tangere [Jesus Lava], "Self-
Appraisal," circa 1950 (CapDoc, Ag.); and Armed Forces of the Philippines, "Case Studies of 11
Top Filipino Communists" (Camp Aguinaldo, mimeo, 1958).

Mariano Balgos and Guillermo Capadocia illustrated a contrasting type of PKP leader in terms of social and economic background, but like the Lava brothers, they were important party theoreticians who conluded that the PKP must lead a revolution.[47] Both Balgos and Capadocia were from working-class families: Balgos's father had been a carpenter in Cavite and Capadocia's was a poor laborer in Negros Occidental. Although neither had much formal education, both men were literate and well-read in Marxist-Leninist political thought. They spent most of their adult life in Manila, Balgos as a skilled typesetter who worked for several Manila newspapers and Capadocia as a jack-of-all-trades whose occupations had included cook and waiter. Both men had been active in labor unions since the 1920s, both were charter members of the PKP and were elected to its first central committee. Like many PKP leaders, these men strongly advocated that the Philippines should become an independent nation. Balgos traced his nationalist convictions back to his father, who had been a sergeant in the 1896 Revolution and who impressed on his son that the Filipino revolutionaries should never have surrendered to the Americans.

For more than twenty years Balgos and Capadocia worked closely together as PKP and labor union leaders (with Capadocia also involved to some extent with peasant unions in Central Luzon), Hukbalahap participants (although Capadocia was not permitted to be fully active because he was suspected of having betrayed fellow party members in 1942), and leaders of the Congress of Labor Organizations (CLO) and the PKP after the war (when Capadocia was reinstated as a party member in good standing).

Balgos was one of those top PKP leaders in 1946 who counseled against the party supporting the HMB. He urged instead that the PKP emphasize labor union activities as laborers were the real proletariat for any revolution that might be in the offing. By 1948 he changed his appraisal and was in the new majority when the party aligned itself with the rebellion. Still, neither he nor Capadocia went underground or joined the rebellion. They continued to work openly as CLO leaders.

After the November 1949 elections, however, each man left his family in Manila to join the HMB and help lead the revolution. Each had the courage of his convictions. Each accepted dangerous assignments to lead HMB "expansion forces"—Balgos to the Bicol region and Capadocia to the island of Panay in the Bisayas, his home region. "A Government that is intolerable to most citizens," wrote Capadocia to labor union members in November 1949, "is wobbly and certainly will tumble down. But we must work to hasten its fall." On Christmas Day 1949, just before going underground,

[47] Sources for these brief biographies include the following: Mariano P. Balgos, Biographical Information (PF, CapDoc, Ag.); H. M. Bonifacio [Mariano Balgos], "Ang Pagtaya sa Aking Sarili" [Self-Appraisal], circa 1950 (CapDoc, Ag.); Luis Taruc, *Born of the People*, pp. 90-92; Armed Forces of the Philippines, "Case Studies of 11 Top Filipino Communists"; Guillermo Capadocia, Biographical Information (PF, CapDoc, Ag.); Araneta, "The Communist Party of the Philippines," p. 158.

Balgos also wrote to CLO members, "our nation is still a servant of American imperialism. The Liberal Party government . . . is only a puppet of Wall Street." Now, as a result of the recent waves of repression, he went on, workers and peasants had no other choice but to unite and "take up arms and join the HMB." "We must," Balgas implored "smash the fascist government of the Liberal Party. We must liberate the Philippines."[48]

If only party leaders such as Balgos, Capadocia, and the Lava brothers believed that the party must lead the peasant rebels into revolution, they would have had little consequence. But such PKP leaders were not alone. Agaton Bulaong, Silvestre Liwanag, Jose de Leon, Luis Taruc, and other "middle-level" PKP leaders—most of whom had been HMB leaders since 1946—agreed that the movement needed more direction. A premise, for instance, of an "Over-All Military Plan" for the guerrilla army's growth that Luis Taruc drafted in August 1950 was that "the whole army must always be solidly Party led and Party controlled." The following month Taruc underlined this view when he listed "Close and firm leadership of the Party in the HMB" as the number one task for the leadership in order to correct the weaknesses within the guerrilla forces.[49] Similarly, Peregrino Taruc—another PKP leader in Central Luzon who had joined the HMB before the PKP aligned itself with the rebellion—worked to enhance the party's leadership. The problems of the country, he said, were national problems whose remedies required a national organization and a "national outlook." "One part of this national outlook," he explained, "was to see America as the basic force holding back the Philippines." Because most Huks joined "more for personal reasons, they were not very ideological; they didn't have a national outlook." It was the job of the national organization, led by the PKP, to educate the Huks—"to make members more national in their outlook."[50]

The top PKP leadership's determination to lead the rebellion, coupled with cooperation from PKP leaders in Central Luzon who were already in the HMB, partially accounted for the strengthening of the HMB's organization in 1949-1951. High-ranking party members headed national committees or "departments" that were responsible for finances, communication, education, organization, and the guerrilla forces. These departments had counterparts, with which national leaders tried to keep in contact, in the Recos and frequently in district committees and field commands. In charge of these national departments during this period were dedicated people like Mateo del Castillo (finance), Iluminada Calonge and Ramon Espiritu (communication), Celia Mariano Pomeroy, William Pomeroy, and Pere-

[48] Guillermo Capadocia, to Lupong Tagapagpaganap ng CLO [CLO Executive Committee], 30 November 1949 (Hernandez Exh. D 2015-2016; CFI, Manila); and Mariano Balgos, "Bukas na Liham sa CLO" [Open Letter to the CLO], 25 December 1949 (PF, CapDoc, Ag.).

[49] Enteng [Luis Taruc], to Coms. of SEC [PKP Secretariat], 30 September 1950 (Politburo Exh. 0 279-280; CFI, Manila); Enteng. to Comrades in the MC [Military Committee], "Over-All Military Plan," 26 August 1950 (Politburo Exh. N 307-317; CFI, Manila).

[50] Interview with Peregrino Taruc, Camp Crame, Quezon City, 8 July 1970.

grino Taruc (education), and Federico Maclang (organization). Each Reco also had a politburo-appointed "supervisor" whose responsibility was to enforce national guidelines for discipline, military methods, finances, and so on. Other high-ranking party members such as Angel Baking worked inside the Philippine government and passed its secrets to the PKP. Meanwhile, PKP leaders in Central and Southern Luzon recruited more HMB guerrillas into the party. According to surviving records, one-third to one-half of the Huks in several field commands in Luzon were also PKP members in 1952.

These and other accomplishments led the central committee and politburo to conclude in late 1951 or early 1952 that the PKP's "biggest triumph was the success of the Party in replacing the HMB and the masses under its supervision. Our struggle for the control of the 'reserve force' in the revolution is [also] succeeding. [And] coordination of military operations is being carried out."[51]

In more sober assessments, however, party leaders in the provinces as well as in the HMB-PKP's headquarters knew that this claim to supervision or control over the HMB had to be qualified. Even at the movement's peak, reports from the field showed, for instance, that one of the most troublesome problems from the national PKP leaders' viewpoint was that leaders of section committees, squadrons, and field commands frequently refused to comply with party directives. This happened even if these local leaders were party members. In many instances, local party leaders and members never received the directives because they had no meetings or refused to attend meetings of the party's local branch, apparently because they saw no need to. Such difficulties reflected a larger problem: PKP leaders in the national departments and Recos failed, despite their numerous efforts, to standardize procedures for recruiting people into the party. Consequently, for instance, the PKP's central committee passed a resolution in 1951 that lambasted lower chapters and branches in the provinces for failing to recruit new members "scientifically," and thus allowing "nearly anyone, just as long as he follows orders, into the Party."[52] Just as was true in earlier years, "members" in the PKP lacked a common understanding of what "membership" meant. It still had one meaning to those who made the party's policies but another to those who helped HMB squadrons in Central Luzon.

More fundamental than these limitations to PKP claims that it controlled the HMB was the precarious alliance in the first place between the PKP, as represented by its policies and top leadership, and the peasant

---

[51] PKP, Central Committee, "Political Resolution of the Central Committee," circa late 1951 or early 1952 (CapDoc, Ag.). By "reserve force," the PKP meant those people, mainly among the lower classes and intellectuals, who were not yet involved in the movement but potentially could be recruited.

[52] PKP, Central Committee, "Kapasiyahang Pang-Organisasion" [Organizational Resolution], Conference of 21 February-21 March 1951 (CapDoc, Ag.).

rebellion itself, as represented by most Huks and their supporters, including many of those who also may have been nominal PKP members. The contrast between the objectives and orientations of the PKP, on the one hand, and those of the peasant movement (including the HMB), on the other, showed this.

The maximum program of the PKP was "to establish socialism in the Philippines," for it believed it had a mission to hasten the switch from a burgeois revolution to a socialist one. The minimum program was "to win the bourgeois revolution" and "establish New Democracy." Among the major reforms that would characterize New Democracy and simultaneously propel the country closer to socialism were these: seize large landholdings and haciendas; redistribute these lands to tenants under a "land to the landless" program; nationalize banks, public utilities, transportation and communication services, and mining and forestry industries; establish a government that represented "the proletariat, peasants, middle class, intellectuals, and progressive bourgeois"; throw out the American imperialists and American military bases. The PKP, as the vanguard leadership for New Democracy, also would set examples for all Filipinos to follow. The result would be a reformed society—one, for instance, that emphasized duty to party and country rather than to family, friends, and townmates, and one that based promotions on merit and knowledge rather than on *kilala, kapit,* and *pakikisama* (who you know, good connections, and good personal relationships). These new values, which PKP documents from 1949 onward urged all members to adopt, would be in keeping with what some top leaders called "scientific humanitarianism" and what Casto Alejandrino, one of the party's leading theoreticians by 1950, called "administrative efficiency."[53]

The enemy, according to the PKP's analysis, was twofold. The first was American imperialism. The central political issue, PKP educational pamphlets often said, was who shall rule the Philippines—"American imperialists or the working class?" American imperialism was the cause of the country's rotten conditions—high prices, low wages, high unemployment, rural impoverishment, undemocratic government. Nothing fundamentally had changed in 1946 when the Philippines became, on paper, independent. American rule had continued, the party said. "Parity rights" for American businessmen were only the most obvious fact to demonstrate the point. And, the party's analysis went on, the PKP gravely erred when it

[53] Alejandrino interview, 12 November 1970. Additional sources regarding the PKP's objectives include Jose Lava, "Milestones"; Jesus Lava interview, 19 August 1970; interview with Peregrino Taruc, Camp Crame, Quezon City, 9 July 1970; PKP, "Ang Partido Komunista" [The Communist Party], August 1949 (Politburo Exh. M 1560; CFI, Manila); PKP, Central Committee, "State of the Nation and Call to Action," 29 March 1950 (Politburo Exh. C 3-4; CFI, Manila); Gaston [Jose Lava], to Com. Bob [William Pomeroy] and Coms. of ED [Education Department], 24 August 1950 (Politburo Exh. N 24-26; CFI, Manila); PKP, "Ang Bagong Demokrasia" [New Democracy], circa 1949 (CapDoc, Ag.); PKP, Secretariat, "Bakahin ang Lahat ng Uri ng Oportunismo sa Sinapupunan ng Partido" [Fight All Forms of Opportunism in the Party], 21 April 1950 (CapDoc, Ag.).

failed to recognize this in 1946 and to begin right then and there "to prepare our organizations for the resumption of the armed struggle." The second enemy was those Filipinos who cooperated with the imperialists. These "tools of imperialism" included many politicians, landlords, and businessmen. Any struggle, however, that fought only these agents of imperialism without also attacking the chief evil itself was bound to fail. So central was this view to the PKP's position that its major policy by 1953 was to wage an "anti-imperialist war above all."[54]

The PKP based its commitment to revolution on more than the economic and political conditions in Central Luzon. Guiding the party's top leaders was Marxist-Leninist thought; inspiring them were the Soviet Union and, to a lesser extent, revolutionary movements in China and Vietnam. To them the Philippine movement was one struggle among many in a revolutionary tide of socialism that would sweep away imperialism and liberate exploited peoples throughout the world. A PKP statement on Labor Day 1950, for instance, said to Filipino workers:

> Because of economic recoveries in the Soviet Union and the New Europe, the victory of New Democracy in China under the leadership of the Communists and with atomic and hydrogen bombs the Soviet Union now has—all these together have forced the imperialists to retreat on all fronts. On the national front [in the Philippines], the national liberation movement is spreading, too, by means of the National Liberation Army [HMB] under the leadership and guidance of the Communists. It is fighting American imperialism and its puppets. And it does not give the enemy a moment's rest.[55]

An important application of the party's orientation was the analysis in early 1950 from which it concluded that a revolutionary situation existed. Although the PKP's enlarged central committee conference that year examined conditions inside the Philippines, it apparently emphasized the situation outside the country. Casto Alejandrino recalled that the party's conclusion "was based largely on an analysis of the U.S. economy, an analysis which actually relied a lot on one by a top Soviet economist, whose name I don't remember."[56] Among other things, this assessment argued that the United States economy was crumbling and consequently it could not afford to bail out the Philippine government, which was deeply in debt. Nor could it assist the Philippines' balance of payments deficit, which was another important part of the PKP's analysis. "Skilled Marxists

---

[54] PKP, "Political Transmission No. 4," December 1952, and PKP, "Organizer's Guide No. 2," February 1953 (CapDoc, Ag.). Additional sources include PKP, "Ang Partido Komunista," August 1949; PKP, Politburo, "Resolution Adopted by the Enlarged Conference of the Politburo," January 1950; PKP, "Coordinate Revolutionary Activities in the Cities and Towns with the Armed Struggle in the Field," 9 May 1950 (CapDoc, Ag.); PKP, Central Committee, "Resolusion sa Pananalapi" [Financial Resolution], 21 March 1951 (CapDoc, Ag.).

[55] PKP, Central Committee, "Panahon na Upang Kumilos" [It's Time to Act], 1 May 1950 (Politburo Exh. F 6; CFI, Manila).

[56] Alejandrino interview, 14 July 1950.

in the party," said Peregrino Taruc as he recalled the party's conference, "argued that the Philippines' dollar reserve was at an all time low—the barest minimum that the economy could withstand. They said if it went any lower, the whole economy would absolutely collapse."[57] This appraisal, coupled with the view that revolutionary movements around the world were growing stronger each month, permitted the PKP to "take too lightly," in Alejandrino's words, the fact that the peasant movement in the Philippines was pretty much isolated to Central Luzon.

The party's leadership predicted that because a revolutionary situation existed, people in other parts of the country, too, would join the movement as HMB expansion forces fanned out. This, in turn, would force the Quirino government either to spread its military thinner and thinner, thus becoming a "great hollow shell that can be cracked to pieces," or concentrate its forces on only "the cities and lines of communication, leaving the entire countryside to us, as happened in China and as is now happening in Indo-China."[58]

Whatever merit the party's concerns about the United States economy may have had, later events proved its evaluation wrong. At the time, however, few in the party's leadership questioned it. When I asked Alejandrino in 1970 why the top leaders had looked at the United States to make a decision about conditions for revolution in the Philippines, he replied, "Yes, that is a question that we've been asking ourselves," referring to himself and other former leaders still incarcerated in the Camp Crame prison, "but only in recent years. We didn't raise that question in 1949 and 1950."[59]

The PKP also contended in 1950 that the movement could not establish "New Democracy" by relying only on elections and other legal methods. Rather, it must emphasize "armed struggle" even though, as party documents later conceded, "we were not completely prepared for it." Conditions had forced the PKP "to launch our armed struggle prematurely."[60] From

[57] Interview with Peregrino Taruc, Camp Crame, Quezon City, 13 July 1970.

[58] PKP, Politburo, "Additional Political-Military Strategic Conceptions," circa 1950; PKP, "Military Strategy and Tactics," circa 1950.

[59] Alejandrino interview, 14 July 1970. According to Alejandrino and Jesus Lava, only one person during the PKP's central committee conference in January 1950 raised serious objections to the analysis and the conclusion regarding a revolutionary situation. That person was Alejandrino. His objections, however, were limited to the party's possible underestimation of American military strength; he feared that it could substantially bolster the Philippine army. And he objected to the view that overthrow of the government could come quickly; he favored, instead, a protracted war. According to Luis Taruc and Alfredo Saulo, however, they, too, questioned the analysis, particularly its heavy reliance on economic trends outside the Philippines, even though they eventually endorsed the final decisions. (Saulo interview, 4 February 1970; Luis Taruc interviews, 27 January and 25 February 1970. Also see Taruc, *He Who Rides the Tiger*, pp. 68-74.)

[60] PKP, Central Committee, "Political Resolution of the Central Committee," circa late 1951 or early 1952; PKP, "Ang Partido Komunista," August 1949; and "Basic Military Training for Our Armed Forces," circa 1950 (Politburo Exh. 0 1030; CFI, Manila).

1950 to 1952, the party apparently believed that armed revolution could quickly topple the government. Later the PKP revised its position, advocating instead a "long, protracted struggle." In both periods, however, armed struggle was primary, even though the party tried after 1952 to combine it with nonviolent methods such as "legal cadres" working within legal organizations. The party had also given up on elections. After the terribly corrupt 1949 election, followed by the Nacionalista Party's endorsement of the re-elected Quirino government and the refusal of NP leader Jose Laurel to support the rebellion, the PKP concluded that the two national parties and their leaders were identical—both Liberals and Nacionalistas "defend the interests of imperialists, feudal landlords, compradores, and big capitalists." Consequently, elections were farces.[61]

PKP objectives and orientations contrasted sharply with those of most peasants and most HMB guerrillas and supporters. Peasants wanted, as this book has tried to show, reforms in the tenancy system. Tenant farmers were not even particularly interested in redistributing or owning land. Villagers in Central Luzon also wanted justice, which they defined according to local, traditional standards: landlords should help them, not abuse and exploit them, and government soldiers and civilian guards should leave them alone, not plunder them. They also wanted the right to have their own organizations. Those who had been in the Hukbalahap wanted the recognition they believed they deserved—or at the very least they wanted government officials and police to stop hounding them as though they were criminals. These objectives, in short, were grounded in local grievances. They were far removed from the justifications and theoretical analysis supporting the PKP's concerns, just as they were less ambitious than was the PKP's vision for fundamental economic, social, and political changes.

PKP leaders recognized, at least to an extent, the gap between the party's objectives and those of most peasant rebels. "The great majority of Huks," Jesus Lava said as he reflected on problems within the movement, "joined because of repression by the Philippine government, American soldiers, and civilian guards. Many felt it was either join or be killed without at least putting up a fight. We didn't have time in the movement to train many of these people nor educate them politically—to raise their consciousness."[62]

On the land issue, Lava continued, "it was the party that propagandized the slogan 'Land for the Landless.' That didn't come from an outcry by the peasants. Few peasants then—or even today—were willing to fight with guns for land. Most really only wanted larger shares of the harvests. We used that slogan as a way to try and teach peasants that they should have

---

[61] PKP, Central Committee, "Establish Underground Local Governments as Organs of Power and Struggle to Overthrow Imperialist-Puppet Rule," circa 1950 (Politburo Exh. 0 702-703; CFI, Manila); and PKP, Central Committee, "Resolusion Ukol sa Hinaharap na Halalan" [Resolution concerning the Forthcoming Election], March 1951 (CapDoc, Ag.).

[62] Jesus Lava interview, 12 August 1970.

their own land." Earlier, in fact, the PKP central committee had rebuked peasant associations, particularly the PKM (Pambansang Kaisahan ng mga Magbubukid), for their failure to demand land redistribution.[63]

Similarly, the PKP wished that more peasants and workers would oppose imperialism. "It was hard," said Peregrino Taruc, speaking as one who had been an instructor in PKP schools, "to make peasants see the connection between their problems and American imperialism. It was especially difficult in Angeles, Pampanga, where so many of the people directly or indirectly earned their livelihood from Clark Air Force Base."[64] Many people, including those in the movement, explained Jesus Lava, "could not understand American imperialism. For one thing, it was something they couldn't visually see. Also, Americans were looked up to, especially because of [their help during] liberation [from the Japanese]. The party and the movement had to work hard to get people to try to see how their problems resulted from imperialism."[65] A 1951 PKP report said,

> Even cadres lacked a full grasp of the imperialist forms and actions in our country. They didn't know if the imperialists are directly or indirectly responsible for the destruction of farmers and workers. [If we can unmask American imperialism] the masses will surely side with us in bringing out the complete elimination of imperialist influence in the country.[66]

The party, therefore, continued to press this issue of imperialism, Jesus Lava said, "because we knew that ultimately all problems [in the Philippines] stemmed from this fact."

Party leaders firmly believed that peasants in the movement had to become more national and revolutionary in outlook. One of the most persistent complaints found among PKP documents was that too many cadres, HMB soldiers, and others in the movement were "undisciplined." This included numerous faults, but among the most serious, the PKP literature argued, was that people put their families, friendships, and local concerns ahead of the movement as a whole and the party itself. Particularly bothersome were those HMB guerrillas and even party cadres who refused to go on missions to other areas, despite orders from higher up, and insisted on staying in their home regions. Party leaders like Jesus Lava and Casto Alejandrino, therefore, would have been displeased with a Huk such as Roberto Aspia of San Ricardo, Talavera. He told me that he had no reason to go to other areas because, "I knew who the bad people were in our region. I knew how to watch out for cattle thieves and civilian guards here. But I didn't know this for other areas, so why should I go elsewhere?" Other Huks used the excuse, according to PKP records, that

---

[63] PKP, Central Committee, "Resolusyong Pampolitika" [Political Resolution], May 1948 (CapDoc, Ag.).

[64] Peregrino Taruc interview, 9 July 1970.

[65] Jesus Lava interview, 12 August 1970.

[66] PKP, "Political Transmissions No. 2," December 1951 (CapDoc, Ag.).

they could not leave their wives and children, or they did not want to leave their fellow Huks in their home regions.

PKP reports frequently attributed these discipline problems to "awaitism" among many rebels. That is, they lacked "devotion to the revolution" or a commitment to engage fully in nationwide armed struggle to overthrow the government. Another explanation was "low political consciousness," insufficient "class consciousness," or, as one document from Pampanga and vicinity reported in 1952, people were not "awake":

> [Concerning the] awakening of the Comrades in the Army [HMB] and the Cadre—the majority are not yet politically and militarily awakened; however, there are improvements. [Concerning the] awakening of the Masses—Still weak. Frankly, the majority still believe in using peaceful means to obtain the goals of the struggle.[67]

In order to correct such discipline problems and to "raise people's consciousness," the PKP prescribed "political education," which would include more study of Marxist-Leninist philosophy, and strong leadership from the party—especially from members who were well-versed in communism. These were reasonable prescriptions, for the PKP had concluded that the necessary "objective conditions" for revolution already existed. If people in the countryside, and in urban areas for that matter, still failed to revolt, then it must be the fault of poor leadership or low politicalization and "false consciousness."

Casto Alejandrino's views on leadership and education reflected the party's position as portrayed in documents from its national offices. When discussing the relationship between leaders and followers, Alejandrino made an analogy to the relationship between a capable rider and a spirited horse.[68] "A spirited horse alone will only cause damage, running wild in no particular direction. But a capable rider can guide the horse to go in a direction that will lead someplace, achieve something. The party was trying to be the capable rider for the masses, who were like the spirited horse." Alejandrino offered another analogy to emphasize his point. It's like red hot iron. The iron is nothing unless molded and shaped by a hammer. The masses in Central Luzon and elsewhere were like the red hot iron, and leaders were wielding the hammer. If done properly, the hammer—the leaders—can turn a revolutionary situation into a revolutionary crisis." When explaining why Huk expansion missions to areas beyond Central Luzon, such as to the Bisayas area, enjoyed little support among the villagers, Alejandrino said that too many "bad elements were taken into the movement"—that is, bandits and thieves. "Our leaders there should have recruited more good elements," he said. I suggested that maybe the "good elements" would not join the HMB because, even though they were poor people, they did not feel exploited; maybe they saw rich

---

[67] Reco 2, Ed [Education Department], "Annual Summary Report, 1952" (CapDoc, Ag.).
[68] Alejandrino interview, 14 July 1970.

people as their benefactors rather than their exploiters. "That may be true," Alejandrino replied. "But good leaders would have been able to educate the people to the realities of their situation and broken down their allegiances [to the rich]."

While emphasizing its leadership and education, the PKP also advised that "the party must learn from the masses" and that the people know best what they should do. In 1950, for instance, party leaders criticized themselves and the PKP generally for having failed in the past to listen well to workers and peasants. As a result, the PKP had issued directives in the 1940s which were out of step with what the people wanted. Consequently, the masses, including "rank and file" party members, simply ignored the party's leaders. Two particularly significant examples that 1950 documents cited were the PKP's "retreat for defense" policy during the Japanese occupation—a policy that most Hukbalahap supporters ignored—and the PKP's position in 1946 that villagers and rank and file party members in Central Luzon should not revolt. From this history, the PKP's top leadership concluded "that the masses and Party members who have had some revolutionary background and experience and who have to bear the brunt of enemy suppression instinctively know when to advance and when to retreat in the face of enemy fire."[69]

The party's prescriptions, in short, were inconsistent. One voice said, we PKP leaders must learn from the people. Another said, we PKP leaders must lead and teach the people lest they fail to see that the revolution is coming. Given this ambiguity, party leaders must have had difficulty judging at any particular time which counsel to heed.

The top PKP leaders tended to insist that only they—particularly the handful in the secretariat—should make the important decisions for both the PKP and HMB. This included, for example, deciding how to spend money and supplies confiscated by HMB guerrillas, defining the "real enemy," defining the "aims of our struggle" because many rank and file party members and Huks did not have this "basic knowledge," and deciding whether the "revolutionary situation" was rising or falling.[70] Often times these decisions and policies, although maybe reasonable according to the party theoreticians' analysis, had little support among party members and Huks generally. In 1950, for instance, the party secretariat said a large portion of the HMB should be converted from a guerrilla army into a "regular army." The plan, however, remained a blueprint, partly because so many Huk squadron leaders and even notable HMB-PKP leaders like Luis

[69] PKP, "Coordinate Revolutionary Activities," 9 May 1950.

[70] PKP, SEC [Secretariat], to Comrades of Politburo-Out, 10 June 1950, and "Overall Plan of Expansion and Development of the Party, HMB, and Mass Organizations," circa July 1950 (Politburo Exh. 0 271-272; CFI, Manila); Greg [Jose Lava], to Comrades of Politburo-Out, 23 September 1950, 14 October 1950 (Politburo Exh. M 31-32, O 341-342; CFI, Manila); PKP, Central Committee, "Resolusion sa Pananalapi" [Financial Resolution], 21 March 1951; PKP, "Paraan sa Pagtatatag ng mga Organisasyong Pang-masa" [Method for Establishing Mass Organizations], 9 May 1951 (CapDoc, Ag.); and "Resolusyon sa Disiplina ng Partido" [Resolution Concerning Discipline in the Party], 21 March 1951 (CapDoc, Ag.).

Taruc opposed it.[71] In 1951, PKP directives said the movement should confiscate land in HMB strongholds in order to show peasants what New Democracy would be like. Again this was not done, for the HMB's strength had never been sufficiently strong to keep out government troops in order to have such "liberated areas." "Better to be alive and not try to take land for themselves than to get killed trying it. That was the peasants' thinking even in HMB strongholds," Luis Taruc explained. Similarly, the 1952 annual report from Reco 2 stated that peasants there were afraid of such proposals.[72] In 1951-1952, the PKP said that it must try to eliminate the "trade union mentality" among workers by abandoning the legal struggle and concentrating instead on "illegal revolutionary forms of organization among workers" in order to elevate workers "to their rightful place as the vanguard of the revolution." But workers had never been militant nor very sympathetic to the peasants' movement in Central Luzon. Moreover, the party tried to force workers into "armed struggle" and "headlong clashes with the forces of the State" at least once, in early 1950, but failed.[73] Such examples indicated that the distance between the top PKP leadership and the majority of peasant rebels or the lower classes generally had not lessened significantly between 1948 and 1951.

The middle-level PKP leaders tended to hold a different view. Although they believed that the PKP's leadership was necessary, they also believed there were serious limits as to how far even well-meaning leaders could push or change rebellious peasants. Compared to the top leadership they leaned toward the view that PKP leaders must learn from the people. Like

[71] The evidence for this and the following two illustrations comes from several sources, the most important of which are cited here and in the following two footnotes: PKP, Politburo, "Resolution Adopted by the Enlarged Conference of the Politburo," January 1950; PKP, "Military Strategy and Tactics," circa 1950; PKP, SEC [Secretariat], to Politburo-Out, 2 September 1950 (Politburo Exh. O 643; CFI, Manila); Enteng [Luis Taruc], "Over-All Military Plan," 26 August 1950; Enteng [Luis Taruc], to Coms. of SEC [PKP Secretariat], 30 September 1950; Luis Taruc interview, 27 January 1970.

[72] PKP, Politburo, "Additional Political-Military Strategic Conceptions," circa 1950; Francisco Rodilla, "From Provisional Revolutionary Governments," *The Communist*, August 1951; PKP, Central Committee, "Resolusion ukol sa Pangsamantalang Pamahalaang Mapanghimag-sik" [Resolution Concerning Provisional Revolutionary Government], March 1951 (CapDoc, Ag.); Peregrino Taruc interview, 13 July 1970; Bulaong interview, 20 July 1970; Luis Taruc interview, 25 February 1970; Reco 2, "Summary of Annual Political Report," January-December 1952.

[73] PKP, Central Committee, "Political Resolution," circa late 1951 or early 1952, and "Resolution on Our Tasks among the Industrial Workers," March 1951 (CapDoc, Ag.); PKP, National Education Department, "Patnubay sa Pagpapataas ng Tempo sa Gawain ng mga Organo ng mga Reco at sa loob ng mga Kampong Pampalagian" [Instruction for Heightening the Tempo of Work in the Recos and Regular Camps], 28 February 1952 (CapDoc, Ag.); PKP, "Coordinate Revolutionary Activities," 9 May 1950; PKP, SEC [Secretariat], to Comrades of Politburo-Out, 29 April 1950 (Politburo Exh. O 319-320; CFI, Manila); Jesus Lava interview, 19 August 1970. Also see Hoeksema, "Communism in the Philippines" for additional evidence that the PKP generally stressed that workers, rather than peasants, were more important to focus on because they were supposed to be more inclined to revolution.

the party's top leaders but unlike most Huks, these middle-level leaders were anti-imperialists and strong nationalists, they favored socialism and the New Democracy, they frequently advocated land redistribution, and they hoped to topple the corrupt government in Manila. Unlike most of the top PKP leaders, however, they had been leaders of the Huk rebellion since 1946, they were closer to the villagers (many were the sons of peasant families), they understood the villagers' outlooks and ways, and they had followings among the peasantry due to their long, intimate involvement with the movement in Central Luzon. Indeed, the fact that they had a base of support among the peasantry was an important reason why they had standing in the PKP hierarchy.

Luis Taruc was a notable example of this type of leader. He was one of the most widely respected peasant leaders in Central Luzon. He also held high positions in the PKP. By the late 1940s, for instance, he was one of nine politburo members and one of thirty-one central committee members. Unlike most PKP leaders in the politburo and other national offices of the party, Luis Taruc was not an intellectual, theoretician, or labor union leader. Rather, his high offices in the PKP reflected his popularity as a peasant leader. In fact, his rudimentary understanding of Marxist-Leninist thought and his reputation among peasants bothered many top PKP leaders. Casto Alejandrino, who had known Taruc since the 1930s when the two men had worked together in the movement in Pampanga, said, "Luis was never a revolutionary, really, despite all the party's efforts to turn him into one. His basic problem was he liked publicity too much."[74] Jesus Lava, the former PKP general secretary, recalled of Taruc, "The party had long been concerned about his tendencies to seek personal glory at the expense of the movement. But the party couldn't discipline him severely for that [at least not in the 1940s and early 1950s] because of his large following. Taruc had great prestige and popularity with the people."[75]

The party did reprimand Luis Taruc for "excessive humanism" and for ignoring party instructions. In 1950, for instance, he reportedly was too generous to cadres in Pampanga, he objected to the party secretariat taking for its own use couriers he had recruited, he objected to higher party officials opening his mail, and he deviated substantially from the prepared text that the party's secretariat had instructed him to follow when a journalist interviewed him at a Huk hideout.[76] Taruc also got into trouble for using kapit, family ties, and pakikisama to get things done rather than

---

[74] Alejandrino interview, 16 July 1970.

[75] Jesus Lava interview, 12 August 1970.

[76] Enteng [Luis Taruc], to O Beria [Federico Maclang], 28 April 1950, May Day 1950, 23 July 1950 (Politburo Exh. M 421-422, M 427-430, N 337-339; CFI, Manila); O Beria, to Enteng, 1 July 1950 (Politburo Exh. N 334; CFI, Manila); Gaston [Jose Lava], to Comrades of Politburo-Out, 6 May 1950, 20 May 1950, 25 June 1950 (Politburo Exh. O 91-92; O 93-95, O 99-101; CFI, Manila); Luis Taruc interview, 27 January 1970; Jesus Lava interview, 12 August 1970. Also see the PKP's critique of Luis Taruc, written in 1954, the year he surrendered, "Life Cycle of Careerism" (CapDoc, Ag.); and William J. Pomeroy, "Portrait of a Turncoat," *Political Affairs* 46 (December 1967):39-41.

going through prescribed channels within the party's organization. "I was also criticized for using Christian teachings when talking to people in Central Luzon," Taruc said. "Christ was a radical, a socialist. And when people said they couldn't join the movement because their destiny while on earth was to be poor but once in heaven they'd get their reward, I explained to them that Christ was a socialist."[77] The party's schools and literature paid no attention to religion, except sometimes to criticize it. "This was a mistake," said Taruc. "Yet I got in trouble for doing what I did."

Taruc later stated that one serious weakness in the party was an insufficient number of leaders who had "a good feel for the people's needs and desires. Not enough party leaders understood peasants, what they wanted, how they wanted to work for it." Another underlying difficulty was different interpretations of what the PKP leadership could do. Taruc and others like him held that "the Communist Party couldn't push people to revolution, or propel people into a revolutionary crisis. The job of a revolutionary leader is only to guide the people's revolutionary anger, not try to create that anger. It can't do the latter. Lava and others figured the party not only could but should."[78]

The Decline: 1952-1956

If there was any single turning point as the rebellion passed from its prime to its decline, it was between late 1951 and the first half of 1952.

"The advances of our struggle in this territory were much less compared to 1951," began a detailed report about Pampanga and other parts of Reco 2 that a PKP politburo supervisor prepared at the end of 1952. "There were many [in Reco 2] who were convinced and used by the enemy. There were many among our comrades who were disappointed and discouraged." The HMB, it said, "decreased in number compared to 1951," largely because of "comrades who died in action, traitors and those who surrendered, few recruits due to the downward trend in battle successes and insufficient care exercised in recruitment." The number of people in towns and barrios who once supported the HMB also "declined significantly." The major reasons were

(a) Weakening of the leaders . . . who are close to the masses. They lack awakening and propaganda. (b) There are many barrio residents who refuse to be organized. Those who were formerly organized no longer wish to speak in the name of the organization out of fear of the enemy and because of the promise they made to the enemy that they will not take sides. (c) There are many [supporters] who allowed themselves to be used by the enemy. (d) The barrio folks evacuated to the towns and the other evacuees no longer communicate with us.

[77] Luis Taruc interview, 27 January 1970.
[78] Luis Taruc interview, 25 February 1970.

The PKP's membership, too, declined due to "comrades who died in action, others who surrendered, and cells [that] were dispersed and never reorganized because of . . . the enemy; others allowed themselves to be made instruments of the enemy."[79]

By 1953, the movement's remaining leaders were powerless to prevent even larger numbers of armed peasants from leaving. And few peasants now joined the Huks, unlike in the past, to replace those who lay dead in the rice fields and on the mountain slopes. By 1955-1956, only widely scattered handfuls of desperate rebels remained.

Benjamin Cunanan, leader of 650 Huks in field command 21 in Pampanga-Tarlac in 1951, only had a hundred men by early 1953 and "only seventy in 1956," he said. "The rest had surrendered or been killed. Mostly surrendered. When I was captured [in 1962], there were fourteen men under my command."[80] So many squadrons of Huks had completely disappeared by the mid-1950s that previously strong field commands and Recos were decimated. When Ignacio Dabu took charge of Reco 1 (centered in Nueva Ecija) in 1954, for instance, he found it had neither many rebels nor barrio and municipal underground groups for support.[81] Not long thereafter, according to Silvestre Liwanag of Pampanga, "Reco 1 was dissolved because it had too few people left. Most had surrendered, quit, died, or been captured."[82] A short while later all of Central Luzon, which previously had three Recos, was placed under one command. Liwanag was in charge. Now the entire Central Plain had fewer Huks than Liwanag had had in his field command along the Pampanga-Bataan border. By the mid-1950s, Peregrino Taruc recalled, the number of people in each of the remaining field commands "had dwindled to between thirty and forty—less than the normal squadron size had been in 1950." And these, he added, "were scattered in groups of only three or five men each."[83]

The situation for Huks in Southern Luzon—principally Laguna and Batangas—was worse. Huks there never had enjoyed the strong village support they knew in Central Luzon. "The initial response," Casto Alejandrino said about people in Southern Luzon, "was the same [as in Central Luzon]—warm, hospitable, and attentive to what the HMB said and did. The difference was in their stability; the support of people in Central Luzon was more stable, more dependable, when times became tough and pressure great."[84] One explanation, according to Cenon Bungay, was that villagers in Southern Luzon, unlike in Central Luzon, had little

[79] Reco 2, "Summary of Annual Political Report," January to December 1952.

[80] Cunanan interview, 11 August 1970. Also Genoveva Dumlao, Sworn Statement to Central Intelligence Bureau, Armed Forces of the Philippines, 17 October 1953 (PF, CapDoc, Ag.).

[81] Ignacio G. Dabu, Unsigned Statements to the Philippine Constabulary, 24, 26, 27, 31 October and 8 December 1960 (CapDoc, Cr.).

[82] Interview with Silvestre Liwanag, Camp Crame, Quezon City, 21 July 1970.

[83] Peregrino Taruc interview, 13 July 1970.

[84] Alejandrino interviews, 14 and 16 July 1970.

political experience and awareness.[85] Similarly, Alejandrino noted that the region's "pockets of strong support" for the Huks were mainly areas where peasant associations had been active in the 1930s. Another explanation was that some recruits were loyal to Jose Laurel, the presidential candidate defeated in the 1949 election. As Batangas was Laurel's home province, some of his followers had joined the Huks in order to strike back at Quirino's administration, which they believed had stolen the election. After Laurel made his peace with Quirino's government, his supporters abandoned the Huks.

Alejandrino, who had been the principal HMB commander for Southern Luzon since 1950, returned to Central Luzon in 1954. The situation in Laguna and Batangas was so dangerous that he and other Huks with him could not remain in even the strongest HMB-support areas there. He felt safer in Central Luzon and managed to elude government troops until 1960 by continually moving around, usually in the company of a dozen bodyguards he called his "security forces." Two former Huks from Southern Luzon also illustrated the Huks' decline there. Faustino Tenorio, a son of a carpenter in San Pablo, Laguna, had joined the HMB in 1947 when he was sixteen years old. He quit, he said, in 1953. "I surrendered because of pleadings from my family and because things were in such a sad state for the Huks. People who before had really supported the movement were by then being taken in by Magsaysay's program."[86] Paulino Huertas, who had joined the Huks in 1950, was the son of a tenant farmer, a man with less than four years of formal education, and a native of Batangas. Between 1953 and 1956 (the year government soldiers captured him), he said, the HMB in Batangas lost the support of the people, the government forces got stronger, and the remaining Huk rebels themselves were getting "tired and run down."[87]

The efforts of some HMB leaders after 1948 to expand the rebellion far beyond Central Luzon were no consolation, either, to the dying rebellion. Huks had never managed to earn sufficient support from peasants in Bicol, Bisayas, Ilocos, and Northern Luzon regions. In part the fault lay with the Huks and national PKP leaders themselves. "The theory of sending our better cadres on expansion missions was not always put into practice," confessed Casto Alejandrino.[88] In fact, sometimes the most poorly trained and undisciplined Huks went. Among them were, in Alejandrino's words, "rascals, including murderers, rapists, and thieves." Jesus Lava gave an illustration. One important reason why the HMB "did not make much headway in the Ilocos area," he said, was that one of the leaders "raped a Negrito woman. This closed off all mountain routes, which went through Negrito territory, making travel for our missions very difficult."[89] Even

[85] Bungay interview, 15 July 1970.
[86] Interview with Faustino Tenorio, Camp Crame, Quezon City, 27 July 1970.
[87] Interview with Paulino Huertas, Camp Crame, Quezon City, 29 July 1970.
[88] Alejandrino interview, 16 July 1970.
[89] Jesus Lava interview, 12 August 1970.

when the Huks were well behaved—and probably most were—their forces still failed to grow. They remained by and large small groups of poorly armed and hungry people who lived in mountainous hideouts and were often isolated from the villagers in the lowlands. They were unable, in short, to export rebellion from Central Luzon. Perhaps one reason was that peasants in Bicol, the Bisayas, and elsewhere were not outraged by their conditions, or perhaps they chose means other than rebellion to protest.[90]

These missions were the last ones for such dedicated revolutionaries as Mariano Balgos and Guillermo Capadocia. In September 1951, government troops killed Capadocia and several men with him at his hideout in the mountains of Panay Island. And in December 1954 they killed Balgos, along with several others, after a pursuit through the mountainous terrain of Bicol that lasted several months.

Why did the Huk rebellion in Central Luzon, which had been going on since 1946, fade away by the mid-1950s? No single answer will do. According to surviving Huk records and the recollections of former participants, there are many reasons. Most are nearly inextricably wound together. Nevertheless, there is considerable consensus about three interrelated ones.

The first can perhaps be best summarized as a general weariness among peasant rebels and their supporters in Central Luzon. "Battle fatigue" were the words Benjamin Cunanan used to describe the Huks' condition in his field command by the early 1950s.[91] Similarly, Silvestre Liwanag portrayed the rebels in the vicinity of the Pampanga-Bataan border as "tired and exhausted." Huks, he said, were able to spend less and less time near friendly barrios and had to spend more time hiding and keeping on the move. "We needed a place to retreat and to recuperate," he concluded, "but we didn't have one, unlike guerrillas in China and Indochina."[92]

Not only were rank and file Huk guerrillas "suffering from battle fatigue as early as 1951," said Alfredo Saulo, who was with the HMB in Central Luzon until 1958, but barrio residents were, too. "Supporting the rebellion," he explained, "was becoming a serious strain for people in Central Luzon": food was scarce, "people didn't have enough time or couldn't farm their crops, and besides that, they were sharing what they did have with the guerrillas."[93] A report from a district committee in Nueva Ecija in October 1951 explained that because living conditions for villagers were so hard, it was increasingly difficult for them to contribute to the movement. Many villagers were even borrowing in order to assist the Huks. By 1953-1954, several Huk commanders reported that peasants in their areas complained

---

[90] The question of why the Huk rebellion failed to stir Filipinos elsewhere certainly deserves more attention. My research, unfortunately, allows me to say no more.

[91] Cunanan interview, 11 August 1970.

[92] Liwanag interview, 21 July 1970.

[93] Interview with Alfredo Saulo, Quezon City, 14 April 1969.

about continually having to give food and supplies to the guerrillas.[94] As more villagers even in Central Luzon became reluctant to feed and help the guerrillas, remaining Huks lost confidence in themselves and peasants they relied on. Then they became more desperate. Consequently, explained Luis Taruc, they made more "mistakes against the people."[95] They began to steal from villagers and even beat up or kill innocent persons. This partly accounted for why Reco 2 reported in 1952 that "there are cases when masses dislike or hate some of us."[96] The Huks were coercing the very ones they were supposed to protect and alienating those they needed for support.

The second major reason was government reforms. Although modest and frequently superficial, these reforms were sufficient to improve the government's image and provide hope for those Huks and rebellion supporters for whom revolt had been a last resort in the face of government and landlord lawlessness. As most rebels were in this category, the government's actions did significantly weaken the HMB.

Among the most important events to improve the government's appearance was the 1951 election. Many had expected the worst from this election, because the one in 1949 had been so blatantly violent and dishonest. The PKP predicted that the Quirino administration and Liberal Party would either cancel the 1951 election or "duplicate the fraud and terror committed in the last elections to assure their electoral victory." Either one, the party said, would "ignite the people's wrath. . . ." Consequently PKP policy was to boycott the election in order to help "make the masses realize the necessity, the absolute necessity, of revolution. . . . We must complete the people's disillusionment regarding the elections."[97] Many Huk leaders in the field commands and Recos urged boycott, too. Contrary to

[94] "Ulat ng D'Com-1" [Report of District Committee No. 1], to Reco 1, 21 October 1951 (CapDoc, Ag.). Reco 10, "Sirkular: Hingil sa Pagharap sa Pangunahing Suliranin ng Masa" [Circular: Concerning the Foremost Problem of the Masses], 29 March 1953 (CapDoc, Ag.); Romeo Soliman (a captured Huk from Central Luzon), miscellaneous documents and his sworn statement to Philippine government officials, 9 August 1954 (PF, CapDoc, Ag.); "Pangtatluhang Buwang Ulat ng FC 102 mula Abril 1954 hanggang Junio 1954" [Quarterly Report of Field Command 102 for April to June 1954], (CapDoc, Ag.)—FC 102 was supposed to be in Batangas or Cavite (which were provinces in Reco 10), but by 1954 some of its members were also in Central Luzon.

[95] Luis Taruc interview, 25 February 1970.

[96] Reco 2, "Summary of Annual Political Report," January to December 1952.

[97] PKP, Politburo, "Additional Political-Military Strategic Conceptions," circa 1950; PKP, Central Committee, "Resolusion Ukol sa Hinaharap na Halalan" [Resolution Concerning the Forthcoming Election], March 1951; Jose Lapuz, "Boycott the National Election," The Communist, August 1951. Edward G. Lansdale, the American counterinsurgency advisor to Magsaysay during the 1950s, certainly exaggerates his importance when he claims he tricked the PKP into its boycott of the 1951 election. If indeed he did slip to the PKP in 1951 a fake document of his own design which argued for the boycott, it was hardly the cause of the party's position. Several party documents written in 1950, including the first one cited here, argued this tactic. Edward Geary Lansdale, In the Midst of Wars (New York: Harper and Row, 1972), p. 92.

238   THE HUK REBELLION

these expectations, however, the 1951 election was relatively peaceful and honest. Even compared to later ones, the one in 1951 was frequently described by Filipinos as among the most legitimate. An immediate effect on peasants in Central Luzon, recalled Luis Taruc and other former Huk leaders, was to "open again elections as alternatives to rebellion."[98]

Similarly, the PKP's top leadership wrote in December that the relatively "peaceful, clean election" had caused people to doubt "the immediate need of armed struggle, especially if we consider the fact that the great majority of the masses greatly favor the existence of peace and order even though they suffer poor living conditions. . . . That is why the moment they sense any reason *not* to lose faith and confidence in elections, they adhere to it immediately. This illusion is hard to eliminate. . . ." This feeling was strong, the PKP later emphasized, even among those who were sympathetic to the movement.[99] And this sentiment spread in 1953 when Ramon Magsaysay, the man villagers credited most for improving the government, won the presidency in another relatively clean election. Seventy percent of the vote in Central Luzon was for Magsaysay.

More than any other reason, peasants in Central Luzon liked Magsaysay, first as secretary of defense (1950-1953) and then as president (1954-1957), because he had personal contact with villagers and because the military became less abusive under his leadership. "When Magsaysay started making reforms in the Philippine army and in the government generally," Jesus Lava said, "it had an impact not only on the movement's mass support but on the armed [Huk] soldiers as well. Many left because repression was ending, and they were not ideologically committed enough to stay in the movement, especially as things grew worse for the Huks."[100] Agaton Bulaong, a major peasant leader in the Huk movement in Bulacan, concluded that a crucial reason why the HMB increasingly lost support among villagers was "the Magsaysay thing." "All the reforms that were promised and partially implemented," he said, "even though small and show-case in nature, were encouraging for people. Many people believed the government; they believed Magsaysay." Especially impressive, he went on, "were the reforms within the government troops, considering how badly government forces and civilian guards treated people before."[101]

Secondary to a better behaved military, from the peasant's viewpoint, but still important to the government's improved image, were numerous rural projects aimed particularly at Central Luzon. They included agricultural

[98] Luis Taruc interview, 27 January 1970.
[99] PKP, "Political Transmissions No. 2," December 1951, emphasis added, and "Political Transmissions No. 5," July 1953 (CapDoc, Ag.).
[100] Jesus Lava interview, 12 August 1970. For an excellent study of Magsaysay's impact on people in Central Luzon, see Frances L. Starner, *Magsaysay and the Philippine Peasantry* (Berkeley: University of California Press, 1961). One of the points Starner makes, which corroborates the evidence I have from Huk records and interviews, is that peasants in Central Luzon appreciated Magsaysay more for reforming the military and for his personal, reassuring style than for agrarian programs he promised or began.
[101] Bulaong interview, 20 July 1970.

extension services, cash credit for peasants, barrio health clinics, agrarian courts to hear grievances between tenants and landlords, new bridges and roads, several hundred "liberty wells," and irrigation canals. Between 1952 and 1955 the government devoted far more attention and money to rural public works and agrarian reform than it had during the previous six years.[102] To many Huk and PKP leaders, such projects were token gestures for propaganda purposes. To the government, they formed part of its new "psychological warfare" against the rebellion. Jose Crisol, one of the designers of this "psych war," said these projects and reforming the military were aimed "at the soft core of the Huk movement—those who were not hard-core communists or Huk leaders, but rather the lower levels of the movement and the mass base."[103] The rural projects, he agreed, were not effective for what they accomplished, for they were, indeed, "very small compared to the total agrarian problem." Rather, they were effective "for the method in which they were publicized and advertised. They gave people hope that the government could do things for them, which they were trying to get by violence and at the risk of their lives."

One of the best advertised programs, which Magsaysay began while secretary of defense, promised homestead lands to Huks who surrendered. This Economic Development Corps (EDCOR) program spent several million pesos and resettled 950 families on land in Mindanao. Many of these families, however, were not from Central Luzon, and less than 250 of them had been in the Huk movement. The EDCOR homesteads, therefore, had no noticeable effect on the number of tenant farmers or Huks in Central Luzon. But this program never intended to accomodate even a modest percentage of Huks. In fact, the government hoped that only a few Huks would accept its offer of land, for it had only a little bit of land available. The intent was to steal from the PKP and HMB the idea of "land for the landless" with a well-publicized experiment that was more than the Huk movement itself had been able to do.[104]

[102] For details regarding these policies, see David O. D. Wurfel, "The Bell Report and After: A Study of the Political Problems of Social Reform Stimulated by Foreign Aid" (Ph.D. dissertation, Cornell University, 1960); Starner, *Magsaysay and the Philippine Peasantry;* Jose V. Abueva, *Focus on the Barrio* (Manila: Institute of Public Administraton, University of the Philippines, 1959); and Jose V. Abueva, *Ramon Magsaysay: A Political Biography* (Manila: Solidaridad, 1971).

[103] Interview with Jose Crisol, Civic Action Program Office, Camp Aguinaldo, Quezon City, 15 December 1969.

[104] Philippines, Economic Development Corps, *Annual Report, 1956-1957,* annex 4, and *Final Report on the Land Settlement Project of the Armed Forces of the Philippines Now Known as Genio Farm, Midsayap, Cotobato,* December 1953-June 1956; Wurfel, "The Bell Report and After," pp. 465, 469; Frate Bull, *Philippine Land Reform: 1950-1958* (Manila: International Cooperation Administration, 1958), p. 18; Roy E. Davis, *Land Settlement and Title Clearance Final Report, 1952-1957* (Manila: USOM/International Cooperation Administration, 1957), pp. 34-35; James P. Emerson, *Land Reform Progress in the Philippines, 1951-1955* (Manila: International Cooperation Administration, 1956), p. 43; Crisol interview, 15 December 1969. For a contrasting assessment of EDCOR's impact on the rebellion, see Alvin Scaff, *The Philippine Answer to Communism* (Stanford, California: Stanford University Press, 1955).

In a similar manner, the handful of new agrarian courts, the government-paid lawyers who assisted tenants in Central Luzon, the government-sponsored credit facilities, and Magsaysay's vows to reduce tenant farmers' rents defused the salient issue of tenancy reform. Much of these efforts came after 1953—after the rebellion had begun to recede. Preceding them, however, were widely publicized promises and a few projects that appealed to villagers. These and Magsaysay's pesonal touch and the image of reform he projected as secretary of defense played on the peasantry's hope that revolt was no longer necessary.

Try as they might, leaders in the PKP and HMB failed to convince villagers that the government's promises and projects would never significantly improve their situation. "The people entertain the wrong impression," complained a PKP directive in 1954, "that the principles of the movement are also similar to the principles of Magsaysay."[105] Similarly, a 1956 report about Central Luzon from remaining Huk and PKP leaders there admitted, reluctantly, that although some villagers were disillusioned by then with the Magsaysay government,

> most of the people have faith and trust in the RM [Ramon Magsaysay] administration. . . . Many have been influenced by deceitful government propaganda, the establishment of 'welfare agencies' (Agricultural Credit and Cooperative Financing Administration, Farmers' Cooperative Marketing Association, Philippine Rural Reconstruction Movement, Rural Improvement Club, Social Welfare Administration) and the promised land for the landless program administered by the Land Tenure Administration.

People also believed, the report continued, that the government was better than previous ones; they said, " 'Magsaysay is good compared to Roxas and Quirino. Now we no longer evacuate, we can go everywhere we want, and we are able to work freely, especially on the farm.' " And villagers credited Magsaysay with reforming the military, as soldiers "don't manhandle people so much as before."[106]

A third major reason for the Huk movement's decline was the government's more effective use of force. Government soldiers damaged HMB forces more than they had been able to do prior to 1952, while simultaneously mistreating villagers less. They managed to do this partly because they were reorganized and retrained. For instance, the government merged the Philippine Constabulary with the Armed Forces of the Philippines, put both under the Department of National Defense (rather than having only the AFP under the Defense Department while the PC was under the Interior Department), formed eleven new "Battalion Combat Teams" that were better equipped and trained than previous military "companies" had been, attached small units to the BCTs that were mobile and whose soldiers were tutored in guerrilla warfare, disbanded the civilian guards,

---

[105] PKP, "Organizer's Guide No. 4," January 1954 (CapDoc, Ag.).

[106] Y-2 Report, "Complete Report of the Situation Obtaining in this Territory," March to October 1956 (CapDoc, Ag.).

and boosted the morale of the troops by paying and feeding them regularly and rewarding them with promotions and additional money for service well done. "Our reforms inside the military," said Crisol, "emphasized professionalism and in-service training." In terms of new military tactics and strategies, he said, "we emphasized small, hard-hitting groups of soldiers to drive deep into Huk areas, all the way to their camps. Connected to this was a whole orientation to commando tactics. These reforms were not only more effective militarily, but less damaging to the civilians."[107] Although not accomplished overnight, government officials did make these changes quickly, beginning in early 1950 and accelerating after Magsaysay became secretary of defense later that year.

Although it never performed in practice as it was supposed to on paper, the reorganized Philippine military did improve enough to make rebellion much more costly to the Huks. For example, the HMB field command encompassing southeastern municipalities of Bulacan wrote in early 1951 that more frequent government military attacks and searches of barrios sympathetic to the rebellion had forced more guerrillas to retreat to mountain bases. Worse still, government troops pursued retreating squadrons into the mountains. The military also stationed troops in numerous barrios, guarded bridges and roads more closely, and conducted daily "propaganda assaults" in towns and villages throughout Central Luzon. As a result, this FC's report went on, morale among the Huks and village supporters "sank low and many people have voluntarily evacuated" to areas where there was no fighting, thus making it more difficult than before for "the HMB to secure livelihood or carry out military plans." Another field command in Bulacan reported at about the same time that it was unable to do much except lie low for weeks at a time because of numerous government troops and spies.[108] Similarly, Huks in Nueva Ecija reported in October 1951 that they had attacked no enemy soldiers for two months, because it was too dangerous for them to move about except in very small groups. Government military operations also had jolted peasants so severely that "many citizens have lost their energy and are too frightened" to help, and villagers feared that Huks who were surrendering would implicate them in the movement.[109] A report written at the same time from Laguna said that government soldiers swarmed over the area and "all routes to and from our supply points are being controlled by them." And although people still believed in the HMB's cause, they now were afraid to join because of the hardships and "strength of the AFP [Armed Forces of the Philippines]."[110] Meanwhile, government soldiers spoiled numerous

[107] Crisol interview, 15 December 1969.

[108] Reco 3, General Headquarters, "Sirkular Blg. 2 sa FC 33 [Circular No. 3 to FC 33], 11 March 1951 (CapDoc, Ag.); "Overall Report of FC 33, HMB," 1 April-20 April 1951 (CapDoc, Ag.); and Reco 3, Headquarters, Executive Officer, "Sirkular No. 3 to FC 32," 1 April 1951 (CapDoc, Ag.).

[109] "Ulat ng D'Com 1" [Report of District Committee No. 1], to Reco 1, 31 October 1951.

[110] "Political Trends Report of FC 45 to Headquarters, Reco 4," 7 October 1951 (CapDoc, Ag.).

plans Huk forces had made. They broke up, for instance, several training sessions Huk leaders had designed for guerrillas from several parts of Central and Southern Luzon. Ignacio Dabu and other HMB military instructors had tried to hold the sessions, but during each attempt enemy troops came too near. Once in June 1951, the Huks had finally managed to hold one day of instruction, only to be routed the next day by soldiers. The Huks had to split up and march nonstop for days through the mountains without food and adequate equipment.[111]

From late 1951 onward, the Huks' predicament worsened. "Many of our cadres have been killed, many have surrendered, and others [have] turned passive," reported the PKP in 1951 or 1952. And in January 1952 the party stated that government military operations had "successfully intimidated the masses" and infiltrated the HMB's network so much that many of the rebellion's links to towns and villages had been "destroyed," forcing Huks "to retreat away from towns it used to hold," and making it impossible for "cadres to stay among the masses."[112] For nearly two months in late 1951, several Huk commanders and their men stumbled through the Sierra Madre mountains, "pursued . . . for one month continuous by three successive [government military] operations, giving them [the Huks] no chance to recover their balance and procure supplies," and suffering cold rains all the while. They were so hungry that at least one man died from eating a poisonous plant, and several Huks became "hot-tempered and defiant," fighting among themselves over scraps of food.[113] During the following months and years, Huk communications mention less and less about victorious encounters with the military or strong support from the barrios. More and more they relate sad news, like the message from Jose de Leon (of Nueva Ecija) in 1953 which said, in part, "Kas. Cecing has surrendered, Kas. Legaspi is dead, Kas. Mabini has long been wounded." Then de Leon inquired if it was true that a certain Huk commander and his wife had surrendered.[114] Increasingly, government troops forced remaining rebels to live in swamps, mountains, and remote parts of Central Luzon where hunger drove them to eat grass, raw snails, rats, and whatever else they could scavenge. "We were defeated in the armed struggle," concluded Silvestre Liwanag, the former Huk leader in Pampanga, after describing the hardships and decimation of the squadrons he had led. "The enemy's military strength was too great."[115]

[111] Cente [Ignacio Dabu], "Report (Partial) to General Headquarters," circa September 1951 (PF, CapDoc, Ag.).

[112] PKP, Central Committee, "Political Resolution," circa late 1951 or early 1952; and PKP, "Magsanay ng mga Kadreng Kikilos ng Legal at Ihanda ang Masa sa Mahayap at Matagal na Pakikibaka" [Train Cadres for Legal Action and Prepare the Masses for a Long and Bitter Struggle], January 1952 (CapDoc, Ag.).

[113] Pemio, to Andoy, 24 March 1952 (PF—Luis Taruc, CapDoc, Ag.). For a moving account of the hardships several Huk and PKP leaders endured in 1951 and 1952 as they tried to elude government soldiers, read William J. Pomeroy's The Forest, especially pp. 165-207.

[114] De Leon, to Tio, 14 August 1953 (PF, CapDoc, Ag.).

[115] Liwanag interview, 21 July 1970.

Why was the Philippine government able in the 1950s to combine military and nonmilitary methods to counter the Huks when apparently it was unable before? One reason must be considered because Huk accounts emphasized it: the economic, military, and technical assistance from the United States government. "Money from the American government financed Magsaysay's programs, including cash handouts to barrios to buy people's support," former Huk Faustino Tenorio said as he discussed reasons why the Huk movement declined. And Americans, he continued, "built up the government's military forces, gave them military advice, and so forth. The government had, for example, American planes and pilots to spot Huks from the air, and it dropped American bombs on Huk areas."[116] Several Huk leaders, such as Peregrino Taruc, Luis Taruc, and Silvestre Liwanag, made the same point, as did numerous analyses by the PKP's top leadership. When the PKP concluded in 1950 that a "revolutionary situation" existed, it anticipated that the United States government would be unwilling and financially unable to aid the Quirino administration. Time having proved this incorrect, the party took the position by 1952-1953 that American aid was the Philippine government's lifeline and that Magsaysay himself was a tool of American government and business interests.

Some evidence suggests that the PKP's revised appraisal was true. And considerable evidence indicates that even if American assistance was not decisive, it was extremely important. First, it cushioned the effects of the government's deficit, which was huge by 1950, and probably saved the government from total economic collapse. Frank Golay, an economist who was not one to exaggerate United States importance in Philippine affairs, wrote,

> By the end of 1949 the government seemed willing to let the military go unpaid and the educational system wither for want of funds, and even to succumb to the Huk rebellion, rather than face up to minimum responsibility for governmental functions. . . . It is a depressing commentary that the reforms, when they did come, were to a considerable extent installed from the outside as a result of the [United States government's] Bell Mission and its recommendations.[117]

Following the Bell Mission report and appropriate legislation to support its recommendations, the American government (particularly the departments of State and Defense) forced the Philippine government to pass new tax laws to generate needed revenues, worked directly with Philippine agencies to plan and administer economic and military programs funded from the new revenues and U.S. monetary assistance, and significantly influenced

---

[116] Tenorio interview, 27 July 1970.

[117] Frank H. Golay, *The Philippines: Public Policy and National Economic Development* (Ithaca, N.Y.: Cornell University Press, 1961), pp. 71-72. Also see the "Bell Report": United States, Department of State, *Report to the President of the United States by the United States Economic Survey [Bell] Mission to the Philippines* (Washington, D.C: Department of State Publication no. 4010, 1950).

the use of aid and "counterpart funds" (which resulted from selling goods imported to the Philippines with U.S. government money and were set aside mainly for agrarian programs).[118]

United States assistance to the Philippines in fiscal years 1951 through 1956 totaled $500 million—$383 million of economic assistance and $117 million of military assistance.[119] This supplemented the $700 million the United States had delivered from 1946 through 1950 to assist Filipinos to rebuild after World War II and to help finance government armed forces. American aid provided roughly half of the funds designated for agrarian projects in the government's "psych war" against the Huk rebellion between 1951 and 1955. And during the first year or two of several projects, American government money accounted for well over half the expenditures.[120] The military assistance that the United States Congress appropriated between 1951 and 1954 was $67 million, which exceeded one-fifth of the Philippine government's "defense and law-and-order" expenditures during the same period.[121] This figure excluded the dollar value of surplus American military equipment transferred to the Philippine military. The United States, reported the agency administering the military aid in December 1951, "is supplying most of the material needed by the [Philippine] armed forces and . . . it shows every indication of continuing to do so during the crisis arising from the Huk activities." And in 1954 the same agency said, "The Philippine armed services have greatly improved in recent years, in large measure through the weapons, gunboats, and aircraft, and the equipment and spare parts which the United States has made available under the mutual security program. U.S. military equipment and training have given substantial support to the Philippine government in its efforts to build a more effective military establishment."[122] Among the weapons and war materials were nearly all the tanks, rifles, pistols, mortars, ammunition, bombs, vehicles, and communications equipment that the Philippine military used against the Huks.

Certainly Filipino military officials considered American assistance very

---

[118] Golay, *The Philippines*, pp. 292-302; David Wurfel, "Foreign Aid and Social Reform in Political Development: A Philippine Case Study," *American Political Science Review* 53 (June 1959):456-482, and "The Bell Report and After."

[119] The annual amounts were reported to me in June 1974 by the U.S. Department of State, Agency for International Development, Statistics and Reports Division, Office of Financial Management, Washington, D.C.

[120] Philippines, National Economic Council, Philippine Council for United States Aid, *The Philippines and FOA Assistance Annual Report for Period Ending June 30, 1954* (Manila: 1954), and Office of Foreign Aid Coordination, *Joint P.I.-U.S. Economic Development Program, Cumulative Report as of June 30, 1958* (Manila: 1958); and Wurfel, "The Bell Report and After."

[121] Philippine government annual expenditures for national defense and law and order were as follows, in millions of pesos: 131 (1951), 186 (1952), 170 (1953), 175 (1954). (Legal exchange during the 1950s was 2 pesos per dollar). A. V. H. Hartendorp, *History of Industry and Trade of the Philippines* (Manila: American Chamber of Commerce of the Philippines, 1958), p. 368.

[122] United States, Mutual Security Program, *Report to Congress*, 31 December 1951, p. 31, and *Report to Congress*, 30 June 1954, p. 39.

useful, if not essential. An officer in the Philippine army during the height of the anti-Huk campaigns said in 1970, for example, "The equipment and weapons my company used were from the United States government. . . . During the 1950s, the quality and quantity of these weapons improved. In fact, they continue to improve until now."[123] Another army officer who fought against the Huks said, "U.S. aid was very important to defeating the Huks. . . . I'd say 30 percent of the credit for stopping the Huks goes to the United States."[124] "Operations in the Philippines," wrote Napoleon Valeriano, an officer in the Philippine military, and Charles Bohannan, an American military advisor to the Philippines during the 1950s, "were blessed by an unusual absence of critical aid problems. . . . Indeed, the prevailing spirit of cooperation [between the Philippines and the United States], and the aid given and used as a result, contributed decisively to the success of the counter-guerrilla effort."[125] Not only were money and materials important, but American advice and training were too, as illustrated by a 1954 article in an official journal of the Philippine military, which said, "The part JUSMAG [Joint United States Military Advisory Group] has played at the request of the Philippine Government in the rebuilding and reorganizing of our Armed Forces since 1950 has been very notable. . . . [The] reorganization of the Philippine Armed Forces may very well be . . . one of its greatest achievements."[126]

Weariness among peasants in Central Luzon, the government's effective use of promises and reforms, and the HMB's inferiority compared to the government military's renewed strength and tactics—these were the major reasons why the Huk rebellion died down. They made it impossible for rebels to concentrate on strengthening their political organization and refining their guerrilla tactics. Rebels had no more time for the movement's work; they were too busy trying to survive. These changes eroded support in the barrios, caused growing numbers of Huks to return to their families, and made it even more costly than before for peasants to revolt. The Philippine military claimed that between 1950 and 1955 it killed over 6,000 Huks, wounded nearly 2,000, captured 4,700, and forced almost 9,500 to surrender and take advantage of its amnesty offers.[127]

More telling than these figures were reports from the remaining Huks themselves. For instance, the small number of Huks with Mateo del Castillo, formerly the president of the PKM and a top leader in the PKP, spent nearly all their time between 1954 and 1956 moving from one remote area to another in Central and Southern Luzon searching for food and

[123] Interview with Col. Florentino Villacrusis, Talavera, Nueva Ecija, 28 June 1970.

[124] Interview with Col. Jose Z. Perlas, Mount Arayat, Pampanga, 26 June 1969.

[125] Napoleon D. Valeriano and Charles T. R. Bohannan, *Counter-Guerrilla Operations: The Philippine Experience* (New York: Praeger, 1962), pp. 76-77.

[126] Philippines, Philippine Armed Forces, *Philippine Armed Forces Journal 7* (May 1954):10.

[127] These rounded figures are based on statistics reported in Hartendorp, *History of Industry and Trade*, p. 368, and Carlos Quirino, *Magsaysay of the Philippines* (Manila: Ramon Magsaysay Memorial Society, 1958), pp. 62, 64.

eluding government soldiers. For months at a time they subsisted on
coconuts and coconut buds. Frequently they were weak from hunger. One
day late in 1956, while several members of the group were foraging for
food, a couple of Huks killed del Castillo. They also took the money he
was carrying as manager of the PKP's finance department. Later his killers
surrendered to government soldiers.[128]

Another small group of Huks in Central Luzon in 1956 suffered similar
hardships: several men died from wounds that became infected, many were
"stricken with disease from June to September," the man to whom they
had entrusted 1,000 pesos deserted in May, they were unable to do any
political work for many months, their contacts with villages were cut off
because "the enemy has succeeded in drawing us apart from the masses and
our weak comrades who are not willing to risk their lives have surrendered
one by one," and many tenants said that things would be better if there
were no Huks so they could till their lands in peace. "Now, whenever we
are marching," wrote one member of the group, "we try to avoid being seen
by civilians. Formerly, we could meet them without fear. What is the
meaning of this? It now appears that we are the criminals like the Japanese
from whom we used to hide." He concluded, "I am completely convinced,
based on what I have seen, that most of the masses want peace, even anti-
democratic peace, at any price. If such is the case, our policy should be
based on that, and the [Communist] Party should help the masses attain
that peace."[129]

Since 1951, leaders in the HMB and PKP had been debating what to do.
Should they try to negotiate a truce? Did they dare trust the government
again after what had happened in previous negotiations? Should they
simply declare an end to the rebellion and return to nonviolent political
methods? Or should they continue to fight? If so, should they prepare for a
"protracted armed struggle?" Was Central Luzon a suitable place to do
that; would the guerrillas be too vulnerable because of the flat terrain?
There was little consensus. And increasingly, leaders found it nearly
impossible to elude government troops long enough to discuss and plan
together. Moreover, mounting hardships that the movement confronted
were wearing down the leaders, too. They began to fight among themselves, accusing each other for this failure or that.

Several important leaders split into two factions over this question of
what to do. And the resulting disagreements themselves, said Benjamin
Cunanan of Tarlac, also "wore down the morale and confidence" of the
remaining Huks. Everyone in his field command knew about the disputes,
but when they asked Cunanan questions, he said he was not "really able to

[128] Mateo del Castillo, Biographical Information (PF, CapDoc, Ag.); Alejandro Gonzales,
Sworn Statement to Central Intelligence Bureau, Armed Forces of the Philippines, 28 November
1956 (PF-del Castillo, CapDoc, Ag.); and Lope Cunanan, Sworn Statement to Philippine
Constabulary, 26 January 1957 (CapDoc, Cr.). Luis Taruc writes that the Huks who shot Mateo
del Castillo also killed one of del Castillo's sons (He Who Rides the Tiger, p. 151).

[129] Oen, to Dureng and Ikto, October 1956 (PF-Jesus Lava, CapDoc, Ag.).

answer them. After all, as an FC commander, I wasn't involved in the decision making higher up, so I didn't know a lot about what was going on there."[130]

One faction's position, which was stated the most consistently in official records of the PKP and by top party leaders like Jesus Lava, was to continue the armed struggle but plan for a protracted revolution that would combine violence with "legal tactics." This position rejected surrender and negotiations.

Those associated with the second faction were leaders such as Ignacio Dabu, Jose de Leon, and Luis Taruc, who were more closely in touch with barrio residents. They said stop the fighting and negotiate. As early as 1952, advocates of this position began to argue that peasants in Central Luzon wanted peace. "The Huks," Luis Taruc said in 1948, "can only hold out as long as it is supported by the masses. No more, no less."[131] In 1953, he said, the Huks no longer had that support. Then in 1954 he wrote, "We don't consider the present administration as we did the past one. We respect the will of the [1953] electorate; that is why we seek peace, democratic peace, with the government." He and others wanted the fighting to stop now, because it was "senseless and expensive in many aspects."[132]

In May 1954, Luis Taruc did what many Huks had been doing during the previous two years. He quit. Unlike most Huks, however, he could not just return to live in the barrios. He had to surrender. After standing trial for crimes against the state, he spent fifteen years in prison. In the meantime, the PKP denounced him for abandoning the revolution.

A few armed Huks remained underground in Central Luzon until the 1960s. Among them were men like Jesus Lava and Casto Alejandrino, who were convinced that in due course another revolutionary situation would develop and that they must be prepared for it and keep alive the spirit of revolution no matter how few their numbers had become. "Revolutionaries don't surrender," Alejandrino said firmly. Had he not been captured in 1960, he said, he would have continued to live as a revolutionary "until I died."[133] Other Huks, like Silvestre Liwanag, continued to live as rebels— less out of a conviction that revolution was inevitable and more because rebellion had become the only way to live. They could not leave without being imprisoned. They survived by stealing from the rich and, in Robin Hood fashion, sharing the confiscations with villagers. Barrio people also gave them food in return for what had become known as "Huk justice." This meant Huks caught carabao rustlers, found rapists, and threatened or killed abusive or corrupt local officials and landlords. A third category of Huks in the 1960s included those who robbed practically anyone or ran

[130] Cunanan interview, 11 August 1970.
[131] *Manila Chronicle,* 11 January 1948, p. 1.
[132] Luis Taruc, to Benigno Aquino, *Manila Times* correspondent, 27 April 1954 (PF, CapDoc, Ag.).
[133] Alejandrino interview, 16 July 1970.

"protection rackets," which thrived on gambling and prostitution near Clark Air Force Base in Angeles, Pampanga. A few Huks reportedly became wealthy this way. Some even began to hobnob with prominent politicians and landlords in Central Luzon.

Scattered bands of revolutionaries, social bandits, and thieves were the only signs of rebellion in Central Luzon by late 1956. Most Huks had returned to eking out a living as tenants and laborers. They expected at least to live in peace now, free from marauding soldiers and civilian guards. Many also immediately joined peasant organizations. Given the choice between using legal and illegal political methods, they preferred the former. They generally had throughout their long struggle. Conditions now seemed to offer that choice again. Their struggle was not over, they said. It had just entered another phase.

Chapter 7
CONCLUSION

THE CONTRAST between Central Luzon in the early 1930s and Central Luzon in the early 1950s is both startling and understandable. It is startling because no one would have predicted that by 1950 thousands of armed peasants would have organized themselves to fight government authorities and their armed forces. And no one would have guessed that several thousand more peasants would be actively supporting these armed rebels through an elaborate network linking one barrio and town to the next. Certainly no villager in 1930 would have imagined such an outcome. The situation by the 1950s is striking, too, because the extent of peasant organization and the degree of peasant unity for political action contrast so starkly with earlier decades. In twenty years, peasant society in Central Luzon changed from having virtually no horizontal political organization to forming large peasant unions and rebelling.

On the other hand, Central Luzon's peasant movement and the Huk rebellion are understandable. Explaining why has been the purpose of this study. The explanation, however, has been neither easily made nor simply put. And undoubtedly there remains more to learn about this revolt. But by now several themes should be clear. A central cause was the disintegration of the traditional landlord-tenant relationship in an area where cash crop cultivation was intense and relied almost exclusively on the tenancy system. Peasants tried to compensate for this fundamental change, but their options were few and inadequate. Tenants also vigorously tried to maintain the traditional system by holding landlords accountable for services usually provided; and they became increasingly organized, pressing for reforms in the tenancy system. These efforts failed either to resurrect the dying system or to satisfy villagers' minimum needs. Any short-term gains they made were typically negated or proved meaningless. Meanwhile, reactions of the government and landed elites became increasingly hostile and violent. Although they conceded a few palliatives, the government and the landed were unsympathetic to the peasants' plight. Organized protest gradually became organized rebellion, primarily as a consequence of the government's and landed elites' repression. From late 1946 to the early 1950s, the Huk rebellion dominated Central Luzon.

In this final section, I would like to emphasize conclusions which are significant, first, for what they say about this particular rebellion. Some of them alter the previous scholarship on the Huk movement. Second, these conclusions are important for what they might say about other peasant revolts in the "Third World" during the twentieth century. My reading of the literature on this subject leads me to believe that the revolt in Central Luzon has parallels elsewhere.[1] Consequently, the conclusions elaborated here may contribute to a general understanding of why and how peasants rebel, although I have no illusions that these cover all cases or that they form a comprehensive framework for studying other rebellions.

The sources I have used in this study permitted an analysis from the peasantry's perspective and an appreciation of what the rebellion meant to villagers. I am satisfied that my analysis shows beyond a reasonable doubt that persons who joined and supported peasant organizations of the 1930s and 1940s as well as the Huk rebellion itself were rational human beings reacting to major political and economic changes, which had brought them unbearable hardship. Standing back now and looking at the whole rebellion and the movement supporting it, I see eight conclusions for discussion. They concern the long-term causes of peasant unrest, the justifications people had for their protest and revolt, the peasants' moderate goals, the preludes to rebellion, the consequences of repression, the three types of leaders in peasant movements, the significance of colonialism for understanding revolt, and the meaning of "a rebellion that failed."

1. A major cause for the unrest was the dramatic deterioration of traditional ties between local elites and peasants. Peasants rebelled not because they were poor and weak while large landowners were wealthy and strong. Traditional rural society in Central Luzon—and so many other parts of Southeast Asia—had been that way for a long time. Rather, a major reason for discontent was that the ties, which previously had bound together the rich and the poor, broke. As a consequence, peasants not only remained poor—and in many cases poorer—but now they were also cut off from people who had provided valuable protection and assistance.

Ties between local elites and peasants had formed what can be called traditional patron-client relationships. Because owning land that other people farmed was a measure of status in Central Luzon—and in many traditional societies—frequently the patrons were landowners (with *big* patrons being the *big* landowners). Their clients were those on whom they relied to work the land and do a variety of other services. In short, the typical patron was a landlord, and the typical client was a tenant farmer. But even small landowners frequently had patrons to whom they were loyal and gave services in return for protection (perhaps even protection against

---

[1] For some of these parallels, see James C. Scott and Benedict J. Kerkvliet, "How Traditional Rural Patrons Lose Legitimacy: A Theory with Special Reference to Southeast Asia," *Cultures et développement,* vol. 5, no. 3 (1973):501-540, and "The Politics of Survival: Peasant Response to 'Progress' in Southeast Asia," *Journal of Southeast Asian Studies 4* (September 1973):241-268.

others making claims on their land), sponsorship at weddings and baptisms, and financial assistance during hard times.

In addition to being a relationship between unequals, traditional patron-
client ties had, judging from Central Luzon, three important charac-
teristics. First, ties between patron and client were numerous, diffuse, and
flexible. Indeed, these qualities were a primary source of the relationship's
strength as far as clients were concerned, for they could call on their
patrons for a wide range of assistance. In this way, a patron became each
client's all-inclusive superior, principal source of assistance, and last resort
when all other things failed. At the same time, the nature of the relationship allowed a patron wide latitude in what he could ask from each client.
Over time, therefore, the relationship became complex, and its complexity
became its strength. Second, the patron-client relationship was a personal,
face-to-face one. This was an important way to keep the ties diffuse and
flexible and prevent the relationship from becoming too specific and rigid.
Third, the relationship was based not on compulsion or force but on
reciprocity. Because of structural conditions, each party had something
that the other needed. For landlords, these conditions included a relative
scarcity of peasants to farm their lands and do supplementary work. For
villagers, the conditions were a need for land to till and the inability of
kinship and the village community to provide sufficient protection against
crop failures and other hardships. For both, the relative absence of
effective impersonal guarantees such as public law for security of family and
property was also an important reason for the development of patron-
client bonds. In order to get what the other had, land-owners and villagers
each had to give something that was considered fair. Hence, theirs was a
symbiotic relationship in which expectations and obligations grew through
practice and personal interaction.

It would be erroneous, of course, to give the impression that years ago
life was rosy for tenant farmers in Central Luzon and other areas where
ties between lord and peasant were paternalistic. On the contrary. Villagers
in San Ricardo told me matter-of-factly about their struggle to turn wild
grasslands and forests into vegetable plots and rice fields. Peasants in
Central Luzon had to work hard the year around just to keep their heads
above water. Like most peasants in the world, their perennial problem was
to satisfy their families' needs and their obligations to other villagers and
the community as a whole while at the same time paying rent, doing work,
and fulfilling obligations to landlords and others of higher status beyond
the village.[2] They rarely had any surplus from their labors. And they lived
about as close to the margin of bare subsistence as one could get
without starving.

Meanwhile, landlords like General Manuel Tinio—the small minority at
the top of the social pyramid—lived in big houses, wore nice clothes,
employed servants, and ate very well. And sometimes they abused their

[2] For a succinct and influential elaboration of this generalization, see Eric R. Wolf, *Peasants*
(Englewood Cliffs, N.J.: Prentice-Hall, 1966), pp. 1-17, 60-95.

relationships with peasants by making illegitimate demands and using force to compel tenants to comply with their wishes.

Two important points to keep in mind, however, are these: First, force was not the normal means to maintain traditional ties between landlords and villagers. Landlords needed peasants who were loyal, not peasants who were simply being forced to obey. A loyal following was a basic part of the patron's status and political power in the locality. Second, their landlords' paternalism was precisely one vital means for peasants to keep their heads above water. A strong patron-client relationship was a kind of all-encompassing insurance policy whose coverage, although not total and infinitely reliable, was as comprehensive as a poor family could get. Consequently, what peasants did for landlords was balanced off, in their eyes, by what landlords did for them. This balance of exchange made the relationship legitimate and just, as far as villagers were concerned, however exploitative it might seem to those on the outside.

Due to land scarcity, large population growth, commercial markets, and other changes in the conditions that had shaped patron-client relations, the traditional balance of exchange went awry. Moreover, this happened quickly, within only a few decades. Had such changes been spread across several centuries, as they were in some other parts of the world, perhaps people in Central Luzon's villages could have coped somehow or would have protested only sporadically and individually or in small groups.

The new conditions allowed local elites to be less dependent on personal followings. More specifically, landlords no longer needed tenants as clients. They simply needed them as workers. They wanted, therefore, to reduce to a minimum their dealings with tenants as people, preferring an employer-employee relationship in which all terms of employment were carefully spelled out and wages were as low as possible in order to maximize profits. Increasingly, large landowners wanted tenants only because there was no other way to farm their lands. Had it been possible, many would have preferred, as Manolo Tinio of Talavera, Nueva Ecija, did, to have machines rather than people work their lands.

Villagers, meanwhile, needed traditional patronage more than ever, lest they succumb not only to such usual hazards as poor harvests or sicknesses, but also to new ones (such as being evicted from their land) resulting from the rapid changes themselves. Most tenants did not even benefit from the expanding market for the crops they grew for the landowners. Peasants who cultivated rice, for example, did not prosper from the expanding rice industry. Rarely did a tenant working for landlords like Manolo Tinio have any surplus to sell. Indeed, few had enough left after sharing with their landowners to feed their own families. Consequently, most had to borrow at interest rates that kept going higher.

2. The second conclusion is that protesting and rebellious villagers believed their actions were justified. Expressed in terms of local problems, their justifications addressed such basic political issues as justice, human rights, and the distribution of resources and wealth. The bases for their

claims were local customs and their understanding of decent human behavior. Previously the elites themselves had supported these customs and standards of morality, but now they refused to.

Simply stated, peasants justified their actions in the 1930s and 1940s on the basis that the landed elites had violated customary obligations to the poor—the "little people," in the villagers' vocabulary. The violations were grave in two respects. First, they were not just occasional lapses affecting a few persons here and there. Rather, they persisted over a number of years and made life significantly more precarious for thousands of villagers in the region. Second, rural elites failed to uphold not just the peripheral and weaker obligations, but also the major ones. It was bad enough, according to peasants in Central Luzon, that landlords increasingly stopped providing pigs and chickens for barrio fiestas, moved out of the villages to live in towns and cities, refused to sponsor their tenants' weddings and baptisms, or forbade tenants to take grain home for their chickens. It was intolerable, however, when landlords began to evict tenants from the land or refused to allow them a large enough share of the harvest to feed their families. From the peasants' point of view, the landlords' most serious transgression was to quit giving "rations" and interest-free loans of rice to those who had no more of their own to eat. To deny rations and loans was tantamount to forcing them to borrow from thick-skinned moneylenders or starve, if not one year then some other year, because inevitably times came when peasants needed to borrow or else not eat.

Rations, certainly, and interest-free loans, probably, were a peasant family's guarantee from their landlord that they could subsist even if their own crop failed. The traditional patron-client relationship obligated the landed elites to guarantee subsistence to peasants working on their lands. Beginning around the 1920s, however, landlords refused. Meanwhile, it was obvious to peasants that most landlords had enough to share with the peasants. They saw many prosper from rice and sugar sales. As far as peasants could tell, therefore, landlords denied the traditional guarantees to subsistence not because they themselves had nothing left to share with villagers but because they no longer wanted to fulfill their obligations. Meanwhile, landlords continued to demand services and rent from their tenants. The previous balance of exchange had become so unbalanced that peasants now felt exploited. Just as they knew when the relationship with their patrons was satisfactory and hence legitimate, so too they knew when the exchange was unbalanced and illegitimate.

The other major justification peasants stated was that they had a right to defend themselves against the abuses and repression of landlords, armed guards, government officials, and soldiers. Furthermore, peasants felt obligated to avenge the mistreatment and murder of relatives and friends who had been victims of landlord and government immorality and lawlessness. On these grounds, peasants justified the Huks' violence against the elites and their armies and looked on the rebels as their own instrument of justice.

It is significant that peasants defended their actions largely in terms of what they considered right and just. Landlords and the government had wronged them; they had treated them unfairly and had violated norms which peasants still regarded as binding. Without this understanding one cannot fully appreciate the rational basis for the peasantry's actions. It is not enough to know, for example, that landlords took 50 or 55 percent of the harvests, that they charged interest on loans, that they did not give rations, that they hired armed guards, that government soldiers arrested peasant union leaders, and so on. One needs to know the cultural context for these facts.[3]

3. Peasant demands were moderate, not radical. Villagers wanted to reform the tenancy system, not eliminate it and appropriate the landlords' lands for themselves. Indeed, the basic objective shared by most peasants who were striking, marching, and rebelling during the 1930s and 1940s was to regain the economic and political security that the traditional tenancy system had previously provided. Consequently, they demanded that landlords live up to their obligations as traditional partons—give rations, give loans without charging interest, guarantee tenants a parcel of land to use for life, increase the tenants' share of the harvest, and stop using armed guards or calling out the Philippine Constabulary against them. Growing out of this struggle were other issues, such as the peasants' right to organize and have their own unions. Even villagers in the Huk rebellion had only moderate aims. In addition to the agrarian reforms they had been talking about before, the rebels in Central Luzon wanted an end to the repression against peasant organization members, former Hukbalahap guerrillas, and villagers in general. They were not rebelling in hopes of overthrowing the government or establishing a revolutionary political system.

Of course, there were exceptions to this generalization. Some in the peasant organizations and Huk movement wanted to take or buy their landlords' lands. Similarly, some villagers believed that toppling the governments of presidents Roxas and Quirino was the only chance peasants had to alleviate their problems. In addition to these exceptions among the peasantry, leaders in the PKM, PKP, and HMB who were not themselves from the peasantry often advocated land redistribution, a socialist economic system, and other radical programs.

What is so striking, however, is that these people were a minority. The radical visions of the few did not become the movement's visions. The movement grew, and it moved from unrest and protest to rebellion. Yet the issues and goals remained as modest in the late 1940s and 1950s as they had been in the 1930s. This was one important reason why the govern-

---

[3] For a brilliant essay that argues the importance of "moral indignation" for understanding political unrest in many contexts, see Peter A. Lupsha's "Explanation of Political Violence: Some Psychological Theories versus Indignation," *Politics and Society* 2 (fall 1971):89-104. I am also impressed with George Rude's discussion of related ideas in *The Crowd in History* (New York: Wiley, 1964).

ment's own moderate reforms of the 1950s had a deadening effect on the Huk rebellion.

Why were peasants content to demand so little? Why, for example, did so few peasants demand that they, rather than their landlords, own the lands they farmed? Some remarks to supplement what has already been said may provide a clearer answer. The first is to ask, why would we expect peasants to demand their own land? Certainly there is no inherent reason for tenants to claim the land they till. Typically what is crucial for peasants is the right to subsistence living from the produce of the land, not a legal title itself. To go a little further, one must consider the matter of justification. Based on village culture, peasants in Central Luzon could amply support their claims that rents should be reduced, they had a right to farm the owners' lands, landlords should pay a fair share of the agricultural expenses, landlords should provide tenants with minimum subsistence, and so on. But nothing in their tradition justified taking land for themselves. Their situation was not one in which they had been suddenly alienated from land they thought was theirs to own. (This was true only for some peasants in those parts of Central Luzon where larger landowners grabbed the lands of homesteaders and small landowners). Rather, it was a situation in which they had been alienated from agrarian elites on whom they thought they had a right to make certain claims. The deterioration of the traditional relations was so recent that peasants in Central Luzon remembered well the paternalistic system. Remnants of patron-client bonds sometimes remained. Consequently, peasants felt that there was a chance to reestablish them.

Other studies have demonstrated that peasants generally try to maximize their security and minimize their risks. Villagers in Central Luzon did the same. The traditional tenancy system, which many peasants in the region either had experienced personally or had known through their parents and grandparents, had provided security and minimized risks. Owning land would not necessarily mean fewer hazards or more safety. Indeed, peasants might well have feared the reverse. Owning land could pose even greater risks—such as having to carry the burden of all expenses for a crop that could easily fail if drought or blight hit. Owning land could also be less secure than tenancy—it implied having only weak or no claims on wealthy persons for rations and loans and no protection against land-grabbers. One possibility would have been for peasants to consider a thorough revolution in which landlords and other elites were stripped of their power once and for all, thereby eliminating many dangers which otherwise might threaten small landowners. But this undertaking in itself was such a gigantic risk that it was scarcely thinkable in the 1930s through the 1950s. There remained other, less dangerous possibilities, including efforts to reconstruct good patron-client relationships with landed elites.

Previous studies, for the most part, have portrayed the Huk movement as being more radical than my findings would allow. Several books frequently cited for their treatment of the rebellion have argued that the Huks wanted to redistribute land and they were revolutionaries who sought to replace the country's government with a communist regime.[4] At the same time, none of these studies discusses the villagers' desire to regain a disappearing relationship with their former patrons. Usually this important point is also absent in interpretations of Philippine history by Filipino leftists.[5] As has been noted, some within the movement, particularly certain leaders, did have a radical vision for the rebellion. It so happens that previous studies have relied heavily on information from these more radical participants in the movement. Or they have used information that the Philippine or United States government has supplied, which almost invariably portrays—often without evidence—the Huks as revolutionaries. These studies, in short, generally have emphasized perspectives other than those of villagers involved in the movement.

4. A fourth conclusion is that long before they rebelled, peasants tried a variety of ways to cope with the drastically changing agrarian conditions and to demand reforms. Rebellion was a last resort after other efforts had failed.

This is another point that previous studies on the Huk rebellion have ignored for the most part. Despite the publication of Luis Taruc's *Born of the People,* whose initial chapters describe the unrest in Central Luzon prior to the revolt, most studies have talked about the rebellion as it if were a sudden explosion of discontent. They scarcely mention the tumultuous decade or more of agrarian unrest prior to the Japanese occupation.[6] This

[4] Uldarico S. Baclagon, *Lessons from the Huk Campaign in the Philippines* (Manila: M. Colcol, 1960); Fred H. Barton, *Salient Operational Aspects of Paramilitary Warfare in Three Asian Areas* (Washington, D.C.: Operations Research Office, Technical Memorandum ORO-T-228, Department of the Army, 1954); Jose M. Crisol, *The Red Lie* (Manila: Barangay Pocketbook, 1954); Louis F. Felder, *Socio-Economic Aspects of Counterinsurgency: A Case Study—Philippines* (Washington, D.C.: Industrial College of the Armed Forces, 1963); Eduardo Lachica, *Huk: Philippine Agrarian Society in Revolt* (Manila: Solidaridad, 1971); Richard M. Leighton, Ralph Sanders, and Jose N. Tinio, *The Huk Rebellion: A Case Study in the Social Dynamics of Insurrection* (Washington, D.C.: Industrial College of the Armed Forces, 1964); Alredo B. Saulo, *Communism in the Philippines: An Introduction* (Quezon City: Ateneo de Manila University, 1969); Alvin H. Scaff, *The Philippine Answer to Communism* (Stanford: Stanford University Press, 1955); Napoleon D. Valeriano and Charles T. R. Bohannan, *Counter-Guerrilla Operations: The Philippine Experience* (New York: Praeger, 1962).

[5] See, for example, Amado Guerrero, *Philippine Society and Revolution* (Manila: Pulang Tala, 1971).

[6] See, for instance, two of the better-known books on the Huk rebellion: Lachica, *Huk,* and Scaff, *The Philippine Answer to Communism.* Although Lachica's book does mention some of the important social and economic conditions, it says little about the peasant organizations and unrest during the 1930s and immediately following the Japanese occupation. To the extent it does mention these, it places heavy and, in my judgment, undue emphasis on the skillfulness of leaders in arousing peasants to act. And when it discusses social and economic conditions, it speaks almost exclusively about the province of Pampanga. A major thesis of the book is that the Huk rebellion was mainly a Pampangan movement. As for Scaff's study, the book makes practically no mention of peasant unrest prior to the Japanese occupation and has no serious discussion of the PKM, Democratic Alliance, and other important aspects of the peasant movement after 1945.

characterization has reinforced the image frequently presented in government accounts that peasants in Central Luzon are an impatient and rowdy bunch. And it has contributed to the notion that Filipino peasants are docile except when they occasionally become hot-headed and explode into an uncontrollable rage. Frequently accompanying such ideas is the claim that "outside agitators"—usually communists—came in and stirred up the quiet countryside until it became a storm of discontent.

My analysis suggests the opposite. Rather than being docile, peasants in Central Luzon were aggressive toward landlords and government officials once they concluded that they were being exploited. But rather than being quick to revolt, peasants tried every possible avenue before resorting to organized violence. Finally, neither the Huk rebellion itself nor the peasant unrest preceding it resulted from outsiders coming into the villagers to start trouble. This revolt's history suggests that such an idea has dubious validity for any peasant movement. When a few Huks tried to export their rebellion to other parts of the Philippines—for example, to the Bisayas and Northern Luzon regions—they failed, apparently because they were outsiders themselves and the political conditions were not bad enough from the viewpoint of villagers there to warrant revolt.

Two themes should be highlighted here to develop this point about rebellion coming at the end of a long struggle. The first is that peasants in Central Luzon turned to collective, public actions the more they realized that alternatives for either coping with or escaping new hardships were unsatisfactory. In the nineteenth and early twentieth centuries, dissatisfied peasants could move from one area to another in search of better landlords. Or they could move to virgin lands, maybe even homestead and become small landowners. Such mobility continued into the 1940s, but the relief it brought declined markedly. Several villagers, for example, had moved to Talavera, Nueva Ecija, in the 1920s and 1930s from Bulacan. They had left Bulacan because their landlords had become strict and unjust; they hoped to find "decent" and "good" landlords in Nueva Ecija. They never did. Many peasants moved several times, from one hacienda to another in an endless pursuit of fair tenancy conditions. Eventually they realized through their own experiences and those of others that bad conditions permeated the region. Meanwhile, population growth had taken its toll on virgin land, to say nothing of financial, legal, and bureaucratic obstacles confronting a peasant family who wanted its own land. Homesteading, in particular, was a realistic hope for only a tiny few. Peasants also tried to adjust by finding work in towns and cities, supplementing agricultural work with odd jobs in the vicinity of their home villages, eating less, and changing their diets (such as substituting cheaper root crops for rice and eating little or no fish or poultry). As one elderly woman in San Ricardo, Talavera, described her family's efforts to survive in the 1930s, they simply "suffered through as best as possible."

Some people did find landowners—typically ones owning only a few hectares—who were less strict and more traditional about their relations with tenants. A small number of peasants even managed to buy a little bit of land in remote parts of Nueva Ecija and Tarlac. Some others became carpenters and day laborers in Cabanatuan, San Fernando, and other towns in Central Luzon. In these ways, a few managed to escape the worst. But most did not. The changes were too sweeping and there were too many people, too few jobs, too little land, and too many obstacles for the majority of Central Luzon's villagers to make do by relying only on normal efforts to adjust.

The other important theme here is that the unrest prior to rebellion took several forms and was a period during which peasants learned the necessity of collective action. Peasants expressed their discontent in various ways. They secretly harvested the fields in order to take what they regarded as rightfully theirs even though the landlords' new regulations called this cheating and stealing. They had strikes, sometimes against just one landlord and other times against all landlords for miles around. They petitioned mayors, governors, congressmen, and presidents. They marched and demonstrated in small groups and large. They took landlords and sugar central owners to court. They even ran candidates for municipal offices and for congress. And in a few significant instances, their candidates were elected. They left no avenues unexplored as they sought to air their grievances and make their demands.

Incidents at the local level were both peaceful and violent. The latter included, for instance, peasants committing arson and attacking the property and persons of the local elites and officials. As the arena of protest widened, shifting from the village to a nearby town or capital city, and as the number of persons in any one incident grew larger, the activities tended to be more peaceful. In part this was because large numbers of violent people would cause more alarm and provoke more violent retaliation from the elites and government. It was also assuredly easier to get large numbers of people to demonstrate peacefully than to storm a government building. Finally, as the size of the arena grew, the movement was linked at the top to intellectuals and politicians who were much more familiar with the range of legitimate avenues and how to use them than those at the base of the movement. Indeed, the peasantry frequently learned about legal recourses and petitioning lawmakers from these leaders, who in turn tried to steer the movement away from local violence and toward peaceful protest.

The avenues of nonviolent protest were more numerous in the Philippines during the 1930s and 1940s than they probably are in many countries. Consequently, the prelude to rebellion in this case may have been more prolonged than would be possible for peasants in most countries. Nevertheless, the general point is that peasants exhaust their recourses before they rebel.

As peasants began to act publicly, they increasingly learned that they experienced many common problems and became acutely aware of the necessity to join together in order to achieve provincial or national influence. Before peasants from several villages or haciendas—or even peasants working on the same hacienda—would join together in public protest, they had to perceive that they shared problems. Historically, this had been rare. Peasant society in the Philippines, as elsewhere, was divided along religious, geographical, and linguistic lines. No inherent reason drove villagers to act together or possess a sense of class consciousness that could be translated into collective action. Even farming for the same landlord did not necessarily create bonds among tenants. Because each peasant typically dealt with his landlord individually, the tenants of a single landlord could each have distinct arrangements. As the traditional system deteriorated, however, relations between a landlord and his tenants became increasingly uniform, a fact best illustrated in Central Luzon by the fading personalism and the growing prevalence of written, highly specific contracts that peasants had to sign. The modern market economy was indeed creating a "class" of persons who shared similar working conditions. As this became apparent to peasants themselves, organizing began to make sense.

Even with the increasing awareness of shared experience, however, numerous obstacles hampered collective action. Remaining ties between peasants and local elites, for example, hindered the formation of peasant organizations. Some villagers tried to survive these hard times precisely by ingratiating themselves with local elites and doing whatever was asked of them, even if it meant fighting other villagers. Consequently landlords, sugar central owners, and local officials could recruit poor people to be strikebreakers, hacienda guards, and soldiers. Appropriate illustrations of these were the Cawalning Capayapaan (Knights of Peace) strikebreakers in the 1930s and the civilian guards in the 1940s. Many of the confrontations in Central Luzon during the agrarian unrest and the HMB rebellion had poor people on both sides. "Little people" in the peasant movement clashed with other "little people" used by landlords and the government.

Working to the peasantry's advantage were preexisting ties among fellow villagers, extended families, and people who had worked each other's fields. In several parts of Central Luzon, customary arrangements for mutual help in farm work even became contingent on participation in the local peasant association. Those who were reluctant to join were denied the benefits of mutual help by villagers who had joined.

Also helping to mitigate cleavages within the peasantry was the peasants' growing awareness that they needed large organizations in order to be heard. Peasants throughout the region learned during the 1930s that they made little or no headway by appealing individually or in small groups to landlords or local officials. Consequently, they began to consolidate, acting together in larger groups and forming organizations that encompassed several villages, municipalities, and provinces. They brought others into their movement by emphasizing shared problems and common bonds, which the changing conditions had created. Demonstrations and strikes, in turn, helped to make others aware that their plight was not unique, thereby giving them more incentive to join too.

The learning process during the agrarian unrest included learning how to organize. Peasants tried to profit from the experience of past failures and successes of collective action. Peasants in an area learned not only from their own efforts, but from those of others as well. From the protests, strikes, and related tactics of villagers elsewhere, peasants in a given locality picked up cues and suggestions that seemed helpful to their own situation. In this way, too, villagers grew to know more about other peasants farther away, thus learning *about* them as well as *from* them. Word of mouth was the most common means of communication. Particularly important, for instance, were those people who moved from one area to the next in search of better land and employment; they passed on what they had seen and understood about organizations and protests elsewhere. As the changing conditions began to homogenize the daily experience of villagers, they also produced a mobile peasantry that could begin to knit them together. With the growth of actual peasant organizations, leaders who traveled from village to village provided more explicit links. Many villages of Central Luzon accumulated collective knowledge about organizing methods, which was passed down from one generation to the next and became part of the village culture. Of course, people used what they had learned when they turned from discontent to revolt.

Unfortunately for the peasantry, its protests brought little relief. Government authorities never took decisive steps in the 1930s or after the Japanese occupation to remedy the peasants' problems. Despite their occasional friendly gestures, the country's presidents and other highly placed persons whom peasants repeatedly approached continued to side with the large landowners, sugar mill owners, and other elite circles. The courts, aside from being an expensive route, proved more responsible to the influential and the wealthy than they did to peasant petitioners. As for the laws that Congress passed, they protected the claims of big landlords more than they helped peasants. Consequently, even if the laws had been fully enforced, which they rarely were, they would have brought the peasantry little satisfaction. Meanwhile, landlords could call on government agencies and the Philippine Constabulary to back up their claims against tenants.

5. What changed the direction of the peasant movement from protest to revolt, however, was not merely discouraging results. Rather, it was repression by the government and agrarian elites. The landlords and government officials' lawless and frequently violent actions forced peasants to resort to organized violence. In the peasantry's view, rebellion was the only alternative left in the face of numerous illegal maneuvers and violent actions against them.

This important point is another one which previous studies of the Huk movement have practically ignored.[7] Even when they have discussed the

---

[7] Scaff *(Philippine Answer to Communism)* has no discussion of the repression. Lachica *(Huk)* barely mentions it; he cites in a few sentences the unseating of Democratic Alliance congressmen-elect and the killing of Juan Feleo (pp. 120-121). The other studies cited in footnote 4 also ignore the repression. Several general studies of Philippine history, however, do discuss the repression, although very briefly: Guerrero, *Philippine Society,* p. 66; Agoncillo and Alfonso, *History of the Filipino People,* pp. 534-536.

landed elites' violence or the government's lawlessness, they have minimized its intensity and its significance for peasants. More often they have
dwelled on the peasantry's violence, which government officials included
among their justifications for countering the "insurgency" with force.
Repression had driven peasants in Central Luzon to rebel on two
occasions. The first was during the Japanese occupation; the second was
during the early years of the new Philippine Republic. When the Japanese
army invaded the Philippines, the entire political situation in Central
Luzon changed within a matter of weeks. No longer could people publicly
organize and criticize. Furthermore, the Japanese soldiers and their allies
in the Philippine Constabulary and municipal police forces were ill-
tempered and often brutal. Because of this repression and the closing of
other outlets for public expression of discontent and because the villagers
disliked the foreign invaders (whose government was even worse than the
Filipino-American one before it), thousands of veterans of the peasant
movement took their organization underground. Gradually, they became
skilled in guerrilla military methods. The result was the Hukbalahap, a
well-organized and effective resistance movement.

After the Japanese occupation, the peasant movement resumed working
through legal channels. The opening of the political system even a little
encouraged peasants to turn away from rebellion. Now, however, their
movement was stronger and more vigorous than before. The leadership
and experience from the Hukbalahap resistance added immeasurably to
what the movement had achieved during the 1930s. Besides that, the
villagers' effective resistance to the Japanese had buoyed their confidence
in their collective power. The result was the PKM (National Peasants
Union)—the largest peasant organization in the country's history up to that
time—and the peasant-supported Democratic Alliance, a political party
which ran eight congressional candidates in Central Luzon in the 1946
election.

As the peasantry's organizations became more powerful, however,
government authorities and local elites became more repressive. Harassment was not entirely new, of course, for the landlords' private armies, in
cooperation with provincial detachments of the Philippine Constabulary,
had frequently abused villagers, broken up strikes, and forcibly evicted
tenants during the 1930s. But in 1945-1946, the repression was significantly
worse. The elites had more to fear because the peasant movement was so
threatening, and they were more hostile because of the bitter animosities
that had built up between them and the Hukbalahap during the Japanese
occupation. The disdainful and destructive way in which returning Americans and the Filipino elites treated Hukbalahap veterans after the Japanese
army had been defeated, the intense harassment of former Hukbalahap
participants and supporters, the abuses against PKM members, the murder
of PKM leader Juan Feleo—all of these and many more contributed
directly to the rebellion. Perhaps the most significant period of repression
occurred during and immediately following the 1946 election campaign.

Government authorities, for example, directed police, constabulary soldiers, and civilian guards—who were on the payrolls of landlords and the government—to raid offices of the Democratic Alliance and PKM, break up political rallies, and beat up peasant leaders and spokesmen. Adding insult to injury, national government authorities, including President Manuel Roxas, manipulated Congress so as to refuse illegally to seat the six Democratic Alliance candidates whom voters in Central Luzon had elected to the House of Representatives.

Repression had become so significant for peasants that it and related issues—such as demands that the government disband the civilian guards— became more important to many villagers than the agrarian issues themselves. Many people joined the HMB guerrillas because of repression rather than because they wanted bigger shares of their harvests or good relations with landlords. Of course, unresolved agrarian issues remained indispensable for understanding why Huk guerrillas and government soldiers fought. A major theme in the HMB's demands, however, was that the government must stop killing and abusing people before peasant leaders would meet again with landlords and government officials to discuss agrarian reform proposals.

Peasants who rebelled in Central Luzon, therefore, did so in desperation. They felt they had no other choice. Rebellion was not a step they had planned to take in order to get what they wanted. It was instead a reaction to an impossible situation. Either they used the military skills many had learned while resisting the Japanese or they would be imprisoned and killed, lose their homes and lands, and leave unavenged the deaths and abuses of relatives and friends. Even as they fought, they continued to try to return to more peaceful and legal avenues. For example, the HMB attempted several times to negotiate a truce. Indicative, too, of the peasants' reluctance to rebel was the fact that the revolt receded in the 1950s as the Philippine army became less abusive and the government disbanded the civilian guards.

6. The sixth conclusion concerns leadership. Leaders never caused the unrest or the rebellion. They only helped to shape it. Sometimes leaders were not even in the lead. Nor could they necessarily tell rank and file participants what to do. Significantly, the movement had not one set of leaders but at least three, which developed as the unrest expanded. Those three types of leaders played different parts; they also reflected important differences within the movement. Generally, leaders varied with respect to their connections to peasant organizations and with respect to their ideologies or outlooks.

One type in the Huk movement, which I call local leaders, were usually peasants themselves who knew intimately the predicaments fellow peasants faced. Their goals were also generally restricted to the immediate concerns of most villagers—to reestablish traditional patron-client relationships and end repression. They became leaders by virture of the respect and esteem they had earned in the eyes of others in the vicinity. They had emerged as leaders from the struggle itself; they were not imposed on the local area from the outside. Geographically, most of these local leaders stayed in their home villages and municipalities. They were officials in local chapters of peasant unions, squadron leaders, underground leaders for the village or municipality, and HMB field commanders. Three examples were Hilario Felipe and Patricio del Rosario (both in Talavera, Nueva Ecija) and Benjamin Cunanan (in southern Tarlac).

A second type of leader included those who were rather distant from the peasants' world and whose goals or outlook only partly complemented and sometimes conflicted with the peasant activists' goals. These were the national or top-level leaders. In most cases, they were not from a peasant background. Or if they were, they had left that background behind them through education, occupation, and residence. Most were urban intellectuals, bureaucrats, lawyers, and other professionals who were sympathetic to the peasants' plight. They offered their services after watching local initiatives, or they were approached by local peasant spokesmen to help with larger organizational tasks. The special contributions of these leaders were their skills and knowledge about taking grievances to court, lobbying with congressmen, petitioning government offices, and using other avenues of protest and appeal that went beyond the villages and municipalities.

Many leaders in this national or top-level leadership group wanted not only to help the peasant movement, but also to push for major economic and political reforms—even radical changes—that went beyond what the peasantry was talking about. The most noticeable leaders of this type were several national officers and theoreticians in the Philippine Communist Party (PKP). Illustrative here were such men as Mateo del Castillo, Jose Lava, Jesus Lava, Mariano Balgos, and Guillermo Capadocia.

A third type of leader shared attributes of both local and national leaders. These middle-level leaders lived in the villages and market towns, maintained close ties to the peasantry, and usually were of peasant background themselves. Typically they were veteran local peasant leaders who had become well-known among peasants in many municipalities or even in much of the region and who traveled around as officers of provincial and regional peasant unions. They were people like Luis Taruc, Cenon Bungay, Agaton Bulaong, Jose de Leon, and Juan Feleo, who reemerged time after time as prominent spokesmen for the peasants' local initiatives and who became leading figures in the Hukbalahap resistance and the HMB rebellion. Partly because of their experience and partly because of their slight removal from village life due to their occupations (such as craftsmen, urban workers, high school teachers, and local government employees) and sometimes education, these middle-level leaders could also understand the intentions of national leaders who were more radical than the peasantry. To some extent, they even shared the national leadership's radical vision of a new order. Many, for example, were officers in the PKP. As a consequence of their position, middle-level leaders often found themselves trying to bridge the gap between local peasant organizations

and the movement's national leadership. They represented the more con-
servative peasant aims to the national leadership while trying to broaden
the peasantry's ideology.

As this study has shown, the PKP did not inspire or control the peasant
movement in Central Luzon during the 1930s and 1940s, the Hukbalahap,
or the Huk rebellion itself. This finding disputes a common argument made
in previous studies and in United States and Philippine government accounts.[8] Frequently these sources have left the impression that the PKP
created or tightly controlled the rebellion. What appears closer to the truth
is that the PKP, as an organization, moved back and forth between
alliance and nonalliance with the peasant movement in Central Luzon. For
example, the PKP was allied for awhile with the peasants' resistance during
the Japanese occupation. Later, because of its "retreat-for-defense policy,"
the party's top leadership decided that the PKP and the Hukbalahap
should lie low. Most peasants in the Hukbalahap, however, continued to
fight, paying little mind to the PKP. After the Japanese occupation, the
PKP again aligned itself with the peasant movement, as did some other
groups that desired certain political reforms, which included but also
exceeded what the peasants in Central Luzon demanded. The formal
manifestation of this collaboration was the Democratic Alliance. When
thousands of peasants turned to rebellion in 1946, however, the PKP
backed away once again from the movement. Two years later, the party
rejoined the peasants, whose rebellion was still raging.

Guiding the party's policies regarding whether or not to join—and try to
lead—the peasants were considerations that reflected its objectives as
defined, for the most part, by its top leadership—especially its theoreticians. Consequently, when the party's top leadership deliberated about
what actions to endorse, they evaluated economic and political conditions
that went far beyond those directly affecting peasants in one region.
Therefore, the party's actions did not always converge with what peasant
activists in Central Luzon wanted and did. One consideration, for example,
was whether to rely on "legal struggle" or on "armed struggle" in order to
pursue radical changes in the country. Using criteria which the party's top
leaders believed were in keeping with Marxist-Leninist theory and evidence
concerning conditions all over the Philippines and in other parts of the
world, the party concluded in 1946 that the time for armed struggle—
revolution—was not ripe. Therefore, it decided not to join or support the
rebellion. In 1948-1949, the conditions were ripening, according to the
party's new appraisal, so the PKP joined the HMB with the idea of taking

[8] See, for example, Scaff, *Philippine Answer to Communism*, chapters 1 and 10; Lachica,
Huk, pp. 103-135; Saulo, *Communism in the Philippines*, pp. 36-39, 44-47; Baclagon, *Lessons
from the Huk Campaign*, pp. 2-4; Felder, *Socio-Economic Aspects of Counterinsurgency;* and
Leighton, *The Huk Rebellion*. William J. Pomeroy, the American Communist Party member
who was in the Philippine Communist Party and the Huk movement until his capture in 1952,
also argues that the PKP led the peasant movement, including the Huk rebellion: *An American-
Made Tragedy* (New York: International Publishers, 1974).

charge of it and pushing the "revolutionary situation" into a full-blown "revolutionary crisis," which would topple the government in Manila.

Another consideration for the PKP was the working class. According to the PKP's theory, workers, not peasants, should be the vanguard of the revolutionary movement. Even though labor unions in Manila in the late 1940s still had not become militant and showed little inclination to support the peasants' struggle, the party's top leadership figured that the PKP could help to push workers into the revolution by taking charge of the peasant rebellion.

Despite the PKP's official positions, however, there were always some who considered themselves party members but did not follow its policies. In short, the party's small membership was not tightly disciplined. Consequently, party members joined the peasants' rebellion in 1946 even though the PKP did not approve, just as there were many members after 1948 who refused to join or support the HMB even though the PKP did. Moreover, even those party members who were in the rebellion did not act in unison. One of the chief complaints of the party's top leaders during the 1950s was that lower echelon party members did not adhere to guidelines and orders coming from the PKP's national offices.

The alliances, when they did occur between peasant organizations or peasant rebels and the PKP, remained tenuous. This was another reason why the party had only limited influence on the course of the peasant movement. First, its ties to the peasant movement were mainly at the upper levels of the movement—primarily through national and middle-level leaders of the Hukbalahap, PKM, and HMB. The party had few roots in the villages and municipalities of Central Luzon. Second, the goals of the PKP, on the one hand, and the main thrust of the peasant movement, on the other, were frequently out of phase and sometimes in conflict with each other. Oversimplified, the party wanted revolution, whereas peasants did not. The party after 1948 wanted to overthrow the Philippine government; peasants only wanted the government to stop its repression. The party wanted to end the tenancy system, redistribute land, set up cooperative farms, nationalize industries, and end American imperialism once and for all. Most peasants in the Huk rebellion, in contrast, wanted to reform the tenancy system, paid little attention to nationalist issues, and saw little connection between their problems and American imperialism. For the PKP, the rebellion was part of a larger struggle for national liberation and radical changes. For peasants, their rebellion was a whole, not a part of something else. And it was an outgrowth of their struggle to survive, which they justified entirely in terms of local values and conditions.

Differences exist between national leaders and local leaders and participants in any peasant movement. And one of the tasks of national leadership is to bring people in the movement closer together by helping to develop consensus on objectives. Certainly, the PKP tried to do this both prior to and during the Huk rebellion. Important to the effort, too, were middle-level leaders, who often played the intermediary between the people in Central Luzon's villages and the national leadership of the PKP. Had the movement more time—had, for example, the Philippine government remained as militarily and politically incompetent as the KMT in China or the French in Vietnam—perhaps the peasantry and the radicals could have moved closer together. As things turned out, however, there was an ironic twist. Peasants and radicals glided past each other, each going the opposite way from the other and from the way each had been going before. The PKP, which only a few years earlier had opposed open rebellion, insisted in the 1950s that the armed struggle must continue because signs for revolutionary upheaval were good. Most peasants in the HMB, in contrast, who had taken up their guns against government and landlord soldiers long before the PKP had consented, began laying down their weapons and turning away from rebellion as the government reduced repression and wooed villagers with promises of reform.

7. Colonialism contributed significantly to the growth of agrarian unrest, with colonial regimes and local elites working hand-in-hand against the peasants' protests and rebellion. The deterioration of traditional patron-client relations in the countryside was, in part, a consequence of colonialism. For one thing, colonial officials relied on local elites in order to rule. In so doing, they strengthened the local elites' power while simultaneously making the elites less dependent on villagers for support and status. Second, the colonial regime's economic policies encouraged and gave monetary incentives for cash crop production. This helped to link the country even more securely than before to the world's capitalistic economy. Landed elites became increasingly concerned about maximizing profits—a concern which pushed them to demand more from workers on their lands while minimizing their costs for labor. Because the interests of the colonial rulers and local elites became so entwined, it is understandable why the two reacted similarly when villagers dared to protest or demand reforms. Together, too, they battled peasant rebels.

Both the American and Japanese regimes were aligned with Filipino elites against poor and propertyless people. Neither regime threatened the economic and political position of the Filipino elites in Central Luzon. The American policy, for example, to title all land strengthened the legal rights of landowners but weakened the traditional rights of land users, which is what most peasants in Central Luzon were. American policies that encouraged sugar production favored the sugar centrals and large landowners, not the tenants and cane cutters. Perhaps most important of all, the armies and police forces, whose job was to keep a law and order weighted heavily in favor of an inequitable status quo, became an extension of the local elites, just as those elites became an extension of the colonial regime. The central government and the local elites became so interlocked that civilian guards, which began essentially as private armies of large landowners, became auxiliary troops for the Philippine Constabulary and municipal police forces during the American regime and the Philippine Republic.

American policies immediately after the Japanese occupation require special mention here. So far as I know, previous scholarship on the Huk movement has paid little attention to the military and administrative reprisals that Americans took against the Hukbalahap. Yet these were blatant and often brutal. The American regime sided with the Hukbalahap's enemies—particularly the big landowners in Central Luzon and the American-affiliated USAFFE guerrilla leaders—and denied the Hukbalahap guerrillas the recognition they deserved for resisting and helping to defeat the Japanese army. Worse than that, from the Hukbalahap's perspective, the American and Filipino authorities disarmed them—sometimes forcibly— and frequently hounded them as criminals. These actions unquestionably were part of the repression which pushed peasants into rebellion.

A final point about colonialism is that it continued to affect what happened in Central Luzon even after the Philippines had become independent of the United States. The Philippine constitution guaranteed this continuation when the "parity amendment"—itself a result of reciprocal back-scratching by Americans and Filipino elites—was added. Beyond that, the United States gave considerable economic, political, and military support to the new Philippine government's anti-Huk campaigns. Although a comprehensive assessment of the amount of support, exactly why it was given, and its degree of importance must await the day when documents reposing in Washington and Manila archives are open to public scrutiny, the available evidence shows that this aid was extremely helpful to the Philippine government. It may have been essential.

8. What did the peasants' rebellion accomplish, if anything? The answer must be tentative, of course, for the meaning of the past changes as the future becomes present. Each generation can look back and find new meanings in old events. Generally, however, the peasant movement's efforts to restore a fading traditional agrarian society brought some limited reprieves, while at the same time increasing the social distance between peasants and their former patrons. Class antagonism, heightened by the struggle itself, made it more difficult, if not impossible, to reestablish traditional relations. Paradoxically, therefore, the struggle that helped to form a peasant class, increase class consciousness among peasants, make peasants more powerful politically, and build new peasant associations, also hastened the decline of the old order, which peasants had set out to restore.

Villagers in Central Luzon attributed several benefits to the Huk rebellion. One was a reduction in rent for many—but certainly not all— tenants. Peasants in Bulacan told a social scientist in 1964, for example, that because of the Huk rebellion, "farm rent dropped from 50 to 45 percent." And, they added "if the next one [peasant uprising] occurred, it would drop to 40 percent."[9] Many people in San Ricardo, Talavera, said that after the Huk rebellion they unilaterally reduced their rent from 55 or

[9] Akira Takahashi, *Land and Peasants in Central Luzon* (Tokyo: Institute of Developing Economies, 1969), p. 77.

50 percent of the harvest to 50 or 45 percent. Landlords did nothing whereas before, according to one elderly tenant, "they would have sent their armed guards and kicked us off the land." Landlords, villagers said, were more cautious and respectful of the peasantry's collective power after the rebellion. People also recalled that interest rates declined a little, at least for a few years after the rebellion, and local officials and courts treated their complaints more sympathetically. Perhaps most important, the Huk movement firmly established the peasantry's right to its own organizations and unions. And the two largest peasant organizations in Central Luzon during the 1960s—the Federation of Free Farmers (FFF) and the Malayang Samahang Magsasaka (MASAKA, Free Farmers Union)—grew directly out of the Huk movement. Many villagers also attributed the reforms of the Ramon Magsaysay era to the Huk rebellion. Without the Huks, people said, Magsaysay and his administration would not have ended the repression and begun agrarian reforms.

Despite these changes, living conditions for people in villages like San Ricardo improved little—if at all—after the revolt. And relations between landlords and tenants never returned to the traditional style. Disputes between the two classes began to surface again even before the guns of the Huks and government soldiers went silent. For instance, newspapers in January 1953 reported about the violence and expectations of violence on several haciendas in Nueva Ecija as a consequence of disagreements between tenants and landlords over crop divisions; reports in December 1953 told of additional serious conflicts in the same province because tenants claimed hacienda guards had prevented them from harvesting rice to feed their hungry families; in June 1954 numerous tenants, through their unions, filed charges in court against landowners for violating agrarian laws.[10] Some of the reforms included in new tenancy laws also pushed landlords and peasants further apart, rather than closer together. Laws, for example, providing for written contracts between tenant and landlord were partly a consequence of the peasant unrest. At first peasants welcomed the contracts but increasingly realized that they strait-jacketed a relationship which ideally was diffuse and flexible. Legislation in the 1950s and 1960s also included provisions allowing share tenants (kasamá) to become leasehold tenants (buwisan), in which case tenants would pay a fixed amount of rent each harvest. But the leasehold system also absolved landlords of all responsibility to help pay agricultural expenses and give loans to their tenants.

The worst change was the trend among large landowners to mechanize. Before the 1950s, mechanized farming in Central Luzon was limited to threshing machines and a few tractors here and there. In the 1950s and 1960s, many large landowners mechanized nearly everything—plowing, weeding, harvesting, and threshing—thereby eliminating the need for tenants. Manolo Tinio in San Ricardo, for example, introduced machinery in

---

[10] *Manila Chronicle*, 11 January 1953, p. 1, 29 January 1953, p. 1, 15 December 1953, p. 1; *Manila Times*, 29 June 1954, p. 1.

1953 that would eventually displace the seventy or eighty tenants who farmed his 216 hectares. In 1970, he had only ten tenants, and by 1974 he expected to have none. Other large landowners in the region were doing the same thing by the end of the 1950s.[11] Replacing tenants with machines and seasonal labor was the final act, for those landowners who could afford it, in the drama of deteriorating relations between peasants and the landed elites in the twentieth century. In San Ricardo mechanized farming, coupled with increased population density, added significantly to the village's poverty.[12]

Many peasants in Central Luzon said the question concerning the rebellion's accomplishments posed a false issue. It implied that those who supported and joined the rebellion had a choice. Most did not. One former Huk in San Ricardo summarized this view well: "Even if we got nothing, that's not important. What's important is that we *had* to fight back. And we fought so well that the big people and the government will never forget us again." The meaning of the revolt to people in Central Luzon's villages goes beyond the weighing of positive and negative, short-term and long-term results. Many in San Ricardo, for instance, said that life in the 1960s was not much better and in some respects worse than it was in the 1930s. They had grave doubts in 1970, however, about launching into rebellion for fear they would suffer worse reprisals than they experienced during the 1940s and 1950s. "Don't be so quick to cry 'revolution,' " cautioned a former Huk in 1970 while speaking with student radicals from Manila who had been preaching to villagers at a meeting of the Talavera chapter of the MASAKA. Despite these considerations, villagers remained proud of what they, their parents, and relatives had done—their peasant organizations of the 1930s, the Hukbalahap, the PKM, and the HMB. This pride was part of the peasant movement's meaning. The movement's success was the movement itself and what it did to people in Central Luzon's villages. "We showed them [the landlords and government] we weren't slaves," an elderly man in Cabiao, Nueva Ecija, said to me as he reflected on his Huk days. "We didn't lie down like whimpering dogs when they started to whip us. We stood up to them and fought for what was rightfully ours." People in San Ricardo agreed. Thus when asked why the rebellion failed, a tenant farmer and veteran of the peasant movement eloquently summarized the sentiments of many others: "No strike, no demonstration, no rebellion fails. Protest against injustice always succeeds."

[11] For an early discussion about this, see L. R. Pamatmat, "A Comment on Farm Mechanization and Tenancy in the Philippines," *Philippine Agricultural Situation* 1 (September 1959):33-36.

[12] Benedict J. Kerkvliet, "Agrarian Conditions since the Huk Rebellion: A Barrio in Central Luzon," in a monograph edited by the author called *Political Change in the Philippines: Studies of Local Politics Preceding Martial Law* (Honolulu: University Press of Hawaii, 1974), pp. 1-76.

ACKNOWLEDGMENTS

I have learned while doing this book how dependent an author is on other people. I wish, as most authors must, that I could adequately thank everyone who assisted me. At the same time, I absolve them of errors I may have made.

Melinda Tria Kerkvliet has been almost as close to this study as I have. She helped with the research, made valuable suggestions, scrutinized my writing, and typed several drafts. Besides all of that, as my wife and closest friend, she has listened to my countless monologues about my work, and shared with me the exhilarations and frustrations of research and writing. I can never adequately express to her my appreciation and love.

I am eternally indebted to people in the Philippines, particularly those in Central Luzon who shared their experiences and knowledge about the history of their region. I am especially grateful to people in San Ricardo, Talavera. They welcomed me into their village and generously gave their time. With their aid, I began to understand the meaning of the rebellion. In Talavera itself, Felipe Bulanadi and his family and Canding Domingo and her household opened their homes to me, taught me a great deal about their province, and introduced me to their relatives and friends, including people in San Ricardo. I shall never forget their generosity. Several other people in Nueva Ecija were especially helpful. Manolo Tinio talked to me for two afternoons about his hacienda. Tomas I. Pagaduan allowed me to read his manuscript on Talavera's history. Juan T. Alano aided my understanding of Central Luzon and arranged for me to meet several tenant farmers and other people who knew much about agrarian conditions in Guimba, Nueva Ecija. Lazaro Francisco shared his knowledge about Nueva Ecija and its peasant movements. Rogelio De Guzman took me to several municipalities and introduced me to tenants, landlords, and local government officials.

In metropolitan Manila and Quezon City, too, many people assisted me. Raul P. De Guzman along with other faculty and staff members of the College of Public Administration at the University of the Philippines kindly permitted me to affiliate with them as a visiting researcher. This, in turn, opened many doors for my research. Many former Huks educated me far more than I can adequately express in this book about themselves and their rebellion. Their integrity and commitment will always be an inspiration. At the Philippines Armed Forces' Camp Aguinaldo and Camp

Crame, the following individuals helped me in 1969 and 1970 to use documents stored there and meet imprisoned Huks: Dominador and Lourdes Arañas, Major Jose F. Bijarias, Colonel Delfin Castro, Judy Collas, Corporal Cecilio R. Contaoi, Tomas Domingo, Major Andrinico Dumlao, Alejandro Melchor, Colonel Prospero T. Ortega, Colonel Ignacio I. Paz, Colonel Valerio Perez, and Sergeant Rod Rodriguez. Staffs at the following offices and institutions were similarly generous: Court of First Instance in Manila, National Library of the Philippines, University of the Philippines Library, Ateneo de Manila University Library, Commission on Elections, and Department of Agriculture and National Resources. I wish to thank Jose Diokno, who was then a Senator, for helping to find court records related to the Huk rebellion; Eden R. Divinagracia and Vita Ventura Dacumos for translating Hiligaynon and Pampangan documents; and Damaso and Paz Tria for their hospitality.

In the United States, the following research depositories and their staffs have been invaluable: University of Wisconsin Library, University of California Library, the Wason Collection at Cornell University, the Asia Collection at the University of Hawaii, and the United States National Archives in Washington, D.C., and the Federal Records Center in Suitland, Maryland.

I thank Daniel F. Doeppers for permission to use his map of the Central Plain, International Publishers for the liberty to cite several passages from books it published, and the Bureau of Coast and Geodetic Survey in the Philippines for authorization to use a portion of its map of Talavera, Nueva Ecija. And I am grateful to Everett Hawkins, Aprodicio A. Lacquian, and Fred R. von der Mehden for their assistance when I was beginning the research for this book.

Financial and other institutional support made my work feasible. Most of the research was done while I had a fellowship from the Foreign Area Fellowship Program (1969-1971). It supported my family and me for seventeen months in the Philippines and six months in the United States while I wrote a dissertation on this topic. Prior to that, the University of Wisconsin Graduate School and the Midwestern Universities Consortium for International Activities paid for international travel and three months of work in the Philippines. More recently, the University of Hawaii paid for research by Lito Asuncion, Evelyn Garcia, and Richard Wojtowicz, who assisted me with additional library work.

The University of Hawaii, especially its Department of Political Science, has contributed in many ways. I shall forever appreciate the numerous favors from Michael J. Shapiro, Robert S. Cahill, and Deane E. Neubauer, chairpersons of the Department while I was writing. They not only helped me to join the University of Hawaii, but they fostered a healthy environment for scholarship and teaching. I also benefited from my colleagues Harry J. Friedman, Robert B. Stauffer, Douglas Bwy, Manfred Henningsen, Oliver Lee, and Glenn D. Paige, who previewed portions of the manuscripts, made provocative observations about the general topic of rebellion, or otherwise took an interest in my work. The first two gentlemen also helped when I was just beginning to research this topic. The Asian Studies Program and the Graduate School at Hawaii paid my travel expenses to two professional conferences where I presented portions of my findings. Lynette Kotake, Jeanette Matsuda, Carole Moon, and Laurene Nakashima typed various drafts. So did Freda R. Hellinger, who also made encouraging comments about my writing. Sandra Lee Yee prepared the maps for publication.

Without the Woodrow Wilson International Center for Scholars in Washington, D.C., I probably would never have had the luxury of doing research in United States government archives, reevaluating my dissertation, and writing this book. For twelve months (1973-1974) the Center supported my family and me and provided excellent facilities. Many people there assisted me, particularly Helen Clayton, Fran Hunter, Marcella Jones, Michael Lacey, Mildred Pappas, Cathy Pitchell, Suzanne Reppert, and Gaenor Willson. James H. Billington, Director, William M. Dunn, Assistant Director, and Robert Packenham, Fellow, kindly agreed to examine critically early drafts of some chapters. I also benefited from my colleagues Peter Braestrup, Carlos Fuentes, Charles S. Hyneman, K. P. Misra, Patrick Morgan, Claire Nader, Roland Stromberg, and Peter Van Ness.

Frank Hursh, Tetsuo Miyabara, Bruce Nussbaum, Daniel B. Schirmer, David R. Sturtevant, David O. D. Wurfel, and two anonymous reviewers for the publishers carefully read part or all of the manuscript. Similarly, Benedict R. O'G. Anderson, Edward Friedman, and William J. Pomeroy, after reading my dissertation, made suggestions and criticisms that later proved helpful when I wrote this book. To these people and all others who have commented on my work, I am grateful even though I did not do everything they advised.

Numerous people, many of whom I have never met, have substantially influenced my thinking about politics and research. I wish to thank, in particular, those who have taken a personal interest in my intellectual growth: Charles W. Anderson, Robert Y. Fluno, Henry Hart, John A. Larkin, Hibbert Roberts, and John Stefanoff. I owe the most, however, to James C. Scott and John R. W. Smail. Through their excellent scholarship, teaching, and friendship, these two humane and generous people have reinforced my interest in peasants and encouraged me to pursue this topic. Besides all of that, they have moved mountains to assist my research and have criticized constructively and in detail my written work. Without doubt, they have made this a better book than it otherwise would have been.

Over the years this study has evolved, many people have contributed in ways they are not aware. Their friendship and concern, particularly when problems arose, will always be remembered. I am especially grateful to Bruce and Kathie Cruikshank, Carolyn and Don Emmerson, Dolly and Joe Endriga, Oscar and Susan Evangelista, Jerene Kerkvliet, Jack and Judy Larkin, Elizabeth and Howard Leichter, May and Oliver Lee, Jean and Lee Miralao, Ellen Reyes, David and Jean Rosenberg, Amy and

Hung-mao Tien, and Dory and Fred Yap. I also thank my son and daughter, Brian and Jodie, for the many special things they have done.

This book is dedicated to my parents and grandparents as a token of my appreciation, respect, and love for them.

GLOSSARY

AMT	Aguman ding Malding Talapagobra; General Workers' Union. A peasant union in the 1930s concentrated in Pampanga and affiliated with the Socialist Party.
anting-anting	Amulet; charm to protect a person from evil and death.
bata	Literally it means "child." Colloquially, it often refers to someone who is thought to be a "pawn" of another person.
bayan	Poblacion, or municipal center.
bigas	Hulled rice.
BUDC	Barrio United Defense Corps. Underground political organizations for the Hukbalahap resistance movement.
cavan	Dry measure for grain. 1 cavan equals 2.18 bushels. A cavan of palay weighs about 44 kilgrams; a cavan of bigas weighs about 56 kilograms.
Cawal ning Capayapaan	Knights of Peace. A peasant organization formed by Pampangan landlords and, in particular, Governor Sotero Baluyut in the 1930s. Landlords employed members of the Cawal as strikebreakers and armed guards.
CIC	Central Intelligence Corps for the American regime in the Philippines, 1945-1946.
CLC	Central Luzon Command. In the early stages of the HMB, this was the principal subdivision for Central Luzon.
CLO	Congress of Labor Organizations. A post-Japanese occupation confederation of labor unions that was confined largely to the metropolitan Manila area.

274

DA	Democratic Alliance. An alliance of several reform-oriented organizations that attempted to elect candidates to local and national offices in 1946.
FC	Field Command. A military unit of the HMB. Each FC was composed of several guerrilla squadrons.
Friends of China	A political organization in the late 1930s that protested Japan's invasion of China. It was closely associated with the League for the Defense of Democracy.
Ganap	Refers to Filipinos who supported the Japanese occupation because they thought the Japanese would liberate the Philippines from colonialism once and for all.
hectare	Metric measure of land area. 1 hectare (ha.) equals 2.47 acres.
HMB	Hukbong Mapagpalaya ng Bayan; People's Liberation Army. This is the full name for the Huk rebellion, including the rebellion's guerrilla forces and political organizations.
Hukbalahap	Abbreviation for Hukbo ng Bayan laban sa Hapon; People's Anti-Japanese Army. This was the anti-Japanese resistance movement, including its guerrilla army.
ilustrado	Member of the Filipino elite.
KAP	Katipunan ng mga Anak Pawis; Association of Toilers. A labor union during the 1930s.
kaingin	Swidden type of agriculture.
kamote	Sweet potato.
kapit	Literally it means "hold" or "take hold." Colloquially, it can mean having "pull" in the right places in government or business.
kasama	Companion; comrade.
kasamá	Tenant farmer who shares a percentage of the crop with the landowner.
katiwala	Overseer on a hacienda or other large landholding.
kilala	Literally it means "know" or an "acquaintance." Colloquially, it often refers to one's "connections" in government or business so as to be able to get around rules and regulations or speed up a procedure that otherwise would take a long time.

komadre	Female sponsor in baptism, confirmation, or wedding.
kompadre	Male sponsor in baptism, confirmation, or wedding.
KPMP	Kalipunang Pambansa ng mga Magsasaka sa Pilipinas; National Society of Peasants in the Philippines. A large peasant organization in Central Luzon during the 1930s.
League for the Defense of Democracy	Also called simply the "League." It was an anti-Fascist organization during the 1930s and was confined mainly to the greater Manila area.
LP	Liberal Party. One of the two major political parties after the Japanese occupation.
maka-Hapon	Pro-Japanese; sympathizer with the Japanese regime in the Philippines.
makapili	Refers to Filipinos whom the Japanese officials used to point out persons suspected of being against the government.
Marrcom	Manila-Rizal Regional Committee. A subdivision of the PKP in the Manila area after the Japanese occupation, primarily concerned with labor union activities and recruiting party members from among union memberships.
MP	Military Police. Sometimes it was also called the Military Police Command (MPC). From 1945 to about 1948, it was equivalent to the Philippine Constabulary.
MASAKA	Malayang Samahang Magsasaka; Free Farmers Union. A peasant organization in Central Luzon during the 1960s and early 1970s.
ninong	Male sponsor at baptism, confirmation, or wedding.
NP	Nacionalista Party. One of the two major political parties after the Japanese occupation and the only major party prior to that.
OD	Organization Department of the Communist Party (PKP).
pakikisama	Preservation of harmony among a group of people who have an ongoing exchange of favors and deeds.

palay	Unhulled rice.
PB	Political Bureau or politburo of the Communist Party (PKP).
PC	Philippine Constabulary. The national police.
PKM	Pambansang Kaisahan ng mga Magbubukid; National Peasants Union. A large peasant organization during the 1940s.
PKP	Partido Komunista ng Pilipinas; Communist Party of the Philippines.
poblacion	Another word for bayan; municipal center.
pulot	Pick up; glean.
rasyon	Ration. Usually a loan of rice to a tenant farmer from the landlord that required no interest payment.
Reco	Regional Committee; sometimes called Regional Command. This was a major subdivision within the Hukbalahap and later the HMB.
Sakdal	A peasant-based association in Central and Southern Luzon in the mid-1930s. It was involved in a brief uprising in 1935.
sari-sari stores	Small stores, typically located in front of the owner's house, that carry everyday needs for sundries and simple cooking. They are noted for extending short-term credit to regular customers.
sitio	Cluster of houses in the countryside that is too small to be a barrio of its own. It is considered to be part of a barrio, although it is physically separated from the other houses in the barrio.
SLC	Southern Luzon Command. In the early stages of the HMB, this was the principal organizational subdivision for Southern Luzon guerrilla forces.
tambuli	Bugle made from a carabao horn or a shell.
Tanggulan	A peasant organization in Central Luzon that ended with a short uprising in the early 1930s.
tao	Person.
telyadora	Threshing machine.
tulisaffe	A pun on the word *tulisan,* meaning "bandit" or "thief," to refer to the USAFFE guerrillas in a derogatory manner.

USAFFE	United States Armed Forces in the Far East during World War II.
usurero	Moneylender.
utang na loob	Literally it means "internal debt." It refers to the cultural norm of reciprocity and obligation between persons, often of unequal social status, who have exchanged favors and services.
walang hiya	Shameless; ungrateful; unscrupulous.
zona	The practice of police or soldiers, especially during the Japanese occupation, to surround a neighborhood, round up the residents, and then arrest suspected criminals and opponents of the government.

BIBLIOGRAPHY

Primary Sources

Captured Documents

These include two collections, one each at Camp Aguinaldo, Headquarters of the Armed Forces of the Philippines, and Camp Crame, Headquarters of the Philippine Constabulary. Both are in Quezon City. Most of the documents originally belonged to the Hukbalahap, the HMB, or the PKP. There are others, however, from the PKM, DA, and CLO. Roughly, the documents fall into the following categories: publications from the various organizations, educational materials used by the organizations, policy directives and plans, reports, and correspondence. Also included are statements made by some members of these organizations after they were captured or had surrendered. They gave these statements, usually under oath, to government authorities. Altogether, I was able to study over seven hundred documents in these two collections. Six out of every seven were in the Camp Aguinaldo holdings. Roughly 60 percent of all documents fall in the 1948-1951 time period. The remaining fraction is divided about equally between 1944-1947 and 1952-1956. Roughly half the documents are in Tagalog, slightly less than half in English, and a tiny fraction in Hiligaynon and Pampangan. Neither collection has any kind of systematic bibliography or index of its holdings.

Court Exhibits

During two well-known trials of people accused of being in the Huk rebellion and/or the PKP during the 1950s, a sizable number of the documents that the military authorities captured from the Hukbalahap, HMB, PKP, and other organizations were submitted as exhibits in court. Some are copies from the documents at Camp Aguinaldo and Camp Crame, but most are not.

The first set includes documents originally used in at least five cases in the early 1950s: Criminal Cases 14071, 14082, 14315, 14344, 14270, Court of First Instance, Manila. All of these later became Supreme Court Cases L 4974-4978. The men and women on trial were among those arrested in Manila during a series of raids in late 1950 that the government authorities planned in order to capture PKP politburo members. Consequently, these cases are often referred to as the politburo trials. At present, the "politburo exhibits" number about 350 documents and are stored in the office of the Clerk of Court, Court of First Instance, Manila. They were once more numerous, but a fire destroyed many of them while on loan to the Philippine Constabulary. What remains are photostatic copies that had been made from some of the originals and other duplicates. These exhibits are documents of the same kinds found in the Camp Aguinaldo collection, although their time-span is much narrower. Almost all are dated 1949 and 1950. After I used them, the University of the Philippines Library retyped and then microfilmed these documents. Interested persons can now read them at that library. The second set of court exhibits is from the trial of Amado Hernandez, Criminal Case 15841, Court of First Instance, Manila (Supreme Court Case L 6025-6026). I refer to these as the "Hernandez exhibits." Hernandez was accused of being a member of the PKP and conspiring to overthrow the government. Hence, the exhibits are relevant to the HMB and PKP, although many are duplicates of ones found among the captured documents and politburo exhibits. Hernandez was a leading officer in the Congress of Labor Organizations, so these exhibits contain records from that organization. Numerous papers originally included among these exhibits have been destroyed due to inadequate storage. I helped to rescue all surviving exhibits and to arrange for them to be microfilmed. The University of the Philippines Library staff recently completed that task; ten reels of Hernandez exhibits are now deposited in that library. The originals remain with the Clerk, Court of First Instance, Manila.

Interviews

Alano, Juan T. Quezon City, 4 February 1970. A former attorney for a peasant organization in Nueva Ecija and long-time resident of that province.

Alejandrino, Casto. Camp Crame, Quezon City, 14 and 16 July, and 5 and 12 November 1970. Imprisoned Huk-PKP leader who was also active in Pampanga's peasant movement in the 1930s.

Bulaong, Agaton. Camp Crame, Quezon City, 20 July 1970. Imprisoned Huk leader.

Bungay, Cenon. Camp Crame, Quezon City, 15 July 1970. Imprisoned HMB leader.

Castello, Oscar. Quezon City, 23 February 1970. CFI judge in Manila who presided over the politburo trial and passed sentence on the accused found guilty.

Castro, Delfin. Camp Aguinaldo, Quezon City, 29 July 1969. Colonel in the armed forces of the Philippines.

Crisol, Jose. Civic Action Program Office, Camp Aguinaldo, Quezon City, 15 December 1969. Former adviser to President Ramon Magsaysay and secretary of defense during the government's anti-HMB campaign in the early 1950s.

Cunanan, Benjamin. Camp Crame, Quezon City, 11 August 1970. Imprisoned HMB leader from Tarlac.

Fernando, Carlos. Camp Crame, Quezon City, 10 August 1970. Imprisoned HMB activist.

Francisco, Lazaro. Cabanatuan, Nueva Ecija, 4 June 1970. Well-known Tagalog novelist and life-long resident of Nueva Ecija. Many of his writings concern the lives of peasants in Central Luzon.

De Guzman, Rogelio. Quezon City, 18 February 1970. An attorney with the Court of Agrarian Relations whose "territory" is southern Nueva Ecija.

Huertas, Paulino. Camp Crame, Quezon City, 29 July 1970. Imprisoned HMB activist.

Lava, Jesus. Camp Crame, Quezon City, 12 and 19 August 1970. Imprisoned Huk-PKP leader.

Lava, Ruth. Quezon City, 6 March 1970. Wife of Vicente Lava.

Liwanag, Silvestre. Camp Crame, Quezon City, 21 July 1970. Imprisoned Huk-PKP leader.

Obrador, Julian. Camp Crame, Quezon City, 27 July 1970. Imprisoned man from Batangas who insists he is innocent of crimes for which he has been tried and convicted (murder and subversion). He says he was never a member of the HMB.

Paz, Romero. Camp Crame, Quezon City, 6 August 1970. Imprisoned HMB activist.

Perez, Valerio. Camp Aguinaldo, Quezon City, 22 July 1969. Colonel in the Philippine Constabulary.

Perlas, Jose Z. Mount Arayat, Pampanga, 26 June 1969. Colonel in the armed forces of the Philippines (now retired).

Rustia, Jose. Quezon City, 21 November 1970. Older brother of Juan Rustia.

Saulo, Alfredo. Quezon City, 14 April 1969, 20 January and 4 February 1970. Former activist in DA, PKP, and HMB.

Tantoco, Glecy Rustia. Manila, 25 November 1970. Daughter of Juan Rustia.

Taruc, Luis. Quezon City, 27 January and 25 February 1970. Former Huk-PKP leader.

Taruc, Peregrino. Camp Crame, Quezon City, 8, 9, and 13 July 1970. Former Huk-PKP leader.

Tenorio, Faustino. Camp Crame, Quezon City, 27 July 1970. Imprisoned HMB activist.

Ventura, Adelina. San Fernando, Pampanga, 26 June 1969. Well-informed life-long resident in Pampanga.

Villacrusis, Florentino. Talavera, Nueva Ecija, 28 June 1970. Former officer in the armed forces of the Philippines during anti-HMB campaign.

Vicencio, Pedro. Camp Crame, Quezon City, 23 July 1970. Imprisoned HMB participant.

Newspapers

Manila Chronicle, 1945-1953.
Manila Times, 1930, 1945-1948, 1953-1954.
Philippines Free Press, 1946-1954.
Star Reporter (Manila), 1945-1946. Issues of this short-lived daily are located in the Library of Ateneo de Manila University, Quezon City.
Tribune (Manila), 1930-1941.

Historical Data Papers

These are histories of municipalities (usually barrio by barrio) that teachers and other local persons prepared in the early 1950s at the request of the Philippine government's Bureau of Public Schools. I examined those papers available in the National Library for municipalities in Central Luzon and parts of Southern Luzon and the Bisayas. In provincial government offices in Cabanatuan, Nueva Ecija, I also found papers for some municipalities not included in the National Library's holdings. Future users should be aware that sometimes the data papers for several municipalities in a province are bound together, but papers for other municipalities in the same province are bound separately. For instance, papers for many munici-palities in Nueva Ecija are in two volumes entitled *Historical Data of Nueva Ecija.* But the papers for the municipality of Talavera are in a separate book, *History and Cultural Life of Talavera and Its Barrios.*

Roxas Papers

Official and personal papers of the late President Manuel Roxas, National Library, Manila. When I used these papers in 1969-1970, they were tied in bundles, which were numbered and labeled according to general topics.

United States National Archives

Because the United States has had close ties with the Philippines, several government archives include records relating to peasant unrest, the Hukbalahap, the PKP, and the Huk rebellion itself. The most useful ones are in the Military Records section of the National Archives in Washington, D.C., and at the Federal Records Center, Suitland, Maryland. Most of them originated with the Department of the Army. When I used these collections in 1973, nonofficial researchers like myself were allowed to examine classified documents dated through December 1947. Classified documents more recent than this date were off limits.

Other collections that were helpful for my work were the Bureau of Insular Affairs Records and the Diplomatic Records, which are deposited in the United States National Archives in Washington, D.C., and the records of the Chief of Military History, Department of the Army, Washington, D.C.

Government Publications

While doing research for this study, I used dozens of Philippine and United States government publications. They were invaluable for statistical as well as textual information.

Unpublished Secondary Sources

Anderson, James N. "Kinship and Property in a Pangasinan Barrio." Ph.D. dissertation, University of California, Los Angeles, 1964.

Araneta, A.S. "The Communist Party of the Philippines and the Comintern, 1919-1930." Ph.D. dissertation, Lincoln College, Oxford, England, 1966.

Castro, Amado Alejandro. "The Philippines: A Study in Economic Dependence." Ph.D. dissertation, Harvard University, 1953.

Crisologo, Fortunato L. "Present Education Practices of the Huks." Master's thesis, University of the Philippines, 1953.

Eala, Godofredo C. "Palay Marketing Practices of Farmers in San Jose and Rizal, Nueva Ecija." Master's thesis, University of the Philippines, Los Baños, 1957.

Echon, Emmanuel J. "Rice Mills and Their Facilities in Nueva Ecija." Master's thesis, University of the Philippines, Los Baños, 1957.

Endriga, Dolores Alano. "Farm Management Potentials of Tenants in a 'Hacienda' Barrio." Unpublished paper, 1967.

Endriga, Jose N. "The Friar Lands in the Philippines during the Spanish and American Regimes." Master's thesis, University of Wisconsin, 1969.

Francisco, Victoria R. "The Government's Program of Social Amelioration with Special Reference to Tenants of Central Luzon." Master's thesis, University of the Philippines, 1951.

Hernandez, Teresita J. "An Analysis of the Social and Legal Aspects of Farm Tenancy in the Philippines." Master's thesis, University of the Philippines, 1954.

Hillam, Ray. "Insurgent Communism: The Problem of Counter-Measures in Malaya, Vietnam, and the Philippines." Ph.D. dissertation, American University, 1964.

Hoeksema, Renze L. "Communism in the Philippines: Historical and Analytical Study of Communism and the Communist Party in the Philippines and Its Relation to Communist Movements Abroad." Ph.D. dissertation, Harvard University, 1956.

Kerkvleit, Benedict J. "Peasant Rebellion in the Philippines: The Origins and Growth of the HMB." Ph.D. dissertation, University of Wisconsin, Madison, 1972.

Larkin, John A. "The Evolution of Pampangan Society: A Case Study of Social and Economic Change in the Rural Philippines." Ph.D. dissertation, New York University, 1966.

Lava, Jose. "Milestones in the History of the Philippine Communist Party." Mimeo, circa 1950. Written under the name Gregorio Santayana, an alias for Jose Lava.

Lopez, Oscar J. "A History of the Communist Movement in the Philippines." Honor's essay, Harvard University, 1951.

Mayfield, William. "The Development of Organized Labor in the Philippines." Master's thesis, University of the Philippines, 1956.

McLennan, Marshall S. "Peasant and Hacendero in Nueva Ecija: The Socio-Economic Origins of a Philippine Rice-Growing Region." Ph.D. dissertation, University of California, Berkeley, 1974.

Montenegro, John. "Sociological Implications of Insecurity of Tenure in Selected Rural Areas of the Philippines." Master's thesis, University of Wisconsin, 1959.

Nemenzo, Francisco, Jr. "The Land for the Landless Program in the Philippines." Master's thesis, University of the Philippines, 1959.

Nydegger, William F. "Tarong: A Philippine Barrio." Ph.D. dissertation, Cornell University, 1960.

Oracion, Lossiete A. "The Communist Struggle in the Philippines." Master's thesis, Far Eastern University (Manila), 1958.

Pagaduan, Tomas I. "Kasaysayan ng Talavera, Nueva Ecija" [History of Talavera, Nueva Ecija]. Unpublished manuscript, 1967.

Paulson, Christopher R. "The Role of Sugar in Philippine Society, 1860-1941." Master's thesis, University of Wisconsin, 1967.

Peredo, Benjamin D. "Cost of Marketing Palay and Rice in Nueva Ecija." Master's thesis, University of the Philippines, Los Baños, 1964.

Pobre, Cesar P. "The Resistance Movement in Northern Luzon, 1942-1945." Master's thesis, University of the Philippines, 1962.

Rojo, Trinidad. "Roots of Red Rebellion." Unpublished manuscript, circa 1967.

Sabelino, Conrado S. "A Study of the Legal Struggle of the Communist Movement in the Philippines." Master's thesis, University of the Philippines, 1958.

Salita, Domingo C. "Land Use in the Province of Pampanga." Master's thesis, University of the Philippines, 1958.

Selden, Mark. "Yenan Communism: Revolution in the Shensi-Kansu-Ninghsia Border Region: 1927-1945." Ph.D. dissertation, Yale University, 1967.

Sibley, Willis E. "Manlad: The Maintenance of Unity and Distinctiveness in a Philippine Village." Ph.D. dissertation, University of Chicago, 1958.

Sicat, Loretta Makasiar. "Quezon's Social Justice Program and the Agrarian Problem." Master's thesis, University of the Philippines, 1959.

Simbulan, Dante C. "The Socialist Movement in the Philippines." Master's thesis, University of the Philippines, 1960.

_____. "A Study of the Socio-Economic Elite in Philippine Politics and Government, 1946-1963." Ph.D. dissertation, Australian National University, 1965.

Stubbs, Roy M. "Philippine Radicalism: The Central Luzon Uprisings, 1925-1935." Ph.D. dissertation, University of California, Berkeley, 1951.

Sturtevant, David R. "Philippine Social Structure and Its Relation to Agrarian Unrest." Ph.D. dissertation, Stanford University, 1958.

Tablante, Nathaniel B. "An Appraisal of the Agrarian Problem and Politics in the Philippines." Ph.D. dissertation, Purdue University, 1956.

Tria, Melinda Castro. "The Congress of Labor Organization (CLO) and Its Relation to the Peasant Movement in Central Luzon." Unpublished paper, Department of Political Science, University of Hawaii, November 1971.

——. "The Resistance Movement in Cavite, 1942-1945." Master's thesis, University of the Philippines, 1966.

Urgena, Cynthia B. "The Colorum Uprisings of Pangasinan." Master's thesis, University of the Philippines, 1960.

Ventura, Mamerto S. "Philippine Post-War Recovery: A Record of United States-Philippine Cooperation and Cross-Purposes." Ph.D. dissertation, Southern Illinois University, 1966.

Wurfel, David O.D. "The Bell Report and After: A Study of the Political Problems of Social Reform Stimulated by Foreign Aid." Ph.D. dissertation, Cornell University, 1960.

Selected Published Secondary Sources

Philippines: General

Abaya, Hernando J. *Betrayal in the Philippines.* New York: A.A. Wyn, 1946.

——. *The Untold Philippine Story.* Quezon City: Malaya Books, 1967.

Abelarde, Pedro E. *American Tariff Policy towards the Philippines.* New York: Kings Crown, 1947.

Abueva, Jose V. *Ramon Magsaysay: A Political Biography.* Manila: Solidaridad, 1971.

Agoncillo, Teodoro A. *The Fateful Years: Japan's Adventure in the Philippines, 1941-1945.* 2 vols. Quezon City: R. P. Garcia, 1965.

Agoncillo, Teodoro A., and Oscar M. Alfonso. *A History of the Filipino People.* Quezon City: Malaya Books, 1967.

Anderson, James N. "Buy-and-Sell and Economic Personalism: Foundations for Philippine Entrepreneurship," *Asian Survey* 9 (September 1969):641-668.

Aquino, Ramon C. *Jose Abad Santos: A Chance to Die.* Quezon City: Almer-Phoenix, 1967.

Buenafe, Manuel. *Wartime Philippines.* Manila: Philippine Education Foundation, 1950.

Castillo, Andres. *Philippine Economics.* Manila: n.p., 1949.

Coquia, Jorge R. *Philippine Presidential Election of 1953.* Manila: Universal Publishing, 1955.

Corpuz, Onofre D. *The Bureaucracy in the Philippines.* Quezon City: University of the Philippines Press, 1957.

——. "Filipino Political Parties and Politics," *Philippine Social Science and Humanities Review* 23 (June-December 1958): 141-158.

——. *The Philippines.* Englewood Cliffs, N.J.: Prentice Hall, 1965.

Ellis, Lippert S. *The Tariff on Sugar.* Freeport, Ill.: Rawleigh Foundation, 1933.

Espiritu, Socorro C., and Chester L. Hunt (eds.). *Social Foundations of Community Development: Readings on the Philippines.* Manila: R. M. Garcia, 1964.

Evangelista, Crisanto. *Patnubay sa Kalayaan at Kapayapaan* [Guide to Freedom and Peace]. Manila: Kalayaan Publications, 1941.

Forbes, William C. *The Philippine Islands*. 2 vols. Boston: Houghton Mifflin, 1928.

Friend, Theodore. *Between Two Empires*. New Haven: Yale University Press, 1965.

————. "The Philippine Sugar Industry and the Politics of Independence, 1929-1935," *Journal of Asian Studies* 22 (February 1963): 179-192.

Golay, Frank H. *The Philippines: Public Policy and National Economic Development*. Ithaca: Cornell University Press, 1961.

Goodman, Grant K. *Four Aspects of Philippine-Japanese Relations, 1930-1940*. New Haven: Southeast Asian Studies, Yale University, 1967.

Grossholtz, Jean. *Politics in the Philippines*. Boston: Little, Brown, 1964.

Grunder, Garel A. and William E. Livezey. *The Philippines and the United States*. Norman: University of Oklahoma Press, 1951.

Guerrero, Amado. *Philippine Society and Revolution*. Manila: Pulang Tala Publications, 1971.

Guthrie, George M. *The Filipino Child and Philippine Society*. Manila: Philippine Normal College Press, 1961.

————. (ed.). *Six Perspectives on the Philippines*. Manila: Bookmark, 1968.

Hartendorp, A. V. H. *The Japanese Occupation of the Philippines*. 2 vols. Manila: Bookmark, 1967.

————. *Short History of Industry and Trade of the Philippines*. Manila: American Chamber of Commerce of the Philippines, 1953.

————. *History of Industry and Trade in the Philippines*. Manila: American Chamber of Commerce of the Philippines, 1958.

Hawley, Amos H. *Papers in Demography and Public Administration*. Manila: Institute of Public Administration, University of the Philippines, 1954.

Henson, Mariano A. *The Province of Pampanga and Its Towns (1300-1962)*. Angeles, Pampanga: n.p., 1963.

Hernandez, Amado. *Mga Ibong Mandaragit* [Birds of Prey]. Quezon City: International Graphic Service, 1969.

Hilado, Emilio Y. *Philippine Labor and Social Legislation*. Manila: Philaw Publishing, 1952.

Jenkins, Shirley. *American Economic Policy Toward the Philippines*. Stanford: Stanford University Press, 1954.

————. "Philippine White Paper," *Far Eastern Survey* 20 (January 10, 1951): 1-6.

Kurihara, Kenneth. *Labor in the Philippine Economy*. Stanford: Stanford University Press, 1945.

Lande, Carl. *Structure of Philippine Politics: Leaders, Factions, and Parties*. New Haven: Southeast Asia Studies, Yale University, 1965.

Larkin, John A. "Place of Local History in Philippine Historiography," *Journal of Southeast Asian History* 8 (September 1967): 306-317.

Lear, Elmer. *The Japanese Occupation of the Philippines: Leyte, 1941-1945*. Ithaca: Southeast Asia Program Data Paper, Cornell University, 1961.

LeRoy, James A. *Philippine Life in Town and Country*. New York: Putman, 1905.

Lynch, Frank. "Social Acceptance," in Lynch (compiler), *Four Readings on Philippine Values*. Quezon City: IPC Papers no. 2, Ateneo de Manila University Press, 1968, pp. 1-22.

Macaraig, Serafin E. *Social Problems*. Manila: Educational Supply Company, 1929.

Malay, Armando J. "The Philippine Guerrilla Press," *Saturday Mirror Magazine*, 12 February 1955.

Montemayor, Jeremias. *Labor, Agrarian, and Social Legislation.* 2nd ed. Manila: Rex Book Store, 1968.
Quirino, Carlos. *Magsaysay of the Philippines.* Manila: Ramon Magsaysay Memorial Society, 1958.
Ravenholt, A. "The Philippines: Where Did We Fail?," *Foreign Affairs* 29 (April 1951): 406-416.
Rivera, Juan. "The Aglipayan Movement," *Philippine Social Science and Humanities Review* 9 (1937): 301-328; 10 (1938): 9-32.
Royama Masamichi and Takeuchi Tatsuji. *The Philippine Polity: A Japanese View.* Trans. Takeuchi Tasuji. New Haven: Southeast Asia Studies, Yale University, 1967.
Sanvictores, Jose. "President Quezon's Social Regeneration Program," *Philippine Social Science and Humanities Review* 12 (November 1940): 275-283.
Seeman, Bernard, and Laurence E. Salisbury. *Cross-Currents in the Philippines.* New York: Institute of Pacific Relations, 1946.
Sison, Jose. *Struggle for National Democracy.* Quezon City: Progressive Publications, 1967.
Steinberg, David J. *Philippine Collaboration in World War II.* Ann Arbor: University of Michigan Press, 1967.
Taylor, George E. *The Philippines and the United States: Problems of Partnership.* New York: Council on Foreign Relations, 1964.
Villacorte, Rolando E. *Baliwag: Then and Now.* Quezon City: Philippine Graphic Arts, 1970.
Wernstedt, Frederick L., and J. E. Spencer. *The Philippine Island World.* Berkeley and Los Angeles: University of California Press, 1967.
Wurfel, David O. D. "Foreign Aid and Social Reform in Political Development: A Philippine Case Study," *American Political Science Review* 53 (June 1959): 456-482.

Rural Philippines: Society, Politics, Economics
Abueva, Jose V. *Focus on the Barrio.* Manila: Institute of Public Administration, University of the Philippines, 1959.
Allen, James S. "Agrarian Tendencies in the Philippines," *Pacific Affairs* 11 (March 1938): 52-65.
Anderson, James N. "Land and Society in a Pangasinan Community," in Socorro C. Espiritu and Charles L. Hunt (eds.), *Social Foundations of Community Development.* Manila: R. M. Garcia Publishing, 1964, pp. 171-192.
Arens, Richard S. V. D. "The Early Pulahan Movement in Samar and Leyte," *Journal of History* 7 (1959): 303-371.
Arnaldo, M. V. "The Agrarian Problems of the Philippines and Their Solutions," *Silliman Journal* 2 (January 1955): 31-50.
Arnaldo, M. V., and J. E. Velmonte. "Five-Year Farm Accounting Study of Tenancies in the College of Agriculture Farm, 1931-1936," *Philippine Agriculturist* 30 (November 1941): 465-491.
Asuncion, Daniel F. "A Study of Marketing Rice in Nueva Ecija," *Philippine Agriculturist* 21 (August 1932): 177-193.
Aurello, Catalino. "Cost of Production of Rice by Philippine Methods, *Philippine Agriculturist* 4 (May 1915): 29-42.
Bulatao, Jaime. "Hiya," *Philippine Studies* 12 (July 1964): 424-438.
Bull, Frate. *Philippine Land Reform, 1950-1958.* Manila: International Cooperation Administration, 1958.

Camus, J. S. *Rice in the Philippines.* Manila: Bureau of Printing, 1921.

Cater, Sonya D. *Philippine Federation of Free Farmers: A Case Study in Mass Agrarian Organization.* Ithaca: Southeast Asia Program Data Paper, Cornell University, 1959.

Coller, Richard W. *Barrio Gacao: A Study of Village Ecology and the Schistosomiasis Problem.* Quezon City: University of the Philippines Community Development Research Council, 1960.

Cook, Hugh L., et al. *Philippine Rice Production in the National Economy.* Manila: International Cooperation Administration, 1958.

Crippen, Harlan R. "Philippine Agrarian Unrest: Historical Backgrounds," *Science and Society* 10 (fall 1946): 337-360.

Cutshall, Alden. "Problems of Land Ownership in the Philippine Islands," *Economic Geography* 28 (January 1952): 31-36.

Dalisay, Amando M. *Development of Economic Policy in Philippine Agriculture.* Manila: Phoenix Publishing, 1959.

——. "Factors Related to Income and Cost of Production of Rice on Tenant Holdings in Cabiao, Nueva Ecija," *Philippine Agriculturist* 26 (February 1938): 730-756.

——. "Types of Tenancy Contracts on Rice Farms of Nueva Ecija," *Philippine Agriculturist* 26 (July 1937): 159-186.

Davis, Ray E. *Land Settlement and Title Clearance.* Manila: International Cooperation Administration, 1957.

Davis, William G. "Economic Limitations and Social Relationships in a Philippine Marketplace: Capital Accumulation in a Peasant Economy," in Robert Van Niel (ed.), *Economic Factors in Southeast Asian Social Change.* Honolulu: Asian Studies at Hawaii Program, Publication no. 2, University of Hawaii, 1968, pp. 1-28.

Diaz, Ralph C., and Horst and Judith von Oppenfeld. *Case Studies of Farm Families, Laguna Province, Philippines.* Los Baños, Laguna: University of the Philippines, circa 1960.

Emerson, James P. *Land Reform Progress in the Philippines, 1951-1955.* Manila: International Cooperation Administration, 1956.

Encarnacion, Vicente, Jr. "Types of Authority in a Benguet Village," *Philippine Journal of Public Administration* 1 (October 1957): 379-391.

Fairchild, George H. *Facts and Statistics about the Philippine Sugar Industry.* Manila: Philippine Sugar Association, 1928.

Fey, Harold E. "Farmers Revolt in the Philippines," *Christian Century* 48 (5 August 1931): 1004.

Firmalino, Tito C. *Political Activities of Barrio Citizens in Iloilo as They Affect Community Development.* Quezon City: University of the Philippines Community Development Research Council, 1959.

Foronda, Marcelino A. "The Canonization of Rizal," *Journal of History* 8 (1960): 1-48.

Francisco, Lazaro. *Ama* [Father]. Typewritten manuscript of a serialized novel appearing in *Liwayway,* 1929.

Gapud, Jose P. "Financing Lowland Rice Farming in Selected Barrios of Muñoz, Nueva Ecija," *Economic Research Journal* 6 (September 1959): 74-82.

Guerrero, Milagros C. "The Colorum Uprisings: 1924-1931," *Asian Studies* 5 (April 1967): 65-78.

Guthrie, G. M., et al. *The Psychology of Modernization in the Rural Philippines.* Quezon City: IPC Papers no. 8, Ateneo de Manila University Press, 1970.

Hainsworth, Reginold G., and Raymond T. Moyer. *Agricultural Geography of the Philippine Islands*. Washington, D.C.: U.S. Department of Agriculture, 1945.

Hardie, Robert S. *Philippine Land Tenure Reform: Analysis and Recommendations*. Manila: U.S. Mutual Security Agency, 1952.

Hartendorp, A. V. N. "The Tayug Colorums," *Philippine Magazine* 27 (February 1931): 563-567.

Healy, G. W. "Usury in the Philippines Today," *Philippine Studies* 3 (June 1955): 136-156.

Hester, Evett D., et al. "Some Economic and Social Aspects of Philippine Rice Tenancies," *Philippine Agriculturist* 12 (February 1924): 367-444.

Hines, Cleve W. *Sugar Industry in the Philippine Islands*. Manila: Bureau of Agriculture, 1914.

Hollnsteiner, Mary R. *The Dynamics of Power in a Philippine Municipality*. Quezon City: University of the Philippines Community Development Research Council, 1963.

———. "Reciprocity in the Lowland Philippines," in Frank Lynch (compiler), *Four Readings on Philippine Values*. Quezon City: IPC Papers no. 2, Ateneo de Manila University Press, 1968, pp. 22-49.

Houston, Charles O. "The Philippine Coconut Industry, 1934-1950," *Journal of East Asiatic Studies* 3 (January 1954): 153-182.

———. "The Philippine Sugar Industry, 1934-1950," *Journal of East Asiatic Studies* 3 (July-October 1954): 370-415.

———. "Rice in the Philippine Economy," *Journal of East Asiatic Studies* 3 (October 1953): 12-85.

Huke, Robert E. *Shadows on the Land: An Economic Geography of the Philippines*. Manila: Bookmark, 1963.

Jacobson, H. *Rice in the Philippine Islands*. Manila: Bureau of Agriculture, 1914.

Jacoby, Erich H. *Agrarian Unrest in Southeast Asia*. Bombay: P. S. Jayasinghe, Asia Publishing House, 1961.

Jocano, F. Landa. *Growing Up in a Philippine Barrio*. New York: Holt, Rinehart, and Winston, 1969.

———. *The Traditional World of Malitbog*. Quezon City: Bookmark, 1969.

Jose, F. Sionil. "The Filipino and His Land," *Sunday Times Magazine*. 3, 10, 17, and 24 November and 1 and 8 December 1957.

———. "The Philippine Agrarian Problem," *Comment* (3rd quarter, 1959): 85-143.

Kalaw, Moises K. "Some Economic Phases of Rice Production in Some Towns of Laguna," *Philippine Agriculturist* 16 (October 1927): 297-306.

Kaut, C. R. "Process and Social Structure in a Lowland Philippine Settlement," *Studies in Asia: 1960*. Lincoln: University of Nebraska, 1960, pp. 35-50.

———. "Utang na Loob: A System of Contractual Obligation among Tagalogs," *Southwestern Journal of Anthropology* 17 (Autumn 1961): 256-272.

Keesing, Felix. *The Ethno-History of Northern Luzon*. Stanford: Stanford University Press, 1962.

Kerkvliet, Benedict J. "Agrarian Conditions since the Huk Rebellion: A Barrio in Central Luzon," in Kerkvliet (ed.), *Political Change in the Philippines: Studies of Local Politics Preceding Martial Law*. Honolulu: University Press of Hawaii, 1974, pp. 1-76.

Larkin, John A. *The Pampangans*. Berkeley and Los Angeles: University of California Press, 1972.

Lasker, Bruno. *Human Bondage in Southeast Asia*. Chapel Hill: University of North Carolina Press, 1950.

Lava, Horacio. *Levels of Living in the Ilocos Region.* Manila: Institute of Pacific Relations, 1938.

Lava, V. G. "Relations between Employer and Employee," *Philippine Agriculturist* 16 (November 1927): 337-340.

Lewis, Henry T. *Ilocano Rice Farmers.* Honolulu: University of Hawaii Press, 1971.

Liao, S. H., S. C. Hsieh, and P. R. Sandoval. "Factors Affecting Productivity in Selected Areas of Philippine Rice Farms," *Philippine Agriculturist* 52 (October 1968): 241-255.

Lynch, Frank. *Social Class in a Bikol Town.* Chicago: Philippine Studies Program Research Series, University of Chicago, 1959.

Manawis, Mariano D. "The Life of the Nueva Ecija Peasant," *Philippine Magazine* 31 (January 1934). Reprinted in *Journal of East Asiatic Studies* 4 (April 1955): 279-281.

Maulit, Dimas A. "Income Ratio Between Rural and Urban Workers in the Philippines," *Economics Research Journal* 10 (September 1957): 83-95.

McLennan, Marshall S. "Land and Tenancy in the Central Luzon Plain," *Philippine Studies* 17 (October 1969): 651-682.

McMillan, Robert T. "Land Tenure in the Philippines," *Rural Sociology* 20 (March 1955): 25-33.

Nurge, Ethel. *Life in a Leyte Village.* Seattle: University of Washington Press, 1965.

Nydegger, W. F. and C. *Tarong: An Ilocos Barrio in the Philippines.* New York: Wiley, 1966.

Padilla, Ambrosio B. *Memo Report for the President of the Philippines Regarding San Pedro Tunasan Estate.* Manila: Bureau of Printing, 1955.

Pamatmat, L. R. "A Comment on Farm Mechanization and Tenancy in the Philippines," *Philippine Agricultural Situation* 1 (September 1959): 33-36.

"The Peasant War in the Philippines," *Philippine Social Science and Humanities Review* 23 (June-December 1958): 373-436.

Pelzer, Karl J. "The Philippine Abaca Industry," *Far Eastern Survey* 17 (24 March 1948): 71-74.

――――. *Pioneer Settlement in Asiatic Tropics.* International Secretariat, Institute of Pacific Relations, 1945.

Peña, Antonio. "Agricultural Conditions in the Philippines, 1921," *Philippine Agricultural Review* 15 (summer 1927): 79-148.

Piron, Jorge. "Land Tenure and Levels of Living in Central Luzon," *Philippine Studies* 6 (September 1956): 391-410.

Polson, Robert A., and Agaton P. Pal. *The Status of Rural Life in the Dumaguete City Trade Area, Philippines.* Ithaca: Southeast Asia Program Data Paper, Cornell University, 1956.

Quiaoit, Bonifacio A. "Cooperative Marketing and the Rice Industry," *Commerce and Industry Journal* 7 (June-July 1931).

Ramsey, Ansil. "Ramon Magsaysay and the Philippine Peasantry," *Philippine Social Science and Humanities Review* 30 (1965): 65-86.

Rivera, Generoso F., and Robert T. McMillan. *An Economic and Social Survey of Rural Households in Central Luzon.* Manila: Philippine Council for U.S. Aid and U.S. Operation Mission to the Philippines, 1954.

――――. *The Rural Philippines.* Manila: Mutual Security Agency, 1952.

Romani, J. H. "The Philippine Barrio," *Far Eastern Quarterly* 15 (February 1956): 229-237.

Runes, I. T. *General Standards of Living and Wages of Workers in the Philippine Sugar Industry.* Manila: Institute of Pacific Relations, 1939.

Sacay, Francisco M. "Cost of Producing Rice, 1926-1927," *Philippine Agriculturist* 16 (September 1927): 253-265.

Sacay, Francisco M., and Martin V. Jarmin. "A Study of Economic and Social Conditions in a Farm Village of Laguna," *Philippine Agriculturist* 31 (September 1947): 44-50.

Sacay, Francisco M., and Florendo R. Naanep. "A Study of Farm, Home, and Community Conditions in a Farm Village of Ilocos Norte as a Basis for Formulating a Program of Rural Education," *Philippine Agriculturist* 29 (December 1940): 555-570.

Salamanca, Bonifacio. "Background and Early Beginnings of the Encomienda," *Philippine Social Science and Humanities Review* 26 (March 1961): 67-86.

Samonte, Vedarto J. "The Commonwealth Government Policy of Small Landholding," *Philippine Social Science and Humanities Review* 10 (August 1938): 231-250.

Schul, Norman W. "Hacienda Magnitude and Philippine Sugar-Cane Production," *Asian Studies* 5 (August 1967): 258-273.

Sibley, Willis E. "Work Partner Choice in a Philippine Village," *Silliman Journal* 4 (3rd quarter, 1957): 196-206.

Sorongon, Arturo P. *A Special Study of Landed Estates in the Philippines.* Manila: International Cooperation Administration, 1955.

Spencer, J. E. *Land and People in the Philippines.* Berkeley and Los Angeles: University of California Press, 1952.

————. "The Philippine Rice Problem," *Far Eastern Survey* 18 (1 June 1949): 25-28.

Starner, Frances L. *Magsaysay and the Philippine Peasantry.* Berkeley and Los Angeles: University of California Press, 1961.

Stoodley, Bartlett H. "Some Aspects of Tagalog Family Structure," *American Anthropologist* 59 (April 1957): 236-249.

Sturtevant, David R. *Agrarian Unrest in the Philippines.* Athens: Center for International Studies, Southeast Asia Series no. 8, Ohio University, n.d.

————. "Epilog for an Old 'Colorum,'" *Solidarity* 3 (August 1968): 10-18.

————. "Guardia de Honor: Revitalization within the Revolution," *Asian Studies* 4 (August 1966): 342-352.

————. " 'No Uprising Fails—Each One is a Step in the Right Direction. . . ,' " *Solidarity* 1 (October-December 1965): 11-21.

————. "Sakdalism and Philippine Radicalism," *Journal of Asian Studies* 21 (February 1962): 199-213.

Sweet, David. "The Proto-Political Peasant Movement in the Spanish Philippines: The *Cofradia de San Jose* and the Tayabas Rebellion of 1841," *Asian Studies* 8 (April 1970): 94-119.

Takahashi, Akira. *Land and Peasants in Central Luzon.* Tokyo: Institute of Developing Economies, Occasional Papers, 1969.

van Oppenfeld, Horst and Judith, J. C. Sta. Iglesia, and P. R. Sandoval. "Farm Management, Land Use, and Tenancy in the Philippines," *Central Experiment Station Bulletin* 1 (April 1957): 1-168.

Velmonte, Jose E. "Farm Ownership and Tenancy in the Philippines," Papers presented before the Conference on World Land Tenure Problems, University of Wisconsin, 18 October 1951.

————. "Farm Security for the Tenant," *Philippine Agriculturist* 26 (October 1937): 395-397.

————. "Farm Tenancy Problems in the Philippines with Particular Reference to Tenancies in Rice-Producing Regions," *Philippine Agriculturist* 27 (December 1938): 515-529.

_____. "The Land Settlement Project at Koronadal after Its First Year, 1939-1940," *Philippine Agriculturist* 30 (August 1941): 239-249.

_____. "Palay and Rice Prices," *Philippine Agriculturist* 25 (October 1936): 382-410.

Velmonte, Jose E., and Alfonso B. Castro. "Economic and Social Survey of Sugar-Cane Tenancies on the Calamba Sugar Estate, Laguna," *Philippine Agriculturist* 30 (September 1941): 314-338.

Wood, R. G. "The Strange Story of the Colorum Sect," *Asia* 32 (1932): 450-460.

Wurfel, David O. D. "Philippine Agrarian Reform under Magsaysay," *Far Eastern Survey* 27 (January 1958): 7-15, and 27 (February 1958): 23-30.

Yen, Y. C. James, et al. *Philippine Rural Reconstruction Movement.* New York: Praeger, 1967.

Hukbalahap, HMB, and PKP

Appelton, Shelden. "Communism and the Chinese in the Philippines," *Pacific Affairs* 32 (December 1959): 376-391.

Baclagon, Uldarico S. *Lessons from the Huk Campaign in the Philippines.* Manila: M. Colcol, 1960.

Barton, Fred H. *Salient Operational Aspects of Paramilitary Warfare in Three Asian Areas.* Washington, D.C.: Operations Research Office, Technical Memorandum ORO-T-228, Department of the Army, 1954.

Bashore, Boyd T. "Dual Strategy for Limited War," *Military Review* 40 (May 1960): 46-62.

Bohannan, Charles T. R. "Anti-Guerrilla Operations," *The Annals* 341 (May 1962): 19-29.

Chapman, Abraham. "Pacification in Central Luzon," *Far Eastern Survey* 15 (28 August 1946): 268.

Chynoweth, B. G. "Lessons from the Fall of the Philippines," *Military Engineer* 46 (September-October 1954): 369-372.

Crisol, Jose M. "Communist Propaganda in the Philippines—1950-1953," *Philippine Studies* 1 (December 1953): 207-222.

_____. *The Red Lie.* Manila: Barangay Pocketbook, 1954.

Entenberg, B. "Agrarian Reform and the Hukbalahap," *Far Eastern Survey* 15 (14 August 1946): 245-248.

Felder, Louis F. *Socio-Economic Aspects of Counterinsurgency: A Case Study—Philippines.* Washington, D.C.: Industrial College of the Armed Forces, 1963.

Fifield, Russell H. "The Hukbalahap Today," *Far Eastern Survey* 20 (January 1951): 13-18.

Giron, Maximo. *Report on Communism in the Philippines.* Manila: *Manila Courier,* 1946.

Hammer, Kenneth M. "Huks in the Philippines," in Franklin Osanka (ed.), *Modern Guerrilla Warfare.* New York: Free Press of Glencoe, 1962.

Jones, Adrian H., and Andrew R. Molnar. "The Philippines, 1946-1951," in *International Defense against Insurgency.* Washington, D.C.: Center for Research in Social Systems, American University.

Jose, F. Sionil. "What's Right with the Huks," *Solidarity* 1 (April-June 1966).

Kerkvliet, Benedict J. "Peasant Society and Unrest Prior to the Huk Revolution," *Asian Studies* 9 (August 1971): 164-213.

Lacaba, Jose F. "The Mills of the Gods," *Philippines Free Press,* 17 January 1970.

Lachica, Eduardo. *Huk: Philippine Agrarian Society in Revolt.* Manila: Solidaridad, 1971.

Lansdale, Edward G. *In the Midst of Wars.* New York: Harper and Row, 1972.

Leighton, Richard M., Ralph Sanders, and Jose N. Tinio, *The Huk Rebellion: A Case Study in the Social Dynamics of Insurrection.* Washington, D.C.: Industrial College of the Armed Forces, 1964.

Mitchel, Edward. "Some Econometrics of the Huk Rebellion," *American Political Science Review* 63 (December 1969): 1159-1171.

Owens, William A. "Will the Huks Revolt," *Asia and the Americans* 46 (February 1946): 53-57.

Peterson, A. H., G. C. Reinhardt, and E. E. Conger (eds.). *Symposium on the Role of Airpower in Counterinsurgency and Unconventional Warfare: The Philippine Huk Campaign.* Santa Monica, California: Rand Corporation, 1963.

"Political Transmission 15," *Philippine Studies* 8 (January 1960): 3-50.

Pomeroy, William J. *The American-Made Tragedy: Neo-Colonialism and Dictatorship in the Philippines.* New York: International Publishers, 1974.

———. *The Forest.* New York: International Publishers, 1963.

———. *Guerrilla and Counter-Guerrilla Warfare.* New York: International Publishers, 1964.

———. *Guerrilla Warfare and Marxism.* New York: International Publishers, 1968.

———. "The Huk Movement in the Philippines," *Eastern World* 18 (September 1964).

———. "Portrait of a Turncoat," *Political Affairs* 46 (December 1967): 39-41.

———. "The Unfinished Revolution in the Philippines," *Folio* (literary supplement of the *Philippine Collegian*), April 1964.

Rizal, Tarciano. "The Communist Movement: A Personal Account," Bangkok: SEATO Headquarters, 1957.

Salmon, Jack D. "The Huk Rebellion," *Solidarity* 3 (December 1968): 1-29.

Saulo, Alfrédo B. *Communism in the Philippines: An Introduction.* Quezon City: Ateneo de Manila University, 1969.

Scaff, Alvin H. *The Philippine Answer to Communism.* Stanford: Stanford University Press, 1955.

Sens, Andrew D. *A Survey of the United States Role in Insurgency Situations in the Philippine Islands, 1899-1955.* Washington, D.C.: Special Operations Research Organizations, 1964.

Shaplen, Robert. "The Huks: Foe in the Philippines," *Collier's,* 7 April 1951.

Smith, Robert Ross. "The Hukbalahap Insurgency: Political, Military, and Economic Factors." Washington, D.C.: Office of the Chief of Military History, Department of Army, 1963.

Starner, Frances L. "Communism and the Philippine Nationalist Movement," *Solidarity* 6 (February 1971): 9-26.

Taruc, Luis. *Born of the People.* New York: International Publishers, 1953.

———. *He Who Rides the Tiger.* London: Geoffrey Chapman, 1967.

Teodoro, Luis V., Jr. "Interview with Jose Lava: The Major Obstacle to National Development," *Graphic,* 11 February 1970.

Thayer, Charles W. *Guerrilla.* New York: Signet, 1963.

Tirona, T. C. "The Philippine Anti-Communist Campaign," *Air University Quarterly Review* 7 (summer 1954): 42-55.

Valeriano, Napoleon D., and Charles T. R. Bohannan. *Counter-Guerrilla Operations: The Philippine Experience.* New York: Praeger, 1962.

van der Kroef, Justus M. "Communist Fronts in the Philippines," *Problems of Communism* 16 (March-April 1967): 65-75.

———. Philippine Communism and the Chinese," *China Quarterly 30* (April-June 1967): 115-148.

Vargas, Jesus, and Tarciano Rizal. *Communism in Decline: The Huk Campaign.* Bangkok: SEATO Headquarters, 1957.

Wells, Henry. "Communism in the Philippines," *American Perspective* 4 (winter 1950): 79-91.

Wurfel, David O. D. "The Philippines—Intensified Dialogue," *Asian Survey* 2 (January 1967): 46-52.

INDEX

Abad Santos, Pedro, 37, 44, 46, 48, 50, 54, 81, 97, 99, 100, 115
biography, 52-53
quoted, 55
AFP (Armed Forces of the Philippines), 240, 241. *See also* Philippine army
Agricultural workers. *See* Laborers, agricultural; Tenant farming
Aklasan, 37
Alejandrino, Casto, 48, 53, 79, 80, 84, 88, 98, 103-104, 108, 109, 112, 114, 130, 151-152, 153, 154, 172, 174, 184, 186, 228, 235, 247
biography, 82-83
quoted, 46-47, 169, 212, 213-214, 215-216, 225, 226, 229-230, 232, 234-235
Alejandrino, Jose, Jr., 48, 53
Algas, Herminio, 134
Americans. *See* United States government
AMT (Aguman ding Malding Talapagobra, or General Workers' Union), 37, 44, 46, 52, 55, 56, 78, 79, 81, 82, 94-95, 98, 102, 128-129
leadership, 47-53
merged with KPMP, 45
see also Popular Front Party
Anak Pawis, 37
Ancajas, Angel Y., 136
Anting-anting (amulets), 206
Aquino, Eusebio, 79, 84, 98
Asedillo-Encallado social bandits, 37-38. *See also* Social bandits
Aspia, Roberto, 165, 166, 206
quoted, 10, 71, 110-111, 122, 123, 126, 150, 156, 157, 165, 201, 205, 207, 208, 228
Atin Na (Ours Now), 37, 47-48

Bagong Sikat, 30-31
Baking, Angel, 223
Balgos, Mariano, 86, 183, 188, 236, 263
biography, 221
quoted, 222
Baluyut, Sotero, 46, 55, 56, 57, 211
Bandits, social, 37-38, 79, 248
Baniaga, Mamerto, 85, 142, 181, 183, 186
quoted, 182
Barrera, Jesus, 140, 149, 179
Basa, Leonardo, quoted, 119, 120
Basa, Tomas, quoted, 167, 205

Bataan province, incidents of unrest (table), 40-41
Bayan, defined, 2
Bell Trade Act of 1946, 150-151. *See also* Parity rights
Bicos, Basilio, 197
Bigas, defined, 5. *See also* Rice
Blue Eagle Guerrilla Veterans, 140-141
Bohannan, Charles, quoted, 245
Bombs, use of, 211
Briones, Alejandro, quoted, 168-169, 177
BUDC (Sandatahang Tanod ng Bayan, or Barrio United Defense Corps), 94-95, 102-103
Bulacan province
described, 1-2
HMB in, 212-213
landlord organizations, 55
peasant unrest in 1930s, 37-39, 40-41, 42
PKM in, 129-131
population, 17-19
see also Central Luzon
Bulaong, Agaton, 85, 112, 169, 174, 183, 186, 222, 263
quoted, 78, 144, 151, 170, 171, 172, 177, 217, 238
Bungay, Cenon, 128, 174, 263
quoted, 113, 135, 144, 150, 168, 172, 173, 175-176, 194, 211, 212, 213, 215, 234-235
Buwan, Alfredo, 156, 166
quoted, 62-63, 64, 67, 68, 75, 107, 109, 120, 121, 123, 157, 207

Caiyod, Manuel, 215
Calma, Tomas, 112
biography, 169-170
Calonge, Iluminada, 85, 222-223
Cando, Jose, 126, 136, 152, 197
quoted, 158
Capadocia, Guillermo, 50-51, 86, 236, 263
biography, 221
quoted, 221
Capitalism
growth of, 17, 18-21
impact of, on rural life, 22-25. *See also* Tenant farming
Carmarines, Valentino, 136
Cassava, 215